JOURNAL OF BIBLICAL LITERATURE

EDITORS OF THE JOURNAL
General Editor: ADELE REINHARTZ, University of Ottawa
Managing Editor: BILLIE JEAN COLLINS, Society of Biblical Literature
Editorial Assistant: GEORGETTE LEDGISTER, Society of Biblical Literature

EDITORIAL BOARD

WILLIAM ADLER, North Carolina State University
DAVID L. BARR, Wright State University
JO-ANN BRANT, Goshen College
ELIZABETH CASTELLI, Barnard College
RICHARD J. CLIFFORD, Boston College
COLLEEN CONWAY, Seton Hall University
JOHN COOK, Asbury Seminary
MARY ROSE D'ANGELO, University of Notre Dame
ESTHER ESHEL, Bar-Ilan University
GEORG FISCHER, Leopold-Franzens-Universität Innsbruck
WIL GAFNEY, Brite Divinity School
FRANCES TAYLOR GENCH, Union Presbyterian Seminary
SHIMON GESUNDHEIT, Hebrew University of Jerusalem
MARTIEN A. HALVORSON-TAYLOR, University of Virginia (Charlottesville)
J. ALBERT HARRILL, Ohio State University
ELSE K. HOLT, Aarhus Universitet
DAVID HORRELL, University of Exeter
ANN JERVIS, Wycliffe College
PAUL JOYCE, King's College London
JONATHAN KLAWANS, Boston University
JENNIFER KNUST, Boston University
MICHAEL A. LYONS, Simpson University
DANIEL MACHIELA, McMaster University
CHRISTL M. MAIER, Philipps-Universität Marburg
SHELLY MATTHEWS, Brite Divinity School
KEN PENNER, St. Francis Xavier University
PIERLUIGI PIOVANELLI, University of Ottawa
MARK REASONER, Marian University
ANNETTE YOSHIKO REED, University of Pennsylvania
THOMAS RÖMER, Collège de France and University of Lausanne
JEAN-PIERRE RUIZ, St. John's University (New York)
ERIN RUNIONS, Pomona College
KONRAD SCHMID, University of Zurich
WILLIAM SCHNIEDEWIND, University of California Los Angeles
CLAUDIA SETZER, Manhattan College
CAROLYN SHARP, Yale University
BRENT STRAWN, Emory University
JOHN STRONG, Missouri State University
ELIZABETH STRUTHERS MALBON, Virginia Polytechnic Institute and State University
STEVEN TUELL, Pittsburgh Theological Seminary
DAVID TSUMURA, Japan Bible Seminary
LAWRENCE M. WILLS, Episcopal Divinity School
DAVID WRIGHT, Brandeis University

The Society of Biblical Literature is a constituent member of the American Council of Learned Societies. *President of the Society:* Athalya Brenner-Idan, Tel Aviv University, Tel Aviv 3448204, Israel; *Vice President:* Beverly Roberts Gaventa, Baylor University, Waco, TX 76798; *Chair, Research and Publications Committee:* John T. Fitzgerald, University of Notre Dame, Notre Dame, IN 46556; *Executive Director:* John F. Kutsko, Society of Biblical Literature, 825 Houston Mill Road, Suite 350, Atlanta, GA 30329.

The *Journal of Biblical Literature* (ISSN 0021–9231) is published quarterly by the Society of Biblical Literature, 825 Houston Mill Road, Suite 350, Atlanta, GA 30329. The annual subscription price is US$55.00 for members and US$220.00 for nonmembers. Institutional and online rates are also available. For information regarding subscriptions and membership, contact: SBL Press, 825 Houston Mill Road, Suite 350, Atlanta, GA 30329. Phone: 866-727-9955 (toll free) or 404-727-9498. E-mail: sblservices@sbl-site.org. For information concerning permission to quote, editorial and business matters, please see the first issue of the year, p. 2. Periodical postage paid at Atlanta, Georgia, and at additional mailing offices. POSTMASTER: Send address changes to SBL Press, 825 Houston Mill Road, Suite 350, Atlanta, GA 30329. Copyright © 2015 by the SBL Press.

JBL is indexed in the following resources:

Arts and Humanities Citation Index
Scopus
ATLA Religion Database
Religious and Theological Abstracts
New Testament Abstracts (ATLA)
Old Testament Abstracts (ATLA)
Periodicals Index online (Proquest)
European Reference Index for the Humanities

PRINTED IN THE UNITED STATES OF AMERICA

Journal of Biblical Literature

Volume 134
2015

GENERAL EDITOR
ADELE REINHARTZ
University of Ottawa
Ottawa, ON K1N 6N5

A Quarterly Published by
SBL Press

EDITORIAL BOARD

WILLIAM ADLER, North Carolina State University
DAVID L. BARR, Wright State University
JO-ANN BRANT, Goshen College
ELIZABETH CASTELLI, Barnard College
RICHARD J. CLIFFORD, Boston College
COLLEEN CONWAY, Seton Hall University
JOHN COOK, Asbury Seminary
MARY ROSE D'ANGELO, University of Notre Dame
ESTHER ESHEL, Bar-Ilan University
GEORG FISCHER, Leopold-Franzens-Universität Innsbruck
WIL GAFNEY, Brite Divinity School
FRANCES TAYLOR GENCH, Union Presbyterian Seminary
SHIMON GESUNDHEIT, Hebrew University of Jerusalem
MARTIEN A. HALVORSON-TAYLOR, University of Virginia (Charlottesville)
J. ALBERT HARRILL, Ohio State University
ELSE K. HOLT, Aarhus Universitet
DAVID HORRELL, University of Exeter
ANN JERVIS, Wycliffe College
PAUL JOYCE, King's College London
JONATHAN KLAWANS, Boston University
JENNIFER KNUST, Boston University
MICHAEL A. LYONS, Simpson University
DANIEL MACHIELA, McMaster University
CHRISTL M. MAIER, Philipps-Universität Marburg
SHELLY MATTHEWS, Brite Divinity School
KEN PENNER, St. Francis Xavier University
PIERLUIGI PIOVANELLI, University of Ottawa
MARK REASONER, Marian University
ANNETTE YOSHIKO REED, University of Pennsylvania
THOMAS RÖMER, Collège de France and University of Lausanne
JEAN-PIERRE RUIZ, St. John's University (New York)
ERIN RUNIONS, Pomona College
KONRAD SCHMID, University of Zurich
WILLIAM SCHNIEDEWIND, University of California Los Angeles
CLAUDIA SETZER, Manhattan College
CAROLYN SHARP, Yale University
BRENT STRAWN, Emory University
JOHN STRONG, Missouri State University
ELIZABETH STRUTHERS MALBON, Virginia Polytechnic Institute and State University
STEVEN TUELL, Pittsburgh Theological Seminary
DAVID TSUMURA, Japan Bible Seminary
LAWRENCE M. WILLS, Episcopal Divinity School
DAVID WRIGHT, Brandeis University

Managing Editor: Billie Jean Collins, Society of Biblical Literature
Editorial Assistant: Georgette Ledgister, Society of Biblical Literature

EDITORIAL MATTERS OF THE *JBL*

1. Contributors should consult the *Journal*'s Instructions for Contributors (http://www.sbl-site.org/assets/pdfs/JBL_Instructions.pdf).
2. If a manuscript of an article is submitted in a form that departs in major ways from these instructions, it may be returned to the author for revision, even before it is considered for publication.
3. Submit an electronic copy of an article to JBL.submissions@sbl-site.org.
4. Communications regarding the *Journal* should be addressed to Adele Reinhartz at jbleditor@gmail.com.
5. Permission to quote more than 500 words may be requested from the Rights and Permissions Department, Society of Biblical Literature, 825 Houston Mill Road, Suite 350, Atlanta, GA 30329, USA (E-mail: sblexec@sbl-site.org). Please specify volume, year, and inclusive page numbers.

BUSINESS MATTERS OF THE SBL
(not handled by the editors of the *Journal*)

1. All correspondence regarding membership in the Society, subscriptions to the *Journal*, change of address, renewals, missing or defective issues of the *Journal*, and inquiries about other publications of the Society should be addressed to Society of Biblical Literature, Customer Service Department, 825 Houston Mill Road, Atlanta, GA 30329. Phone: 866-727-9955 (toll-free) or 404-727-9498. E-mail: sbl@sbl-site.org.
2. All correspondence concerning the research and publications programs, the Annual Meeting of the Society, and other business should be addressed to the Executive Director, Society of Biblical Literature, The Luce Center, 825 Houston Mill Road, Atlanta, GA 30329. (E-mail: sblexec@sbl-site.org).
3. Second Class postage paid at Atlanta, Georgia, and at additional mailing offices.

Journal of Biblical Literature

Volume 134
2015

GENERAL EDITOR
ADELE REINHARTZ
University of Ottawa
Ottawa, ON K1N 6N5

A Quarterly Published by
SBL Press

EDITORIAL BOARD

WILLIAM ADLER, North Carolina State University
DAVID L. BARR, Wright State University
JO-ANN BRANT, Goshen College
ELIZABETH CASTELLI, Barnard College
RICHARD J. CLIFFORD, Boston College
COLLEEN CONWAY, Seton Hall University
JOHN COOK, Asbury Seminary
MARY ROSE D'ANGELO, University of Notre Dame
ESTHER ESHEL, Bar-Ilan University
GEORG FISCHER, Leopold-Franzens-Universität Innsbruck
WIL GAFNEY, Brite Divinity School
FRANCES TAYLOR GENCH, Union Presbyterian Seminary
SHIMON GESUNDHEIT, Hebrew University of Jerusalem
MARTIEN A. HALVORSON-TAYLOR, University of Virginia (Charlottesville)
J. ALBERT HARRILL, Ohio State University
ELSE K. HOLT, Aarhus Universitet
DAVID HORRELL, University of Exeter
ANN JERVIS, Wycliffe College
PAUL JOYCE, King's College London
JONATHAN KLAWANS, Boston University
JENNIFER KNUST, Boston University
MICHAEL A. LYONS, Simpson University
DANIEL MACHIELA, McMaster University
CHRISTL M. MAIER, Philipps-Universität Marburg
SHELLY MATTHEWS, Brite Divinity School
KEN PENNER, St. Francis Xavier University
PIERLUIGI PIOVANELLI, University of Ottawa
MARK REASONER, Marian University
ANNETTE YOSHIKO REED, University of Pennsylvania
THOMAS RÖMER, Collège de France and University of Lausanne
JEAN-PIERRE RUIZ, St. John's University (New York)
ERIN RUNIONS, Pomona College
KONRAD SCHMID, University of Zurich
WILLIAM SCHNIEDEWIND, University of California Los Angeles
CLAUDIA SETZER, Manhattan College
CAROLYN SHARP, Yale University
BRENT STRAWN, Emory University
JOHN STRONG, Missouri State University
ELIZABETH STRUTHERS MALBON, Virginia Polytechnic Institute and State University
STEVEN TUELL, Pittsburgh Theological Seminary
DAVID TSUMURA, Japan Bible Seminary
LAWRENCE M. WILLS, Episcopal Divinity School
DAVID WRIGHT, Brandeis University

Managing Editor: Billie Jean Collins, Society of Biblical Literature
Editorial Assistant: Georgette Ledgister, Society of Biblical Literature

EDITORIAL MATTERS OF THE *JBL*

1. Contributors should consult the *Journal*'s Instructions for Contributors (http://www.sbl-site.org/assets/pdfs/JBL_Instructions.pdf).
2. If a manuscript of an article is submitted in a form that departs in major ways from these instructions, it may be returned to the author for revision, even before it is considered for publication.
3. Submit an electronic copy of an article to JBL.submissions@sbl-site.org.
4. Communications regarding the *Journal* should be addressed to Adele Reinhartz at jbleditor@gmail.com.
5. Permission to quote more than 500 words may be requested from the Rights and Permissions Department, Society of Biblical Literature, 825 Houston Mill Road, Suite 350, Atlanta, GA 30329, USA (E-mail: sblexec@sbl-site.org). Please specify volume, year, and inclusive page numbers.

BUSINESS MATTERS OF THE SBL
(not handled by the editors of the *Journal*)

1. All correspondence regarding membership in the Society, subscriptions to the *Journal*, change of address, renewals, missing or defective issues of the *Journal*, and inquiries about other publications of the Society should be addressed to Society of Biblical Literature, Customer Service Department, 825 Houston Mill Road, Atlanta, GA 30329. Phone: 866-727-9955 (toll-free) or 404-727-9498. E-mail: sbl@sbl-site.org.
2. All correspondence concerning the research and publications programs, the Annual Meeting of the Society, and other business should be addressed to the Executive Director, Society of Biblical Literature, The Luce Center, 825 Houston Mill Road, Atlanta, GA 30329. (E-mail: sblexec@sbl-site.org).
3. Second Class postage paid at Atlanta, Georgia, and at additional mailing offices.

Other scholars have likewise gone this way of foregrounding contextual and so-called literary criticism of the biblical text as is. This has been happening recently not only in New Testament studies but also in Hebrew Bible/Old Testament studies, in religion and theology studies, and even ancient Near Eastern and Septuagint studies. This, to a great extent, is the liberating *Zeitgeist:* paradoxically, recognition of the global promotes the uniqueness of the individual and the limited communal. Fernando, you have been a pioneer at the forefront of this scholarly evolution, perhaps revolution, with a clear and balanced voice that was and is heard far beyond the realm of New Testament studies. I can't imagine the publication of such projects as the *Global Bible Commentary*,[3] the Texts@Contexts series,[4] International Voices in Biblical Studies,[5] and similar collections, not to mention courses and lectures and papers, without your influence and trailblazing work.

This interpretive/critical trajectory is, even now, not without opposition. It is dangerous: it unseats established authority and authorities, provokes and challenges accepted politics. It moves away from the Eurocentrism in scholarship that the Northern Hemisphere has adopted so enthusiastically ever since the nineteenth century. However, the trend can no longer be denied.

You are the president of the Society of Biblical Literature this year (2014). The SBL has evolved far from its beginnings in the late nineteenth century as a professional organization mainly by and for American, Christian, largely Protestant, European-influenced, male preachers and academics. It has expanded the scope of its mission, "fostering biblical scholarship," far beyond its beginnings, in the directions that you have worked hard to make acceptable. The SBL now promotes a "big tent" policy, designed to break out of its original exclusive mold to recognize the diversity of critics, scholars, readers, and learners who participate in its activities as members. In other words, the SBL is coming of age. You have been a part of this growth process through your earlier service on the SBL Council; on the Nominating Committee and editorial boards; in publishing and in program units. Through your service as well as your scholarship, you have helped expand the scope of the Society's mission. Nominating you for the Society president is further evidence of this process, and a positive sign for the future.

So thank you for all your work. May it continue apace, for your insistence on what should be done and how it can—inter alia—be done, and for being with us tonight. The floor is yours.

---

[3] *Global Bible Commentary*, ed. Daniel Patte et al. (Nashville: Abingdon, 2004).

[4] In the Texts@Contexts series published by Fortress Press, see *Genesis*, ed. Athalya Brenner, Archie Chi Chung Lee, and Gale A. Yee (2010); *Exodus and Deuteronomy*, ed. Athalya Brenner and Gale A. Yee (2012); *Leviticus and Numbers*, ed. Athalya Brenner and Archie Chi Chung Lee (2013); and *Joshua and Judges*, ed. Athalya Brenner and Gale A. Yee (2013).

[5] An SBL Press, peer-reviewed online series: http://ivbs.sbl-site.org/home.aspx.

Criticism in Critical Times: Reflections on Vision and Task

FERNANDO F. SEGOVIA
f.f.segovia@vanderbilt.edu
Vanderbilt University, Nashville, TN 37240

The problematic addressed in this study is the vision and task of biblical criticism today. The introduction describes its context and rationale: a series of key anniversaries in 2014, involving critical times of the twentieth century, that bring to bear historical, geopolitical, and spatial dimensions of meaning upon our own critical times as well as my term as president of the Society of Biblical Literature. The introduction further sets forth its objective: the felt imperative need for a response to our critical times as a critic. The main body of the study develops an initial response in four major steps: first, analysis of presidential addresses given in critical times of yesteryear, with a focus on the years of the Great War (1914–18), as signifier for the perceived function of biblical criticism in society and culture; second, exposition of the spectrum of opinion regarding the pursuit of critical inquiry in a variety of discursive frameworks, with a focus on intellectual studies, in order to situate the rhetorical choice adopted by former presidents and allow for a different, more activist role; third, analysis of the global state of affairs as the context for critical inquiry today, with a focus on global economics, as a prerequisite for an engaged critical stance; and fourth, search for a theoretical framework appropriate for engaging our critical times, involving not only critical theories of world order from the Global North but also alternative theories from the Global South. The conclusion offers an interpretive project for our times in keeping with the various dimensions of the response, arguing for a fusion of the critical and the political, the biblical and the worldly.

Acceptance of the nomination to serve as president of the Society of Biblical Literature in 2014 immediately set off a process of reflection on my part regarding an appropriate topic for the main function of such a charge, the presidential address. With the passage of time, three ideas, all having to do with various social-cultural dimensions of my term, gradually established themselves as primary in my mind. Eventually, they came together, upon much reflection, in the final determination of the topic. I should like to begin by identifying these converging vectors, doing so by way of chronological emergence and appropriation. They involve, respectively, historical, geopolitical, and spatial dimensions of meaning, although all three such dimensions are present in all three vectors. As such, they involve—individually as well as collectively—a critical reading of the global scene, my own location and stance within it, and my identity and role as a biblical critic. In the end, such reflections led me to the question of critical vision and task as a worthy, indeed imperative, topic for my address, for which I have chosen "Criticism in Critical Times: Reflections on Vision and Task" as the title.

The first insight was historical in character, which led to a juxtaposition of critical times involving relations among global powers in the West. I realized that my term would coincide with major anniversaries of global conflicts during the course of the twentieth century: (1) the Great War (1914–18)—the centenary of the declaration of war in 1914; (2) the Second World War (1939–45)—the seventy-fifth anniversary of the outbreak of war in 1939 and the seventieth of D-Day in 1944, the beginning of the end for Nazi Germany and the Axis; and (3) the Cold War (1947–89/91), a confrontation that would engender multiple regional wars and local clashes—the twenty-fifth anniversary of the beginning of the end in 1989, with the collapse of the communist regimes throughout Eastern Europe, symbolically culminating with the fall of the Berlin Wall in November.[1]

I became aware that it had fallen upon me, as the first president from outside the West, to recall and observe such events. I realized that I could do so only as an outsider-insider. The trajectory for me was clear. The Great War marked the beginning of a relentless descent, through sustained advances in warfare technology, into ever more extreme levels of barbarity, carnage, and destruction. Such a path of destruction would engulf not only the old great powers of Europe and the new power of the United States of America but also the rest of the world in its wake. This path has continued beyond the Cold War into our own days, as the North Atlantic Treaty Organization (NATO) has assumed the role of a global patrol force—the First Gulf War (1990–91), the Second Gulf War (2003–11), and now in 2014 the war with the Islamic State.[2] This path has brought to a climax the civilizational crisis of the West that began with the Great War, with no sense of what is to come and much less how to manage it. In this existential quandary I find that we are all together—insiders, outsiders, and outsiders-insiders alike.

Subsequently, a geopolitical insight emerged, which brought together critical times having to do with the state of affairs of the Two-Thirds World and its differential relations of power with the One-Third World. My term, I realized, would

---

[1] I say the beginning of the end because what began in 1989 with a wave of revolutions that brought down the communist regimes ended in 1991 with the formal disbanding of the Warsaw Pact on 25 February and the dissolution of the Union of Soviet Socialist Republics on 26 December.

[2] On this point, see Immanuel Wallerstein, "NATO: Danger to World Peace" (15 November 2014), http://www.iwallerstein.com/nato-danger-to-world-peace/.

parallel the sixtieth anniversary of a foundational period in the discursive and material emergence of the Third World (1952–55): (1) In 1952, the term appeared for the first time, coined by Alfred Sauvy as *"le tiers monde,"* in a piece written for the French socialist weekly *L'Observateur*.[3] (2) In 1954, the French Far East Expeditionary Corps in Indochina suffered a decisive defeat at the hands of the Viet Minh forces of Ho Chi Minh at Dien Bien Phu, bringing to a close the First Indochina War (1946–54) and ushering in, after the Geneva Accord of 1955 and the partition of Vietnam, the Second Indochina War (1955–75).[4] (3) In 1955, the Bandung (Indonesia) Conference took place, bringing together the newly independent countries of Africa and Asia in a first attempt to chart a middle, independent course between the dialectics of capitalist and socialist modernism.[5]

I became conscious of the fact that I was to be the first president from the Global South, or what was popularly known from the 1950s through the 1970s as the Third World.[6] This was the world of my origins and primary culture. It is to its diaspora in the Global North that I belong, as a first-generation immigrant and an inescapably transnational subject. This was, therefore, the first time that the Society had ventured outside the parameters of the Euro-American world of the North Atlantic. I had thus become a marker of the tectonic demographic changes taking place throughout the world since the 1960s, whose impact began to reach the Society in the late 1970s and early 1980s, as the field of studies expanded into Africa and the Middle East, Asia and the Pacific, Latin America and the Caribbean.

The last insight was spatial in nature, which led to the conjunction of critical times involving borders and migrations, nations and the Other. I realized that my term would coincide with the fiftieth anniversary of a similarly foundational period in the country and its relations with Latin America and the Caribbean (1963–65):

---

[3] Alfred Sauvy, "Trois mondes, une planète," *L'Observateur* 118 (14 August 1952), 14. See also idem, "Note sur l'origine de l'expression 'tiers monde' par Alfred Sauvy," *Le Magazine de l'homme moderne*, http://www.homme-moderne.org/societe/demo/sauvy/3mondes.html.

[4] Southeast Asia was one of many areas of the Third World where the United States and the Soviet Union engaged in geopolitical struggle for control during the late 1940s and the 1950s. See Robert J. McMahon, *The Cold War: A Very Short Introduction*, Very Short Introductions (Oxford: Oxford University Press, 2003), 64–74, esp. 70–72.

[5] On the Bandung Conference, see Robert J. C. Young, *Postcolonialism: An Historical Introduction* (Oxford: Blackwell, 2001), 182–92, esp. 191–92. Young sees the conference, attended by twenty-nine African and Asian countries, as a foundational moment for postcolonialism, given its constitution as a political pressure group reflecting an "independent transcontinental political consciousness in Africa and Asia" (p. 191). Out of it would eventually come the Movement of Non-Aligned Countries in 1961 and the Tricontinental in 1966, which brought together Africa, Asia, and Latin America.

[6] On the concept of the Third World, its origins and variations and trajectory, see M. D. Litonjua, "Third World/Global South: From Modernization, to Dependency/Liberation, to Postdevelopment," *Journal of Third World Studies* 29 (2012): 25–56; Marcin Wojciech Solarz, "'Third World': The 60th Anniversary of a Concept That Changed History," *Third World Quarterly* 33.9 (October 2012): 1561–73.

(1) In 1963, the assassination of President John Fitzgerald Kennedy signified what Jon Margulis has called the "last innocent year" before the sixties.[7] (2) In 1964, the Civil Rights Act was enacted, a landmark of the civil rights struggle, and the progressive government of President João Goulart of Brazil was overthrown, the first of many military coups to follow in Latin America, which would ultimately lead to the establishment of a web of repression across much of the continent, known as Operation Condor.[8] (3) In 1965, the Immigration and Nationality Act abolished the restrictive immigration laws of the 1920s, which had favored western and northern Europeans, paving the way for the massive demographic transformation still under way, in which Latin Americans and Caribbeans have played a leading part.[9]

I became aware that the city of San Diego would serve as the venue for the annual meeting of the Society during my term, where only a few miles to the south stands the westernmost end of the long and freighted border between the United States of America and the Estados Unidos Mexicanos. It is a border that serves as the signifier for a deeper discursive-material border with the whole of Latin America and the Caribbean and, ultimately, for a global divide between haves and have-nots. This deeper border I had traversed, across the Florida Straits, in July of 1961, at the height of the Cold War, as an adolescent and a child of political refugees. In so doing, I was following the trek of millions of Latin Americans who had made and would make their way to the north, becoming thereby a member of a minoritized ethnic formation within the nation-state of the United States. I was also joining the path of untold millions of human beings from the South who had searched and would search for refuge in the North.

In pursuing these converging social-cultural dimensions regarding my term, I was struck by how contemporary discussions regarding such vectors of meaning, surrounding major anniversaries of landmark events, approached these critical times of the past as having direct significance and relevance for the present, drawing upon them to shed light on the critical times of today.

Thus, analysis of the Great War and its ramifications reached into the present and future not only of Europe but also of the globe.[10] It turned for counsel and

---

[7] Jon Margulis, *The Last Innocent Year: America in 1964. The Beginning of the "Sixties"* (New York: Morrow, 1999).

[8] On Operation Condor, see J. Patrice McSherry, *Predatory States: Operation Condor and Covert War in Latin America* (Lanham, MD: Rowman & Littlefield, 2005).

[9] Indeed, a decisive signifier of such ongoing transformation is the new policy on immigration, with Latinos/as foremost in mind, announced by President Barack Obama just prior to the beginning of this annual meeting; see Michael D. Sheer, "Obama, Daring Congress, Acts to Overhaul Immigration," *New York Times*, 21 November 2013, A1, http://www.nytimes.com/2014/11/21/us/obama-immigration-speech.html.

[10] Such comparisons have continued. See, e.g., Margaret MacMillan, "The Rhyme of History: Lessons of the Great War," The Brookings Essay (14 December 2013), http:/www.brookings.edu/research/essays/2013/rhyme-of-history#; Dominique Moïsi, "The Return of the

direction to the uncertain situation involving the great powers at the beginning of the twentieth century, highly charged and precarious, in dealing with the equally shifting and uncertain situation of the great powers at the beginning of the twenty-first century, no less charged and precarious. Similarly, scrutiny of the Global South turned to the concept of the Third World in the second half of the twentieth century. It looked for enlightenment and guidance to the problematic of the Third World in the dialectical world order of industrial capitalism in coming to terms with the fate of the Global South within the neoliberal world order of global capitalism.[11] Further, analysis of the border with Mexico and the phenomenon of Latino/a immigration, and of borders and migration in general, reached back to the decade of the 1960s. It sought wisdom and insight, from within a context of paranoic fear of the Other and massive projects of national security involving militarization and snooping, in the discourse of civil rights, the liberal attitude toward immigration, and the trajectory of relations with Latin America.[12]

Given such emphasis on significance and relevance for the present, I came to see that this convergence of vectors of meaning and association of events regarding my term deserved, even demanded, a response on my part as a biblical critic. What should I as a critic do in the face of our critical times? How should I conduct my métier? This I saw as a daunting task, but imperative nonetheless. I shall attempt to formulate an initial response to this question.

I. Presidential Preoccupations in Critical Times of Yesteryear

I begin my response by tracing the topics pursued by former SBL presidents in their addresses to the Society during the critical times in question.[13] Such a sense

---

Sleepwalkers," Project Syndicate (25 June 2014), http://www.project-syndicate.org/commentary/dominique-moisi-asks-whether-today-s-leaders--unlike-their-counterparts-in-2014--can-avert-a-global-catastrophe.

[11] See, e.g., Arif Dirlik, "Global South: Predicament and Promise," *Global South* 1 (2007): 12–23.

[12] See, e.g., Antonia Darder and Rodolfo D. Torres, "Latinos and Society: Culture, Politics, and Class," in *The Latino Studies Reader: Culture, Economy & Society*, ed. Antonia Darder and Rodolfo D. Torres (Malden, MA: Blackwell, 1998), 3–26; and, in the same volume, Edna Acosta-Belén and Carlos E. Santiago, "Merging Borders: The Remapping of America," 29–42, and Rosaura Sánchez, "Mapping the Spanish Language along a Multiethnic and Multilingual Border," 101–25. See also Ramón Grosfoguel, Nelson Maldonado-Torres, and José David Saldívar, eds., *Latinos/as in the World System: Decolonization Struggles in the 21st Century U.S. Empire*, Political Economy of the World-Systems Annual (Boulder, CO: Paradigm, 2006).

[13] The information on presidents and presidential addresses has been gathered from a variety of sources, among which the following are salient: Ernest W. Saunders, *Searching the Scriptures: A History of the Society of Biblical Literature, 1880–1980*, BSNA 8 (Chico, CA: Scholars Press, 1982); John H. Hayes, ed., *Dictionary of Biblical Interpretation*, 2 vols. (Nashville: Abingdon, 1999).

of rhetorical choice will serve as a telling signifier for the wider problematic regarding the function of criticism with respect to social-cultural context. Presidential addresses in general, as Patrick Gray has noted in his study of the genre, have gone in two directions: speaking either to the few or to the many, that is, taking up a specific question within a specialized area of research or turning to a general question touching upon the field of studies as a whole.[14] I shall focus here on the years of the First World War. What were the concerns of choice on the part of former SBL presidents as Europe and the world plunged ever deeper into an abyss of unparalleled violence and utter inhumanity?

In 1914, the president was Nathaniel Schmidt (1862–1939), a native of Sweden who had immigrated to the United States in 1884. He was Professor of Semitic Languages and Literature at Cornell University (1896–1932). His topic was "The Story of the Flood and the Growth of the Pentateuch."[15] Charles Cutler Torrey (1863–1956) became president in 1915, speaking on "The Need of a New Edition of the Hebrew Bible." He served at the time as Professor of Semitic Philosophy and Comparative Grammar at Yale University (1900–1932).[16] Morris Jastrow Jr. (1861–1922) followed in 1916, a native of Poland and son of a prominent rabbi and scholar; Jastrow had immigrated as a young child with his family in 1866. A professor of Semitics at the University of Pennsylvania (1884–1919), he spoke on "Constructive Elements in the Critical Study of the Old Testament."[17] Warren J. Moulton (1865–1947) became president in 1917, speaking on "The Dating of the Synoptic Gospels." For many years he was associated with Bangor Theological Seminary, where he served as Hayes Professor of the New Testament Language and Literature (1905–33) and as president (1921–33).[18] In 1918, the president was James A. Montgomery (1866–1949), Professor of Hebrew and Aramaic at the University of Pennsylvania and the Philadelphia School of Divinity (1909–38). His topic was "Present Tasks of American Biblical Scholarship."[19]

---

[14] Patrick Gray, "Presidential Addresses," *JBL* 125 (2006): 167–77. This distinction I do not see as a binomial, since addresses dealing with particular areas of research do mention from time to time the ramifications of the positions advanced for the field in general.

[15] The address was not published in *JBL*, and, to the best of my knowledge, it was not published elsewhere. Before coming to Cornell, Schmidt had been Professor of Semitic Languages and Literature at Colgate University (1888–96).

[16] The address was not published in *JBL*, and, again, to the best of my knowledge, it was not published elsewhere. Before his appointment at Yale, Torrey had been Professor of Semitic Languages at Andover Theological Seminary (1892–1900).

[17] Morris Jastrow Jr., "Constructive Elements in the Critical Study of the Old Testament," *JBL* 36 (1917): 1–20.

[18] Warren J. Moulton, "The Dating of the Synoptic Gospels," *JBL* 37 (1918): 1–19. Before Bangor, he taught for a few years in the Semitic and Biblical Department at Yale University (1888–1902). See the *In Memoriam* notices by Charles C. Torrey, Millar Burrows, and William F. Albright, "In Memoriam Warren Joseph Moulton, 1865–1947," *BASOR* 107 (1947): 1, 5–7.

[19] James A. Montgomery, "Present Tasks of American Biblical Scholarship," *JBL* 38 (1919):

These were all learned scholars. Their topics entertained major disputed questions of their time. With one exception, however, none made reference to the war and the global state of affairs in their presentations. The one voice to do so was that of Montgomery. Shortly after the signing of the Armistice (11 November), he invoked the Great War in crafting a vision for American scholarship, analyzing its present moorings[20] and envisioning its future paths[21] (26 December). His reflections are worth examining, given their incisive and unusual, yet ultimately contradictory, character.

For Montgomery, the global framework functions as the context for rather than object of discourse. The crisis provides the grounds for a twofold call. On the one hand, in a biting critique of his fellow scholars, whom he chides for having had nothing to say about or contribute to the war effort, he calls for a committed study of the Bible as a document that is quintessentially religious in character, that has much to say regarding the human condition, and that stands for the values of Western civilization at its best and hence of the victorious Allies in particular. On the other hand, in a sharp challenge to his assembled colleagues, whom he upbraids for their constricted focus on philology and science, he calls for a most expansive agenda of historical research (philological, historiographical, archaeological) alongside a finely tuned program of public dissemination. In the end, the two parts of the vision fail to come together. The first call, grounded in a mixture of unabashed liberal humanism and outright religious (Protestant) sentiment, remains totally

---

1–14. See also Penn Biographies, James Alan Montgomery (1866–1949), http://www.archives.upenn.edu/people/1800s/montgomery_james_a.html.

[20] The context is sharply drawn: (a) a rejection of all things German, including German scholarship; (b) a denunciation of biblical scholarship for its failure to play any role in the war; (c) a critique of American scholarship for the narrowness of its focus; and (d) an exposition of the weaknesses of such scholarship.

[21] The vision is, in principle, expansive. (A) Montgomery calls for a turn to French and British scholarship, whose countries are described as "racially, politically and intellectually our nearest neighbors, bound to us now by a brotherhood knit in blood." One finds throughout, it should be noted, a strong essentialist strain of racial-ethnic discourse, including a reference to "uncivilized races," apparently meaning those outside the fold of Europe ("Present Tasks," 8, 4). (B) He asks scholars to see themselves "first as citizens of the human polity" and to take up the call of the world upon all "to pool their interests and capitals," such as "the science of the Bible," in the pursuit of causes that have "worth-value, spiritual or material" (pp. 1, 2). (C) He outlines such a cause for scholarship by returning to the reason for the study of the Bible: "its assumed value to humanity" (p. 2). Thus, technical expertise must be at the service of the "philosophy of the Bible," which stands "for just those things for which we and our Allies have fought and triumphed"—challenging all human idolatry, "every human thing which would set itself in the seat of God," and providing ideals for the kingdom of God, "right and peace," "natural humanity and sane democracy," "idealism" in contrast to "realities" (pp. 4–5). (D) Montgomery calls for American scholarship to intensify the historical study of the Bible along any number of lines and to sharpen the communication of the results of such study outside academic circles. In the end, the vision is, in practice, limited: it is by far this last point that prevails.

undeveloped, while the second, grounded in a vigorous sense of American leadership, is amply outlined. As a result, what is meant as an imperative corrective to the previous, overriding focus on science in the field loses its impact, vanishing anew under a renewed emphasis on research without any theoretical integration of the religious, human, and civilizational values upheld. Historicism emerges thereby as the key to the future.

This set of addresses is no different from those delivered during the critical times to follow: the Second World War and the Cold War, whether at the beginning, during the rise of the Third World (1952–55), or at its height, the eruption of the sixties (1963–65). They all reveal a sharp disconnect, in sustained and systematic fashion, between what was going on in the academic-scholarly world of the Society and what was taking place in the social-cultural world of national/international affairs. Most were devoted to specialized questions, with no consideration whatever of the wider context of criticism, local or global. Those that opted for a broader optic of the field did not have their respective critical times in mind at all or did so only in passing and by way of material background. Only Montgomery reflected seriously on the global state of affairs and its discursive ramifications for the field. Even here, however, there was no proper theorization or incorporation of the urgent recommendations proposed. In sum, in critical times presidents have kept the world of criticism and the world of politics quite apart from each other.

II. The Function of Criticism as Problematic

In this second part of the response, I turn to the problematic regarding critical vision and task as such, approaching it from a variety of discursive frameworks other than biblical criticism: intellectual, historical, and literary studies. My aim is to situate the rhetorical choice followed by presidential addresses within a comprehensive spectrum of opinion regarding the pursuit of critical inquiry. In effect, former presidents have unreflectively assumed a position within a spectrum of opinion regarding the task of criticism—its nature and role in society and culture. It is imperative, therefore, to examine the design and parameters of any such spectrum—its structural principles and defining boundaries. Here I foreground the category of the intellectual.

The task of the intellectual in the analysis of society and culture is neither self-evident nor determinate. Although it was advanced more than twenty years ago now, I find no better point of entry into this question than Edward W. Said's BBC Reith Lectures of 1993, "Representations of the Intellectual."[22] This was a

---

[22] Edward W. Said, *Representations of the Intellectual: The 1993 Reith Lectures* (New York: Vintage Books, 1996; orig. ed., New York: Pantheon, 1994). Said (1935–2003), University Professor at Columbia University at the time, was a foremost cultural critic, at home in any number of

reflection on the intelligentsia and thus on criticism writ most large in the modern world. Toward the end of the twentieth century, Said undertook a genealogy of the intellectual beginning with the early part of the century. In so doing, he engaged in dialogue with a wide number of figures, positions, and writings through the century, not only in Europe and the West but also in the Third World.

The genealogy yields a spectrum of opinion ranging from the numerous-collaborationist to the selective-oppositional, with a key theory as representative of each pole—Antonio Gramsci and Julien Benda, respectively.[23] At the populist pole, Gramsci allowed for a wide variety of intellectuals, with a distinction between traditional and organic. The former, encompassing functionaries associated with traditional institutions (teachers, priests, administrators), stayed at a distance from society, carrying out their task in routinarian fashion through the years. The latter, involving functionaries in modern institutions (technicians, experts, organizers), were actively involved in society, seeking ever greater influence and power. At the restricted pole, Benda portrayed intellectuals as members of a small, heroic circle, pursuing truth and justice rather than their gain, advancement, or favor with power. Such pursuit entailed not retreat from the world but rather resolute engagement with it, in opposition to corruption, oppression, authoritarianism throughout.

This genealogy Said updates to his own times, the modern world of the late twentieth century. The world of intellectuals, he argues, has turned out largely along the lines predicted by Gramsci. With the growth of the knowledge industry and the proliferation of new professions, there are engaged intellectuals to be found in the production and distribution of knowledge throughout a host of institutions. They work as professionals who, assigned a specific function within such institutions, work for the benefit of the institutions. In such a world the contrarian, moral ideal of Benda has by and large vanished. Indeed, rather than speaking to the world at large in terms of what is true and just, intellectuals today speak to one another within their respective institutions by way of an abstruse and exclusionary language.

Within this general mapping and contemporary scenario, Said opts for Benda's ideal, although in revised fashion. The intellectual, he argues, must be "an

---

discursive frameworks. In the introduction (pp. ix–xix) he provides a sharp analysis of the Lectures as a cultural phenomenon.

[23] For Gramsci (1891–1937), Said relies on his *Quaderni del carcere* or *Prison Notebooks*, written from 1929 to 1935, while in prison under the Fascist regime in Italy. They were not published until the 1950s in the original and the 1970s in English translation: *Selections from the Prison Notebooks of Antonio Gramsci*, ed. and trans. Quintin Hoare and Geoffrey Nowell-Smith (New York: International, 1971). For Benda (1867–1956), he relies on *La trahison des clercs*, originally published in 1927 and updated in 1946. It was first translated into English in 1928: *The Treason of the Intellectuals*, trans. Richard Aldington (New York: Morrow, 1928); it was published in 1955 as *The Betrayal of the Intellectuals*, trans. Richard Aldington, introduction by Herbert Read (Boston: Beacon, 1955).

individual with a specific public role in society that cannot be reduced simply to being a faceless professional, a competent member of a class just going about her/his business."[24] The intellectual task, therefore, is defined as representing a message to and for a public. Such representation has a sharp, double edge to it: first, to question, expose, challenge any type of settled doctrine or attitude on the part of the status quo, local or global; second, to do so on behalf of what is excluded or marginalized, whether issues or persons. Such representation further entails a distinctive, twofold way of acting: first, it must be contextual and personal in mode, bringing together the private and public spheres at all times; second, it must be cosmopolitan and moral in scope, appealing to universal principles regarding humanity as espoused by the global community.[25]

It is in the matter of praxis that Benda is reconceptualized and reformulated. On the one hand, Benda remained resolutely, unconsciously European in his position—Europe as the center of and for the world. After mid-century, such an assumption was no longer possible: with the rise of the Third World, such factors as ethnicity, nationality, and continent had to be taken into account in representation. On the other hand, Benda never expanded on the concepts of justice and truth, their origins or meaning—such principles remained abstract. After mid-century, such a vision was no longer tenable: with the emergence of the United Nations, a series of accords and treaties giving flesh to such principles had to be assumed in representation, such as the United Nations Declaration on Human Rights of 1948.

In the end, for Said, the world is political to the core, full of beckoning representations, and it proves impossible for the intellectual to escape from politics, whether it be "into the realms of pure art and thought or, for that matter, into the realms of disinterested objectivity or transcendental theory."[26] Intellectuals inevitably adopt a position in representation, no matter where they stand in the spectrum. This position can oscillate between the professional-accommodationist, entrenched within the apparatus and horizon of an organization, and the amateur-protesting, opening up to a world in conflict and siding with truth and justice at all times.

---

[24] Said, *Representations of the Intellectual*, 11.

[25] Said summarizes such principles: "that all human beings are entitled to expect decent standards of behavior concerning freedom and justice from worldly powers or nations, and that deliberate or inadvertent violations of these standards need to be testified and fought against courageously" (*Representations of the Intellectual*, 11–12). It is a position that he sees as reasserting a "grand narrative of emancipation and enlightenment" in the face of postmodernism and its emphasis on "local situations and language games": "For in fact governments still manifestly oppress people, grave miscarriages of justice still occur, the co-optation and inclusion of intellectuals by power can still effectively quieten their voices, and the deviation of intellectuals from their vocation is still very often the case" (p. 18).

[26] Said, *Representations of the Intellectual*, 21.

This spectrum of the intellectual life is very similar, mutatis mutandis, to those offered in historiography by Gabrielle Spiegel in her 2009 presidential address to the American Historical Association, "The Task of the Historian,"[27] and in literary criticism by both Terry Eagleton in his 1996 overview of literary theory, "Political Criticism," and Vincent Leitch in his recently published essay on "The Tasks of Critical Reading."[28] What are the consequences of such a spectrum across a variety of discursive frameworks for my response? In largely pursuing pressing questions of the discipline while bypassing pressing questions of the world, as they overwhelmingly did in critical times, presidential addresses assumed a political stance of abstraction from the realm of global affairs into the realm of scholarship. In so doing, they ensconced themselves in the dynamics and mechanics of a discipline devoted to the construction of biblical antiquity and deploying historiographical principles of objectivity and impartiality. The point to keep in mind is that any spectrum of opinion allows for a gamut of other positions and that any position must be acknowledged and theorized. In other words, things need not have been, and need not be, this way, as, alas, James Montgomery grasped all too well in 1918.

III. Critical Analysis of the Global State of Affairs

The third part of my response calls for critical analysis of our own times. If critics are to adopt an activist position within the spectrum on critical task, to address their social-cultural context, and to marshal the resources of their field in this endeavor, then it is indispensable to secure a firm grasp on the global state of affairs today. That our times are perceived as critical, and universally so, should go without saying. Wherever one looks, such is the verdict. Such is certainly the case with respect to any area of society and culture. It is also the case in terms of their overall conjunction as a world system. Indeed, it is not at all unusual to portray our

---

[27] Gabrielle M. Spiegel, "The Task of the Historian," *AHR* 114 (2009): 1–15. At the time, Spiegel was the Krieger-Eisenhower University Professor of History at the Johns Hopkins University. A medievalist by training, Spiegel has multiple interests, among which lies a concern with theory and practice in historiography; on this, see her edited volume, *Practicing History: New Directions in Historical Writing after the Linguistic Turn*, Rewriting Histories (New York: Routledge, 2005), esp. her "Introduction" (pp. 1–31). See also Spiegel, *The Past as Text: The Theory and Practice of Medieval Historiography*, Parallax (Baltimore: Johns Hopkins University Press, 1997), esp. part 1, "Theory."

[28] Terry Eagleton, *Literary Theory: An Introduction*, 2nd ed. (Minneapolis: University of Minnesota Press, 1996), 169–89. See also his historical trajectory of criticism, *The Function of Criticism: From the Spectator to Post-Structuralism* (London: Verso, 1984), and his exposition of Marxist literary criticism, *Marxism and Literary Criticism* (Berkeley: University of California Press, 1976), esp. 37–58 (ch. 3, "The Writer and Commitment"). Vincent Leitch, *Literary Criticism in the 21st Century: Theory Renaissance* (London: Bloomsbury, 2014), 33–49 (ch. 3, "The Tasks of Critical Reading").

narrative points to a series of financial crises that have called into question any dream of an integrated world economy ruled solely in terms of the market and capital.[35] Here one should keep in mind that López is writing prior to the Great Recession of 2008. The narrative also foregrounds the differential consequences of neoliberal policies, which have only served to heighten social ills and accentuate social contradictions. Thus, while the interests of the elite have been protected and furthered, a series of setbacks for the working and middle classes has resulted: lower wages and fewer benefits, an increase in unemployment alongside a decrease in job security, a reduction of social services for the working poor.[36] Indeed, as many economists now argue, it has been the poor, the disadvantaged, and the marginalized who have paid the price of the project, among whom minorities and immigrants are the greatest number by far.[37]

For López, therefore, the Global South of yesteryear, the South of colonial discourse and postcolonial studies, has become the Post–Global South of today, the South of subalterns throughout the world, who are keenly aware that the project of globalization has failed utterly and that they embody the margins of "the brave new liberal world of globalization." This Post–Global South thus moves beyond the North–South divide of yore, insofar as such subalterns are to be found, as immigrants and minorities, throughout the global cities of the geographical North as well. They have been dis-placed from the geographical South and find themselves dis-jointed in the geographical North, at once put to use and set at a distance, despite a host discourse of "multiculturalism, rights, and tolerance of social difference." Immigrants—broadly understood as including descendants—become thereby both "avatar and pariah—simultaneously a product of globalization and a scapegoat for its many failures."[38]

From an academic-scholarly point of view, therefore, the task is to explore the subjectivity and agency of subalterns—those who live in the débris of global capitalism, without access to its benefits—through the development of a postglobal

---

[35] The list is worth reproducing: "These setbacks include the Asian, Russian, and Brazilian economic crises of 1997–8; the end of the U.S. market boom in 2000; the attack on the World Trade Center on September 11, 2001; the exposed multibillion-dollar scams of Enron and other major corporations, culminating in their collapse; the Argentine fiscal crisis; and the current crises and infrastructural meltdowns in Iraq and New Orleans" (López, "[Post] Global South," 4).

[36] Here López has recourse to the work of David Harvey, *A Brief History of Neoliberalism* (Oxford: Oxford University Press, 2005).

[37] Among the poor, the disadvantaged, and the marginalized, López points out, lie also the white working poor and shrinking middle class, who see globalization as a threat to the nation—politically, economically, and culturally. What emerges out of such anxiety is often an extreme form of nationalism that leads to racism, signified by discrimination and violence against immigrants and minorities. "As they so often do in our literal wars," he remarks, "the immigrant and the working-class white native thus become the unacknowledged and largely unwitting foot soldiers of globalization" ("[Post] Global South, 3).

[38] López, "(Post) Global South," 3–4.

discourse. For López, globalization calls forth—as rapidly as it unfolds—opposition. The reason is clear. On the one hand, its wreckage is unquestionable: "widespread poverty, displacement and diaspora, environmental degradation, human and civil rights abuses, war, hunger, disease"—present in a Post–Global South that includes not only the geographical South but also the metaphorical South present in the geographical North. On the other hand, the struggle for survival is equally undeniable: the emergence of subaltern cultures and economies by way of ethnic, religious, or national identity construction—a spectrum of transnational groups working out of the same logic of opposition. Postglobal discourse is to take up, therefore, in inter- and multidisciplinary fashion, the "condition" of such groups: the who—the question of identity, local or global; the why—the logic of globalization; and the how—the cultures of opposition. Its aim in so doing is to search for a "glimpse" of the future—the potential for "a postglobal politics and economics of inclusion and enfranchisement."[39]

Very similar accounts of our sense of fragility and menace in the post–Cold War era emerge in the discourses and critiques regarding climatological projections and international migration, as drawn, respectively, by Dipesh Chakrabarty in "The Climate of History: Four Theses"[40] and Khalid Koser in his volume entitled *International Migration.*[41] The result is an analytic description of the times in postist fashion. What López characterizes as the postglobal, from the perspective of economics, Chakrabarty describes as the posthuman, from the perspective of climate change, and Koser as the postnational, from the perspective of world migration. These studies expose but three of the major problematics affecting the global state of affairs. There are many others, as previously mentioned, all accompanied by similar analytical accounts of peril and tenuousness. Further, as all such studies variously indicate, these problematics are closely interdependent and mutually

---

[39] Ibid., 7.

[40] Dipesh Chakrabarty, "The Climate of History: Four Theses," *Critical Inquiry* 35 (2009): 197–222. Chakrabarty is the Lawrence A. Kimpton Distinguished Service Professor of History, South Asian Languages and Civilizations and the College at the University of Chicago. He is a scholar of wide-ranging interests, with a particular concern for matters of method and theory in the areas of modern South Asia studies, subaltern studies, and postcolonial studies.

[41] Khalid Koser, *International Migration: A Very Short Introduction*, Very Short Introductions (Oxford: Oxford University Press, 2007). Koser, deputy director and academic dean at the Geneva Centre for Security Policy, is an expert in the subject of migration with a long trajectory of publications and an extensive record of administrative positions. Among such positions, the following should be noted: chair of the UK Advisory Panel on Country Information, editor of the *Journal of Refugee Studies,* and vice-chair of the World Economic Forum Global Council on Migration. In 2014 he was named Member of the Order of the British Empire (MBE) in recognition of his work with refugees and asylum seekers in the United Kingdom. Khalid also holds a professorship in Conflict, Peace and Security at the United Nations University–Maastricht Economic and Social Research Institute on Innovation and Technology and its School of Governance (UNU-MERIT) in the Netherlands.

reinforcing. The result is precisely that prevailing sense of the times as uniquely critical, best described perhaps as a crisis of the world system.

What ramifications do such assessments of individual crises and overall assertion of an interlocking global crisis bear for my response? These accounts point, without exception, to the impact of such problematics, both singly and jointly, on the academic-scholarly realm, not only with respect to individual fields of study but also with regard to the full gamut of fields of study—the duty to integrate and respond in some way. That such a verdict applies to religious studies in general and biblical studies in particular should go without question.[42] If critics are to pursue the pressing questions of the world and assume a political stance of engagement in the world, pointed knowledge of the global state of affairs is of the essence. To begin with, there is need for thorough acquaintance with the crises at hand, as conceptualized and formulated, discussed and debated, in their respective discursive and critical trajectories. Beyond that, there is need for a theoretical framework capable of dealing with the intersecting nature of a crisis of the world system. Such impact, I should point out, James Montgomery grasped, within the terms of his own modernist context, perfectly well in 1918.

IV. A Theoretical Framework for Engaging Our Times

In the fourth part of my response, I turn to the demand for a proper theoretical framework for engaging our times. Given the global state of affairs in the post–Cold War era, a critical framework is needed that can properly embrace and address—beyond focalized problematics and responses—the conjunction of so many crises and challenges, so many corresponding discourses and critiques, in intersectional fashion, in order to keep the system as such in mind at all times. A crisis of the world system demands the adoption of a world theory and hence a dialogue with global studies. Only then can a critic successfully construct an activist position within the field, pointedly engage the social and cultural context, and profitably bring to bear the resources of the field on such an undertaking.

There are two lines of thought that I find crucial in this regard. One has to do with developments in social theory in the Global North that theorize the global nature of the contemporary world scene. Here I draw upon Steven Seidman's

---

[42] Here the 2012 presidential address of Otto Maduro to the American Academy of Religion is very much to the point, "Migrants' Religions under Imperial Duress: Reflections on Epistemology, Ethics & Politics in the Study of the Religious 'Stranger,'" *JAAR* 82 (2014): 35–46. Maduro addresses the ramifications of the migration crisis, through the lens of migration from Latin America to the United States, for the social study of religion as an academic-scholarly field, since such study lies itself embedded in this context of global crisis. Such ramifications, Maduro argues, scholars can ignore altogether or address directly.

ongoing overview of social theory.[43] Three "revisions and revolts" vis-à-vis the classical tradition are outlined, the third and most recent of which is assigned the title of "Theories of World Order."[44] The other involves a strand of social theory in the Global South, with representation in the Global North as well, that approaches the global nature of the world today through the optic of the South. Here I foreground the work on "epistemologies of the South" by Boaventura de Sousa Santos."[45]

In the classical tradition, from Auguste Comte to Max Weber, Seidman argues, the nation-state—a state with a common identity based on common descent and culture—was viewed as the basic unit of modern social life and analysis, and change in nation-states was explained in terms of internal factors. In recent times, a number of theorists have pointed to a relative decline in the primacy of the nation-state and a corresponding change in the global order. The reason adduced for such a change of fortune is external: the growth of a transnational order with dynamics and mechanics that go beyond the boundaries of nationalism. Globalization emerges thereby as the primary element of present-day social life and analysis. How this new global order is evaluated differs considerably. There is, to be sure, the highly positive view of neoliberalism, centered on economics. At the same time, Seidman points to three analytical traditions highly critical of this hegemonic approach.

The first tradition, associated with the London School of Economics, is represented by David Held and Mary Kaldor.[46] Globalization is seen as a mixture of

---

[43] Steven Seidman, *Contested Knowledge: Social Theory Today*, 5th ed. (Chichester: Wiley-Blackwell, 2013). Seidman, professor of sociology at the State University of New York at Albany, is a distinguished social theorist, with expertise in a number of areas. This overview of social theory has been going on for two decades, the first edition of the volume having been published in 1994.

[44] Seidman, *Contested Knowledge*, 267–301 (part 6, "Revisions and Revolts: Theories of World Order"). The other two movements include "The Postmodern Turn" and "Identity Politics and Theory" (parts 4 and 5, respectively).

[45] Boaventura de Sousa Santos, "Introducción: Las epistemologías del Sur," in *Formas-Otras: Saber, nombrar, narrar, hacer*, ed. Alvise Vianello and Bet Mañe, Colección Monografías (Barcelona: CIDOB, 2011), 9–22. De Sousa Santos is professor emeritus of sociology at the University of Coimbra, where he is also the director of the Center for Social Studies. A renowned social theorist, his research encompasses a broad variety of fields of study. See also his *Epistemologies of the South: Justice against Epistemicide* (Boulder, CO: Paradigm, 2014); and *Una epistemología del sur: La reinvención del conocimiento y la emancipación social*, Siglo XXI Editores (Buenos Aires: CLACSO, 2009).

[46] David Held is presently master of University College and professor of politics and international relations at Durham University in the United Kingdom. Previously, he had been the Graham Wallas Professor of Political Science at the London School of Economics. His publications on globalization are extensive. The following are among the most recent: *Gridlock: Why Global Cooperation Is Failing* (London: Polity, 2013); and *Cosmopolitanism: Ideals and Realities* (London: Polity, 2010).

economic, social, and political dimensions. It is potentially positive, provided that the social and political dimensions are activated. The vision is one of a global civil society and democratic order—with chaos as the alternative. Immanuel Wallerstein and Manuel Castells stand as the voices of the second tradition, linked to the theory of world systems. [47] Globalization emerges as a junction of politics and economics, the present stage of the world economy of capitalism, within the world system of modernity. It is altogether negative, with inequality at the core, and in profound crisis since the 1960s. The vision is one of utter transformation—in the face of collapse or dystopia. The third tradition, associated with empire and imperialism, brings together Michael Hardt and Antonio Negri, Michael Mann, and David Harvey.[48] Globalization is regarded as a mixture of economics and geopolitics,

---

Mary Kaldor is professor of global governance in the Department of International Development and director of the Civil Society and Human Security Research Unit at the London School of Economics and Political Science. Among her many works on globalization are *Global Civil Society: An Answer to War* (Cambridge, UK: Polity, 2003; and *New and Old Wars: Organised Violence in a Global Era*, 3rd rev. and updated ed. (Stanford, CA: Stanford University Press, 2012).

[47] At present, Immanuel Wallerstein is senior research scholar at Yale University. After appointments at Columbia University (1958–71) and McGill University (1971–76), Wallerstein joined Binghampton University, State University of New York, as Distinguished Professor of Sociology and director of the Fernand Braudel Center for the Study of Economies, Historical Systems, and Civilizations. His theory of world systems, which has now seen four volumes and remains unfinished, is summarized in *World-Systems Analysis: An Introduction* (A John Hope Franklin Center Book; Durham, NC: Duke University Press, 2004).

After appointments at the University of Paris (1967–79) and the University of California, Berkeley (1979–2003), Manuel Castells joined the University of Southern California as University Professor and the Wallis Annenberg Chair Professor of Communication Technology and Society at the Annenberg School of Communication. He is also professor of sociology and director of the Internet Interdisciplinary Institute at the Open University of Catalonia (UOC) in Barcelona. His major work is *The Information Age: Economy, Society, and Culture,* 3 vols. (Oxford: Blackwell, 1996–98).

[48] Michael Hardt, a literary critic and political philosopher, is professor of literature and Italian at Duke University and professor of philosophy and politics at the European Graduate School (Saas-Fee, Canton Wallis, Switzerland). Antonio Negri, a political activist and philosopher, taught first at the University of Padua and then, while in exile in France, at the Université de Paris VIII and the Collège Internationale de Philosophie (1983–97). Together, Hardt and Negri have written a series on empire today: *Empire* (Cambridge: Harvard University Press, 2001); *Multitude: War and Democracy in the Age of Empire* (New York: Penguin Books, 2004); and *Commonwealth* (Cambridge: Belknap Press of Harvard University Press, 2009).

Michael Mann is professor of sociology at the University of California at Los Angeles, where he has taught since 1987, after appointments at the University of Essex (1971–77) and the London School of Economics and Political Science (1977–87). He is well known for the multivolume work *The Sources of Social Power,* 4 vols. (New York: Cambridge University Press, 1986, 1993, 2012, 2013). This theoretical framework on power he brings to bear on the United States in *Incoherent Empire* (London: Verso, 2003).

David Harvey, an expert in geography and critical social theory, became Distinguished

involving either an international, transnational Empire (Hardt and Negri) or a national, statist empire anchored by the United States (Mann; Helder). It is potentially positive, though decidedly more visionary than realistic, along the lines of a Counter-Empire of Resistance (Hardt and Negri) or the utter transformation of the United States (Mann; Helder)—with dystopia as the alternative.

For de Sousa Santos, the theories of the North, be they hegemonic or critical, prove woefully inadequate. It is to the epistemologies of the South, in their struggle for a better world, that one must look. These have as point of departure a form of injustice that grounds and contaminates all others, at work since the inception of modern capitalism—cognitive injustice. This revolves around the belief that there is but one valid form of knowing, modern science, which is advanced as perfect knowledge and is largely the product of the Global North. In the face of such epistemic exclusivism, the epistemologies of the South clamor for new modes of production, new valorization of valid knowledges, and new relations among different forms of knowing. This they do from the perspective of social groups and classes that have suffered systematic destruction, oppression, and discrimination at the hands of capitalism, colonialism, and resultant unequal formations of power.[49]

The premises of the epistemologies of the South are radically different. First of all, they view the understanding of the world as much broader, by far, than that of the West. As such, the social transformation of the world can take place in ways, modes, and methods beyond the imagination of the West. Second, they affirm that the diversity of the world is boundless, along any number of lines.[50] In the face of hegemonic knowledge, such diversity remains invisible. Lastly, they take such diversity as defying any sort of general theory. Rather, its activation and transformation, theoretical as well as empirical, demand a plurality of knowledges and, ultimately, a general theory that accounts for the impossibility of a general theory. Only through such a plurality of knowledges, grounded in their own historical trajectories and not the universal history of the West, can a vision of utopia arise for the future of the world.

What are the consequences of such a panoply of world theories for my response? These accounts bring out, against a common specter of impending chaos,

---

Professor of Anthropology at the City University of New York in 2001 (2001–), after appointments at various institutions, including John Hopkins University (1969–87, 1993–2001) and Oxford University (1987–93). For his work on imperialism, in relation to postmodernity and globalization, see *The New Imperialism* (Oxford: Oxford University Press, 2003); and *Brief History of Neoliberalism*.

[49] These are worth citing: market exchange, individual property, the sacrifice of the land, racism, sexism, individualism, the placement of the material over the spiritual, and all other *monocultivos* ("monocultures") of mind and society that seek to block a liberating imagination and sacrifice the alternatives. See de Sousa Santos, "Las epistemologías del Sur," 16.

[50] These include different ways of thinking, feeling, and acting; different types of relations among human beings and between human beings and nature; different conceptions of time, of viewing the past, present, and future; and different forms of collective life as well as of the distribution of goods and resources.

the broad diversity of approaches to the world system and the crisis at hand. If critics are to deal with the intersecting nature of the crisis in the world system, they have no option but to examine and address such a crisis from a variety of perspectives, theorizing in the process their own locations in and perception of the world. They must engage the angles of vision of the Global North, its hegemonic as well as critical discourses. They must eschew cognitive injustice and embrace diversity in understanding and transforming the world. They must, therefore, engage the angles of vision of the Global South, its array of epistemologies and histories. Throughout, they must develop a utopian vision of the future that has a better world for all in mind, especially those who have been and continue to be the most deprived and the most excluded. Ultimately, they must imagine new projects of interpretation that embody such ideals. The need for such a type of project James Montgomery sensed ever so well in 1918, again within the modernist and eurocentric boundaries of his context; yet he failed to find or develop a proper theoretical framework for its execution.

V. Imagining an Interpretive Project for Our Times

I should like to conclude by imagining one such project of interpretation that would be in keeping with the various elements of my response to the question of critical vision and task. Such a project requires the disposition of a new grand model of interpretation. For some time now, I have approached the critical trajectory and repertoire of the field in terms of a set of six paradigms—historical, literary, sociocultural, ideological, cultural, and religious-theological.[51] I have described them as closely related to other fields of study in the academy and thus, to one degree or another, as interdisciplinary in character.[52] The proposed paradigm is no exception. A proper designation for it I do not find easy to capture, but I would

---

[51] Such umbrella models I have described as follows. First, as paradigms, these movements encompass a variety of approaches within their angles of vision: the approaches possess a number of discursive features in common, although each has its own method and theory as well. Second, they emerge in the field in largely, although not entirely, sequential fashion: the process of development reveals a theoretical logic at work as well as impinging material factors. Third, these movements, while distinctive and competing, are not necessarily mutually exclusive: the discursive boundaries are often porous and interactive.

[52] With the passage of time, the interdisciplinary character of criticism has multiplied and intensified. To begin with, critical dialogue with corresponding fields and discourses outside biblical criticism has become ever more explicit, extensive, and sophisticated. At the same time, to be sure, all such fields and discourses have become quite diverse in their own right. In addition, critical dialogue across grand models of interpretation in biblical criticism has become more common and pronounced as well. Lastly, the problematic of critical dialogue with a range or even the totality of fields of study or grand models of interpretation has become more pressing, in an effort to move away from atomization and toward intersectionality.

offer, as a working suggestion, that of global-systemic.[53] Its objective, scope, and lens could be described as follows.

The objective is ambitious: to bring the field to bear upon the major crises of our post–Cold War times, in both individual and converging fashion. Such conjunction would entail two analytical dimensions. First, it would require interaction with by now well-established discourses regarding each crisis. Second, it would demand interchange with discourses addressing the convergence of crises, the global state of affairs, by way of world theories from the North and alternative theories from the South. The scope is expansive: the world of production (composition, dissemination, interchange) as well as the world of consumption (reception, circulation, discussion). It would thus encompass the following foci of attention: (1) the texts and contexts of antiquity; (2) the interpretation of these texts and contexts, and the contexts of such interpretations, in the various traditions of reading the Bible, with a focus on modernity and postmodernity; and (3) the interpreters behind such interpretations, and their corresponding contexts.[54] The lens is wide-angled: interaction with the other grand models of interpretation as imperative, determined at any one time by the specific focus of the inquiry in question, since all such angles of inquiry are applicable—in one way or another, to one degree or another—to the analysis of the individual crises as well as the global crisis. In effect, just as historical, literary, sociocultural, ideological, cultural, and religious dimensions crisscross the global-systemic, so does the global-systemic impact upon and intersect with all such dimensions.

Needless to say, this is a tall order. The proposed undertaking demands a critical movement: a joint effort on the part of critics who regard such preoccupations as very much a part of the critical task and stand ready to integrate them into their academic and professional lives and work. Such a movement, moreover, needs to be as diverse as possible, so that the effort proves equal to the problematic and task. I would highlight two kinds of diversity. On the one hand, religious-theological diversity: the view of the Bible and its corresponding mode of reading. No one stance need serve as the driving force behind this undertaking; rather, the entire of spectrum of opinion on this matter can take part. On the other hand, geographical-spatial dimension: the global parameters and perspectives of the field of studies today. No one area of the world should set the pace and tone of the undertaking by itself.

For such a critical movement to prosper, a number of measures would prove helpful. Some would be material in nature. Perhaps a network of digital communication and publishing ventures on the part of interested critics could be established.

---

[53] As the first part of the hyphenated designation, "global" names the terrain or sphere of action—the material context; the second part, "systemic," points to the mode or angle of pursuit—the discursive context.

[54] Epistemically, these foci may be approached not as independent but as interdependent realms: the representations of the texts and contexts of antiquity as re-presentations of antiquity in modernity and postmodernity on the part of situated and interested interpreters.

Perhaps a major academic-scholarly center in each area of the world would be willing to serve as a nerve center in this regard. Perhaps the Society itself could serve as an overall coordinating center, given its extensive network of connections and publications. Others would be discursive. Perhaps such an undertaking could begin with a focus on one crisis in particular. Perhaps it could devise a model for carrying out the proposed conjunction with global studies.

Perhaps I am just dreaming. However, I find that various efforts and ventures along these lines are already under way, showing that concern and interest do exist and establishing a discursive trajectory in the process. Dreaming or not, I find that I have no choice but to follow in this path—as an outsider-insider in the West, as a child of the Global South, and as an international migrant. I should like to conclude by recalling two further anniversaries taking place this year, which I find very much to the point in this regard.

The first is partly fictive and partly real. I am referring to a key dystopic novel of the twentieth century—George Orwell's *Nineteen Eighty-Four*, published in 1949. This year represents the sixty-fifth anniversary of its publication and the thirtieth of its narrative setting. Its elements of Big Brother, doublethink, and newspeak—among many others—have been more than surpassed in our days. In fact, their counterparts today constitute yet another of our crises, the total loss of privacy through total multioptical surveillance.

In the year 1946, between the conclusion of the Second World War and the appearance of the novel, Orwell wrote a piece entitled "Why I Write."[55] There are various reasons why authors write, he states, and they are all to one degree or another present in their work.[56] For him, it was political purpose that predominated after 1936–37—the Spanish Civil War (1936–39).[57] From that point on, he declares, "Every line of serious work that I have written ... has been written, directly or indirectly, *against* totalitarianism and *for* democratic socialism, as I understand it."[58] In so doing, he adds, he has sought to make "political writing into an art"—a fusion of the political and the esthetic.[59] His last novel, *Nineteen Eighty-Four*, emerges as a climax of such resolve.

---

[55] George Orwell, "Why I Write," in *Collected Essays* (London: Mercury Books, 1961), 435–42. The essay was originally published in the last issue of a short-lived English literary magazine, *Gangrel* 4 (Summer 1946).

[56] These are sheer egoism, aesthetic enthusiasm, historical impulse, and political purpose. These, he states, "exist in different degrees in every writer, and in any one writer the proportions will vary from time to time, according to the atmosphere in which he is living" (Orwell, "Why I Write," 437).

[57] The political purpose is described as follows: "Desire to push the world in a certain direction, to alter other people's idea of the kind of society that they should strive after" (Orwell, "Why I Write," 438.)

[58] Orwell, "Why I Write," 440.

[59] Ibid. The conclusion to the essay is pointed: "And looking back through my work, I see that it is invariably where I lacked a *political* purpose that I wrote lifeless books and was betrayed into purple passages, sentences without meaning, decorative adjectives and humbug generally."

The second is altogether real. I have in mind a landmark volume of poetry by the Chilean poet Pablo Neruda—*Canción de gesta* (*Epic Song*), which, though published in 1960, took a different turn in composition during 1959 as a result of the triumph of the Cuban Revolution.[60] This year is the fifty-fifth anniversary of both the Revolution and Neruda's paean to Cuba as the future for all of Latin America. Neruda had written politically engaged poetry before and would do so afterwards as well,[61] but *Canción de gesta* marks an important shift in his life and work.[62] Its emphasis on solidarity calls to mind yet another crisis of our days, the loss of human values and pathos through untrammeled self-interest and competition.[63]

Following upon the 20th Congress of the Communist Party of the Soviet Union in 1956, in which Nikita Khrushchev (1894–1971) denounced the policies of Josef Stalin (1878–1953), Neruda underwent a personal and political crisis. It was with the hope of the Cuban Revolution that he began to forge a new political cosmovision of marxist humanism, away from real socialism and toward democratic socialism. In this work he takes on the role of epic troubadour, as described in the preface: "For my part I here assume yet again, and with pride, my duties as a poet of public service, that is, a pure poet."[64] This poetic voice involving historical

---

[60] The first edition of the volume—minus its final poem—was published in Cuba: Pablo Neruda, *Canción de gesta* (Havana: Imprenta Nacional de Cuba, 1960). As the preface to the first edition indicates, and as outlined by Ferro González ("Isla en el canto de un poeta," *A contra corriente: Una revista de historia social y literatura de América Latina* 8.1 [Fall 2010]: 321–31), the volume, consisting of forty-two poems, was written in three stages: (a) its initial focus was on the status and struggle of Puerto Rico (1958)—written in Chile, at Neruda's home in Isla Negra; (b) then it turns to Cuba and the Caribbean in general (1959)—undertaken while Neruda was residing in Venezuela and during the first year of the Cuban Revolution; and (c) finally, the volume was completed in 1960 (April 12) aboard the mail steamer *Louis Lumière* en route to Europe. The volume is dedicated as follows: to the liberators of Cuba, Fidel Castro and his companions, and the people of Cuba; to all those in Puerto Rico and the Caribbean who struggle for freedom and truth under constant threat from the "United States of America of the North."

[61] Prior to *Canción de gesta* one finds, for example: *España en el corazón: Himno a las glorias del pueblo en la guerra* (1937) and *Tercera residencia, 1935–1945* (1947). Following upon it, for example, is *Incitación al Nixoncidio y alabanza a la Revolución Chilena* (1972) and, posthumously, *Elegía* (1974).

[62] On context, literary as well as political, see the study by Greg Dawes, "*Canción de gesta* y la 'Paz Furiosa' de Neruda," *Gramma* 21.47 (2010): 128–62.

[63] See Paul Verhaeghe, *What about Me? The Struggle for Identity in a Market-based Society* (Melbourne: Scribe, 2014). See also George Mombiot, "Sick of This Market-Driven World? You Should Be," *Guardian*, 5 August 2014, http://www.theguardian.com/commentisfree/2014/aug/05/neoliberalism-mental-health-rich-poverty-economy.

[64] "Por mi parte aquí asumo una vez más, y con orgullo, mis deberes de poeta de utilidad pública, es decir de puro poeta." The volume, he writes, represents "a direct and directed weapon, a fundamental and fraternal aid that I give to our brother peoples for each day of their struggles" ("Este libro no es un lamento de solitario ni una emanación de la oscuridad, sino un arma directa y dirigida, una ayuda elemental y fraternal que entrego a los pueblos hermanos para cada día de

witness and political engagement is explained in the poems: a "pure poet" is one who brings poetry and politics together, form and content, beauty and commitment.[65] This fusion he describes in the poem "Ask Me Not" as follows: "I have a pact of love with beauty / I have a pact of blood with my people." Its task he sets forth as follows: "we must do something on this earth / because in this planet we were birthed / and one must see to the affairs of human beings / because we are neither birds nor dogs."[66]

In the light of contemporary events, both writers, one in the Global North and the other in the Global South, found that they had to pursue their craft as they did, that they could not do otherwise. I see no reason why, in the face of our own contemporary times, we biblical critics should not aim for a similar conjunction of the scholarly and the political. The goal is not a displacement of the other paradigms of interpretation: Who would want to lose such wisdom and knowledge? Who would want to abandon such important problematics and discussions? The goal, rather, is the construction of a new paradigm in conversation with all others. One that would bring closely together biblical criticism and the global scene. One that would foreground sustained theorization of critical vision and task as well as the global state of affairs. A paradigm, in sum, from and for the unique, indeed unprecedented, critical times in which we find ourselves.

As a field of studies and as a learned organization, we owe global society and culture no less. In 1918 James Montgomery, a voice from the Global North, argued precisely the same point: critics should see themselves first as "citizens of the human polity" and answer the call of the world. Today, ninety-five years after its publication in 1919, I, a voice from the Global South, would reiterate that call. I find no better way to do so than by invoking Neruda. If I may be allowed to paraphrase the great Neruda: We have all made a pact of love with criticism; let us now make a pact of blood with the world.

---

sus luchas"). The edition I use is the following: *Canción de gesta: Las piedras de Chile*, ed. Hernán Loyola, De Bolsillo, Biblioteca – Contemporánea (Barcelona: Random House Mondadori, 2010). All translations are mine; for an English translation, see *Song of Protest*, trans. and introduction by Miguel Algarín (New York: Morrow, 1976). Algarín, it should be noted, is one of the poets comprising the Nuyorican Poets.

[65] See esp. Poem 15, "Vengo del Sur" (I Come from the South); Poem 22, "Así es mi vida" (Thus Is My Life); Poem 29, "No me lo pidan" (Ask Me Not); and Poem 43, "Meditación sobre la Sierra Maestra" (Meditation on the Sierra Maestra).

[66] The title of the poem, "Ask Me Not," has in mind critics who would want him to write poetry of a different nature, without reference to the politics of the day. The lines cited form part of his response and rejection: "debemos hacer algo en esta tierra / porque en este planeta nos parieron / y hay que arreglar las cosas de los hombres / porque no somos pájaros ni perros." He ends by saying "tengo un pacto de amor con la hermosura: / tengo un pacto de sangre con mi pueblo."

RECENT BOOKS *from* EERDMANS

SECRET SCRIPTURES REVEALED
*A New Introduction to
the Christian Apocrypha*
Tony Burke
"Tony Burke has long established himself as a master of the Christian apocrypha.... [Now] he has made his massive knowledge of the field available to a broad general audience in a readable, informed, and enjoyable overview that will be long cherished by both beginners and devotees."
— Bart D. Ehrman
ISBN 978-0-8028-7131-2 • 170 pages
paperback • $18.00

FOUR GOSPELS, ONE JESUS?
A Symbolic Reading
Third Edition
Richard A. Burridge
This new edition contains updated suggestions for further reading and a substantial new Afterword in which Burridge reflects personally on his book's genesis, development, and reception over the years.
ISBN 978-0-8028-7101-5 • 235 pages
paperback • $20.00

**THE FIRST EPISTLE
TO THE CORINTHIANS**
*New International Commentary
on the New Testament*
Revised Edition
Gordon D. Fee
Fee's revised edition is based on the improved, updated (2011) edition of the NIV, and it takes into account the considerable scholarship on 1 Corinthians over the past twenty-five years.
ISBN 978-0-8028-7136-7 • 1044 pages
hardcover • $65.00

**THE JESUS MOVEMENT
AND ITS EXPANSION**
Meaning and Mission
Seán Freyne
"This book ... is distinguished by its grounding in the archaeological *realia* of ancient Galilee, but it also contains a notable discussion of the sayings tradition and ranges on into the second century. A fitting capstone to a fine scholarly career."
— John J. Collins
ISBN 978-0-8028-6786-5 • 495 pages
paperback • $35.00

At your bookstore,
or call 800-253-7521
www.eerdmans.com

**WM. B. EERDMANS
PUBLISHING CO.**
2140 Oak Industrial Drive NE
Grand Rapids, MI 49505

The Divining Snake: Reading Genesis 3 in the Context of Mesopotamian Ophiomancy

DUANE E. SMITH
duane@telecomtally.com
Pomona, CA 91767

This article argues that the snake in Gen 3 is best understood within a cultural context that included Mesopotamian ophiomancy. Reading the snake in Gen 3 in this context leads to understanding Hebrew טוב ורע as meaning "good fortune and ill fortune." The article reviews ophiomancy as reflected in omen series *Šumma Ālu ina mēlê šakin* and other Mesopotamian omen and ritual texts. Of the hundreds of snake omens, forty some deal with the ominous behavior of snakes acting in the presence of a man and a woman. These omens provide instructive parallels for the interaction of the snake in Gen 3 and the first couple. They also provide evidence for the cultural context of the snake's role as a communicator of YHWH's mind if not YHWH's will. With several well-attested examples of polysemy and alliteration in Gen 2–3, ancient authors and readers no doubt perceived an unstated relationship between נָחָשׁ ("snake") and נִחֵשׁ ("divination"). Hebrew טוב and רע have overlapping semantic ranges with Akkadian *damqu* and *lemuttu*. Good fortune and ill fortune are within those overlapping ranges. Scholars have long noted parallels between Gen 2–3 and other Mesopotamian traditions, most notably Gilgamesh and Adapa.

The snake, הנחש, of Gen 3 has long been a crux. How should one understand this snake? In his commentary on Genesis, Umberto Cassuto listed and rejected a variety of candidate answers to this question. Among his rejected answers was "serpents used for 'divining' future events." In this article, I argue that Cassuto and others have passed over the interpretive virtues of such an understanding too lightly.[1] I argue that the snake and its message are best understood within a cultural

---

[1] Umberto Cassuto (Moshe David), *A Commentary on the Book of Genesis*, Part 1, *From Adam to Noah, Genesis I–VI*, trans. Israel Abrahams (Jerusalem: Magnes, 1972), 140; Heinz-Josef Fabry, "*naḥaš*," *ThWAT* 4:384–85; Ann Jeffers, *Magic and Divination in Ancient Palestine and Syria*, SHANE 8 (Leiden: Brill, 1996), 75; Carole R. Fontaine, "The Strange Face of Wisdom in the

context that includes Mesopotamian ophiomancy. Drawing on omens from *Šumma Ālu ina mēlê šakin* (hereafter *Šumma Ālu*) and other Mesopotamian divination texts, I will first illustrate and explain the Akkadian evidence; I will then discuss how this evidence might inform our understanding of the snake in Gen 3; and, finally, I will justify such an understanding by showing that Mesopotamian ophiomancy was part of the cultural substrate out of which Gen 3 emerged. I delay this last topic to the end of the article because it depends, in part, on evidence and arguments developed in the discussion of the first two topics.

I. Mesopotamian Ophiomancy

Our most extensive source for Mesopotamian ophiomancy is the approximately five hundred snake omens witnessed on tablets 22 through 26 of the Akkadian omen series *Šumma Ālu*. This evidence is supplemented by several additional snake omen collections that are not readily associated with series *Šumma Ālu* but are clearly in the same tradition.[2] The evidence for Mesopotamian ophiomancy is

---

New Testament: On the Reuse of Wisdom Characters from the Hebrew Bible," in *Recycling Biblical Figures: Papers Read at a NOSTER Colloquium in Amsterdam 12-13 May 1997*, ed. Athalya Brenner and Jan Willem van Henten, STAR 1 (Leiden: Deo, 1999), 205–29, esp. 217; Reuven Kimelman, "The Seduction of Eve and Feminist Readings of the Garden of Eden," *Women in Judaism: A Multidisciplinary Journal* 1.2 (1998): n.p., http://www.utoronto.ca/wjudaism/journal/journal_index2.html; David Nimmer, "Rabbi Banet's Charming Snake," *Ḥakirah, the Flatbush Journal of Jewish Law and Thought* 93.2 (2009): 69–108, esp. 75; James H. Charlesworth, *The Good and Evil Serpent: How a Universal Symbol Became Christianized*, AYBRL (New Haven: Yale University Press, 2010), 244–45. It is just possible that Maimonides implied a relationship between the snake and divination in *Guide to the Perplexed* 2.30.217 ("There is a meaning in this name [Samaël]), as there is also in the name naḥash ['serpent'])." See José Faur, *Homo Mysticus: A Guide to Maimonides's Guide for the Perplexed* (Syracuse, NY: Syracuse University Press, 1998), 59, 210 n. 45, who surveys the rabbinic tradition on the relationship between the snake and divination.

[2] Rosel Pientka-Hinz provides a detailed account of snakes in Mesopotamian literature ("Schlange A", *RlA* 12:202–18). Of particular importance to our discussion is his review of Mesopotamian snake omens and exorcism literature (pp. 212–13). Unless otherwise noted, I have used the composite Akkadian text in Sally M. Freedman, *If a City Is Set on a Height: The Akkadian Omen Series Shumma Alu ina mele Shakin*, 2 vols., Occasional Publications of the Samuel Noah Kramer Fund 17, 19 (Philadelphia: University of Pennsylvania Museum of Archaeology and Anthropology, Babylonian Section, 1998, 2006), vol. 2, tablets 23–40. Normalizations and translations, while dependent on Freedman and others, are mine. I also follow her tablet and omen numbering conventions (ibid., 1:19–23). In addition to Akkadian omens and exorcism literature, we have medical texts with prescriptions for curing snakebites (note in this regard Num 21:5–6 and, from Ugarit, *KTU* 1.100 = RS 24.244); references to snake-charming rituals (compare Jer 8:17 and Qoh 10:11); fables (Etana Legend; Benjamin R. Foster, *Before the Muses: An Anthology of Akkadian Literature*, 3rd ed. [Bethesda MD: CDL, 2005], 533–43); and mundane references to snakes.

further augmented by a number of *namburbi* rituals and prayers against negative portents of ominous snake behavior.³ *Šumma Ālu*, as preserved in multiple manuscripts from the Ashurbanipal Library and elsewhere, once consisted of as many as 120 numbered tablets.⁴ Most of these tablets, while often fragmentary, are extant. The series as a whole deals with terrestrial events—everything from the location of cities to animal and insect behavior, to fungal patterns, to plants, to things that might happen during ritual processions.⁵ Each tablet contains approximately one hundred omens—some significantly fewer, some more. The omens are structured as conditional clauses (if P then Q). Most often each omen has but a single, sometimes complex, protasis and a single apodosis. However, a number of the omens have several apodoses. In a few cases multiple apodoses contradict one another.⁶

³ See Stefan M. Maul, *Zukunftsbewältigung: Eine Untersuchung altorientalischen Denkens anhand der babylonisch-assyrischen Löserituale (Namburbi)*, BaF 18 (Mainz: von Zabern, 1994), 270–303; Irving L. Finkel, "On Late Babylonian Medical Training," in *Wisdom, Gods and Literature: Studies in Assyriology in Honour of W. G. Lambert*, ed. Andrew R. George and Irving L. Finkel (Winona Lake, IN: Eisenbrauns, 2000), 137–224, esp. 206–7; Erica Reiner, *Astral Magic in Babylonia*, TAPS 85.4 (Philadelphia: American Philosophical Society, 1995), 83 n. 338; and Duane E. Smith, "A Namburbi against the Evil of a Snake: Shamash 25," in *Reading Akkadian Prayers and Hymns: An Introduction*, ed. Alan Lenzi, ANEM 3 (Atlanta: Society of Biblical Literature, 2011), 421–32. Other incantations cited by Finkel are not formally *namburbi* prayers but are nonetheless within the corpus of Mesopotamian snake-divination traditions (Irving L. Finkel, "On Some Dog, Snake and Scorpion Incantations," in *Mesopotamian Magic: Textual, Historical, and Interpretative Perspectives*, ed. Tzvi Abusch and Karel van der Toorn, AMD 1 [Groningen: Styx, 1999], 211–52).

⁴ That the Ashurbanipal Library version of the series once filled at least 107 tablets is certain. However, the colophon of VAT 13805 from Assur reads in part ⌊DU⌋B 1 ME 20 KAM *ana* DIŠ URU *ina* SUKUD-*e* GAR [... M]U.ŠID.BI.IM, "Tablet 120 of *Šumma Ālu ina Mēlê Šakin* [... l]ines of text." Compare the colophon of the related K.3074 + K.1104 (*CT* 40:38), [DU]B 1 ME 20 KAM *ana* DIŠ URU *ina* SUKUD-*e* GAR [... M]U.ŠID.BI.IM, "[Tab]let 120 of *Šumma Ālu ina Mēlê Šakin* [... l]ines of text." See the discussion in Nils P. Heeßel, *Divinatorische Texte*, vol. 1, *Terrestrische, teratologische, physiognomische und oneiromantische Omina*, Ausgrabungen der Deutschen Orient-Gesellschaft in Assur 1, WVDOG 116 (Wiesbaden: Harrassowitz, 2007), 3, 110–11; Ann Kessler Guinan, "A Severed Head Laughed: Stories of Divinatory Interpretation," in *Magic and Divination in the Ancient World*, ed. Leda Jean Ciraolo and Jonathan Seidel, AMD 2 (Leiden: Brill, 2002), 7–40, esp. 12; and Walther Sallaberger, "Das Erscheinen Marduks als Vorzeichen: Kultstatue und Neujahrsfest in der Omenserie Šumma ālu," *ZA* 90 (2000), 227–62, among others. In addition to Nineveh and Assur, tablets from series *Šumma Ālu* have been discovered at Kalḫu, Babylon, Borsippa, and Sippar. Precursors, clear excerpts from series *Šumma Ālu*, and very similar omens that are not so clearly associated with the canonical series are known from many other sites. These tablets range in date from Old Babylonian *Šumma Ālu* precursors (early to mid-second millennium BCE) to 228 BCE.

⁵ Other such series include *Šumma Izbu*, on malformed births; *Enuma Anu Enlil*, on meteorology and astrology; *Bārûtu* (*manzāzu, padānu*, and *pān tākalti*) on extispicy; ᵈ*Ziqīqu*, on dreams; and several others dealing with everything from moles to "body language."

⁶ For example, omens involving snake behavior with multiple and/or contradictory apodoses include *Šumma Ālu* 22:37, "[If ... a snake] enters a [ho]le, either (*lu*) a prominent person

Occasionally an omen or group of omens will be followed by an apotropaic procedure to mitigate undesirable portents. The overwhelming majority, if perhaps not quite all *Šumma Ālu* omens, are *omina oblativa*, "casually met with omens," as opposed to *omina impetrativa*, "sought out omens." Frederick Cryer calls such omens "surprise encounters."[7] *Šumma Ālu* is organized by protasis theme. Tablets 22–63 deal with the ominous behavior of land animals in general (zoomancy), and tablets 64–79 deal with the ominous behavior of birds (ornithomancy).[8] Tablets 22–26 are devoted to the ominous behavior of snakes. No part of *Šumma Ālu* tablets 27–29 has been identified with certainty. Neither their incipits nor their contents are known. For this reason, it is uncertain if one or more of these tablets also contained snake omens. The first omen in the ophiomancy subseries of *Šumma Ālu* (tablet 22:1) reads:

> DIŠ *ina* ITI.BARA₂ UD.1.KAM₂ NA *la-am* TA GIŠ.NA₂ GIR₂-*šu*₂ *ana* KI GAR-*nu* MUŠ TA ḪABRUD.DA E₃-*ma la-am ma-am-man* IGI LU₂ IGI LU₂ BI *ina* ŠA₃ MU BI UG_x *šum*₄-*ma* LU₂ BI TI.LA *ḫa-šiḫ* SAG.DU *u*₂-*ḫar-ra-ar*₂ TE.MEŠ-*šu*₂ *u*₂-*gal-lab* ITI.3.KAM₂ *uš-ta-pa-aš*₂-*šaq-ma* TI-*uḫ*[9]

> If, on the first of (the month of) Nisānu, before a man has put his foot out of bed onto the ground, a snake comes out of a hole and, before anyone sees (it), it sees the man, that man will die within that year; if that man desires to live, he should ??? (his) head, (and) shave his cheeks; he will suffer for three months but he will live.

Notice that this first snake omen contains a procedure for mitigating the full force of the misfortune that the omen's apodosis entails. If one follows the procedure, there will be three months of suffering, but death will be avoided. While we do not always know the mitigating ritual or procedure, it appears that, given enough time, inconvenience, and expense, many unfavorable portents could be avoided or deflected with appropriate ritual. Following this first snake omen are twenty-two omens involving various snake activities in the month of Nisānu and then fourteen omens involving snake activities during several subsequent months. Like the majority of the omens in *Šumma Ālu*, these omens lack an associated mitigating procedure.

The central thesis of this article depends on the thematic breadth of *Šumma Ālu* snake omens rather than on any particular omen that exhibits a direct parallel

---

will have no rival or (*lu*) a commoner, his calamity will be removed;" or strikingly 22:38, "[If on] the day he prays, a snake slithers under a man and lies down […]; alternatively (KIMIN), his property will be taken away; alternatively (KIMIN), he will eat bounteous food."

[7] Frederick H. Cryer, *Divination in Ancient Israel and Its Near Eastern Environment: A Socio-Historical Investigation*, JSOTSup 142 (Sheffield: JSOT Press, 1994), 162.

[8] Freedman, *If a City*, 2:3.

[9] Following the convention of *CAD*, I read the BAD sign UG_x rather than UG₇. On the uncertainty of the meaning of *ḫarāru*, see *CAD* Ḫ, 91–92 (*ḫarāru* A). BM 129092, an unpublished commentary, reads *ú-ḫar-ra-ár*, perhaps related to *ḫarāru*, "to dig or groove." See Freedman, *If a City*, 2:8; and *CAD* Ḫ, 91 [*ḫarāru* B].

with the activity of the snake in Gen 3. None exhibits such a direct parallel. Therefore it is necessary to document this thematic breadth. Being generally less complex and less lacunose than many omens, omens 52–92 of *Šumma Ālu* tablet 22 provide a useful sequence to further this necessity. The following is but a sample.

22:52   DIŠ MUŠ *ana* IGI NA *i-mu-ut* ŠUB-*at* EN KA-*šu₂* IGI-*mar*

If a snake dies in front of a man, he will see the downfall of his adversary.

22:53   DIŠ MUŠ *ana* IGI NA *it-ta-pa-aṣ* EN KA-*šu₂* GAZ-*ak*

Is a snake flops about (strikes in all directions?) in front of a man, he will kill his adversary.

22:54   DIŠ MUŠ *ana* IGI NA *iz-qu-up lit-ti u ki-šit-ti* ŠU

If a snake stands in front of a man—victory and booty of conquest.

22:55   DIŠ MUŠ *ana* IGI NA DU.DU *mi-lum₂ ana* KUR

If a snake wanders about in front of a man—irrigation of the land.[10]

22:56   [DIŠ] MUŠ *ana* IGI NA KAŠ₄-*um* KUR-*ad₂* A₂.AŠ₂

If a snake runs in front of a man—attainment of desire.

But not all the omens in this sequence have positive portents. Most do not. For example,

22:64   DIŠ MUŠ *ana* IGI NA *sa-dir* NA BI NIG₂.GA-*šu₂ i-gam-mar ina* NU DUG₂ *lìb-bi* DU.MEŠ

If a snake is regularly in front of a man, that man will deplete his resources (property); he will live (go about) unhappily.

Notice that 22:52 shows polysemy: IGI, *pan(u)*, "face," and IGI, *immar* (*amāru*), "he will see." The play between IGI, *pan(u)*, "face," and IGI, *immar*, "he will see," provides a weak hermeneutical connection between the protasis and the apodosis of this omen. The scribe did not save a single sign by writing IGI with the phonetic complement *mar* in 22:52. While still following convention, the scribe saved, at best, a couple of wedges. Far from a majority of omens evidence such wordplay. But polysemy, polyphony, and even more complex linguistic interrelationships do occur in Mesopotamian omens more often than can be accounted for by chance alone. Scott Noegel and Eckart Frahm, among others, have demonstrated that such wordplay often functions as a hermeneutical link between an omen's protasis and its apodosis.[11] As both Noegel and Frahm argue, the ability to draw inferences from

---

[10] *Mitum ana māti*, lit., "flood in the land." A *milum* is the seasonal flood or cresting of a river. While not without its dangers, *milum* has a positive connotation as a source of irrigation. See *CAD* M/2, 69–72.

[11] For examples of stronger hermeneutical uses of polysemy and polyphony, see Scott B. Noegel, *Nocturnal Ciphers: The Allusive Language of Dreams in the Ancient Near East*, AOS 89

polysemy and polyphony was a scribal virtue in the ancient Near East. I will address polysemy in the Hebrew of Gen 3 when I consider the possible play between Hebrew נָחָשׁ ("snake") and נִחֵשׁ ("practice divination") along with its nominal forms below.

Over forty extant omens from *Šumma Ālu* involve a man, a woman, and one or more snakes. Many are too fragmentary for detailed study. Representative of the more readable omens of this type are:

23:28a   DIŠ MUŠ *ana bi-rit* NITA *u* MUNUS ŠUB-*ma* NU E₃ [EN KA?]-*šu*₂ GAZ(?)-[*ak*?]

If a snake falls between a man and a woman and it will not leave, he will kill(?) his adversaries(?).[12]

23:29   DIŠ MUŠ *ana* MURU₂ DAM *u* DAM ŠUB-*ut-ma* DU₈ [...-*z*]*u-uz-zu* DAM *u* DAM TAG₄.ME UG_x.UG_x

If a snake falls in the middle of a husband and wife and leaves [...] they stand, husband and wife will divorce; they will die.

23:30   DIŠ MUŠ *ana* MURU₂ DAM *u* DAM ŠUB-*ut-ma* BI SU X i [. . .] DU₈ SILIM.MI GAL₂-*šu*₂ KUR X X

If a snake falls in the middle of a husband and wife and it replaces(?) [...] it leaves, there will be peace for him; the land will be [...].[13]

23:31   [DIŠ] MUŠ *ana* MURU₂ DAM *u* DAM ŠUB-*ma ina* GU.DU [. . .*b*] *i-ri-šu*₂-*nu* ŠUB-*ut-ma* IGI.ME-*šu*₂ TAG₄-ME-*m*[*a* . . .]

(New Haven: American Oriental Society, 2007), 9–45. See, in addition, idem, "Fox on the Run: Catch a Lamassu by the Pun," *NABU* 73 (1995–96): 101–2; Eckart Frahm, "Reading the Tablet, the Exta, and the Body: The Hermeneutics of Cuneiform Signs in Babylonian and Assyrian Text Commentaries and Divinatory Texts," in *Divination and Interpretation of Signs in the Ancient World*, ed. Amar Annus et al., OIS 6 (Chicago: Oriental Institute of the University of Chicago, 2010), 93–141; and Alasdair Livingstone, *Mystical and Mythological Explanatory Works of Assyrian and Babylonian Scholars* (Oxford: Clarendon, 1986), 45, 88, 102. Gebhard J. Selz provides a useful discussion and nearly complete set of bibliographic references in "Texts, Textual Bilingualism, and the Evolution of Mesopotamian Hermeneutics," in *Between Text and Text: The Hermeneutics of Intertextuality in Ancient Cultures and Their Afterlife in Medieval and Modern Times*, ed. Michaela Bauks, Wayne Horowitz, and Armin Lange, JAJSup 6 (Göttingen: Vandenhoeck & Ruprecht, 2013), 47–65.

[12] My reconstruction is based on *Šumma Ālu* 22:53.

[13] See *tašmû* (*u*) *salimu* (SILIM.MU) *ina māti ibašši* in *CT* 39:22:2 (*Šumma Izbu*) VI:21; *CT* 39:30:33 (*Šumma Ālu*); *CAD* S, 100–101. Compare Erle Leichty, *The Omen Series Šumma Izbu*, TCS 4; Locust Valley, NY: Augustin, 1970), 112 (tablet 8:91'). Freedman renders this simply, "If a snake falls in the middle of husband and wife and gets away, [...], there will be goodwill for him" (*If a City*, 2:38–39).

[If] a snake falls in the middle of a husband and wife and falls behind
[...] among them and they see it, they will divorce an[d ...].

23:32   [DIŠ] MUŠ *a-šar* NITA *u* MUNUS KI DUR$_2$.MEŠ *lu* GUB.MEŠ
[*u*$_4$(?)]^{14}]-*mi-šu-nu i-dab-bu-bu* IGI.MEŠ-*ma ig-dar-ru*^{15} TAG$_4$.
[MEŠ]

[If] where a man and woman are sitting or standing while discussing
their [days], they see a snake and it attacks (?), they will divorce.

23:33   [DIŠ M]UŠ *a-šar* NITA *u* MUNUS KI DUR$_2$.MEŠ-*ma* x x –*ma* IGI.
MEŠ-*šu*$_2$ TAG$_4$.M[EŠ]-*ma* NITA TI-*q*[*i*$_2$]

[If a snake], where a husband and wife are sitting and ... and they see
it, they will divorce, and the husband will take away (the property?).

23:34   [DIŠ MUŠ] *a-šar* NITA *u* MUNUS GUB-*zu i-dab-bu-bu*! IGI NITA *u*
MUSUS [KUD.]MEŠ TAG$_4$.MEŠ

[If a snake] appears where a man and woman are standing conversing,
the man and woman will separate; they will divorce.

23:35   [DIŠ MUŠ *a-šar* NITA] *u* MUNUS DUR$_2$.MEŠ-*ma* DUMU.MEŠ E$_2$
ARAD *u* GEME$_2$ NIGIN.MEŠ-*ma ana bi-ri-šu-nu* ŠUB-*ut* EN E$_2$ UG$_x$-
ma E$_2$ BIR

[If, a snake] falls among [a man] and woman sitting with the children
of the house, (with) the servant and maid surrounding (them), the
owner of the house will die, and the house will be dispersed.

As *Šumma Ālu* 23:30 witnesses, not all such omens have negative portents. Some,
like 23:23, even portend the birth of a male child.

DIŠ MUŠ *ra-man-šu*$_2$ *ik-kal* GAR-*un* ZU$_2$ GIG$_2$ NA [KUN(?)]^{16} *ina*
KA-*šu*$_2$ DAM NA NITA U$_3$.TU

If a snake eats itself, causing tooth (induced) [tail(?)] pain(?) by its
mouth, a man's wife will give birth to a male child.

---

^{14}This reconstruction is but a suggestion.

^{15}*Ig-dar-ru* is problematic. Freedman tentatively suggests that it might be a Gt of *gerû*, "to be hostile" (*If a City*, 2:39).

^{16}It is not obvious how one should understand ZU$_2$.GIG NA. On ZU$_2$.gig (toothache) = *zakigâ*, see *za-ki-ga-a* in RS 17.155 and duplicate (*Ugaritica*, vol. 5, MRS 16 [Paris: Geuthner, 1968], 17:36). Here I take it to mean a pain caused by a tooth. While not without problems, I read NA as the Sumerian 3rd sg. locative pronoun. Exactly how one should gloss it in Akkadian is unclear. Note ni-e NA = *šu-u* (EA IV 105; see *CAD* Š3, 153) and na-a NA = *šu-u* (A IV/2:223′, 222). Freedman, perhaps wisely, simply reads ka mi na without attempting to interpret the text (*If a City*, 2:38). My restoration of KUN = *zibbati*, "tail," is completely speculative. Freedman reads the omen, DIŠ MUŠ *ra-man-šu*$_2$ *ik-kal* GAR-*un* ka mi na [...] *ina* KA-*šu*$_2$ DAM NA NITA U$_3$.TU (*If a City*, 2:38).

In other cases the portent seems to me particularly strange and unexpected. For example 24:1:

> DIŠ MUŠ *ina* UGU GIŠ.NA₂ NA NA₂-*iṣ* DAM LU₂ IGI.MEŠ-*ša*₂ GUR.
> MEŠ-*ma* DUMU.MEŠ-*ša*₂ *ana* KU₃.BABBAR SUM-*in*
>
> If a snake lies on a man's bed, the man's wife will be distracted and sell her children for silver.

What we see in these omens is a rather systematic listing of a range of possible snake activities that were each thought to portend some outcome or outcomes. While most portend separation, divorce, dismantling of the household, even death, others portend positive outcomes.

In addition to *Šumma Ālu*, there are a number of other witnesses to Mesopotamian ophiomancy. Nils Heeßel published a modern edition of four tablets from Assur that contain snake omens with the same formal structure and general content as *Šumma Ālu* snake omens but are not obviously part of that series.[17] VAT 10116 + 10145:8 provides an example,

> DIŠ MUŠ.MEŠ *ina* E₂ DINGER *ana m*[*a-g*]*al* ŠUB.ŠUB.MEŠ-*ni*[18] *ša*₂
> NIR.DA-*a* SI.A *ana*! E₂ DINGER! *ana* E₂.GAL KU₄-ME-*ni*
>
> If snakes often(?) fall in a temple, those who are extremely guilty will enter the temple (or) the palace before me(?).

The omens in lines 8–14 of this tablet plus a few seemingly out-of-place omens deal with ominous behavior of snakes in a temple. Other omens deal with snakes in a man's house, in his path, in a field, and, more generally, on the ground. VAT 10523, also from Assur, witnesses a few omens involving a man, a woman, and a snake. Rev. II:11, for example:

> [DIŠ MU]Š *a-na bi-rit* NITA U MUNUS ŠUB-*ut lu i+na-bit*₂ *lu ina ze-nu-ti* TAR.MEŠ
>
> If a snake falls between a man and a woman: either he will flee or they will separate in hatred.

While this omen is very similar in content, it is not witnessed in these words in any extant tablet in *Šumma Ālu*. We see in these texts, as well as in the more obvious

---

[17] See Heeßel, *Divinatorische Texte*, 1:13 (VAT 10116 + 10145), 14 (VAT 10523 + A 10) and 15 (VAT 10805). Heeßel's tablets 9 (VAT 10481 + VAT 10905b + VAT 12918 etc.), 11 (A 453 + A 536 + A 2410 + A 2438), and 12 (VAT 13812 + VAT 13827) reflect duplicates and/or excerpts of varying lengths from *Šumma Ālu* tablets 22–25.

[18] The Akkadian word represented by this group is no doubt plural and likely a *-tan-* form, "continuously fall." On ŠUB.MEŠ-*ni*, see *CT* 29:48-48, "Stars fell repeatedly(?) (ŠUB.ŠUB.MEŠ-*ni*) from the sky"; A. Leo Oppenheim, *The Interpretation of Dreams in the Ancient Near East, With a Translation of an Assyrian Dream Book*, TAPS NS 46.3 (Philadelphia: American Philosophical Society, 1956), 283, 328, "If stars ŠUB.MEŠ-*ni* (fall) upon a man."

Šumma Ālu duplicates and excerpts from Assur, a dynamic ophiomancy tradition that extended from before the Neo-Assyrian period. As I will show, the Mesopotamian ophiomancy tradition continued from as early as the Old Babylonian period well into late antiquity.

Namburbi rituals and associated prayers are another source for understanding Mesopotamian ophiomancy. *Namburbi* rituals are apotropaic in that they were used to deflect or mitigate the negative portents of omens. Snake activity in the context of human activity had consequences, lives were thought to be changed sometimes in rather dramatic ways. But various gods, notably Shamash, if properly approached, could set aside these negative portents. VAT 5 witnesses a prayer of the type found in *namburbi* rituals:

> O Shamash, king of heaven and earth, Lord of truth and justice, Lord of the Anunna-gods, Lord of the spirits of the dead, whose consent no god can change, whose command cannot be altered, O Shamash, reviving the dead (and) releasing the captive is in your hands.
>
> O Shamash, I, your servant, so-and-so, son of so-and-so, whose personal god is Marduk and (whose) personal goddess is Zarpanitum, stand before you. I seize your hem.
>
> *On account of the evil of a snake, which I saw enter my house and hunt, I am afraid, anxious, and constantly in fear.*
>
> From this evil save me, that I may proclaim your greatness, (and) praise your glories, (and that) those who see me may sound your praises, (and) forever praise your glories!

No extant *Šumma Ālu* omen exactly matches the case of a snake seen entering someone's house *and* hunting prey. *Šumma Ālu* 23:106 mentions a snake entering someone's house resulting in a negative portent, "If a snake enters a man's house, that house will be abandoned," and several omens address snakes hunting specific kinds of prey.[19] But none mentions a snake both entering a house and hunting. The ritual associated with this prayer is unknown. VAT 5 contains only the prayer.[20] However, more complete *namburbi* rituals against the evil of a snake witness a variety of procedures.[21] It is possible to glean an idea of the ritual of which the

---

[19] E.g., *Šumma Ālu* 25-26 ii 6′, 16′, 22′.

[20] For fuller treatments of this prayer, see Smith, "Namburbi," 431 (the source of this translation); and Maul, *Zukunftsbewältigung*, 296-97, 542. Reiner also discusses snake omens and *namburbi* rituals (*Astral Magic*, 83 n. 338).

[21] Maul published eight examples of *namburbi*s against the evil of a snake (*Zukunftsbewältigung*, 270-303), and Finkel published two other examples (BM 43090+ and BM 42559+ ("On Late Babylonian Medical Training," 206-7). On the stock phrase "I am afraid, anxious, and constantly in fear (*palḫāku adrāku u sutādurāku*)," see Werner Mayer, *Untersuchungen zur Formensprache der babylonischen "Gebetsbeschwörungen*," StPohl, Series Maior 5 (Rome: Biblical Institute Press, 1976), 73.

VAT 5 prayer may have been a part from the related text 80-7-19,88.[22] This *namburbi* ritual involves a practitioner drawing water at sunset, mixing barley, emmer, and lentils with silver and gold. In a secluded place "they" make a reed altar to Shamash and place bread, honey, and ghee on and around it. Carnelian, lapis lazuli, and several other stones plus copper, tin, silver, and gold are dipped in oil and made into a necklace for the supplicant. At this point the tablet becomes nearly unreadable, but eventually the supplicant recites an incantation similar to VAT 5's prayer. While closely parallel, the prayer of the 80-7-19,88 *namburbi* does not appear to witness exactly the same prayer as does VAT 5.

Scholars have suggested two ways in which ancient Mesopotamian divination was understood. One understanding was theological. The gods make their will and mind (or the will and mind of other gods) known to humans through omens. While no snake omen or narrative concerning a snake omen directly witnesses this or any other mechanism, we can reasonably surmise a theological mechanism from the petitions to the gods in *namburbi* rituals and, by analogy, with other Mesopotamian divination traditions. For example, it is said of Shamash, *ina libbi immeri tašaṭṭar šīra*, "On the exta of a sheep you inscribe the omen."[23] A common figure for the process is of a literate god writing on the media at hand. As we will see in more detail, "writing" was not the only figure for how the gods communicated their will and mind.[24] Sometimes omens "spoke." Ea's response to Enlil's anger about Atraḫasis's learning of the coming flood illustrates another way of expressing a theological mechanism, "It was not I who disclosed the secret of the great gods. I caused Atraḫasis to have a dream, and so he heard the secret of the gods."[25] Ea induced a dream that revealed the secret of the great gods.

But Ea's response can be understood cosmologically as well as theologically. Ea did not disclose the plans of the gods so much as he allowed Atraḫasis to experience those plans by other means. Ann Jeffers suggests that we should understand divination within a cosmic framework, "How is anyone able to foretell the future but in a world where signs, any signs, are part of the whole, and therefore can be interpreted because the sign incarnates and reflects the whole situation at the moment when it is read."[26] The cosmos aligns with the will and mind of the gods, modifying the stuff of the world in ways that both the gods and properly trained humans can understand.

Whatever the mechanism, the Mesopotamians saw human knowledge of divination as of divine origin. Again we lack explicit evidence in the case of ophiomancy. We do have evidence of how humans came to know other forms of

---

[22] 80-7-19,88, obv. 7–rev. 15. See Maul, *Zukunftsbewältigung*, 278–82.
[23] K.2824 and duplicates.
[24] On this, see Noegel, *Nocturnal Ciphers*, 271.
[25] Gilgamesh Epic XI:200; translation of Benjamin R. Foster, *The Epic of Gilgamesh: A New Translation, Analogues, Criticism* (New York: Norton, 2001), 91.
[26] Jeffers, *Magic and Divination*, 128.

divination. From K.2486 + K.3646 + K.4364 we learn that Shamash and Adad taught the antediluvian king Enmeduranki divine secrets including several forms of divination:

> Enmeduranki [king of Sippar],
> The beloved of Anu, Enlil [and Ea].
> Šamaš and Adad [brought him in]to their assembly,
> Šamaš and Adad [honored him],
> Šamaš and Adad [set him] on a large throne of gold,
> They showed him how to observe oil on water, a mystery of Anu, [Enlil, and Ea],
> They gave him the tablet of the gods, the entrails, a secret of heaven and underworld.
> They put in his hand the cedar-(rod), beloved of the great gods.

And, in turn, Enmeduranki taught divination to the men of Nippur, Sippar, and Babylon.[27] What Lambert called "A Catalogue of Texts and Authors," reads in part:

> [The Exorcist's] Corpus; The Lamentation-priests' Corpus; When Anu and Enlil;
> [(If) a] Form; Not Completed Months; Diseased Sinews;
> (If) the Utterance [of the Mouth]; The King, the Storm(?), whose Aura is Heroic; Fashioned like An
> [These] are of the mouth of Ea.

The other referenced treatises in this ancient catalogue are all assigned to human origin. While one might wonder about the role of Ea as the direct author of the referenced texts, it is clear that the author/compiler of this catalogue and of K.2486+ saw the gods as the ultimate source of human knowledge of divination.[28]

Whether we think in theological or cosmological terms, ophiomancy was surely an important and pervasive part of Mesopotamian divination. It was first in order among the omens concerning the behavior of land animals in *Šumma Ālu*. Among the ominous activities of animals in general, only that of birds was more thoroughly catalogued.

II. THE SNAKE IN GENESIS 3

With this Mesopotamian ophiomancy tradition in mind, I now turn to the snake in Gen 3. Like *omina oblativa*, the snake appears unexpectedly and interrupts

---

[27] Wilfred G. Lambert, "Enmeduranki and Related Matters," *JCS* 21, Special Volume Honoring Professor Albrecht Goetze (1967): 126–38.

[28] K2248:1–4. Wilfred G. Lambert, "A Catalogue of Texts and Authors," *JCS* 16 (1962): 59–77, esp. 72–73. Francesca Rochberg thinks in terms of divine authority rather than divine authorship ("Continuity and Change in Omen Literature," in *Munuscula Mesopotamica: Festschrift für Johannes Renger*, ed. Barbara Bock, Eva Cancik-Kirschbaum, and Thomas Richter, AOAT 267 [Münster: Ugarit-Verlag, 1999], 415–25).

the narrative of life in the garden. An important element of that life is the divine instruction on what can and cannot be eaten (Gen 2:16b–17):

Of every tree of the garden you may eat;	מכל עץ הגן אכל תאכל
but as for the tree of knowledge of good and bad,	ומעץ הדעת טוב ורע
you must not eat of it;	לא תאכל ממנו
for as soon as you eat it you will certainly die.	כי ביום אכלך ממנו מות תמות

The snake engages the woman concerning YHWH's instruction, in due course says to her, לא מות תמתון, "you will not die" (Gen 3:4) and continues:

For God knows	כי ידע אלהים
that on the day you eat of it	כי ביום אכלכם ממנו
your eyes will be opened	ונפקחו עיניכם
and you will be like gods	והייתם כאלהים
who know good and bad.	ידעי טוב ורע

The snake communicates the mind, if not the will, of God. As a narrative, none of this has the form of a Mesopotamian snake omen. It is a different genre. But if we read these lines in the context of Mesopotamian ophiomancy, we see the role of the snake for what it is—the theological and/or cosmological vehicle through which the true mind of God becomes known.

Beyond the negation of the punishment for breaking the divine command, the snake's speech reveals YHWH's underlying motivation. YHWH worries that humans will become like gods, ידעי טוב ורע ("who know good and bad"). The terms רע and טוב have traditionally been understood here as having moral connotations or, less traditionally, when taken together, as a merism for "everything."[29] But looking at the breadth of the semantic ranges of these words and reading them in the context of divination, "fortune" and "misfortune" provide more helpful understandings. In this light I suggest that ידעי טוב ורע means "those who know the results of divination," those who know fortune and misfortune, possibly even those who know the skill of divination.

We have already seen that Mesopotamian snake omens can have either good or bad portents. While this is implicit in the extant snake omens, an extispicy omen makes this point explicitly.[30]

---

[29] The idea that טוב ורע is a merism for "everything" goes back at least to Gerhard von Rad, *Genesis: A Commentary*, trans. J. Marks, OTL (Philadelphia: Westminster, 1972), 86–87. See, more recently, Helen Kraus, *Gender Issues in Ancient and Reformation Translations of Genesis 1–4* (Oxford: Oxford University Press, 2011), 22; and Carol L. Meyers, *Rediscovering Eve: Ancient Israelite Women in Context* (Oxford: Oxford University Press, 2013), 79–80.

[30] Rm² III.103 obv. 17–18 A and duplicates as published by Ulla Koch-Westenholz, *Babylonian Liver Omens: The Chapters Manzāzu, Padānu and Pān Tākalti of the Babylonian Extispicy Series Mainly from Aššurbanipal's Library*, CNIP 25 (Copenhagen: Museum Tusculanum

BE SILIM MAŠ₂ *ina* UGU MAŠ₂ *e-ṣir ša*₂ *ana* SIG₅ *u* ḪUL DUG₄-*u*₂ IGI.MEŠ-*ša*₂ *ana* 15 *ša*₂ GAR.MEŠ-*ma* SIG₅ *ana* 150 GAR.MEŠ-*ma* BAR-*tum*

If the well-being(?) of the *ṣibti* is drawn over the *ṣibti*: they speak (DUG₄-*u*₂ = *iqbû*) of good (SIG₅ = *damqi*) and evil (ḪUL = *lemutti*); features that are placed on the right are favorable (*damiqtu*); (those) on the left are unfavorable (*aḫītu*).

My proposed understanding of טוב and רע in Gen 3:4, and for that matter in Gen 2:17, is semantically parallel with this omen's use of *damqu* and *lemuttu* when associated with the position of the SILIM MAŠ₂ (*šulum ṣibti*) vis-à-vis another part of a liver. *Damqu* and *lemuttu* have no obvious cognates in Hebrew. However, their semantic ranges overlap those of Hebrew טוב and רע. The Akkadian cognate of Hebrew טוב is *ṭūbu* as a noun, *ṭābu* as an adjective. Akkadian *damqu* and *ṭābu* are equated with each other and with Sumerian si-ig [SA₆] in the lexical text A I/4.[31] Proverbs 13:21 provides evidence for טוב and רע meaning good and bad fortune respectively, "Misfortune [רע] pursues sinners, but the righteous are favorably [טוב] rewarded."[32] In Job 30:26 we read, "When I expected good fortune [טוב], misfortune [רע] came. I hoped for light, but darkness came." These usages are well within the meaning of the Hebrew. Likewise, רעה in Amos 3:6b, "Can misfortune [רעה] come to a town if YHWH has not caused it?" is indicative of misfortune rather than evil intent or moral deficiency. Passages like Prov 13:21, Job 30:26, and Amos 3:6 do not involve divination. They do show that the semantic ranges of טוב and רע support the connotations of good and bad fortune. First Kings 22:8, 18, use טוב and רע to mean good and bad fortune in a context where prophecy functions much as does divination—to provide guidance to a king. In a cultural context that included Mesopotamian ophiomancy, Gen 3 portrays the snake as portentous and in so doing makes the connection with divination—with knowing favorable and unfavorable fortune.

Scholarly consensus on the formative period of Gen 2–3 remains elusive. For example, in recent work, Carol Meyers points to the Iron Age as the origin of these chapters, while John Van Seters argues that his Yahwistic source, which includes Gen 2–3, originated in the exilic period; and David Carr argues that much the same

---

Press, 2000), 45, 134. Koch-Westenholz renders SILIM MÁŠ, *šulum ṣibti*, "the wellbeing of the increment" and identifies the *ṣibtu* with the *processus papillaris*.

[31] A I/4 Section C 24–26. See *CAD* Ṭ, 19. *Damqu* and *ṭābu* stand in parallel in *CT* 16: 14 iii 43–44 (*CAD* Ṭ, 20). Patrick R. Bennett considers both Akkadian *damqu* and *ṭābu* to be within the same semantic range as Hebrew טוב (*Comparative Semitic Linguistics: A Manual* [Winona Lake, IN: Eisenbrauns, 1998]). Note that *re-e-ú* in the Akkadian lexical text Erimḫuš Bogazkoy A i:37-37 (*CAD* R, 302) is likely a West Semitic loanword.

[32] Modern understandings of טוב and רע in Prov 13:21 go back at least to Crawford H. Toy, *A Critical and Exegetical Commentary on the Book of Proverbs*, ICC (New York: Scribner's Sons, 1899), 276.

material came out of a process that culminated in the Persian period.³³ Of course, Meyers would concede later developments, and both Van Seters and Carr acknowledge the incorporation of earlier traditions. Because Mesopotamian ophiomancy traditions continued from long before our Assyrian sources³⁴ into, as I will show, late antiquity, the thesis of this article holds whether one places the date of the composition of Gen 2–3 as early as the monarchic period or as late as the Persian period. There are those who would place chs. 2–3 in the Hellenistic period. For example, based on what he sees as parallels with Berossus's *Babyloniaca* and other Hellenistic texts, Russell Gmirkin dates our texts to ca. 273–272 BCE.³⁵ Because Mesopotamian-style ophiomancy was known in late antiquity, a Hellenistic date for the composition of Gen 3 in itself does not argue against the thesis of this article. However, the specific nature of Gmirkin's argument for the Hellenistic period certainly renders direct Mesopotamian influence extremely problematic. Conversely, if the thesis of this article holds, it partially undermines Gmirkin's analysis. In what follows, I use "early exponents" to indicate those oral proponents, writers, editors, compilers, commentators, and readers who participated in the formative period of the text whenever and over whatever period such exponents were active.

Having considered how one might understand the activity of the snake in Gen 3, I turn to the issue of the snake as the craftiest of field animals (ערום מכל חית השדה). Genesis 3:1 tells us, "Now the snake was the *craftiest* field animal that YHWH God created." On what basis should we accept this statement? To be sure, this particular snake was able to dupe the woman: הנחש השיאני ("The snake duped me"; Gen 3:13 NJPS). This may well indicate that this snake is crafty, but it does not answer our question about the snake as the craftiest field animal in general. Whatever motivated the tradition to make this claim may well be lost. However, I suggest that a pervasive belief in the ominous powers of snakes within a shared culture led to the claim in Gen 3:1a and to the large number of snake omens in *Šumma Ālu* and elsewhere, as well as to the relatively large number of *namburbi* rituals against

---

[33] The three scholars cited here are but representative of those who share similarly diverse thoughts on the non-P material in the Pentateuch. See Meyers, *Rediscovering Eve*, 66; John Van Seters, *The Pentateuch: A Social-Science Commentary*, Trajectories 1 (Sheffield: Sheffield Academic, 1999), 159; and, more recently, idem, "The Report of the Yahwist's Demise Has Been Greatly Exaggerated!" in *A Farewell to the Yahwist? The Composition of the Pentateuch in Recent European Interpretation*, ed. Thomas B. Dozeman and Konrad Schmid, SymS 34 (Atlanta: Society of Biblical Literature, 2006), 145; David M. Carr, "The Rise of Torah," in *The Pentateuch as Torah: New Models for Understanding Its Promulgation and Acceptance*, ed. Gary N. Knoppers and Bernard M. Levinson (Winona Lake, IN: Eisenbrauns, 2007), 39–56, esp. 40, 54–56.

[34] Freedman references an unpublished Old Babylonian omen tablet, BM 109228, that mentions mice, pigs, chickens, and, importantly for our considerations, snakes (*If a City*, 1:13).

[35] Russell E. Gmirkin, *Berossus and Genesis, Manetho and Exodus: Hellenistic Histories and the Date of the Pentateuch*, LHBOTS 433, Copenhagen International Series 15 (New York: T&T Clark, 2006), 245–46. See Joyce Rilett Wood, review of *Berossus and Genesis*, by Russell E. Gmirkin, *JHebS* 8 (2008): http://www.jhsonline.org/reviews/reviews_new/review313.htm.

the evil of snakes. As already mentioned, of all the animals, only birds—which Gen 2:19 calls עוֹף הַשָּׁמַיִם, "bird(s) of the air," as opposed to חַיַּת הַשָּׂדֶה, "field animals"—are better represented among the Mesopotamian animal divination texts.[36]

How did early exponents of Gen 3:1 understand עָרוּם? The LXX glosses the Hebrew as φρονιμώτατος ("sage," "thoughtful," "intelligent").[37] Most manuscripts of Targum Onkelos read עָרִים, cognate with Hebrew עָרוּם. Because עָרִים is a rather rare lexeme in Aramaic it is likely the preferred reading as the *lectio difficilior*. But several manuscripts of Targum Onkelos read חכים, "wise."[38] All such renderings point to a semantic range at the union of wise and skillful.[39] It is also possible that the choice of the Hebrew word עָרוּם was influenced by alliteration with עִירֹם ("naked") in this verse and אָרוּר ("damned") in Gen 3:14. See also עֲרוּמִּים meaning "(both) naked" in Gen 2:25. While the text refers to the man and the woman as naked, it is not much of a stretch to see the snake as עִירֹם also. עָרוּם and אָרוּר apply solely to the snake. While not unambiguously attested, "portentous" appears to be within the semantic range of Hebrew עָרוּם. Based on the sheer number of Akkadian snake omens and "portentous" very likely being within the semantic range of Hebrew עָרוּם, my suggestion, simply put, is that the early exponents of Gen 3 perceived snakes as more portentous than any animal except birds.

Scholars have long remarked on a possible linguistic association between the most common Hebrew noun for snake, נָחָשׁ, and the verb נִחֵשׁ, "practice divination," along with its nominal reflex נַחַשׁ ("divination").[40] Semitists are divided on a possible cognate relationship between these words.[41] However, a cognitive association between נָחָשׁ and נִחֵשׁ does not require that they be linguistic cognates in the

---

[36] Echoes of bird divination are seen in Job 12:7 and in the accounts of Noah releasing birds as harbingers of dry land.

[37] Elsewhere, the Old Greek glosses עָרוּם with συνετός ("intelligent," "wise," Prov 12:23); πανοῦργος ("good sense," Prov 13:16, 14:8, 22:3, 27:4), φρόνησις ("purpose," "intention," Job 5:12), and δυναστεία ("power," "domination," Job 15:5). Compare φρόνιμοι ὡς οἱ ὄφεις, "as wise as serpents," in Matt 10:16.

[38] עָרִים is the reading preferred of Alexander Sperber, *The Bible in Aramaic: Based on Old Manuscripts and Printed Texts*, 3 vols. (Leiden: Brill, 2004), 1:4 (1235); however, as Sperber notes, *Biblia Hebraica* (Lisbon, 1491), *Biblia Hebraica* (Izar, 1490), and *Biblia Sacra Complutensis* (1516–17) read חכים ("wise").

[39] An association between snakes and wisdom in the ancient Near East has long been demonstrated. See, e.g., Karen Randolph Joines, "The Serpent in Gen 3," *ZAW* 87 (1975), 1–11, esp. 4–5.

[40] See, among others, Charlesworth, *Good and Evil Serpent*, 244–45, 438; Jeffers, *Magic and Divination*, 75; Fontaine, "Strange Face of Wisdom," 217; Kimelman, "Seduction of Eve"; Nimmer, "Rabbi Banet's Charming Snake," 75; Fabry, *ThWAT* 4:384–85. On the rabbinic tradition, see Faur, *Homo Mysticus*, 59, 210 n. 45.

[41] On the possible etymologies of נָחָשׁ and נִחֵשׁ, see, among others, *HALOT* 2:690–91; Alexander Sperber, "Zu Gen. 30, 27b," *OLZ* 16.9 (Sept. 1913): 389; John Gray, *I & II Kings: A Commentary*, OTL (Philadelphia: Westminster, 1963), 591; Nahum Waldman, "A Note on Genesis 30:27b," *JQR* 55 (1964–65): 164–65; Leonid Kogan, "Genealogical Position of Ugaritic: The Lexical

formal sense. Being polysemous and polyphonic as they were written—and, in the case of the noun נָחָשׁ ("divination") nearly homonymous—is enough to motivate a cognitive association. I have already mentioned the עָרוּם ("crafty")/עֵירֹם ("naked")/ אָרוּר ("damned") triplet. In addition, the pairing of הָאָדָם ("the Adam") with הָאֲדָמָה ("the clay"); אִשָּׁה ("woman") with אִישׁ ("man"); and חַוָּה ("Eve") with חַי ("living") shows a penchant for polysemy and alliteration on the part of the early exponents of Gen 2–3. That these early exponents would have perceived an association between נָחָשׁ, and נָחֵשׁ, even without its being explicit, is all but certain.

I suggest that among the reasons the early exponents of Gen 2–3 chose to keep the association between נָחָשׁ and נָחֵשׁ implicit is the biblical prohibition against unauthorized forms of divination by the followers of Israel's God: Lev 19:26: לֹא תְנַחֲשׁוּ, "you shall not practice divination"; and Deut 18:10: "Let there not be found among you ... one who is ... a מְנַחֵשׁ [diviner]." Or, to quote Num 23:23, "Lo, there is no augury [נַחַשׁ] in Jacob, no divining [קֶסֶם] in Israel" (NJPS). John Hobbins correctly says, "The inspection of entrails and the flight of birds has no place in biblical faith."[42] Except in the limited sense argued here, neither does the interpretation of snake activity. Nevertheless, as Isa 14:29 and Jer 8:17 suggest, in somewhat different ways, snakes can be messengers of God.[43] No tradition forbids what it does not know.

Apart from our snake, Balaam's jenny is the only animal in the Hebrew Bible that speaks. She speaks in an unambiguous divination context (Num 22–24). Having tried other means of communication, the jenny finally speaks of the divine messenger that even Balaam, the great seer, could not see. Note that the Akkadian word used to describe the means of communicating in the extispicy example discussed above is *iqbû*, "they speak." Just as Balaam's jenny used speech to expose something God sought to reveal, Gen 3 uses the snake's speech to expose something that God sought to hide.

III. The Case for a Mesopotamian Ophiomancy Context

What warrants my claim that the early exponents of Gen 2–3 saw in the snake a reflex of divination informed by Mesopotamian ophiomancy? Three lines of evidence and argument support this claim: First, in other passages, the Hebrew Bible is certainly cognizant of Mesopotamian divination in general. In Gen 30:27 we read

---

Dimension; Lexical Isoglosses between Ugaritic and Canaanite," *Sef* 70.1 (Jan.–June 2010): 7–50, esp. 34.

[42] John F. Hobbins, *Habakkuk*, Virginia Theological Seminary Bible Briefs (2012), http://www.vts.edu/ftpimages/95/download/FM.Hobbins.Habakkuk.pdf, p. 4. See also Deut 13:2–6 with regard to oneiromancy.

[43] See Charlesworth, *Good and Evil Serpent*, 437–38. The same can perhaps be said of Moses's and Aaron's staff, which becomes a snake/crocodile(?) in Exod 4:3 (נחש) and 7:10–13 (תנין).

times as uniquely critical, beyond all critical times of the twentieth century, severe as these were.

What are "our times"? Where does the contemporary global state of affairs begin? If the Cold War marked the course of an era, extending over the second half of the century, its end signifies the beginning of a new epoch. The dialectical struggle unto death between East and West, the two superpowers and their corresponding blocs of nations, came to an end with the collapse of the East in 1989/91. We find ourselves, therefore, in a state of affairs best described for now in postist terms —the era of the post–Cold War.

Here a twofold development should be kept in mind. There ensued at first a period of vibrant optimism, bordering on the utopian, if not the millennial. The work of Francis Fukuyama stands as a perfect signifier of this moment. Writing in 1989, he argues that the march of liberal democracy, politically and economically, has proved triumphant, signaling perhaps the "End of History."[29] Peace and progress would now prevail for all, given no competing vision in sight. This initial effervescence would not last long. In time, a period of grave pessimism began to emerge, ultimately entrenching itself in global consciousness. The work of Fukuyama again serves as an ideal indicator of the times. Writing twenty-five years later, and with the anniversary in mind, he offers a chastened assessment of the End of History, still optimistic but only in the long range and with the right corrective measures.[30] Other voices, writing on the anniversary, prove far more dismissive of such claims and far more somber regarding future prospects.[31] The reason for such a shift within the post–Cold War era is not hard to ascertain.

During this past quarter of a century, crisis has followed upon crisis, fueling an ever-widening and ever-deepening sense of dis-order. Such dis-ease has involved any number of interlinked developments across society and culture, local and global alike: geopolitical multipolarity and multijousting; political paralysis or breakdown at the level of the nation-state; global economic meltdown and inequality;

---

[29] Francis Fukuyama, "The End of History," *National Interest* (Summer 1989). At the time, Fukuyama, a former analyst at the RAND Corporation, was deputy director of the State Department's policy planning staff. This theory was expanded in a later volume, *The End of History and the Last Man* (New York: Free Press, 1992).

[30] Francis Fukuyama, "At the 'End of History' Still Stands Democracy," *Wall Street Journal*, 7–8 June 2014, C1–2, http://online.wsj.com/articles/at-the-end-of-history-still-stands-democracy-1402080661. At present, Fukuyama is a senior fellow at the Freeman Spogli Institute for International Studies at Stanford University. See further his *Political Order and Political Decay: From the Industrial Revolution to the Globalization of Democracy* (New York: Farrar, Straus & Giroux, 2014).

[31] See, e.g., Timothy Stanley and Alexander Leesep, "It's Still Not the End of History," *The Atlantic*, 1 September 2014, http://www.theatlantic.com/politics/archive/2014/09/its-still-not-the-end-of-history-francis-fukuyama/379394/?single_page=true; and Mario Vargas Llosa, "Las guerras del fin del mundo," *El País*, 7 September 2014, http://elpais.com/elpais/2014/09/04/opinion/1409856348_817996.html.

radical ecological transformation; seismic population trends and reactions; explosion of violence at all levels. One could go on. The result has been a pervasive sense of disorientation, powerlessness, uncertainty. Such has been the consensus across the ideological spectrum, in terms of both critique and construction: on the left, much reinvigorated, pressing for substantial structural changes; on the right, thoroughly dismayed, advocating the strong assertion of structural power; and in the center, straddling the fence, pressing for corrective structural reforms.

This sense of fragility and threat I have sought to capture by way of three particular discourses and critiques: global economics, climatological projections, and worldwide migration. I highlight global economics here. For this I turn to a highly incisive and programmatic piece by Alfred J. López, "The (Post) Global South."[32] It advances, on the one hand, a critical account of globalization as a process involving three stages: construction, deconstruction, alternatives (possibilities for a different future, both already at work and yet to come).[33] What emerges as a result is a vision of the Global South as a postglobal reality and signifier of subalternity across boundaries, material and discursive alike. The piece calls, on the other hand, for a broadly based analysis of this reality: the development of a postglobal discourse that draws upon the full spectrum of fields of studies in the academy.

Globalization, López argues, emerged in the 1980s and accelerated through the 1990s as the global master narrative. It is thus, in effect, the hegemonic discourse of the post–Cold War era. The narrative presents the process of globalization, as generated and sustained by the economic policies of neoliberalism, as yielding such growth as to lift the entire world in its wake, from the very rich to the very poor. Such growth requires the development of an integrated world economy, based on free trade and free markets and governed by the laws of exchange. Such growth not only would benefit those individuals directly engaged in the process but also would solve all social ills and thus resolve social contradictions.[34]

The reality behind this narrative, López continues, proved quite different, leading to a counter-narrative that exposes the downside of the project. This

---

[32] Alfred J. López, "The (Post) Global South," *Global South* 1 (2007): 1–11. López is professor of English at Purdue University and a scholar with interests in postcolonial, Caribbean, and globalization studies. See also his *Posts and Pasts: A Theory of Postcolonialism*, Explorations in Postcolonial Studies (Albany: State University of New York Press, 2001); and his edited volume, *Postcolonial Whiteness: A Critical Reader on Race and Empire* (Albany: State University of New York Press, 2005).

[33] These stages are at once sequential and simultaneous, given the speed that marks the project of globalization.

[34] Among its proponents stand prominent voices, such as Anthony Giddens (*Runaway World: How Globalization Is Reshaping Our Lives* [London: Profile Books, 1999]) and Joseph Stieglitz (*Globalization and Its Discontents* [New York: Norton, 2003]; and idem, *Making Globalization Work* [New York: Norton, 2006]). Both believe that globalization can be rescued and made to work for all.

that Laban learned through divination that YHWH had blessed him. Laban is said to be an Aramean from Nahor in the Aram-Naharaim (Paddan-aram) region of northwestern Mesopotamia. The text gives no indication of the type of divination that Laban used to make this determination. Ezekiel 21:26–27 (21–22) recounts how Nebuchadnezzar employed belomancy (arrows), teraphim(?), and extispicy to determine the military course and outcome of his attack on Jerusalem. The residents of Jerusalem (Ezek 21:28 [23]) regarded this שוא בקסום [בקסם] ("as empty divination").[44] Ezekiel proclaims that in so doing Nebuchadnezzar brought memory of the Jerusalemites' guilt. Daniel 4 tells of Belshazzar's dream and its interpretation. Daniel 5 recounts an unsolicited omen in the form of writing that an hand drew on a plaster wall. Belshazzar's sages could not interpret it but Daniel could. With the possible exception of Nebuchadnezzar's use of divination, the text does not take a negative stance toward these cases of divination. Yet, also in each of these cases, the omens are sought by or presented to foreigners rather than Israelites.[45] There are certainly misplaced and anachronistic elements in some or all of these accounts; still, they strongly suggest that the biblical tradition was well aware of foreign, specifically Mesopotamian, divination.

Second, it is now almost trite to note that the early exponents of Gen 2–3 knew and were influenced by other Mesopotamian traditions, most notably the Epic of Gilgamesh. Both Gilgamesh and Gen 2–3 include a plant (bush or tree) of life, and both accounts feature a snake in a prominent role, though the roles differ in the two works.[46] Scholars have also noted parallels with Adapa.[47] David Carr speculates, correctly I think, that the "garden of Eden" story reflects the "central values

---

[44] The use of קסם rather than נחש is likely due to differing modes of divination. While certainty is impossible, one might speculate that קסם indicated *omina impetrativa* while נחש indicated *omina oblativa* or something of this nature.

[45] Note also Isa 2:6, ועננים כפלשתים // מקדם [(?)מקסם], "[diviners?] from the East" // "soothsayers like the Philistines." Representing a somewhat different tradition, the Old Greek of Isa 2:6 has "their country ... was filled with divinations [κληδονισμῶν] as it had been at the beginning" [NETS]. The Hebrew Bible also reports on divination among the Moabites (Num 22:7), the Midianites (Num 24:1), the Philistines (1 Sam 6:2, Isa 2:6), and the Egyptians (Gen 40:4b–19 passim). In the context of Egypt, note also Joseph's silver cup, והוא נחש ינחש בו, "and he by divination divines with it" (Gen 44:5).

[46] See John A. Bailey, "Initiation and the Primal Woman in Gilgamesh and Genesis 2–3," *JBL* 89 (1970): 137–50; Joseph Blenkinsopp, "Gilgamesh and Adam: Wisdom through Experience in *Gilgamesh* and in the Biblical Story of the Man, the Woman, and the Snake," in *Treasures Old and New: Essays in the Theology of the Pentateuch* (Grand Rapids: Eerdmans, 2004), 85–101; and Judith E. McKinlay, *Reframing Her: Biblical Women in Postcolonial Focus*, Bible in the Modern World (Sheffield: Sheffield Phoenix, 2004), 6; and recently Thomas Römer, "Le jardin d'Eden entre le ciel et la terre," *JA* 300 (2012): 581–93, esp. 591.

[47] E.g., Giorgio Buccellati, "Adapa, Genesis and the Notion of Faith," *UF* 5 (1973): 61–66; William H. Shea, "Adam in Ancient Mesopotamian Traditions," *AUSS* 15 (1977): 27–41; Niels-Erik Andreasen, "Adam and Adapa: Two Anthropological Characters," *AUSS* 19 (1981): 179–94; John Daniel Bing, "Adapa and Immortality," *UF* 16 (1984): 53–56.

of the Mesopotamian [scribal] curriculum."[48] Becoming a diviner was one of the "postgraduate" options for the advanced scribe. Given the other well-established Mesopotamian influences, it should be no surprise that Mesopotamian divination traditions were part of the cultural substrate that informed the early exponents of Gen 2–3.

Third, Mesopotamian ophiomancy was known over great chronological and geographical continua. Mesopotamian ophiomancy traditions originated during or before the Old Babylonian period[49] and continued into late antiquity. Referring specifically to the prohibition against diviners in Deut 18:10, b. Sanh. 65b says this about the forbidden מנחש, "one who divines":

> A Menahesh [מנחש] is one who says: So and so's bread has fallen out of his hand; his staff has fallen out of his hand; his son called after him; a raven screamed after him, a deer has crossed his path; a serpent [נחש] came at his right hand or a fox at his left.

Šumma Ālu witnesses three of these rabbinic examples about which a מנחש is concerned. In 79:3 ravens scream; in 23:16–17 snakes are on the right and the left; and in an excerpt foxes are on the right and left.[50] The other examples are well within the scope of a Mesopotamian diviner's portfolio. There is no evidence that the rabbis knew Šumma Ālu or any direct literary successor. Still, as is evident from the passage quoted above, they knew of those who practiced divination in the Mesopotamian tradition of Šumma Ālu; they knew of the type of ophiomancy witnessed in Šumma Ālu. As Amar Annus notes, many rabbinic omens clearly have Mesopotamian origins. Annus cites this omen regarding a snake: "If a snake fell on the bed, it says: he is poor, but he will end up being rich, if (the woman) is pregnant, she will give birth to a boy, if she is a maiden, she will marry a great man" (t. Šabb. 6:16).[51] Not only were these traditions long lived, they were also very widespread. By at least the sixth century BCE and likely a century or two earlier, knowledge of Mesopotamian ophiomancy had spread as far west as Ionia. Homer, Il. 12.200–207,

---

[48] David M. Carr, *Writing on the Tablet of the Heart: Origins of Scripture and Literature* (Oxford: Oxford University Press, 2005), 60–61.

[49] Note the unpublished Old Babylonian tablet containing snake omens referenced by Freedman, *If a City*, 1:13.

[50] Egbert von Weiher, *Spätbabylonische Texte aus Uruk*, vol. 2, Ausgrabungen der deutschen Forschungsgemeinschaft in Uruk-Warka 10 (Berlin: Mann, 1983), #33:6–7.

[51] Amar Annus, "On the Beginnings and Continuities of Omen Science in the Ancient World," in idem, *Divination and Interpretation of Signs*, 1–18, esp. 9–10. See also Sifre Deut. 171 and Sifra, Kedoshim 6. Elements of the rabbinic omen cited by Annus have parallels in Šumma Ālu 22:75, "If a snake falls on a man, a rich man will become poor or a poor man will become rich; that man will be infected." Cf. Šumma Ālu 22:76. Šumma Ālu 22:75 is witnessed in six manuscripts, including multiple witnesses from Kuyunjik and one from Sultantepe (STT 2: 321 i 26).

contains a very close parallel with three *Šumma Ālu* omens (24:20–22) where a bird carries and drops a snake.[52]

The Hebrew Bible's cognizance of Mesopotamian divination, the influence of other Mesopotamian traditions, and the extent over space and time that Mesopotamian ophiomancy was known all support the thesis that the early exponents of Gen 2–3 understood the snake within a cultural context that included Mesopotamian divination traditions. This understanding may well have been nuanced by other traditions, including native Hebrew traditions, but was not completely concealed by them.[53]

The well-attested influence of other learned Mesopotamian traditions and the geographical and chronological range over which *Šumma Ālu*-like ophiomancy was current in antiquity make it all but certain that ophiomancy was part of the cultural substrate that informed the early exponents of Gen 3. This high probability is strengthened by the implied play on נָחָשׁ ("snake") and נָחֵשׁ ("practice divination"); and by the forty-plus omens in *Šumma Ālu* whose protases involve a man, a woman, and a snake. The early exponents of Gen 3 wrote, read, edited, and understood the snake in the context of these Mesopotamian ophiomancy traditions—traditions that existed in their cultural substrate from at least the Iron Age until late antiquity. In Gen 2, God wills that humankind not know good and bad fortune. The snake in Gen 3 frustrates that will. Over time other interpretations came to overshadow this understanding.

---

[52] See Duane E. Smith, "Portentous Birds Flying West: On the Mesopotamian Origin of Homeric Bird-Divination," *JANER* 13 (2013): 49–85. Also note that Herodotus (*Hist.* 1.78) mentions snake/horse divination in Lydia. Xenophon writes, "Never put yourself or your army in danger contrary to snake [ἱερά] or bird [οἰωνούς]" (*Cyr.* 1.6.44). On ἱερά meaning "snake," see Aristotle, *Hist. an.* 607a31, "There is a certain very small snake [ὀφίδιον], which some call ἱερόν that the really big snakes avoid." One cannot be completely certain of the origin of these later examples, but each of them would be at home within the Mesopotamian divination tradition.

[53] For example, passages such as Deut 1:39 and 1 Kgs 3:7–9 imply a merism for "discernment" in טוב ורע and similar formulations. In addition, both Mesopotamian and Egyptian sources often associate the snake with immortality. The snake of Gilgamesh XI:309–311 steals the plant that makes one young and in so doing steals immortality. This association no doubt also colored the early understanding of the snake in Gen 3. On this see, e.g., Joines, "Snake in Gen 3," 1–3, on both the Mesopotamian and Egyptian material. I thank an anonymous *JBL* reviewer for pointing out these likely additional influences on the early exponent's understanding of both the snake and its role in Gen 3.

fp fortress press
scholarship that matters

fresh encounters!

Paul within Judaism
Restoring the First-Century Context to the Apostle
MARK D. NANOS and MAGNUS ZETTERHOLM, editors

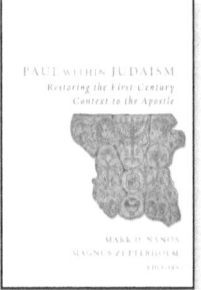

Renowned international scholars seek to describe Paul and his work from "within Judaism," rather than on the assumption that in practice Paul left behind aspects of Jewish living after his discovery of Jesus as Christ (Messiah). A coherent alternative to the "New Perspective."
9781451470031 360 pp pbk $39

Jesus' Sermon on the Mount
Mandating a Better Righteousness
JACK R. LUNDBOM

"[Lundbom] not only draws upon the Old Testament and rabbinic sources to exegete Jesus' Sermon on the Mount but also interprets the Sermon in light of centuries of Christian insights, so as to proclaim the mandate of holy living for our generation today. A highly academic yet readable and practical book."
—K. K. YEO, Garrett-Evangelical Theological Seminary
9781451493023 208 pp pbk $49

The Gospel on the Margins
The Reception of Mark in the Second Century
MICHAEL J. KOK

"Controlling abundant primary evidence with fine analysis of biblical and patristic scholarship, Michael J. Kok reopens the question of Mark's ambiguous authority in second-century Christianity."   —C. CLIFTON BLACK
Princeton Theological Seminary
9781451490220 240 pp pbk $49

Available wherever books are sold or
800-328-4648
fortresspress.com   **fp**

A Rejoinder concerning Genesis 3:6 and the NJPS Translation

DAVID E. S. STEIN
editor@davidesstein.name
6275 Canterbury Dr., Unit 202, Culver City, CA 90230

This rejoinder counters the thrust of an article published in this journal in late 2013, "Blaming Eve Alone: Translation, Omission, and Implications of עמה in Genesis 3:6b," by Julie Faith Parker (*JBL* 132, no. 4: 729–47). That critique focused largely on the NJPS translation's rendering, which it assailed. Four flaws in the earlier piece are now adduced, covering every aspect of its argumentation. This rejoinder holds that (1) the NJPS translators' alleged *motive* for interpretive bias is lacking; (2) the prior author's understanding of the narrated events is not supported by the Hebrew text's *grammar* and *syntax*; (3) the *nature* of the NJPS translation was misconstrued, so that it was judged according to the wrong criteria; and (4) even if NJPS had rendered this passage as advocated by the earlier article, such wording *would not hinder* misogynistic interpretations. The NJPS has not misled readers in this instance, nor has it created an opening for misogyny. Rather, the NJPS rendering of Gen 3:6b accurately reproduces the text's depiction, while remaining true to that translation's approach.

Julie Faith Parker, in her article "Blaming Eve Alone: Translation, Omission, and Implications of עמה in Genesis 3:6b" (*JBL* 132, no. 4 [2013]: 729–47), assails the Jewish Publication Society translation (NJPS) of Gen 3:6: ותקח מפריו ותאכל ותתן גם לאישה עמה ויאכל, "she took of its fruit and ate. She also gave some to her husband, and he ate." Regarding the prepositional phrase that depicts Adam as עמה ("with her"), Parker asserts that NJPS misleads readers by omitting a direct rendering—because this encourages their "blaming Eve alone" for bringing humankind to sin (pp. 730, 747). Yet that assessment does not withstand scrutiny, on four counts.

First, a motive hardly exists for the NJPS's alleged crime. Jewish translations have little reason to downplay Adam's culpability. The classical and widespread rabbinic term for the fateful feast of forbidden fruit is חטאו של אדם הראשון ("*Adam's sin*").[1] If traditional Jewish interpretation has downplayed anything, it is Eve's leadership role.

---

[1] In English, see, e.g., Ephraim E. Urbach, *The Sages: Their Concepts and Beliefs*, 2nd ed.,

Second, the Hebrew text's grammar and syntax do not support Parker's view that עמה implies that Adam could have intervened to stop Eve from eating the fruit. Our verse does not specify that Eve's acts of eating and of sharing with Adam occurred at the same time or place.[2] Yet it could easily have done so.[3] Rather than "excusing Adam from responsibility" as Parker claims (p. 732), the NJPS accurately reproduced the text's depiction of Eve's two distinct acts.

Third, contra Parker (p. 743), the NJPS is not a "formal equivalence" translation.[4] Word-for-word expectations do not apply. As a sense-for-sense translation, the NJPS *by design* avoids rendering individual Hebrew words whose import is clear from the idiomatic English wording.[5]

Finally, Adam's whereabouts while Eve ate the forbidden fruit have no bearing on the misogynistic interpretations that (justifiably) trouble Parker. In the narrative itself, Adam is held accountable not for failing to stop Eve but for eating the fruit (v. 17). All fifty-nine translations cited by Parker state explicitly that Adam ate the fruit. Interpreters who blame Eve for Adam's own disobedience thus depart from the text's plain sense. And if those interpreters did not learn from the unhappy outcome after Adam already attempted to blame Eve (v. 12), surely no construal or rendering of עמה in our verse will dissuade them from doing so.

---

2 vols., Publications of the Perry Foundation in the Hebrew University of Jerusalem (Jerusalem: Magnes, 1979), 1:421–26.

[2] Each act is expressed via its own past narrative (*wayyqtl*) conjugation, a construction that is temporally and spatially imprecise. Nor does the conjunction גם, which reintroduces Adam, prove that he was present during the previously mentioned event (cf. Gen 38:7, 10). And the complement containing עמה modifies only its own clause's predicate, regarding the act of sharing. In short, Eve's "giving" may well have occurred later and/or in another part of the garden.

[3] By saying, for example, ותאכל היא ואישה ("she ate—she and her partner"); cf., e.g., Gen 13:1, 33:6. The text's ancient audience probably inferred that Adam was *not* present during Eve's initial eating, because they surely knew that alternative wording to *explicitly* note his presence was readily available to the text's composer(s).

[4] Its translators made this point repeatedly. For example, their 1962 preface justified the new translation on the grounds that prior ones "rendered the Hebrew to a considerable extent word for word rather than idiomatically" (n.p.). Their declared goal was "to discard ... literal, mechanical translation" (Harry M. Orlinsky, ed., *Notes on the New Translation of the Torah* [Philadelphia: Jewish Publication Society, 1969], 13).

[5] A typical example of the NJPS's not reproducing a prepositional phrase is the succinct rendering "and took wives" for ויקחו להם נשים (Gen 6:2).

The Fearsome Sword of Genesis 3:24

MURRAY H. LICHTENSTEIN
mhlpg@comcast.net
Emeritus, Hunter College, City University of New York, New York, NY 10017

In Gen 3:24, the way to the "tree of life" in the garden of Eden is said to be guarded by the biblical cherubim, as well as by a similarly intimidating, uniquely depicted sword. The latter is said to be in a continuous, apparently revolving motion and has what seems to be a fiery appearance. This passage was the subject of a Critical Note by Ronald S. Hendel in *JBL* 104 (1985), which, in essence, interpreted the fiery aspect of the weapon as representing the presence of a sword-bearing, quasi-divine being belonging to YHWH's mythic entourage. The present discussion takes issue with Hendel's approach, concentrating rather on the sword as an independent, inanimate entity and defining in detail the terminology employed in its description. It goes on to suggest that the biblical imagery corresponds to, and may possibly derive from, the design of ancient Persian scythed chariot wheels, as described in Greek historical accounts.

According to Gen 3:24, Adam and Eve were denied access to the "tree of life" by the presence of guardian cherubim stationed at the entrance to the garden of Eden. These כְּרֻבִים are to some extent the functional equivalents of the deified *kurību* figures installed in the temples built by the Assyrian king Esarhaddon.[1] But also guarding the entrance to the garden was a uniquely depicted sword, about which much remains unclear, regarding both how it looked and how it functioned. The sword in question is said to be moving in a manner described as מִתְהַפֶּכֶת. The latter has been variously translated as "turn(ing) this way and that, every way"

---

[1] Riekele Borger, *Die Inschriften Asarhaddons, Königs von Assyrien*, AfO Beiheft 9 (Graz: privately published, 1956), 33:10; 87:24. The *kurību* figures positioned at the temple gateway appear alongside representations of lions and fearsome mythological creatures. In their company, the *kurību* would have the same intimidating effect as the biblical כרבים stationed at the entrance to the garden of Eden in Gen 3:24. Cf. the colossal *šēdu* and *lamassu* orthostats placed at the entrance to a temple and termed its "guardians"; see Maximilian Streck, *Assurbanipal und die letzten assyrischen Könige bis zum Untergange Ninivehs*, 3 vols., VAB 7 (Leipzig: Hinrichs, 1916), 2:54, vi: 58.

(BDB); "whirling" (NEB); "revolving" (AB [Speiser], NAB, WBC [Wenham]); "ever turning" (NJPS), and the like.

In his brief note on Gen 3:24 in *JBL* 104 (1985), Ronald S. Hendel identifies the movement of the sword more precisely as "the motion that a sword makes in the hand: a constant thrusting and slashing, the whirl of swordplay."[2] A somewhat different image, however, is suggested by some of the standard renderings sampled above, which depict a considerably smoother, more regular movement. Indeed, the LXX renders the Hebrew verb by στρέφειν (in the middle voice), indicating here a continuous rotation, such as that of revolving heavenly bodies. Similarly, in Judg 7:13 Gideon overhears a dream in which a barley cake moves through the Midianite camp until it hits and upends a tent. Here, as in Gen 3:24, the movement is described by Hebrew מִתְהַפֵּךְ, once again rendered in the LXX by Greek στρέφειν, and depicts what is clearly the tumbling or rolling of the barley cake toward the tent.

The actual phrase in Gen 3:24 is לַהַט הַחֶרֶב הַמִּתְהַפֶּכֶת, further specifying that the revolving sword has what is termed לַהַט as its most prominent feature. While the word לַהַט has been interpreted quite literally as "fiery, flaming" (LXX φλόγινος), in all likelihood it was not the sword itself that was afire or emitting flames per se. Rather, as surmised by E. A. Speiser, the fire was actually "a metaphorical description apparently of the bolt-like or glinting blade."[3] That is, the reference to fire actually refers to the effect or impression created by the movement of the sword's blade, perceived as blazing or flashing before one's eyes.

Flashing, lightninglike blades of swords and spearheads are featured, for example, in the Akkadian Erra Epic, I:3–5: "Ishum, famed slaughterer, whose hands are well-suited to bear his fierce weapons, and make his terrible spears (or: axes) flash like lightning (*šubruqu*)...."[4] Closely related to the use of the Akkadian verb *barāqu* ("to flash") in this passage is the imagery in Deut 32:41, ברק חרבי, "the lightning of my sword," and Hab 3:11, ברק חניתך, "the lightning of your spear." In Nah 3:3 the same phrase, ברק חנית, is used together with להב חרב, "the flame of a sword," a combination that is especially relevant for understanding the imagery of Gen 3:24.

Both the "flame" of the divine sword and its "lightning" are specific references to its blade, as is clear, for example, from Ezek 21:14–15 (Eng. 9–10): "Say, 'A sword! A sword sharpened and highly burnished; sharpened for the slaughter, burnished that its polish be that of lightning.'" The same metaphorical point is repeated in v. 33 (Eng. 28): "You shall say, 'A sword! A sword bared for slaughter, polished to

---

[2] Ronald S. Hendel, "'The Flame of the Whirling Sword': A Note on Genesis 3:24," *JBL* 104 (1985): 671 n. 6.

[3] E. A. Speiser, *Genesis: Introduction, Translation, and Notes*, AB 1 (Garden City, NY: Doubleday, 1964), 25.

[4] Aptly cited by Hendel, "'Flame of the Whirling Sword,'" 674. For an English translation of the complete passage in context, see Benjamin R. Foster, *Before the Muses: An Anthology of Akkadian Literature*, 2nd ed., 2 vols. (Bethesda, MD: CDL, 1996), 2:758.

perfection (?), to flash as lightning." So, too, in Judg 3:22, להב ("flame") clearly refers to the blade of Ehud's sword, which, when thrust into King Eglon's belly, is completely enveloped by his fat, even to the hilt. The term "flame" also denotes the bladelike spearhead of a lance or javelin in Job 39:23, paralleling חרב ("sword") in the preceding verse. Similarly, in 1 Sam 17:7 the word להבת is used for the six-hundred-shekel iron head of Goliath's lance, that is, its cutting edges. Also to be noted is the specialized terminology employed in the War Scroll from Qumran when dealing with ritually inscribed spearheads:

> And they shall write on the blade [לוהב] of the missile: "Lightning-bolt of the spear [ברקת חנית] of God's might" ... And they shall write on the third missile: "Flame [שלהובת] of the sword which devours the sinful dead by the judgment of God." (1QM VI, 2–3)[5]

The poetic equation of the *blade* of a weapon and a fiery *flame* is well known from the idiomatic usage they share, such as with the verb אכל ("to consume"). It is further evident, for example, in the figurative use of the term "tongue" in both Akkadian and Hebrew, imagery that suggests the shape common to both blade and flame. Thus, Akkadian *lišānu* is used in Esarhaddon's annals in relating how the north wind had blown the threatening "tongue" (EME = *lišānu*) of fire away from the king's position and toward his enemy.[6] The same word "tongue" is also used for the iron "blade" (EME = *lišānu*) of a dagger offered as a royal gift.[7] Analogously, Hebrew attests to לשון אש ("a tongue of fire") in Isa 5:24, and לשון is likewise applied to those who have "sharpened their tongues like a sword" in Ps 64:4 and 57:5, "their tongue is a sharp sword."

In contrast to the well-attested association of the blade of a weapon with the term להב, the employment of להט in that context is less self-evident. At the outset, one notices the assonance, as well as the orthographic similarity of להב and להט, features that might increase the likelihood of an interchange of the two, be it deliberate or inadvertent. This possibility remains, even though להט is not attested as a noun elsewhere in the Hebrew Bible.[8] It is, however, most suggestive that the two words are often combined and employed together in the same passage:

---

[5] For text and commentary, see the still invaluable Yigael Yadin (ed. and trans.), *The Scroll of the War of the Sons of Light against the Sons of Darkness* (Oxford: Oxford University Press, 1962), 285.

[6] Borger, *Die Inschriften Asarhaddons*, 104:6.

[7] EA 22, ii: 16, for which see William L. Moran, ed. and trans., *The Amarna Letters* (Baltimore: Johns Hopkins University Press, 1992), 53.

[8] Postbiblical Hebrew usage, however, does include the nominal form. The remarks of some of the medieval Jewish commentators are to the point. Thus, commenting on Gen 3:24, Rashi treats להט as a noun: "The revolving sword has a להט to terrify him from re-entering the garden." On the same verse, Ibn Ezra is more specific, identifying it as the blade of the sword: "The כרובים are the well-known angels, and in their hands is a sword having a two-edged *blade* [להט]." The

Joel 1:19:	ולהבה להטה כל־עצי השדה,	"and flames set ablaze all the trees of the plain"
Joel 2:3:	ואחריו תלהט להבה,	"while, behind it, flames are ablaze"
Ps 83:15:	וכלהבה תלהט הרים,	"and like flames setting the hills ablaze"
Ps 106:18:	להבה תלהט רשעים,	"flames set the wicked ablaze"

In these verses, the two roots are so closely associated in context that the metaphorical usage of the one may well have been extended to the other in Gen 3:24.

Whatever the case, it remains clear from context that the להט ("blazing") of the revolving sword refers to none other than its flamelike flashing blade. Thus, Hendel's identification of להט as "an animate divine being, a member of Yahweh's divine host, similar in status to the Cherubim" is highly questionable. The same may be said of his further assertion that "in Israelite tradition, Reshep belongs to the same class of beings as the *lahat* in Gen 3:24; they are both 'fiery' members of Yahweh's divine entourage."[9] It will be observed that in Hab 3:5, the personified רשף ("plague") appears parallel to דבר ("pestilence") and in Deut 32:24 it is parallel to רעב ("famine") but is not attested in parallelism with "fire." So, too, in Ugaritic mythology, the god Rashap is never identified with or even specifically associated with fire. Significantly, even when Hebrew רשף is in fact associated with fiery phenomena, it is in the form of lightning bolts (// "hail"; Ps 78:48), flaming arrows (Ps 76:4, Song 8:6), or even sparks (Job 5:7), all of which appear in the plural.

An as-yet-unaddressed, but nevertheless intriguing question is whether the fearsome weapon depicted in Gen 3:24 derives from the realia of warfare in the ancient Near East. The image of a revolving sword with flashing blade might very well have an actual counterpart in the scythed chariot, said to have been introduced between 467 and 458 BCE by Artaxerxes I.[10] The swordlike scythes extended at an angle from the axle of the chariot wheels, and, when the chariot was in motion, the blade of the scythes rotated together with the wheel. In so doing, it is possible that the rapid rotation of the blade of the scythe might well have produced a visual effect not unlike flashing or blazing flames. It is thus not hard to imagine that the regular

---

latter interpretation finds support in Targum Onkelos on Gen 3:24, where להט החרב המתהפכת is rendered by Aramaic שנן חרבא דמתהפכא, "the *blade* of the revolving sword."

[9] Hendel, "'Flame of the Whirling Sword,'" 673–74. The Ugaritic passage KTU 1.2.I.32–33, cited by Hendel as a reference to a previously unknown pair of fiery divine beings, "a flame, two flames," actually describes Yamm's two messengers before El; they are fiery in aspect, and "their [tongue (!)] is a sharpened sword." For the passage, see Mark S. Smith, "The Baal Cycle," in *Ugaritic Narrative Poetry*, ed. Simon B. Parker, WAW 9 (Atlanta: Scholars Press, 1997), 100. Hendel ("'Flame of the Whirling Sword,'" 672) credits P. D. Miller Jr. with identifying the cherubim and flaming sword of Gen 3:24 with "Canaanite fiery messengers," having emended the text of Ps 104:4 to read as a supposed reference to two divine agents named אֵשׁ [וְ]לַהַט, "Fire and Flame." It must be stressed, however, that, beyond the poetic metaphor in Ps 104 and its proposed emendation, the existence of two such beings is purely conjectural.

[10] Alexander K. Nefiodkin, "On the Origin of the Scythed Chariots," *Historia: Zeitschrift für alte Geschichte* 53 (2004): 369–78.

rotation of the scythe and the startling, fearsome appearance of its blade constitute possible prototypes for the terrifying weapon depicted in Gen 3:24. In his account of Persian weaponry, the ancient Greek historian Xenophon portrays Cyrus the Great as having boasted, "What would you have done, if you heard that chariots are coming … and that scythes of steel have been fitted to axles, and that it is the intention to drive these into the ranks of the enemy?" Further on, in the same account, Xenophon records, "and, where scythes caught them, men and weapons were cut to shreds" (*Cyr.* 6.2.17; 7.1.31 [Miller, LCL]).

From a visual point of view, the proposed correspondence between the "blazing" blade of the revolving sword in Gen 3:24 and the burnished cutting edge of the scythe on the revolving Persian chariot wheel is certainly striking yet, by itself, inconclusive. The question of any direct influence on the passage in Genesis must rest with whether its author could possibly have seen or known of the Persian chariot wheel. Indeed, positing the dependence of the biblical imagery on this novel modification of Persian chariots necessarily implies a mid-fifth-century BCE date for the composition of Gen 3:24, which raises questions of its own. That issue, however, calls to mind the mention of priestly trousers in, for example, Exod 28:42 and Lev 6:3 and its novel interpretation by S. David Sperling as conclusive evidence for dating those passages to the Persian period—that is, no earlier than the sixth century BCE.[11] For now, at least, the question must remain open as to whether the appearance of the Persian scythed chariot wheel has any bearing on the date of our passage. Nevertheless, the present suggestion does, at the very least, afford a more workable way of visualizing the flashing blade of the revolving sword of Gen 3:24 than what has been advanced in previous explanations.[12]

---

[11] See his erudite and thoroughly convincing demonstration in "Pants, Persians, and the Priestly Source," in *Ki Baruch Hu: Ancient Near Eastern, Biblical, and Judaic Studies in Honor of Baruch A. Levine*, ed. Robert Chazan, William W. Hallo, and Lawrence H. Schiffman (Winona Lake, IN: Eisenbrauns, 1999), 373–85.

[12] Hendel ("'Flame of the Whirling Sword,'" 672) provides a convenient summary and brief discussion of previously advanced interpretations of the sword, some of which take it as a stylized representation of a lightning bolt, and others as some kind of divinely wielded weapon. It will be noted, however, that neither image, taken by itself, manages to account adequately for *both* the blazing appearance *and* the revolving motion of the biblical sword.

NEW FROM BAKER ACADEMIC

978-0-8010-4887-6 • 320 pp. • $28.99p

COMING APRIL 2015

"Karl Kuhn's groundbreaking monograph on Luke-Acts will reset modern interpretation of these books and influence New Testament studies for years to come."—**Mark Allan Powell**, Trinity Lutheran Seminary

978-0-8010-3190-8
448 pp. • $30.00p

Mikeal Parsons, a leading scholar on Luke and Acts, offers a practical commentary on Luke that is conversant with contemporary scholarship, draws on ancient backgrounds, and attends to the theological nature of the texts.

978-0-8010-3275-2 • 256 pp. • $30.00p

COMING APRIL 2015

"Peter Oakes has delivered the goods in his much anticipated Galatians commentary. Despite the many difficult passages in Galatians, Oakes provides a judicious and magisterial treatment of the text."—**Michael F. Bird**, Ridley College

Ḃ Baker Academic

Available in bookstores or by calling 800.877.2665 | Visit our blog: **blog.bakeracademic.com**
Subscribe to *E-Notes*, our enewsletter, at **bakeracademic.com**

Two Translations of HSS V 67 and Their Significance for Genesis 16, 21, and 30

KERRY D. LEE
kerry.d.lee.jr@gmail.com
Crosby, TX 77532

In two different treatments of the Nuzi contract HSS V 67, E. A. Speiser provided two different transliterations and translations of a key phrase without giving his reasons for the revision. It turns out that the text in question is damaged, rendering one particular cuneiform sign nearly unreadable. The significance of Speiser's revision for biblical studies is that, depending on which reading is taken, this text provides some legal background either for the concern that a full wife might send away the children of a secondary wife (as in Gen 21) or for the phenomenon of surrogate motherhood (i.e., the identification of the child of a secondary wife as in some way the child of the full wife; see Gen 16 and 30). Though some biblical scholars have noted Speiser's two translations, no one so far has engaged in a technical discussion of the primary text in order to understand the revision. Rather, scholars have sometimes simply chosen the reading that fits better with their purposes (usually Speiser's earlier reading). This article examines the original cuneiform text of HSS V 67 in order to ascertain, using orthographic and linguistic data, which of Speiser's two readings is the more likely. Speiser's revised reading proves to be the correct one, meaning that HSS V 67 does not provide a legal background for the concern that a full wife might send away the sons of a secondary wife (e.g., Gen 21).

The phenomenon in Gen 16 and 30, in which Sarai, Rachel, and Leah give their handmaidens to their husbands as substitute mothers, has been convincingly situated within the larger context of ancient Near Eastern law, specifically in clauses found in numerous marriage contracts from all over Mesopotamia and from both the first and second millennia BCE. Even so, the situations in Genesis are not an exact match for any extant marriage contract. The nature of the relationship between the barren woman and her handmaiden's children, the status of the children, the rights of the wife over the handmaiden, and the role of the husband in all of this vary from contract to contract, such that we can only conclude that the general phenomenon of surrogate motherhood was in reality a flexible practice whose precise terms were dependent on each context.

With regard to the relationship between mother and the handmaiden's children, E. A. Speiser depended heavily on texts from Nuzi for his interpretation (he was involved in the expedition, led by Edward Chiera, that discovered these texts). Speiser has been rightly criticized for overstressing the Nuzi parallels, but even so these texts remain an essential part of the textual data for reconstructing the ancient Near Eastern legal background for the Hebrew Bible and especially for Genesis.[1]

Speiser's use of one text, HSS V 67,[2] is of interest because he offers two different translations at different points in time but does not give his reason for changing his translation. In a 1930 monograph, he translates and discusses at length this text, which is moderately unusual in being a combination adoption and marriage contract.[3] The situation is that one man, Shurihilu, is adopting his nephew, Shennima, and as part of the deal is giving to him as wife Gilimninu, who is probably Shurihilu's daughter.[4] Lines 19–22 are the critical segment, and Speiser translates thus: "And if Gilimninu does not bear, Gilimninu a woman of the Lullu as wife for Shennima shall take. As for the (the concubine's) offspring, Gilimninu shall [*not*] send (them) away." This would appear to provide some legal background for the events of Gen 21, when Sarah sends away Hagar and Ishmael (or, rather, demands that Abraham send them away—this distinction is not to be disregarded, but it is not the subject of the present article), as a witness that such action was not inconceivable in some parts of the ancient Near East.

Later on, however, in his commentary on Genesis, Speiser translates line 22 differently: "Gilimninu herself shall have authority over the offspring."[5] This translation makes this contract simply one of many texts showing that the children of a substitute mother were sometimes considered to be legally the children of the full wife, a situation we find in Gen 16:2 and 30:3. So which translation is correct? Does

---

[1] For both a critique and a balanced assessment of the value of the Nuzi texts for the study of the ancestral narratives, see esp. ch. 10 of Thomas L. Thompson, *The Historicity of the Patriarchal Narrative: The Quest for the Historical Abraham*, BZAW 133 (Berlin: de Gruyter, 1974), 196–297.

[2] Edward Chiera, ed., *Texts on Varied Contents*, vol. 1 of *Excavations at Nuzi: Conducted by the Semitic Museum and the Fogg Art Museum of Harvard University, with the Cooperation of the American School of Oriental Research at Bagdad*, HSS 5 (Cambridge: Harvard University Press, 1929).

[3] E. A. Speiser, *New Kirkuk Documents Relating to Family Laws*, AASOR 10 (New Haven: American Schools of Oriental Research, 1930), 31.

[4] Thompson points out that this is an assumption and not explicitly stated (*Historicity of the Patriarchal Narratives*, 270 n. 319). However, a comparable text (Cyril J. Gadd, "Tablets from Kirkuk," *RA* 23 [1926]: 49–161, no. 51) also is a combination adoption and marriage contract with a few similar provisions, and here the fact that the bride is the adopter's daughter is explicit. Furthermore, in both contracts the obvious concern of the adopter is to make sure that the sons of the bride receive inheritance preference of some sort. In HSS V 67, Gilimninu's connection to Shurihilu as daughter is an assumption, but it is a very defensible one.

[5] E. A. Speiser, *Genesis: Introduction, Translation, and Notes*, AB 1 (Garden City, NY: Doubleday, 1963), 120.

this phrase provide background only for Gen 16 and 30, or does it also reflect the ethics operative in Gen 21?

Speiser notes in his commentary that there was need for an updated treatment of HSS V 67, but he does not offer any in-depth discussion of what sort of update he means. Essentially, what he does differently in the commentary boils down to a revision of his reading of the fourth-to-last and second-to-last signs on line 22. In the former context he transliterates *Gi-li-im-ni-nu l[a] ú-ma-ar*, but in the second *Gi-li-im-ni-nu-m[a] ú-wa-ar*. The fourth-to-last sign is damaged. Only its last downward stroke is discernible, so it could be either *la* (Borger 055) or *ma* (Borger 342).[6] In the former case, the symbol is a negative particle *la*. In the latter, it is an emphatic particle suffixed to "Gilimninu," possibly because it is stipulating a change in custody over the children from the handmaiden to Gilimninu. Either is a guess from context.[7]

The second-to-last sign is completely readable (𒈠). This sign, three horizontal strokes of equal length, justified on the left side, and bounded on the right by a downward stroke, is the standard *ma* sign (Borger 342). The standard sign for *wa* (Borger 383) is very different. As with most cuneiform signs, there are a number of variants, but no list of variants I have encountered yet shows a variant of Borger 383 that looks anything like Borger 342.[8] This would argue against Speiser's second reading (last word being *uwâr*). However, according to René Labat, *ba* (Borger 005) also has syllabic value *wa*.[9] The tendency for "b" sounds to be represented by "w"

---

[6] Riekle Borger, *Assyrisch-babylonische Zeichenliste*, 3rd ed., AOAT 33/33A (Kevelaer: Butzon & Bercker; Neukirchen-Vluyn: Neukirchener Verlag, 1986).

[7] To my knowledge, no one has discussed the textual or lexicographical bases for these alternative readings. Rather, the practice has been typically to note both translations and then select one based on the implications for the writer's exegesis of Genesis. Thompson adeptly covers the implications of either reading, but overall his treatment of the text assumes Speiser's first reading (*Historicity of the Patriarchal Narratives*, 252–59). Likewise, John Van Seters finds Speiser's later translation obscure and opts for the former without looking into the textual issues behind the two translations ("The Problem of Childlessness in Near Eastern Law and the Patriarchs of Israel," *JBL* 87 [1968]: 405–6 and n. 15). Speiser's first translation is what appears in *ANET* (p. 220). Outside of biblical studies and slightly more recently, Katarzyna Grosz translates the phrase similarly to Speiser's second translation, but the issue of the damaged sign is passed over ("Dowry and Brideprice in Nuzi," in *In Honor of Ernest R. Lacheman on His Seventy-fifth Birthday, April 29, 1981*, ed. Martha A. Morrison and David I. Owen, SCCNH 1 (Winona Lake, IN: Eisenbrauns, 1981), 161–82, esp. 166–67). Other contracts from Nuzi that make reference to this exact adoption, such as HSS V 48 (Speiser, *New Kirkuk Documents*, 66–67), neither concern nor contain clauses approximating the phrase in question.

[8] Neo-Assyrian variants tend to look like ⸢𒈠⸣, whereas Old Babylonian variants tend to look something like 𒈠. The variants show some degree of uniformity, involving in most cases two short strokes diagonal down-right, a downward stroke, and a horizontal stroke vertically centered.

[9] René Labat, *Manuel d'épigraphie akkadienne: Signes, syllabaire, idéogrammes*, 4th ed. (Paris: Imprimerie Nationale, 1963), 250, 267.

signs, and vice versa, has been specifically noted in relation to the Nuzi texts.[10] Furthermore, Babylonian variants of this sign show a tendency toward vertical leveling on the left side such that they are indistinguishable from Borger 342.[11] Therefore, both *umâr* and *uwâr* are plausible readings of the last three signs of line 22.

Both forms look like third masculine/feminine[12] singular D-stem present tense forms of a middle-*aleph* root or a geminate root. There are two possibilities. Speiser's original reading appears to have supposed *marāru* (root *mrr*), which in a causative D-stem would mean "to expel." However, this verb is not attested in the D-stem, only in G- and Š-stems.[13] The other possibility is *wâru(m)* (= *âru*/*mâru*; root *wʾr* or *mʾr*).[14] The D-stem is widely attested in this verb,[15] carries the general meaning "to govern" or "to command," and is more likely the word in line 22.[16] This estimation is likely what motivated Speiser's revision of his transliteration and translation. Interestingly, the fact that *wâru* also occurs as *mâru*[17] renders irrelevant the question of which sign, *ma* or *ḫa* = *wa*, is intended. Speiser's revision ultimately

---

[10] Moshé Berkooz, "Language Dissertation No. 23: The Nuzi Dialect of Akkadian: Orthography and Phonology," *Language* 13 (1937): 5–64, esp. 46–52.

[11] Arthur Amiaud and Lucien Méchineau, *Tableau comparé des écritures babylonienne et assyrienne archaïques et modernes avec classement des signes d'après leur forme archaïque* (Paris: V. Goupy et Jourdan, 1887), 89. On the other hand, Assyrian variants evolved so that the horizontal strokes were staggered—the middle being leftmost, the bottom center, and the top rightmost, with only the bottom and top strokes touching the downward stroke on the right. While the Nuzi dialect does have some features in common with Old Assyrian, it is fundamentally a Babylonian dialect (Berkooz, "Nuzi Dialect," 9).

[12] In the Babylonian dialects, gender distinction in the third person verbs in the present, perfect, and preterite tenses drops out. Feminine forms in Old Akkadian were preserved only in the Assyrian dialects. See Arthur Ungnad, *Grammatik des Akkadischen*, rev. Lubor Matous (Munich: Beck, 1969), §52d. Another explanation for the gender confusion is the possible influence of Hurrian on the Nuzi dialect. Either way, the verb can only refer to Gilimninu.

[13] *CAD* 10/1: 268; *CDA*, 197. It appears to be a word borrowed from Ugaritic, and its attestation in Akkadian texts is rather limited. See also entry "/m-r(-r)/ (I)" in Gregorio del Olmo Lete and Joaquín Sanmartín, *A Dictionary of the Ugaritic Language in the Alphabetic Tradition*, trans. Wilfred G. E. Watson, 2 vols., HdO 67 (Leiden: Brill, 2003), 2:577.

[14] These are variants of the same word. See *CAD* 1/2: 318–23; *CDA*, 25, 199, 435.

[15] As early as the Old Akkadian period. It is attested also in Old Assyrian and in Babylonian down to Standard Babylonian.

[16] Van Seters argues that the text makes sense only if Speiser's original reading is maintained: "The fact that the slave-girl's children could not inherit equally with Kelim-ninu's children clearly indicates that they have *no* relationship to her" ("Problem of Childlessness," 404–5). However, custodianship, the meaning of the verb *wâru*, is not the same as adoption, for which one usually finds the phrase *ana mārūti leqû/nadānu*, "to take/give into sonship." No legal fiction has necessarily been instituted by Gilimninu's custodianship.

[17] According to *CDA*, especially in Middle and Standard Babylonian. This exchange is, once again, specifically noted by Berkooz in the Nuzi dialect ("Nuzi Dialect," 46–52).

needed only to correct his guess as to the damaged fourth-to-last symbol. Speiser's second translation ("Gilimninu herself shall have authority over the offspring") is correct. This contract, therefore, does not bear witness to a precedent concern about a woman desiring to send away the sons of a substitute mother. If Gen 21 has a background in ancient Near Eastern law, it is not found in HSS V 67. Rather, this contract is part of an already large body of evidence from the ancient Near East that shows the practice of substitute childbirth (as also found in Gen 16 and 30). It also reveals the sometimes uncertain status that the children born in such circumstances inherited, being connected to the full wife in some way but not guaranteed full status as coheirs of the father.

Evangelically Rooted.   *Critically Engaged.*

GENESIS ON ITS OWN TERMS

272 pages, paperback, 978-0-8308-2461-8, $17.00

The Lost World of Adam and Eve
Genesis 2–3 and the Human Origins Debate

John H. Walton

What if the creation account in its ancient Near Eastern context actually makes no claims regarding Adam and Eve's material origins? Walton's groundbreaking insights into this text create space for a faithful reading of Scripture along with full engagement with science, creating a new way forward in the human origins debate.

"In this groundbreaking work the author places Adam and Eve firmly where they belong—in the cultural and textual world of the ancient Near East. Scholarly and readable, the text seen through Near Eastern eyes provides fascinating new insights into the question of human origins. The fine chapter by N. T. Wright provides the 'icing on the cake.'"

Denis Alexander, emeritus director of The Faraday Institute for Science and Religion, St. Edmund's College, Cambridge

Visit **ivpacademic.com** to request an exam copy.

Follow us on Twitter   Join us on Facebook   800.843.9487 | ivpacademic.com

Vengeance and Vindication in Numbers 31

KEN BROWN
Ken.Steven.Brown@gmail.com
Whitworth University, Spokane, WA 99251

In much of the Pentateuch, Moses's word and YHWH's will are practically indistinguishable, but this equation seems to break down in the latter half of Numbers, where Moses himself is explicitly condemned for rebellion (20:12; 27:13-14). In line with that shift, this article argues against the widespread assumption that Moses's command to slaughter the Midianite women and boys in Num 31:17-18 fulfills YHWH's call for "vengeance" (נקמה) in 31:1-2. Reinterpreting a surprisingly diverse range of earlier biblical legislation, Num 31 will be seen to juxtapose two sequences of divine command, fulfillment, and voluntary extension (31:1-18; 31:25-54), in which Moses's demand in 31:13-18 is contrasted with the officers' gift to the sanctuary in 31:48-54. Both can be seen as additional responses to YHWH's נקמה, but the first emphasizes its punitive side, demanding vengeance on the enemy, while the second takes up the liberating side of נקמה, celebrating the vindication and redress of Israel. In the end, it is not Moses's call for slaughter that is granted lasting significance but the officers' generous gift to the sanctuary.

The story of Moses's birth amid Israel's "ruthless" oppression in Egypt is one of the best known in the Hebrew Bible, thanks in part to Pharaoh's heartless command "Every son that is born you shall throw into the Nile, but every daughter you may allow to live" (Exod 1:22).[1] Yet there is another "slaughter of the innocents" that has received far less notice. In Num 31 we meet Moses at the end of his life (v. 2b), commanded by YHWH to "avenge the Israelites on the Midianites" (v. 2a), according to the NRSV. Moses's own wife was a Midianite (Exod 2:15-22, Num 10:29-32); but not only does Moses send an army against them (Num 31:3-12), he even angrily objects to the preservation of the captives after the battle (31:13-16). Like Pharaoh, Moses now demands that they also "kill every male among the

---

A version of this paper was presented at the Society of Biblical Literature International Meeting, Amsterdam, 25 July 2012. Thanks to Craig Broyles, Nathan MacDonald, and the members of the Early Jewish Monotheisms research group in Göttingen for valuable feedback on earlier drafts.

[1] Except where otherwise noted, all translations are my own.

children, and kill every woman who has known a man..., but every child among the women ... keep alive for yourselves" (31:17–18). Unlike Exod 1–2, Num 31 raises no lament over the fate of these women and children and tells no tales of their miraculous escape. "Vengeance," it appears, has been served. But has it?

In Num 31:16, Moses justifies his command by appealing to the Midianites' role in the apostasy and plague recounted in Num 25, and commentators have generally accepted that explanation and concluded that the text portrays the utter destruction of Midian as the fulfillment of YHWH's call for "vengeance."[2] Horst Seebass has questioned that consensus, noting that the slaughter of the Midianite women and boys is nowhere granted explicit divine sanction and asking whether this implies a "distance" over against Moses's command.[3] Seebass does not commit to that line, but there is a great deal of evidence to support it. Through an examination of the chapter's overall structure and reuse of earlier traditions, I will argue that Num 31 as a whole portrays Moses's demands in vv. 13–18 as an extension *beyond* YHWH's requirements, not as their fulfillment.

Numbers 31 does not simply recount a historical event; it reapplies and reformulates a wide range of earlier biblical legislation in novel and surprising ways.[4] While critical English-language scholarship has often considered the chapter

---

[2] E.g., Gordon J. Wenham, *Numbers: An Introduction and Commentary*, TOTC (Downers Grove, IL: InterVarsity, 1981), 210; Timothy R. Ashley, *The Book of Numbers*, NICOT 4 (Grand Rapids: Eerdmans, 1993), 591, 595; Baruch A. Levine, *Numbers: A New Translation with Introduction and Commentary*, 2 vols., AB 4, 4A (New York: Doubleday, 1993, 2000), 2:464, 466–70; Ludwig Schmidt, *Das vierte Buch Mose: Numeri 10,11–36,13*, ATD 7.2 (Göttingen: Vandenhoeck & Ruprecht, 2004), 188. Few studies center on Num 31 specifically, but see Susan Niditch, "War, Women, and Defilement in Numbers 31," *Semeia* 61 (1993): 39–57; David P. Wright, "Purification from Corpse-Contamination in Numbers XXXI 19–24," *VT* 35 (1985): 213–23; Christopher T. Begg, "Josephus' and Philo's Retelling of Numbers 31 Compared," *ETL* 83 (2007): 81–106.

[3] "Deutet der Text eine Distanz Jahwes gegenüber Moses Maßnahmen in 13–18 an? Sie bliebe höchstens sehr zurückhaltend, da Jahwe Mose nicht zurechtweist und die anschließende Beuteverteilung ausgesprochen zustimmende Züge zeigt" (Horst Seebass, *Numeri*, 3 vols., BKAT 4 [Neukirchen-Vluyn: Neukirchener Verlag, 2003–7], 3:318; cf. 3:290–318). These reservations will be addressed below.

[4] No location is named, and the battle is not described (Num 31:1–8; cf. Josh 13:21–22), which serves only as a platform for detailed discussions concerning the captives and plunder (31:9–54). The chapter is therefore commonly identified as "midrash" (e.g., Rüdiger Schmitt, *Der "Heilige Krieg" im Pentateuch und im deuteronomistischen Geschichtswerk: Studien zur Forschungs-, Rezeptions- und Religionsgeschichte von Krieg und Bann im Alten Testament*, AOAT 381 [Münster: Ugarit-Verlag, 2011], 150–57; George Buchanan Gray, *A Critical and Exegetical Commentary on Numbers*, ICC 4 [Edinburgh: T&T Clark, 1912], 418–19; John Sturdy, *Numbers*, CBC 5 [Cambridge: Cambridge University Press, 1976], 214–15). To call Num 31 "midrash" is imprecise (so Seebass, *Numeri*, 3:297–98, 316–17; cf. Lieve M. Teugels, *Bible and Midrash: The Story of 'The Wooing of Rebekah' (Gen. 24)*, CBET 35 [Leuven: Peeters, 2004], 135–69) but rightly stresses its prominent use of earlier texts. For methodological discussions, see esp. Bernard M. Levinson, *Deuteronomy and the Hermeneutics of Legal Innovation* (Oxford: Oxford University Press, 1997); Benjamin D.

Priestly,[5] its reinterpretations not only of Priestly but also of Deuteronomic and other traditions suggest that its final form is late and post-Priestly, as German scholarship has long recognized.[6] In particular, Moses's command to execute the Midianite women and boys will be seen to reinterpret both YHWH's command in 31:2—already fulfilled in 31:7—and the war regulations in Deut 20:10-15, which are closely followed in Num 31:7-12. Similarly, this whole sequence of divine command, fulfillment, and extension in 31:1-18 is paralleled in the second half of the chapter, where a voluntary gift to the sanctuary by "the officers" in 31:48-54 also goes beyond YHWH's commands regarding the distribution of the plunder in 31:25-30, which are explicitly fulfilled in 31:31-47. Like Moses's demand, the officers' gift lacks explicit divine approval, and its reapplication of the census regulations in Exod 30:11-16 is no less innovative than Moses's reinterpretation of Deut 20.

Yet these two extensions beyond YHWH's command are not simply parallel; they are set in contrast. They embody two very different responses to the threat of apostasy and plague, the former focused on the enemy, the latter on Israel itself. This reflects a tension first introduced between YHWH's initial call for "vengeance" (נקמה) in 31:2 and Moses's reformulation of it in 31:3. Though the two verses are generally assumed to be equivalent, they are not. Moses's restatement emphasizes YHWH's נקמה *on* (ב) Midian, but YHWH's own command highlights Israel's נקמה *from* (מן) the Midianites. As Jacob Milgrom notes, the two expressions carry distinct nuances: Moses's indicates retribution or punishment on the enemy, but, despite the usual translations, YHWH's probably calls for the vindication or redress of Israel itself.[7]

Moses's call for the complete destruction of the enemy in 31:13-18 is a natural corollary to his interpretation of YHWH's נקמה, but the rest of the chapter adheres instead to YHWH's more positive use of the term, with its consistent focus on the collection, purification, and distribution of the plunder. The officers' gift in vv. 48-54 completes that theme, leaving Moses's call for slaughter an outlier in the chapter. Moreover, while both Moses's demand and the officers' gift go beyond YHWH's commands, the former is not expressly carried out, while the latter is explicitly

---

Sommer, *A Prophet Reads Scripture: Allusion in Isaiah 40-66* (Stanford, CA: Stanford University Press, 1998).

[5] E.g., Philip J. Budd, *Numbers*, WBC 5 (Waco, TX: Word, 1984), 327-29; Levine, *Numbers*, 2:445.

[6] Most recently, Seebass, *Numeri*, 3:290-99, 315-18; Ulrich Fistill, *Israel und das Ostjordanland: Untersuchungen zur Komposition von Num 21,21-36,13 im Hinblick auf die Entstehung des Buches Numeri*, ÖBS 30 (Frankfurt am Main: Lang, 2007), 112-13; cf. 157-59; Reinhard Achenbach, *Die Vollendung der Tora: Studien zur Redaktionsgeschichte des Numeribuches im Kontext von Hexateuch und Pentateuch*, BZABR 3 (Wiesbaden: Harrassowitz, 2003), 615-22; cf. also Gray, *Critical and Exegetical Commentary on Numbers*, 419-20.

[7] Jacob Milgrom, *Numbers* במדבר: *The Traditional Hebrew Text with the New JPS Translation*, JPS Torah Commentary (Philadelphia: Jewish Publication Society of America, 1990), 255-56.

accepted by Moses and Eleazar the high priest and brought into the tent of meeting as a permanent memorial for Israel before YHWH (31:51–54). Numbers 31, therefore, not only contrasts Moses's demand with the actions of the officers (vv. 14, 48–54) and the priests (vv. 6, 13, 21–54) but also uses this subtly to challenge Moses's own interpretation of YHWH's commands, opening up space for a wider reinterpretation of biblical legislation by subsequent leaders of Israel.

I. Structure and Parallelism

Numbers 31 has often been thought to form a chiasm, but this demands a parallel between vv. 1–12 and vv. 48–54, which is not obvious, and downplays the parallel divine commands in vv. 1–2 and vv. 25–30, which divide the passage in half.[8] Therefore, while the chapter bears some features of a chiasm, it falls more naturally into a parallel structure (see next page).

Each half begins with a direct divine command with parallel introductory formulae: "YHWH spoke/said to Moses, saying" (vv. 1, 25; the first is reformulated by Moses in vv. 3–4).[9] Each is followed by explicit depictions of Moses's and the people's obedience "as YHWH commanded Moses" (כאשר צוה יהוה את־משה; vv. 7, 31, 41, 47).[10] Then each climaxes in an unexpected extension beyond that command, centering on Moses and "the officers..., the commanders of the thousands and the commanders of the hundreds" (vv. 14, 48).[11] The central section, in which Eleazar introduces a novel set of purity regulations, is unparalleled (vv. 19–24).[12] Thus, the chapter forms a kind of diptych, in which the command, fulfillment, and

---

[8] For instance, Milgrom's structure is (A) vv. 1–12; (B) vv. 13–24; (B′) vv. 25–47; (A′) vv. 48–54 (*Numbers*, 491–92; similarly, Thomas Staubli, *Die Bücher Levitikus, Numeri*, NSKAT 3 [Stuttgart: Katholisches Bibelwerk, 1996], 331; followed by Schmitt, *Der "Heilige Krieg,"* 150). Seebass rejects such chiastic arrangements (*Numeri*, 3:289–90).

[9] YHWH speaks nowhere else, and the speeches in 31:15, 21, 49 use other formulae.

[10] Cf. also 31:21; sections B and B′ are also linked by the terms בהמה (appearing here only in 31:9, 11, 26, 30, 47), בזז (31:9, 32, 53), מלקוח (31:11, 12, 26, 27, 32; elsewhere only in Isa 49:24–25), and אדם (31:11, 26, 28, 30, 35, 40, 46, 47).

[11] These figures appear nowhere else in Numbers (see n. 64 below), and their introduction is repeated in full in 31:14 and 48 (more briefly in 31:52, 54). Corresponding introductory formulae are used also in 31:15 (ויאמר אליהם משה) and 31:49 (ויאמרו אל־משה).

[12] This ABC-D-A′B′C′ structure would be a modification of the expected ABC-A′B′C′ pattern (on which, see Jerome Walsh, *Style and Structure in Biblical Hebrew Narrative* [Collegeville, MN: Liturgical Press, 2001], 35–45) and requires an implicit break between 31:18 and 19, which is widely acknowledged, often attributed to the later addition of 31:19–24 (e.g., Martin Noth, *Numbers: A Commentary*, trans. James D. Martin, OTL [London: SCM, 1968], 230–31). Be that as it may, the lexical and structural parallels between A and A′, B and B′, and C and C′ are not matched by any chiastic arrangement and imply that the final structure of the text is not simply ad hoc, even if it is secondary. A similar but less detailed parallel arrangement is recognized by Seebass (*Numeri*, 3:290).

extension of the war against Midian in vv. 1–18 are paralleled and contrasted with the command, fulfillment, and extension of the distribution of the plunder in vv. 25–54. There are no references to YHWH's speech or command in either concluding section, and each can be seen as a point where YHWH's demand has been exceeded.

Structure of Numbers 31

A Command 31:1–2	YHWH commands Moses (וַיְדַבֵּר יהוה אֶל־מֹשֶׁה לֵּאמֹר; 31:1) to "נקם the נקמה of the Israelites *from* the Midianites" (31:2).	
31:3–4	Moses commands Israel (וַיְדַבֵּר מֹשֶׁה אֶל־הָעָם לֵאמֹר; 31:3a) to prepare for war "to exact the נקמה of YHWH *on* Midian" (31:3c).	
B Obedience 31:5–12	The war and its results, performed "as YHWH commanded Moses" (כַּאֲשֶׁר צִוָּה יהוה אֶת־מֹשֶׁה; 31:7).	
C Extension 31:13–18	Moses commands the officers and commanders (פְּקוּדֵי הֶחָיִל שָׂרֵי הָאֲלָפִים וְשָׂרֵי הַמֵּאוֹת; 31:14) to kill the women and boys.	
D Purification 31:19–24	Purification regulations, "which YHWH commanded Moses" (אֲשֶׁר־צִוָּה יהוה אֶת־מֹשֶׁה; 31:21), expanded by Eleazar (31:21–24).	
A´ Command 31:25–30	YHWH commands Moses (וַיֹּאמֶר יהוה אֶל־מֹשֶׁה לֵּאמֹר; 31:25) to count and divide the plunder.	
B´ Obedience 31:31–47	The count and division of the plunder, "as YHWH commanded Moses" (כַּאֲשֶׁר צִוָּה יהוה אֶת־מֹשֶׁה; 31:31, 41, 47).	
C´ Extension 31:48–54	The officers and commanders (הַפְּקֻדִים אֲשֶׁר לְאַלְפֵי הַצָּבָא שָׂרֵי הָאֲלָפִים וְשָׂרֵי הַמֵּאוֹת; 31:48; cf. 52, 54) bring an additional gift to Moses.	

II. Numbers 25–31 and the Tension between Divine Command and Human Initiative

Numbers 31 is not explicitly connected to either ch. 30 or ch. 32 but rather follows from the Baal-Peor incident in ch. 25, particularly the divine command in 25:16–18:

> YHWH spoke to Moses, saying, "Be hostile to the Midianites and strike them, for they have been hostile to you when they deceived you in the matter of Peor, and in the matter of Cozbi, daughter of the chieftain of Midian, their sister, who was killed on the day of the plague [הַמַּגֵּפָה] as a result of the matter of Peor."

This provides a justification for war that is missing from Num 31:1–2, as Moses makes explicit in 31:16, repeating the allusions to "the plague" (המגפה) and "the matter of Peor."[13] More importantly, ch. 25 sets a precedent for ch. 31 in its depiction of Moses's actions over against those of the priest Phinehas, who appears in 25:7–13 and 31:6.[14] Chapter 25 appears to be a composite of at least two layers, the earlier of which does not mention Midianites and seems to have portrayed Moses as the hero, quickly responding to a divine command to slay the guilty (25:1–5*).[15] In the present form of the text, however, the deed is never done, and we suddenly find Moses and the people weeping before the tent of meeting as Cozbi appears with the son of a prominent Israelite (25:6). While Moses remains inactive, Phinehas slays the couple (25:7–8), ending the previously unmentioned plague (25:8–11). This act fulfills no divine command, yet it is claimed to secure "atonement" for Israel and earns Phinehas "a covenant of eternal priesthood" (25:13).

Jonathan Grossman argues that this establishes a tension between divine command and human initiative that plays out across the rest of chs. 25–31.[16] Itamar Kislev discusses a further example in 27:12–23, where Moses's death is anticipated and tied to his rebellion at Meribah (27:13–14; cf. 20:12, 24).[17] Numbers 27 not only explicitly condemns Moses but also addresses the problem of Israel's subsequent leadership in a surprising manner. Here Moses asks YHWH to name a successor, but YHWH responds by directly subordinating Joshua to Eleazar (27:19–22).[18] This not only maintains the more prominent position of the priesthood established

---

[13] An allusion to some form of Num 25 is universally recognized, though the precise nature of the two chapters' interdependence is debatable (see, e.g., Seebass, *Numeri*, 3:290–92; Fistill, *Israel und das Ostjordanland*, 101–2).

[14] Outside the genealogy in Exod 6:25, Phinehas appears in the Pentateuch only in these two passages. He appears also in Josh 22:13–32, 24:33, Judg 20:28, 1 Chr 5:30, 6:35, 9:20, Ezra 7:5, and Ps 106:30 (see Barbara E. Organ, "Pursuing Phinehas: A Synchronic Reading," *CBQ* 63 [2001]: 203–18).

[15] Fistill, *Israel und das Ostjordanland*, 84–103; Achenbach, *Die Vollendung der Tora*, 425–42; Seebass, *Numeri*, 3:115–17; Schmidt, *Das vierte Buch Mose*, 145–48; Budd, *Numbers*, 277–78.

[16] Jonathan Grossman, "Divine Command and Human Initiative: A Literary View on Numbers 25–31," *BibInt* 15 (2007): 54–79. Grossman suggests that Phinehas's role in ch. 25 also "served as a veiled criticism of Moses' conduct as leader" (p. 73; similarly, Milgrom, *Numbers*, 214; Seebass, *Numeri*, 3:124), though that is not explicit in ch. 25 as it is in chs. 20 and 27. Much less likely is Josebert Fleurant's claim that the Midianite killed was Moses's own wife, and that P "whitewashed" this ("Phinehas Murdered Moses' Wife: An Analysis of Numbers 25," *JSOT* 35 [2011]: 285–94).

[17] Itamar Kislev, "The Investiture of Joshua (Numbers 27:12–23) and the Dispute on the Form of the Leadership in *Yehud*," *VT* 59 (2009): 429–45; cf. Grossman, "Divine Command and Human Initiative," 65–69.

[18] Note, for example, the repeated demand (27:19, 21, 22) that Joshua "stand before" (עמד לפני) Eleazar, an expression generally used of a subordinate before a superior (e.g., Deut 1:38, Gen 41:46, 43:15, Num 35:12, Deut 29:14[15]). See Kislev, "Investiture of Joshua," 437–40; and further points in Grossman, "Divine Command and Human Initiative," 67–69.

in ch. 25 but also undermines any simplistic equation of Moses's intent with YHWH's.

Numbers 31 takes up and extends both of these themes, as Phinehas and Eleazar continue to play key roles throughout the chapter, while Moses's own position is relativized. Using the same expression as in 27:13, ch. 31 begins with another reminder of Moses's approaching death and directly ties this to YHWH's call for נקמה in 31:2. Leaving the term untranslated for now, the verse reads literally: "נקם the נקמה of the Israelites from [מאת] the Midianites; afterward you will be gathered to your people."[19] This linkage to Moses's death is not incidental, as it recalls those earlier instances of tension between YHWH's and Moses's perspectives, setting the stage for Moses's reformulation of YHWH's command in 31:3. As in chs. 25 and 27, Moses's response is here juxtaposed with YHWH's intent, and a closer comparison reveals subtle but significant differences between the two.

III. YHWH's Commands and Moses's Interpretation in Numbers 25:16–18 and 31:1–3

Though the divine commands in Num 25:16–18 and 31:1–2 are often equated with the whole of what follows in ch. 31, this is not as straightforward as is generally assumed.[20] Taken on its own, 25:16–18 is ambiguous: "Be hostile [צרר] to the Midianites and strike them [נכה], for they have been hostile [צרר] to you" certainly does not have to be read as a call for extermination. The verb צרר indicates treating someone as an enemy, but it can do so in a variety of contexts.[21] That it is here portrayed as a reciprocal response offers little help, since the account mentions only one Midianite, and even her role is ambiguous.[22]

The sense would appear to be clarified by the parallel with נכה, which likely means "kill," given its use of Phinehas's slaying Zimri and Cozbi (25:14–15, 18). But when applied to a people group, נכה only sometimes implies the destruction of the entire population (e.g., Num 21:35, Deut 7:2). Often it indicates nothing more than the defeat of its army. The latter usage is especially common in Chronicles, a work

---

[19] Both Num 27:13 and 31:2 use the expression אסף אל־עמיך, "you will be gathered to your people," which appears elsewhere in Numbers only in the account of Aaron's death, which is *also* explicitly tied to the rebellion at Meribah (20:23–26; noted by Levine, *Numbers*, 2:450; cf. 1:494, 2:349; Budd, *Numbers*, 330; cf. 228, 306—though neither allows this to influence his reading of Num 31).

[20] Contra Budd, *Numbers*, 280; Ashley, *Book of Numbers*, 524; Staubli, *Die Bücher Levitikus, Numeri*, 308; Schmidt, *Das vierte Buch Mose*, 151–52; Wenham, *Numbers*, 210.

[21] Cf. Exod 23:22, Num 10:9, 33:55, Deut 28:52, 2 Chr 28:20, Neh 9:27, Ps 129:1–2, Isa 11:13, Jer 10:18, Amos 5:12, Zeph 1:17. See צרר II in *HALOT* 2:1058–59.

[22] Numbers 25:1–5 mentions only *Moabites* and stresses primarily the sin of Israel, while Cozbi is the only Midianite in view in 25:6–15; see Helena Zlotnick Sivan, "The Rape of Cozbi (Numbers XXV)," *VT* 51 (2001): 69–80; Seebass, *Numeri*, 3:116–24.

with long-noted connections to the late stages of Numbers.[23] Chronicles omits nearly every instance of mass slaughter from the Deuteronomistic History, while preserving and even adding numerous wars in which enemy armies are defeated, often using נכה, but the civilian populations are not killed.[24] The same usage is found in Num 14:45, where Israel is "defeated" (נכה) by the Amalekites and Canaanites, but obviously not exterminated. In that light, the use of צרר and נכה in Num 25:17 leaves open whether YHWH is demanding the military defeat of Midian, as described in 31:7–12, or the extermination of Midian in toto, as demanded in 31:13–18.

What, then, of the divine command in Num 31:1–2? Instead of צרר and נכה, here the key terms are נקם and נקמה, which are generally translated with "avenge" and "vengeance." Though this suggests to many English speakers a kind of vigilante justice and excessive violence, H. G. L. Peels has argued that, when used of and by God, נקם typically indicates the establishment or maintenance of justice.[25] This often entails the punishment of the guilty, but it can also emphasize the vindication or even liberation of the innocent. For instance, Isa 34–35 illustrates these two senses with elaborate accounts of judgment and restoration: ch. 34 anticipates "a day of נקם" (34:8) with imagery of utter devastation. By contrast, ch. 35 parallels "your God will come with נקם" with "he will come and save you [ישע]" (35:4), describing the restoration of the blind and lame, streams in the desert, and the return of the redeemed to Zion.[26]

Milgrom has suggested that a tension between such vindicating and punitive

---

[23] Some terminological connections between Chronicles and Num 31 will be noted at various points below; see also Heinrich Holzinger, *Numeri*, KHC 4 (Tübingen: Mohr Siebeck, 1903), 148–49; Gray, *Critical and Exegetical Commentary on Numbers*, 420; Levine, *Numbers*, 2:470–72; Achenbach, *Die Vollendung der Tora*, 622.

[24] Such wars are retained from DtrH (e.g., 1 Chr 14:11–16, 2 Chr 21:9–10) and added (e.g., 1 Chr 20:1–3, 2 Chr 28:5–17). For example, 1 Chr 18:2 takes nearly verbatim from 2 Sam 8:2a + e the claim that David "defeated [נכה] Moab, and the Moabites became servants to David, and brought tribute," while omitting the intervening claim that David executed two-thirds of the prisoners (2 Sam 8:2b–d). Only twice in Chronicles is נכה connected with the slaughter of civilians (1 Chr 4:41, 2 Chr 25:11–13), neither of which is praised.

[25] H. G. L. Peels, *The Vengeance of God: The Meaning of the Root NQM and the Function of the NQM-Texts in the Context of Divine Revelation in the Old Testament*, OtSt 31 (Leiden: Brill, 1995), 265–66 et passim. See also Edward Lipiński, "נָקַם *nāqam*; נָקָם *nāqām*; נְקָמָה *nᵉqāmâ*," *TDOT* 10:1–9; G. Sauer, "נקם *nqm* to avenge," *TLOT* 2:767–69; George E. Mendenhall, *The Tenth Generation: The Origins of Biblical Tradition* (Baltimore: Johns Hopkins University Press, 1973), 69–104; Walter Dietrich, "Rache: Erwägungen zu einem alttestamentlichen Thema," *EvT* 36 (1976): 450–72.

[26] Similarly, Isa 59:17–20, Deut 32:35–36; see Mendenhall, *Tenth Generation*, 99–100; Peels, *Vengeance of God*, 148–60, 118–23. Much has been written on Isa 34–35; see the well-balanced discussion of Brevard S. Childs, *Isaiah*, OTL (Louisville: Westminster John Knox, 2001), 249–58, who sees these chapters as a contrastive diptych that serves, at least in its final form, to link Isa 1–33 to Isa 40–66.

senses of נקם can also be perceived between the divine command in Num 31:1–2, which uses נקם plus נקמה with מן, and Moses's restatement in 31:3, which uses נתן plus נקמה with ב: "The verb *nakam* bears two closely associated meanings: to redress past wrongs and to exact retribution. The former takes the preposition *min*, 'from,' the latter the preposition *be*, 'on.'"[27] Milgrom does not attempt to justify this distinction, however, so a review of the lexicographical evidence is in order.

That נקם or נקמה with ב indicates retribution or punishment *on* someone is clear in every context where it appears.[28] Many of these texts stress the death or complete destruction of those to whom the expression is applied. For example, "I will stretch out my hand against Edom [עַל־אֱדוֹם] and cut off from it human and animal. I will make it desolate; from Teman to Dedan, they shall fall by the sword. I will exact [נתן] my נקמה on Edom [בֶּאֱדוֹם], by the hand of my people Israel" (Ezek 25:13b–14a). Read in that light, Moses's command to "equip from among you men for battle and go against Midian [עַל־מִדְיָן] to exact [נתן] YHWH's נקמה on Midian [בְּמִדְיָן]" (Num 31:3) probably expects a similarly devastating attack, as Moses's anger at the preservation of the captives in 31:13–18 seems to confirm.[29]

But does YHWH's command imply the same thing? Despite Milgrom's distinction, some occurrences of נקם or נקמה with מן do appear to imply a retribution comparable to that seen above (esp. Judg 16:28, Jer 46:10).[30] Nonetheless, other occurrences emphasize the vindication or deliverance of the victim more than the destruction of the guilty.[31] For instance, Jeremiah prays, "You know, O YHWH— remember me and attend to me and נקם me from my persecutors [מֵרֹדְפַי]. In your forbearance do not take me away. Know that I suffer insult on your account" (Jer 15:15). The emphasis is squarely on Jeremiah's wish for vindication and rescue, and

---

[27] Milgrom, *Numbers*, 255. Typically, the one for whom נקם is taken is the direct object of the verb, or is attached to a construct form of נקמה, while a preposition introduces the one "on" (ב), "from" (מן), or "against" (ל or על) whom נקמה/נקם is taken (cf. Lipiński, *TDOT* 10:1–2, though he does not distinguish in meaning between these prepositions).

[28] See Judg 15:7; 1 Sam 18:25; Ps 149:7; Jer 5:9, 29; 9:8[9]; 50:15 (cf. 50:28; 51:1–11); Ezek 25:12–17.

[29] Mendenhall suggests that Ezek 25:12–14 stands behind Num 31:2–3, without acknowledging that the expression in Num 31:2 is different (*Tenth Generation*, 99).

[30] The expression appears also in Judg 11:36; 1 Sam 14:24; 24:13[12]; 2 Sam 4:8; Esth 8:13; Isa 1:24; Jer 11:20; 15:15; 20:10, 12. Some of these indeed respond to "past wrongs" (e.g., 2 Sam 4:8, Isa 1:24; Milgrom, *Numbers*, 255), but most instead respond to a present, deadly threat. The expression נקם דם מיד occurs in 2 Kgs 9:7 (with a punitive sense), but this probably should not be equated with the other uses of נקם with מן.

[31] This usage is stressed by Mendenhall (*Tenth Generation*, 69–104, esp. 82–88). Peels (*Vengeance of God*, 9–11, 39–41, 267–68, following Wayne T. Pitard, "Amarna *ekēmu* and Hebrew *nāqam*," *Maarav* 3 [1982]: 5–25) rightly objects to Mendenhall's attempt to link this to the maintenance of a covenant, but Peels still affirms that the term can carry a sense of "*liberating vengeance*: נקם as retribution that brings liberation to the oppressed" (*Vengeance of God*, 266; emphasis original).

YHWH's response in 15:19–21 is framed in those terms, promising to save (ישע), rescue (נצל), and deliver (פדה).³² Similarly, 1 Sam 24:9–16[8–15] uses נקם in parallel with שפט and contrasts it with personal retaliation: "May YHWH judge [שפט] between me and you; may YHWH נקם me from you [ממך], but my hand will not be against you [בך]" (24:13[12]; cf. 24:16[15]). This is generally translated "may the LORD avenge me on you" (NRSV),³³ but the context of a threat on David's life, his explicit rejection of violence, and the use of מן all suggest instead the sense: "May YHWH vindicate me from you."³⁴

Therefore, while נקם with מן is not always used in this way, it can carry the sense of vindication or redress *from* an aggressor, while נקם with ב virtually always indicates retribution or punishment *on* a guilty party. With Milgrom, then, YHWH's command in Num 31:2 can be translated, "Seek the vindication [or redress] of the Israelites from the Midianites," while Moses's restatement in 31:3 should be read: "to exact YHWH's retribution on Midian."³⁵ In support of this, note that the direct object of YHWH's command is "the נקמה of the Israelites," while Moses drops this reference to Israel and focuses his command on Midian, *against* whom war is mustered (על־מדין), and *on* whom the נקמה of YHWH is executed (במדין). That these commands are set side by side, with parallel introductory formulae, invites their comparison and implicitly raises a question about the nature of YHWH's נקמה.³⁶

If Num 31 is a response to the events at Baal-Peor, is the primary force of YHWH's

---

³² So Mendenhall, *Tenth Generation*, 97, followed by John Bright, *Jeremiah: A New Translation with Introduction and Commentary*, 2nd ed., AB 21 (Garden City, NY: Doubleday, 1965), 110–12; cf. 87. Peels acknowledges that this wish for "vengeance upon the pursuers" implies "the liberation of the oppressed prophet," but he unnecessarily ties this to "the punishment of the enemy" (*Vengeance of God*, 230; cf. 224–34; similarly, Jack R. Lundbom, *Jeremiah 1–20: A New Translation with Introduction and Commentary*, AB 21A [New York: Doubleday, 1999], 742), who notes parallels in the complaint psalms.

³³ Most commentators follow this without discussion, but, as Walter Brueggemann notes, the "juridical language" indicates a wish to be "vindicated and acquitted" and a need to be rescued (*First and Second Samuel*, IBC [Louisville: John Knox, 1990], 170; similarly, Mendenhall, *Tenth Generation*, 83–84). Peels also emphasizes the "judicial" force of David's call for נקם, though he ties it to "punishing judgment," despite acknowledging the parallel in Jer 15:15 (*Vengeance of God*, 256).

³⁴ Cf. the sequel in 2 Sam 4:8–12 (on which, see Brueggemann, *First and Second Samuel*, 234–35).

³⁵ Derived from Milgrom (*Numbers*, 255–56), though oddly he then confuses this distinction by attributing YHWH's command to Israel, and Moses's to YHWH (p. 256). Ashley (*Book of Numbers*, 590–91) follows Mendenhall in translating *both* expressions with "vindication," though this does not stop him from claiming that such a YHWH war demands חרם.

³⁶ Achenbach thinks the parallel introductions portray Moses as the ideal prophet (*Die Vollendung der Tora*, 616), but, as Robert Alter emphasizes, the juxtaposition of such "repetitions with significant variations" is often contrastive and can indicate "some unexpected, perhaps unsettling, new revelation of character or plot" (*The Art of Biblical Narrative* [New York: Basic Books, 1981], 97–98; cf. 63–113).

command indeed retribution *on* Israel's enemy, as Moses states, or is it the vindication or redress of Israel *from* Midian, as YHWH's expression could indicate?

Such a distinction is borne out by the shape of the following account. Outside of Moses's commands, the destruction of Midian is reported in a bare four verses (31:7-10), while the remainder of the chapter is focused on the vindication and redress of Israel, as seen in the vast plunder secured and its carefully calculated distribution to the army, people, priests, and Levites (31:11-12, 25-47; further exceeded in 31:48-54). Yet the significance of this contrast is not merely structural; it establishes a tension between divine command and human response that will recur throughout the chapter. To see this, we will consider in turn how each section of the chapter applies, modifies, or extends earlier divine commands, beginning with the reinterpretations of Deut 20 in Num 31:7-18.

IV. Deuteronomy 20, Judges 21, and the Threat of חרם in Numbers 31:7-18

Deuteronomy 20:10-18 includes two contrasting sets of war regulations. The first is applied to nations "very far from you" and requires that Israel kill the men but take the women, children, and livestock as plunder (vv. 10-15). The second is limited to "the Hittites and the Amorites, the Canaanites and the Perizzites, the Hivites and the Jebusites" (v. 17) and demands the destruction (חרם) of "everything that breathes" (vv. 16-18).[37] Midian is not among the nations listed in Deut 20:17, and accordingly the battle in Num 31:7-12 closely follows the pattern for nations "very far from you," repeating most of the key terms from Deut 20:14 to describe the plunder.[38] This also fits the command in Num 25:17, as the term נכה used there is applied to the males in Deut 20:13 but not to the women and children. Thus, Num 31:7-12 appears to carry out Num 25:17 and 31:2 by way of Deut 20:13-14, diverging from Deuteronomy on only two points: First, the offer of peace is omitted (Deut 20:10-12), presumably in consequence of the divine commands in Numbers. More importantly, the cities and camps are burned (Num 31:10), which is not mentioned in Deut 20. This is often taken as an indication of חרם, since the burning of cities

---

[37] On חרם, the practice of devoting people or cities to YHWH, usually by complete destruction, see esp. Norbert Lohfink, "חָרַם *ḥāram;* חֵרֶם *ḥērem,*" *TDOT* 5:180-99; Philip D. Stern, *The Biblical Ḥerem: A Window on Israel's Religious Experience,* BJS 211 (Atlanta: Scholars Press, 1991); Joel N. Lohr, *Chosen and Unchosen: Conceptions of Election in the Pentateuch and Jewish-Christian Interpretation,* Siphrut 2 (Winona Lake, IN: Eisenbrauns, 2009), 208-25; Nathan MacDonald, *Deuteronomy and the Meaning of "Monotheism,"* 2nd ed., FAT 2/1 (Tübingen: Mohr Siebeck, 2012), 108-23.

[38] In both Deut 20:13-14 and Num 31:7-11, they kill "every male" (כל־זכור/כל־זכר), then plunder (בזז) the women (נשים), children (טף), and cattle (בהמה) from the cities (ערים) as spoils (שלל). Though Num 31:7 and Deut 20:13 use different expressions to refer to slaying the males, the sense is identical. Allusion here is accepted by Levine, *Numbers,* 2:465-70; Schmidt, *Das vierte Buch Mose,* 187; Seebass, *Numeri,* 3:295, 302; Achenbach, *Die Vollendung der Tora,* 615, 617-18.

is often associated with the destruction of their inhabitants.³⁹ The burning of *non-Israelite* cities is never commanded in the Pentateuch, however, and, of course, the army does not kill the Midianite civilians, as חרם would demand.⁴⁰ If the burning of the cities and camps raises the specter of חרם, therefore, it does so without actually implementing or requiring it.

This is in keeping with the rest of the Priestly-influenced literature in the Pentateuch, where the practice of חרם is very rare and is typically confined to civil rather than military contexts.⁴¹ In Numbers particularly, the only explicit war-חרם is in 21:1–3, where it is presented as a desperate vow rather than a divine command.⁴² Why, then, does Moses object to the preservation of the captives in Num 31:13–18?

He claims shock that they allowed the women to live, when "they were the ones who, on Balaam's advice, caused the Israelites to act faithlessly against YHWH in the matter of Peor, so that the plague came upon the congregation of YHWH" (31:16). This maintains the same shift in blame from the daughters of the Moabites to the Midianites first introduced in 25:16–18 but then goes further, condemning all of the women, where Num 25 mentioned only one.⁴³ Still more curiously, Moses then commands them to kill the male children—who have had no role at all before now—only then adding that they should also kill the nonvirgin women (31:17–18). While commentators sometimes link this to the demands of חרם, this is not simply an extension of Deut 20:16–18 to Midian, as in that case all the captives and livestock would have to be killed (Deut 20:16).⁴⁴

Instead, as Baruch Levine suggests, this seems to be a reinterpretation of Deut 20:13–14 itself, including the male (זכר) children (טף) with "all the males [כל־זכור]" to be killed, rather than with "the women and children [טף]" to be spared.⁴⁵ If so,

---

³⁹ See Achenbach, *Die Vollendung der Tora*, 618; Schmidt, *Das vierte Buch Mose*, 187.

⁴⁰ Apostate Israelite cities are to be burned, along with all the plunder (Deut 13:17[16]; cf. Judg 20:48), but against outside enemies the command is to burn only the idols, not the cities (Deut 7:5, 25; 12:3; cf. also Exod 32:20, Deut 9:21). Only in Josh 6:24, 8:28, and 11:11 are non-Israelite cities burned in connection with חרם, and 11:13 even claims that Hazor was the only city burned. More often, cities are burned without explicit connection to חרם (e.g., Judg 18:27; 1 Sam 30:1–3[!]; 1 Kgs 9:16; Isa 1:7; Jer 32:29; 34:2, 22; 37:8–10).

⁴¹ Cf. Lev 27:28–29, Num 18:14//Ezek 44:29b. On the Priestly-influenced use of חרם, see Stern, *Biblical Ḥerem*, 125–35; Jacob Milgrom, *Leviticus 23–27: A New Translation with Introduction and Commentary*, AB 3B (New York: Doubleday, 2001), 2392–96. Norbert Lohfink goes so far as to deny that there is any war at all in P (*Theology of the Pentateuch: Themes of the Priestly Narrative and Deuteronomy*, trans. Linda M. Maloney [Minneapolis: Fortress, 1994], 195–210; similarly, Schmitt, *Der "Heilige Krieg,"* 149–50).

⁴² See Seebass, *Numeri*, 2:305–10; Stern, *Biblical Ḥerem*, 135–38.

⁴³ See n. 22 above; Seebass, *Numeri*, 3:291–92, 296–97.

⁴⁴ Contra Ashley, *Book of Numbers*, 591, 595; Seebass especially denies that this is an ideal "toragemäßen Jahwekrieg" (*Numeri*, 3:290; cf. 296, 304, 316; so also Schmitt, *Der "Heilige Krieg,"* 151, 157, both responding to Achenbach, *Die Vollendung der Tora*, 615).

⁴⁵ Levine, *Numbers*, 2:469–70. Niditch thinks this reflects a belief that virgin girls are in a

this directly reverses Num 31:7–12, which assumes that "all the males" (כל־זכר; 31:7) does not include the children (טף; 31:9).⁴⁶ The surprising thing about this reversal, however, is that 31:7–12 was explicitly carried out "as YHWH commanded Moses" (31:7), while Moses's own reinterpretation is nowhere attributed to divine command.⁴⁷ In fact, this command to kill all but the virgin girls is without precedent in the Pentateuch.

There is one חרם-war, however, that precisely parallels Moses's command. In Judg 21, as in Num 31, exactly twelve thousand men are sent to attack the Israelite town of Jabesh-Gilead (Judg 21:10; cf. Num 31:4–5). They are told to "devote to destruction [חרם] every male and every woman who has known by sleeping with a male" (Judg 21:11), including the children (טף; Judg 21:10). Meanwhile, the "young girls who had not known a man by sleeping with a male" are saved and given to the tribe of Benjamin for wives (Judg 21:12). These descriptions of the women and girls are virtually identical to those in Num 31:17–18.⁴⁸ Most commentators, therefore, find a direct literary link between these passages, though the direction in which it runs is debated.⁴⁹

"blank-state" and so capable of acceptance into the people of God, while males—even from birth—are "small men" and thus enemies ("War, Women, and Defilement," 51). This is an interesting possibility, though it lacks explicit confirmation in Numbers or outside it.

⁴⁶ Levine, *Numbers*, 2:470.

⁴⁷ This contrast is further heightened by the fact that Phinehas was sent to accompany (or lead?) the army in 31:6, yet he disappears entirely from 31:13–18, where Moses instead addresses the "officers" and "commanders." Given the contrasting roles of Moses and Phinehas in Num 25, might Phinehas's presence at the battle implicitly support the army's actions and therefore undermine Moses's?

⁴⁸ The expressions are inverted, however:
וכל־אשה ידעת איש למשכב זכר and
וכל הטף בנשים אשר לא־ידעו משכב זכר in Num 31:17–18, but
וכל־אשה ידעת משכב־זכר and
נערה בתולה אשר לא־ידעה איש למשכב זכר in Judg 21:11–12.

This way of describing virgins occurs elsewhere in the Hebrew Bible only in Judg 11:39, of Jephthah's daughter (והיא לא־ידעה איש), and in Gen 19:8, of Lot's daughters (שתי בנות אשר לא־ידעו איש). See Cynthia Edenburg, "The Story of the Outrage at Gibeah (Jdg. 19–21): Composition, Sources and Historical Context" (in Hebrew; PhD diss., Tel Aviv University, 2003), 305–6.

⁴⁹ Some argue that Judg 21 is older, and that Num 31:14–18 uses it to reinterpret Deut 20:10–18 (e.g., Achenbach, *Die Vollendung der Tora*, 615, 620; Seebass, *Numeri*, 3:296, 304, 317), while Edenburg suggests that originally Judg 21 did *not* recount the destruction of Jabesh-Gilead, and that 21:2–5, 10–11 + 12b are secondary and dependent on Num 31 ("Story of the Outrage," 96–97, 303–10; cf. also Levine, *Numbers*, 2:466; Robert G. Boling, *Judges: Introduction, Translation, and Commentary*, AB 6A [Garden City, NY: Doubleday, 1975], 291; Carolyn Pressler, *Joshua, Judges, and Ruth*, WeBC [Louisville: Westminster John Knox, 2002], 256; Walter Groß, *Richter*, HTKAT [Freiburg im Breisgau: Herder, 2009], 874). Alternatively, if the partial חרם was added to *both* Num 31 and Judg 21 secondarily, that could imply a closer link between the final forms of these texts than simple one-sided dependence.

Either way the comparison is not flattering to Moses. Like Num 25, the story recounted in Judg 19–21 centers on the danger of apostasy, but its tale of civil war and escalating violence also emphasizes the tragedy that can result from the indiscriminate application of חרם.⁵⁰ The whole account is highly ironic: the Israelites set out to avenge the rape of one woman, only to authorize the rapes of six hundred more.⁵¹ They regret the results of one slaughter, so they commit another to repair it.⁵² In fact, the Israelites destroy Jabesh-Gilead for no other reason than that it was the one town that refused to join their attack against Benjamin, yet they do this to save Benjamin from that very attack. Nowhere does YHWH command or condone these actions, and the account ends with the wry conclusion: "In those days … everyone did what was right in their own eyes" (Judg 21:25).⁵³

That this is the closest parallel to Moses's command in Num 31:13–18 hardly casts him in a comfortable light, as virtually all of the connections between these passages are confined to Moses's own words and the people's obedience in Num 31:3–6 and 31:13–18.⁵⁴ Like the people's actions in Judg 21, Moses's command is nowhere granted divine approval. On the contrary, it challenges the practice explicitly credited to divine command in Num 31:7–12. Like the destruction of Jabesh-Gilead, Moses's call for slaughter is implicitly subverted by its larger context.

---

⁵⁰ This is emphasized by Groß, who notes the Israelites' equally distraught reaction to their victory as to their initial defeats (cf. Judg 20:18, 23, 26–28; 21:2–3; *Richter*, 870–71).

⁵¹ Note that נערה ("young girl") and בתולה ("virgin") appear in Judges only in 21:12 and in the account of the rape in 19:3–9, 24 (Tammi J. Schneider, *Judges*, Berit Olam [Collegeville, MN: Liturgical Press, 2000], 281; cf. xviii–xix, 280–83). This is even clearer in 21:15–24, in which the elders tell the Benjaminites to "lie in wait" (ארב) and "seize" (חטף) one maiden each from a festival at Shiloh (21:20–21). Outside of war, ארב and חטף are always associated with violence against the innocent (e.g., Judg 16:2, Ps 10:9, Prov 1:11, Mic 7:2), as is גזל in Judg 21:23 (cf. Judg 9:25, Gen 31:31, Lev 5:21[6:2], Prov 22:22, Isa 61:8; see Pressler, *Joshua, Judges, and Ruth*, 256–57; Daniel I. Block, *Judges, Ruth*, NAC 6 [Nashville: Broadman & Holman, 1999], 581–83).

⁵² Cf. Judg 20:46–21:3 with 21:10–12; Phyllis Trible, *Texts of Terror: Literary-Feminist Readings of Biblical Narratives*, OBT 13 (Philadelphia: Fortress, 1984), 82–84; Susan Niditch, *Judges: A Commentary*, OTL (Louisville: Westminster John Knox, 2008), 211; Block, *Judges, Ruth*, 569, 583–86; Pressler, *Joshua, Judges, and Ruth*, 256; Groß, *Richter*, 877.

⁵³ See Block, *Judges, Ruth*, 583; Schneider, *Judges*, 284. Though Boling thinks Judg 21:25 has "a positive thrust after the ingenious solution of problems in the final scenes" (*Judges*, 293), this is belied by the subversive nature of the foregoing account and by the use of the same expression in Judg 17:6, where it follows the making of an idol, and in Deut 12:8, where it describes how Israel is *not* to behave upon entering the land.

⁵⁴ There are two exceptions: כל־זכר (Judg 21:11) appears in Num 31:7 and 31:17, but this is a common Priestly expression and merely contrasts the latter two verses. On the other hand, פקד with מן with the meaning "missing from" in Judg 21:3 and Num 31:49 is relatively rare (Edenburg, "Story of the Outrage," 308–9). This could support the suggestion that Num 31:13–18 and 31:48–54 were added together (see below). Note that Judg 21:3 and Num 31:49 directly contrast.

V. THE PURIFICATION AND DISTRIBUTION OF THE PLUNDER IN NUMBERS 31:19–47

There is no account of the execution of Moses's command. Instead, he immediately turns in 31:19-20 to the need for purification, only to be interrupted by Eleazar in 31:21–24. As David P. Wright notes, both Moses's and Eleazar's purification regulations draw on those found in Num 19:11–22, but Eleazar's especially represent a significant innovation, now requiring that captured plunder be passed through fire or water in addition to the sprinkling stipulated in 19:17–19.[55] Wright concludes that the attribution of this regulation to Eleazar instead of Moses is intended to minimize any suspicion of human invention,[56] but the juxtaposition with Moses's own innovation in 31:13–18 suggests a further motive. That Moses's command is not attributed to YHWH but Eleazar's *is* described as that "which YHWH commanded Moses" (31:21b) seems to reflect the more prominent role of the priests seen in Num 25 and 27, striking a balance between respect for Mosaic tradition and the priesthood's authority to clarify biblical law.[57] That increased authority is also reflected in Eleazar's more prominent role in the rest of 31:25–54. Whereas Moses alone spoke and acted in 31:14–18 (despite Eleazar's presence in 31:13), Moses and Eleazar are *together* addressed by YHWH in 31:26, *together* fulfill YHWH's command in 31:31, 41, and *together* accept the officers' gift in 31:51, 54.

Equally significant, this second sequence of command and fulfillment may even imply that Moses's demand in 31:17–18 had not been carried out, as YHWH and the narrator both repeatedly describe the captives as אדם (31:26, 28, 30, 35[!], 40, 46, 47).[58] The term אדם appeared already in 31:11 to refer to all the captives together—male and female—and as far as I am aware it is nowhere else used of a group of women alone, as would be required if Moses had been obeyed. That

---

[55] Wright, "Purification from Corpse-Contamination," 216–23. The words זאת חקת התורה ("this is the statue of the law") in 31:21 are found elsewhere only as the introduction to Num 19:2, while the requirement to purify oneself on the third and seventh days in 31:19, 24 derives from 19:11–12. The purification by fire or water in 31:23 is unique.

[56] Wright, "Purification from Corpse-Contamination," 223; similarly, Milgrom, *Numbers*, 260.

[57] A similar explanation was suggested by Sifre Num. 157.12, which first recounts Rabbi Eleazar ben Azariah's view that Moses "made a mistake" in his anger, which Eleazar corrected, then observes that others think Moses himself gave Eleazar authority to speak on such (ritual) matters, in anticipation of his death (also noted by Milgrom, *Numbers*, 260).

[58] The command concerning the distribution of the plunder is yet another case of legal innovation, as its closest parallel is the "fixed rule" concerning the division of the spoils attributed to David in 1 Sam 30:23–25, apparently modified in accordance with the tithe formulas in Num 18:21–29 (see Levine, *Numbers*, 2:459–60, 470–71).

tension no doubt motivated the gloss in 31:35b, which attempts to restrict אדם to the virgin girls, but this is almost certainly secondary:

ונפש אדם מן־הנשים אשר 35	35 And the people <u>from the women</u>
לא־ידעו משכב זכר כל־נפש	<u>who had not known by sleeping with a</u>
שנים ושלשים אלף	<u>male,</u> all the people, 32,000.

אשר לא־ידעו משכב זכר is taken verbatim from 31:18b, but there it was introduced much more naturally with הטף בנשים ("the children among the women"), while נפש אדם מן־הנשים ("the people from the women") is much more awkward. The addition also badly overbalances the verse, and the closing כל־נפש ("all the people") seems to be a repetitive resumption.[59] If the gloss is removed the remaining text (ונפש אדם שנים ושלשים אלף; 31:35*) parallels 31:32c–34 and corresponds exactly to the halves reported in 31:40 and 46:[60]

31:32a-b ויהי המלקוח יתר הבז אשר בזזו עם הצבא	31:32a-b And the booty, other than the plunder that the army plundered, was
32c צאן שש־מאות אלף ושבעים אלף וחמשת־אלפים	32c 675,000 sheep
33 ובקר שנים ושבעים אלף	33 and 72,000 cattle
34 וחמרים אחד וששים אלף	34 and 61,000 donkeys
35* ונפש אדם שנים ושלשים אלף	35* and 32,000 people
...	...
40a ונפש אדם ששה עשר אלף	40a and 16,000 people
...	...
46 ונפש אדם ששה עשר אלף	46 and 16,000 people

If Num 31:35b is a later gloss, then the original form of 31:25–47 showed no awareness that the women and boys had been killed. This could support the common conclusion that 31:13–18 is itself secondary,[61] but, more importantly, it confirms that Moses's command is an extension beyond YHWH's requirements, at least as those were initially conceived. After all, the gloss modifies only Moses's response in 31:35, while the references to the captives as אדם in YHWH's command remain

---

[59] Surprisingly, this gloss goes unmentioned in the commentaries (though see Schmidt, *Das vierte Buch Mose*, 189), perhaps because the MT is followed by the ancient versions here.

[60] The expression appears also in 1 Chr 5:21, which reports the plunder from another YHWH war, ending with "and 100,000 people" (ונפש אדם מאה אלף).

[61] See Holzinger, *Numeri*, 148; Milgrom, *Numbers*, 492; Staubli, *Die Bücher Levitikus, Numeri*, 331. This would also explain the divergent backgrounds of Num 31:7–12 and 31:13–18 and might be further supported by the reference to this incident in Josh 13:21–22, which does not mention killing women and children (the reference to "the rest of the slain" in Josh 13:22 [אל־חלליהם] parallels Num 31:8 [על־חלליהם], not 31:14–18; see Achenbach, *Die Vollendung der Tora*, 617–18 n. 16). That the Midianites were not in fact executed to the last woman and boy is evident also from Judg 6–8, which Num 31:48–54 may have in view (see esp. Judg 8:24–28; Levine, *Numbers*, 2:471; Seebass, *Numeri*, 3:297; Achenbach, *Die Vollendung der Tora*, 617, 620). If Num 31:13–18 (or 31:14–18) is secondary, 31:48–54 was probably added at the same time, while 31:19–20 is either later, as it lacks an introduction of the speaker, or perhaps originally followed 31:13 (+ 15a?).

untouched (31:26, 28, 30). Even with the gloss, then, 31:13–18 remains an unexpected modification of the divine word.[62]

VI. THE GIFT OF THE OFFICERS AND THE VINDICATION OF ISRAEL

Grossman argues that Num 31:48–54 provides yet another place where Moses takes a passive role, as other leaders of Israel are praised for their initiative. In this case the officers and commanders bring a substantial offering of gold to the sanctuary, over and above the contribution already made by divine command.[63] What Grossman overlooks, however, is that this account is directly linked to 31:13–18 by the presence of "the officers who were over the thousands of the army, the commanders of the thousands and the commanders of the hundreds" (31:48; cf. vv. 52, 54). These figures appear elsewhere in Numbers only in 31:14, where they were the objects of Moses's anger, and their repeated full introduction in 31:48 marks a strong connection between these two sections.[64] Further, each section centers on leaders of Israel giving up additional plunder, and neither attributes this to divine command.[65]

The two sections are not simply parallel, however, as their portrayals of Moses and the officers are reversed. In the first, Moses addresses the officers while they remained silent (ויאמר אליהם משה; 31:15); in the second, the officers address Moses while he remains silent (ויאמרו אל־משה; 31:49). In the first, Moses's command was not explicitly obeyed; in the second, "Moses and Eleazar the priest took the gold from the commanders of the thousands and of the hundreds, and brought it into the tent of meeting as a memorial for the Israelites before YHWH" (31:54; cf. v. 51). Therefore, while neither Moses's command nor the officers' gift fulfills a divine command, the latter is explicitly accepted, whereas the former was not.

---

[62] This also ameliorates Seebass's caution regarding such a reading (see *Numeri*, 3:318). The more difficult question is whether this harmonizing gloss was added by the same person who composed 31:13–18 (or 31:14–18), or only by a later scribe—and thus, whether the gloss can be taken as evidence of the original redactor's stance toward Moses's demand. But if 31:32b and 31:53 are also secondary (see Bruno Baentsch, *Exodus-Leviticus-Numeri*, HKAT 2 [Göttingen: Vandenhoeck & Ruprecht, 1903], 657, 659; Schmidt, *Das vierte Buch Mose*, 189–90), they would seem to postdate both 31:13–18 and 31:48–54*, which could imply that 31:35b does as well.

[63] Grossman, "Divine Command," 74–76.

[64] The term פקדים ("officers") appears mostly in census reports, where it means "the registered" (Exod 30:13–14, 38:25–26, throughout Num 1–4, 7:2, 2 Kgs 12:12[11; *ketiv*]; cf. 12:5–6[4–5]). "The commanders of the thousands and of the hundreds" is most common in Chronicles (1 Chr 13:1; 15:25; 26:26; 27:1; 28:1; 29:6; 2 Chr 17:14; 23:1, 9, 14, 20; 25:5; but cf. Exod 18:21, 25; Deut 1:15; 1 Sam 8:12; 22:7; 2 Sam 18:1; 2 Kgs 11:19).

[65] Milgrom notes that the presence of the officers and the absence of the "command-execution structure" evident in the rest of the passage connect 31:14–18 with 31:48–54, but the only significance he finds in this is "a sign they were inserted by the same editor" (*Numbers*, 492).

That being the case, it should not be overlooked that these two sections also parallel the two senses of נקמה suggested above: Moses's command in 31:3 focused on the enemy *against* whom war was mustered and *on* whom retribution was demanded, and the same is true of his command in 31:13–18. Moses says nothing of the Israelites' victory, focusing instead on the remaining enemies to be destroyed. By contrast, YHWH's command in 31:1–2 can be read as a call for the vindication or redress of the Israelites *from* the Midianites, and the officers' gift similarly is directed toward the preservation and remembrance of their own people: "Your servants have counted [נשאו את־ראש] the warriors under our command, and not one of us is missing. So we have brought as YHWH's offering the gold articles each of us found … to make atonement for our lives [לכפר על־נפשתינו] before YHWH" (31:49–50).

This reflects the census regulations in Exod 30:11–16, which require that any census (כי תשא את־ראש; Exod 30:12), must result in a half-shekel tax "to make atonement for your lives" (לכפר על־נפשתיכם; 30:15, 16), lest a plague come upon Israel (30:12).[66] In addition to these lexical links, Moses's and Eleazar's acceptance of the gift and its deposit in the tent of meeting (אהל מועד) as a memorial (זכרון) for the Israelites before YHWH (לבני־ישראל לפני יהוה; Num 31:54) all draw language from Exod 30:16.[67]

If Exod 30:11–16 stands behind Num 31:48–54, however, the latter is no more a direct application of that text than Moses's command was a direct application of Deut 20.[68] Exodus 30:11–16 is a divine command concerning a census of all Israel, demanding half a shekel of silver per man, no more and no less (Exod 30:15), as Exod 38:25–28 confirms. By contrast, the officers' count involves only their own twelve thousand men, while their gift of 16,750 shekels of gold far exceeds the required sum.[69] Moreover, the distribution of the spoils had already included precisely calculated "contributions for YHWH" (תרומת יהוה; Num 31:29, 41), so the

---

[66] This link is widely accepted (see Levine, *Numbers*, 2:462–63; Schmidt, *Das vierte Buch Mose*, 190–91; Seebass, *Numeri*, 3:312–14). Michael Fishbane doubts that Exod 30 stands behind Num 31 ("Census and Intercession in a Priestly Text (Exodus 30:11–16) and Its Midrashic Transformation," in *Pomegranates and Golden Bells: Studies in Biblical, Jewish, and Near Eastern Ritual, Law, and Literature in Honor of Jacob Milgrom*, ed. David P. Wright et al. [Winona Lake, IN: Eisenbrauns, 1995], 105–6; similarly, Ashley, *Book of Numbers*, 599–600; cf. Seebass, *Numeri*, 3:314), but while the differences he notes are important (see below), the direct literary parallels are too detailed to be dismissed.

[67] There are other lexical connections as well: הפקדים (Num 31:48, Exod 30:13–14), תרומה (Num 31:52; Exod 30:13, 14, 15), שקל (Num 31:52; Exod 30:13 [4x], 15), and the expression לקח מאת (Num 31:51, 54; Exod 30:16). It is also notable that the sanctuary is אהל מועד in Num 31:54 and Exod 30:16, but משכן in Num 31:30, 47.

[68] Fishbane is correct about this ("Census and Intercession," 106), but that is no reason to conclude that Exod 30:11–16 is not in view, as Fishbane himself discusses numerous comparable reapplications of older traditions (pp. 107–11; see also idem, *Biblical Interpretation in Ancient Israel*, rev. ed. [Oxford: Oxford University Press, 1986], esp. 281–440).

[69] See Milgrom, *Numbers*, 265; Seebass, *Numeri*, 3:312.

use of the same term in all three sections marks a clear pattern of command (31:29), fulfillment (31:41), and voluntary extension (31:52).[70] This is, therefore, a further act of devotion over and above that commanded in 31:25–30 and accomplished in 31:31–47, which confirms the pattern traced above in 31:1–18. But whereas Moses's unexpected demand found its closest parallel in the highly subversive account of Judg 21, the officers' additional gift parallels not only Exod 30:11–16 but also the voluntary offerings of "the registered" (הפקדים) honored in Num 7:2,[71] as well as those of other "commanders of the thousands and of the hundreds" in 1 Chr 26:26 and 29:6, as Levine observes.[72]

Beyond all this, however, the connection between the officers' gift and Exod 30 suggests a deeper significance to their action, which brings the passage full circle. For the explicit purpose of the כפר in Exod 30:12 is to avert a plague (נֶגֶף), and in Num 31 a plague (מגפה) was precisely what the war was meant to resolve, as Moses himself recognized in Num 31:16. The connection is explicit also in Num 25, where Phinehas's earlier plague-averting action was specifically claimed to secure atonement (כפר) for Israel (Num 25:7–13; cf. 25:18).[73] Therefore, if Num 31 is framed as נקמה for the apostasy and plague at Baal-Peor, Moses's and the officers' actions embody two very different responses to that incident, one linked to the complete destruction of the enemy, the other to the atonement and remembrance of Israel. Where Moses angrily demands vengeance *on* Midian for its role at Baal-Peor, the officers' gift vindicates Israel *from* Midian by averting the plague and reaffirming their commitment to YHWH's sanctuary.

VII. Conclusions

It is generally assumed that Moses's command to kill the Midianite women and boys fulfills YHWH's call for vengeance in Num 31:1–2, but both the structure of the chapter and its reinterpretations of earlier texts imply that Moses is introducing a novel extension beyond YHWH's demand. The preservation of the captives by the army in 31:7–12 not only is introduced by an explicit claim that the battle was conducted "as YHWH commanded Moses" (31:7), but it also closely corresponds to the regulations in Deut 20:13–14. Moses's reinterpretation of Deut 20 in 31:13–18 is accorded no such explicit divine sanction, while the repeated references

---

[70] See Grossman, "Divine Command and Human Initiative," 75.

[71] The term הפקדים is the same form used to mean "officers" in Num 31:14 and 48.

[72] Levine argues that this reflects Persian-period interest in supporting the sanctuary (*Numbers*, 2:470–72; followed by Seebass, *Numeri*, 3:314; see also Budd, *Numbers*, 334; Kislev, "Investiture of Joshua," 440–43). All subsequent allusions to Exod 30:11–16 are similarly tied to the sanctuary (cf. Exod 38:25–28, 2 Kgs 12:5–6[4–5], 2 Chr 24:6, Neh 10:33–40[32–39]; Fishbane, "Census and Intercession," 103–11; John I. Durham, *Exodus*, WBC 3 [Waco, TX: Word, 1987], 403; Christoph Dohmen, *Exodus 19–40*, HThKAT [Freiburg im Breisgau: Herder, 2004], 276).

[73] All three use *piel* forms of כפר with על (Exod 30:15, 16; Num 25:13; 31:50).

to the captives as אדם in 31:25–47 may even imply that Moses was not obeyed. The late gloss in 31:35b attempts to resolve this tension, but even then it modifies only Moses's response, not YHWH's command itself.

At the same time, this reflects a wider pattern of divine command, fulfillment, and unexpected extension seen also in the officers' contribution to the sanctuary in 31:48–54. Their reapplication of Exod 30:11–16 is no less innovative than Moses's demand, yet the two actions seem to be contrasted. While Moses's reinterpretation is most closely paralleled by the highly subversive account of the destruction of Jabesh-Gilead in Judg 21, the officers' gift most closely parallels the voluntary offerings of other leaders of Israel praised in Num 7 and 1 Chr 26 and 29. Moreover, while Moses's demand is not explicitly obeyed, the officers' gift is explicitly accepted by Moses *and Eleazar*. This reflects the more prominent role attributed to the priesthood throughout Num 25–31, seen also in Phinehas's role in Num 25:7–13 and 31:6, and in Joshua's subordination to Eleazar in 27:19–22, as well as in Eleazar's introduction of novel purification regulations in 31:21–24 and his position alongside Moses throughout 31:25–54.

Thus, the chapter as a whole presents a range of approaches to the interpretation of biblical law. At points it simply reformulates the law itself, as in Eleazar's extension of Num 19 in 31:21–24, but at other points Moses, the army, and the officers *reapply* particular laws in subtle and contrasting ways. Rather than directly challenging Mosaic authority, Num 31 follows chs. 25 and 27 in juxtaposing Moses's interpretations with those of other leaders of Israel. In so doing, the text does not merely reapply specific laws; it creates space for further reinterpretations by subsequent leaders, especially the high priest.

These contrasting reinterpretations may have resulted from secondary redaction, but they are not mere accidental relics. They form a deliberate pattern of command, fulfillment, and extension repeated in both halves of the chapter, and reflect back on the divergent uses of נקמה by YHWH and Moses at its outset. Moses emphasized vengeance or retribution on the enemy in 31:3, and his call for slaughter continues that interpretation. But YHWH emphasized the vindication or redress of Israel itself in 31:2, and the overwhelming emphasis on the proper handling of the plunder in the rest of the chapter maintains that focus. The officers' gift completes the theme by reaffirming Israel's loyalty to YHWH and the sanctuary, while their wish for atonement also brings the passage full circle, responding to the threat of plague used to justify the war in the first place.

The text therefore creates a kind of diptych, setting these two expressions of excessive zeal for YHWH's נקמה in parallel and contrast. Perhaps, one might argue, both Moses's command and the officers' gift are meant to reveal complementary reactions to Yhwh's נקמה, much as Isa 34–35 paired the punitive and redemptive connotations of נקם, but the larger shape of the chapter implies a sharper contrast. For in the end Moses's call for slaughter remains unfulfilled, while the officers' gift secures a permanent "memorial for the Israelites before Yhwh."

Merab, Saul's Mute and Muffled Daughter

ORLY KEREN
orlyke@kaye.ac.il
RAMBAM 68/12, Beer Sheva 8424336, Israel

HAGIT TARAGAN
targan@bgu.ac.il
Hamuchtar 7/13, Beer Sheva 8430511, Israel

Merab, Saul's older daughter, is first mentioned in the genealogy of the royal family in 1 Sam 14:49. Merab's name returns only twice after that, in the short episode of her proposed betrothal to David in 1 Sam 18:17–19. Merab's fleeting appearance here may lead us to wonder about her life and character. At first she is presented as a princess and a potential bride for David; in the end, she is the wife of Adriel the Meholathite. Merab, present yet absent, is not the only character in this scene. Also involved are the two men who in practice govern her destiny: Saul and David. Hovering above the voices of these two men as they haggle over her fate is Merab's silence, which is not broken even when she is given to Adriel the Meholathite. Merab is just one more item in the list of conditions that Saul sets for David in their dialogue—but meant, in fact, to be a death trap for her intended husband. Nowhere in this proposal of marriage is there any reference to her feelings or emotions. Both Merab and Adriel are enveloped in silence and are ostensibly not involved in the events linked to the house of Saul. The article examines the figure of Merab, daughter of Saul and wife of Adriel the Meholathite. Underlying the discussion are the questions about her place in the story and the very need for her to appear in it.

Merab is mentioned by name only three times in the Bible: the first time in the summary of Saul's career (1 Sam 14:49), and twice more in the brief episode of 1 Sam 18:17–19.[1] Merab's cameo appearance in this episode leaves us wondering

---

Because it was not possible to adhere consistently to any standard English translation of the Bible, the renderings here are often taken from or based on the NJPS and occasionally the RSV, but are, ultimately, our own.

[1] For the derivation of the name Merab and its meanings, see BDB, 5619; *HALOT*, 5625. The MT always employs the spelling מרב. The LXX has μεροβ, as does Josephus; the Vulgate has "Merob." In 4QSam^a (4Q51), the name is given as מרוב. See also Scott C. Layton, "The Hebrew Personal Name Merab: Its Etymology and Meaning," *JSS* 38 (1993): 193–207.

about the events related to her life and character, given that she is introduced as the king's daughter and the bride intended for David the warrior, and only two verses later winds up married to Adriel the Meholathite.[2]

The first half of v. 17 deals with Merab, but she is not alone. The men who in practice control and will continue to control her destiny are also present: "Then **Saul** said to **David**, … I [**Saul**] will give her to you [**David**] for a wife." For the balance of this verse and the next verse, Merab is only one item in the conditions that Saul sets for David in their dialogue, in which Merab is intended to be simultaneously a bride and a death trap for her groom.

At the time of the marriage offer (1 Sam 18:17–18), Merab seems to be both present and absent. Hovering above the voices of Saul and David, who are negotiating over her fate, is her silence—a silence that is not broken even when she is "given to Adriel the Meholathite for a wife" (v. 19). There is no reference to her feelings or emotions;[3] Merab, like her husband, Adriel the Meholathite, is wrapped in silence, apparently excluded from the adventures of the house of Saul.

Despite the brevity of the episode, the narrator managed to cram in all the tension latent in the description of Saul's plan to kill David (v. 17b). Readers wonder: will the plot succeed? Will his marriage to Merab be David's undoing?

This article looks at Merab, daughter of Saul and wife of Adriel the Meholathite. The discussion rests on several questions: What is Merab's place in the text and why is her inclusion there essential? In addition to these overt references, can we find allusions to Merab's presence in the shadows in the background of the chronicles of the house of Saul?

I. First Samuel 18:17–19: Narrative Structure

The story of Merab is limited to 1 Sam 18:17–19. This extremely short episode, whose topic is Saul's attempt to marry off Merab to David, is complete and self-contained;[4] Merab appears only here and has no presence in the framing episode (18:1–5, 6–9, 10–13, 14–16, 20–30). The episode begins with Saul's plans for his older daughter, Merab, and ends with what he actually does with her. It fits perfectly into the series of incidents (18:1–30) that, on the one hand, describe Saul's hostility toward David and his plans to kill him, starting with his first attempt to strike down

---

[2] On "king's daughter," see Shoshana Arbeli-Raveh, *The King's Daughter and Political Marriage in Antiquity* (in Hebrew; Tel Aviv: Archeological Center, 2000), 173.

[3] Nor is there any expression of Merab's feelings when her younger sister Michal weds David (1 Sam 18:20–27).

[4] The Merab episode (18:17–19) is omitted in Codex Vaticanus of the LXX and in Josephus's *Antiquities*. See Josephus, *Jewish Antiquities, Books VII–VIII*, trans. Ralph Marcus, LCL (1934; repr., Cambridge: Harvard University Press, 1950), 263. That the entire episode is missing from these two sources is a strong argument in favor of its originality.

David directly and continuing with his subsequent attempt to use Michal to eliminate him (18:20–21; 19:11, 17). On the other hand, the episodes that precede (18:1, 6–7, 12, 16) and follow (18:20, 28) describe all those who love David: Jonathan (v. 1), the women of all the towns of Israel (vv. 6–7), the Lord (v. 14), all Israel and Judah (v. 16), and Michal (v. 20). Our episode (vv. 17–19), in contrast to all the others, is devoid of emotions, with neither hatred nor love.

The frame in which the episode is set is bracketed by the phrase "give[n] as a wife," found in both the first and third verses (vv. 17, 19). These verses also indicate the great change in Merab's destiny, from the pinnacle of being David's potential bride to the reality of marriage to Adriel the Meholathite—this time without negotiations or terms set for the match.

The Structure of the Episode

Verses 17–19 alternate the statements and names of David and Saul with remarks by the narrator:

> v. 17. **Saul:** Then **Saul** said to **David**, "Here is my daughter, the older one, Merab; I will give her to you for a wife; only be valiant for me and fight the Lord's battles."
>
> **Narrator:** For Saul thought, "Let not my hand be upon him, but let the hand of the Philistines be upon him."
>
> v. 18. **David:** And **David** said to **Saul**, "Who am I, and who are my kinsfolk, my father's family in Israel, that I should be son-in-law to the king?"
>
> v. 19. **Narrator:** But at the time when Merab, **Saul's** daughter, should have been given to **David**, she was given to Adriel the Meholathite for a wife."

The dialogue about Merab seems to have been carefully designed by the narrator, who begins with Saul addressing David (v. 17) and continues chiastically with David addressing Saul (v. 18):

<u>Saul</u>—David—**Narrator**

David—<u>Saul</u>

Narrator—<u>Saul</u>—David

The episode begins with a marriage proposal—Saul's plan to marry Merab to David: "**Then Saul said to David, 'Here is my daughter, the older one, Merab; I will give her to you for a wife'**" (v. 17) and concludes with Merab's marriage to Adriel the Meholathite: "**She was given to Adriel the Meholathite for a wife**" (v. 19). The information provided at the end of the episode refers to Merab in the third person and reinforces readers' sense that her marriage to Adriel was arranged without her.

In the first part of v. 17, Saul presents Merab, even before he names her, as "my daughter, the older one,"[5] a phrase that ostensibly expresses both gentleness and pride.[6] The first person possessive "my daughter," accompanied by the adjective "older," accords her the appropriate status as a princess—both the elder[7] and the chosen one.

Later in the verse, the accusative pronoun "her" also refers to Merab and emphasizes her status as promised to David. Here Merab is identified not only by her name but also by three additional distinguishing terms: "my daughter," "the older one," and "her."[8] This sequence may reflect Saul's feelings when he offers his daughter in marriage to David, his mortal enemy, as if he cannot let go and give her away. The gradual stages here—"my daughter," "the older one," and "her"—may be meant to help Saul get used to the idea, as noted above. It is also possible that this order is meant to help readers understand Saul's dilemma: Will he really give his older daughter in marriage to David, whom he wants to see dead? Here we have a gradual movement, proceeding from the most intimate term, "my daughter," to the less intimate "her."[9]

At the end of this episode (v. 19), the narrator refers to Merab as "Saul's daughter,"[10] to remind readers of her lineage. But he also finds it necessary to insist that there has been a change in her status and family affiliation: Merab, formerly known as the daughter of the king, is now identified by reference to her husband,[11] Adriel the Meholathite.

---

[5] The adjective "older" attached to Merab in this verse would have been appropriate in 1 Sam 14:49, in contrast to Michal, the "younger." For more on גדול/ה as a definite adjective, with a range that includes the comparative and the superlative, see *IBHS*, 269. See also Frederick E. Greenspahn, *When Brothers Dwell Together: The Preeminence of Younger Siblings in the Hebrew Bible* (New York: Oxford University Press, 1994), 64; and Amnon Shapira, "Jacob and Esau: A Multivocal Reading," in *Studies in Bible and Exegesis 4*, ed. R. Kasher, M. Tzipor, and Y. Zefati (in Hebrew; Ramat Gan: Bar-Ilan University Press, 1997), 260.

[6] "Ostensibly," because we soon discover that Saul plans for Merab to be widowed, so that his apparent gentleness toward Merab is actually a show.

[7] The adjective בכירה occurs in three biblical stories: four times in the episode of Lot and his daughters (Gen 19:31, 33, 34, 37); in the Jacob saga—Laban said, "It is not so done in our country, to give the younger before the *firstborn*" (Gen 29:26); and in 1 Sam 14:49.

[8] The biblical narrator frequently changes the pronoun used with regard to a character as a sign of a changed perspective toward him/her. See Meir Sternberg, "The Delicate Balance in the Story of the Rape of Dinah" (in Hebrew), *Hasifrut* 4.2 (1973): 200. Here, the first person of "my daughter" is replaced by "to you," suggesting that what is now mine will become yours.

[9] See Yaira Amit, "Gradualness as a Rhetorical Device in Biblical Literature," in *Homage to Shmuel: Studies in the World of the Bible*, ed. Z. Talshir, S. Yonah, and D. Sivan (Beer Sheva: Ben-Gurion University Press; Jerusalem: Bialik Institute, 2001), 24–25, 27. Meir Weiss calls this literary device "internal monologue" and views it as the author's manipulation and intervention ("The Narrative Art in the Bible" [in Hebrew], *Molad* 20 [1972]: 403–4).

[10] Jan P. Fokkelman asserts that every occurrence of the term "Saul's daughter" identifies both Merab and Michal (*Narrative Art and Poetry in the Books of Samuel: A Full Interpretation Based on Stylistic and Structural Analyses*, vol. 2, *The Crossing Fates* (Assen: Van Gorcum, 1986), 243.

[11] On betrothal scenes in the Bible, see Esther Fuchs, *Sexual Politics in the Biblical Narrative*:

Merab's transition from one family and class status to another is also emphasized by the repeated use of the root נתן,[12] first as nominal absolute infinitive and then as a passive verb that encompasses her name and family: "But at the time when Merab, Saul's daughter, **should have been given** [lit., at the time of the giving of Merab] to David, she **was *given*** to Adriel the Meholathite for a wife."

The linguistic variation emphasizes that Merab is being pushed outside the family circle, and, in practice, outside the palace:

| Here | is my daughter, the older one, Merab; | her | I will give to you | for a wife. |
| But *at the time of the giving* | of Merab, Saul's daughter, to David, | she | was given to Adriel the Meholathite | for a wife. |

Saul's speech (v. 17) can be divided into three parts. The first, the marriage proposal, is short and to the point. The other two add supplementary details, engage in double-speak, and expose Saul's violent intentions toward David.

The narrator quotes Saul's proposal to David directly, beginning with the deictic "here." The content of his proposal shows that, on the one hand, Saul relies on David and offers him the opportunity to be a valiant warrior, fight the LORD's wars, and become the king's son-in-law. On the other hand, he seeks his death. Saul, addressing David directly for the first time, leaves nothing vague about his intentions. He links the two elements—a wife and death—with the goal of "rewarding" David with both of them.[13] There is an implicit condition in Saul's words, although the standard indicators of a conditional sentence are missing. The first clause, as noted, is direct and to the point, but the second clause has two parts, with the second—"and fight the LORD's battles"—clarifying and elucidating the first part—"only be valiant for me."[14] Despite the clarification, David's role in the deal is vague; it is impossible to know if and when he will fulfill his mission and be rewarded by marriage to Merab.[15] Saul knows very well that the condition he sets for David cannot be realized; this demonstrates that Saul does not really intend to fulfill his promise and give his daughter Merab to David.

Reading the Hebrew Bible as a Woman, JSOTSup 310 (Sheffield: Sheffield Academic, 2000), 112; and Victor P. Hamilton, "Marriage," *ABD* 4:559–68.

[12] According to Fuchs (*Sexual Politics in the Biblical Narrative*, 112), the bride was viewed as movable property, so the verbs generally attached to her are לקח ("take") for the groom and נתן ("give") for the father.

[13] According to Fokkelman (*Crossing Fates*, 235–45), Saul has the ability to bridge the gap between marriage and violence, as reflected by the strange parallel in his words here: "I will **give her to you for a wife** ≠ only be valiant for me and **fight the LORD's battles**" (18:17).

[14] For use of אך as a restrictive adverb, see *IBHS*, 670.

[15] On Saul's offer of Merab to David, see David J. A. Clines, "Michal Observed: An Introduction to Reading Her Story," in *Telling Queen Michal's Story: An Experiment in Comparative Interpretation*, ed. David J. A. Clines and Tamara C. Eskenazi, JSOTSup 119 (Sheffield: JSOT Press, 1991), 28, 31.

The trio of Saul–David–Merab is expanded by the addition of the deity—"and fight the Lord's battles"—an addition that supports the notion that Saul's proposal to marry his daughter to David is genuine, a way of anchoring the contract and validating the agreement between them. Saul is being cynical when he inserts "the Lord" into the equation. He already knows that God is with David and is well aware that David is a valiant warrior. In his despair, he tries to send David to fight the Lord's battles as part of his scheme: "Let not my hand be upon him, but let the hand of the Philistines be upon him" (18:17).

In contrast to what might be seen as an ideal situation and a clear advantage for Saul should he marry his daughter to David, the picture that emerges from his thoughts actually points in the opposite direction, to hypocrisy.[16] Saul *says* that he wants to marry his daughter to David, but he also wants to kill him.[17] This is true even though the idea of David's death is latent in Saul's proposal, given that a king who sends another into battle has in practice already sentenced him to death.[18] So it is clear that there is a contradiction between Saul's proposal, "be valiant for me," and the scheme he has in mind: "Let not my hand be upon him."[19] The festive atmosphere of the start of this episode is dissipated at once: the narrator shares Saul's thoughts[20] and then vanishes after David's refusal, which relates not to Merab but only to himself (v. 18).[21]

Saul offers David the opportunity to marry Merab and become the king's son-in-law. David does not reply to Saul's proposal that he be a valiant warrior and fight the Lord's battles, but he does decline Saul's offer of Merab (v. 18).[22] He ascribes

---

[16] According to Frank Polak, this is a technique of presenting unspoken thoughts (*Biblical Narrative: Aspects of Art and Design* [in Hebrew; Jerusalem: Bialik Institute, 1994], 15). Antony F. Campbell sees a connection between the parts of the proposal—first the bait (v. 17a) and then the trap (v. 17b) (*1 Samuel*, FOTL 7 [Grand Rapids: Eerdmans, 2003], 196). See Moshe Garsiel, "The Relationship between David and Michal, Daughter of King Saul" (in Hebrew), in *Studies in Bible and Exegesis 10*, ed. M. Garsiel, R. Kasher, A. Frisch, and D. Elgavish (Ramat Gan: Bar-Ilan University Press, 2011), 119.

[17] See Uriel Simon, *Reading Prophetic Narratives*, trans. Lenn J. Schramm (Bloomington: Indiana University Press, 1997), 93–129, on the episode of David, Bathsheba, and Uriah (2 Sam 11–12). See also Walter Brueggemann, "Narrative Coherence and Theological Intentionality in 1 Samuel 18," *CBQ* 55 (1993): 233–34.

[18] Walter Brueggemann, *Power, Providence, and Personality: Biblical Insight into Life and Ministry* (Louisville: Westminster John Knox, 1990), 30.

[19] Fokkelman, *Crossing Fates*, 228.

[20] See Shimon Bar-Efrat, *Narrative Art in the Bible*, BLS 17 (Sheffield: Almond Press, 1989), 63; and Garsiel, "David and Michal," 118. The narrator shares Saul's thoughts with readers on three occasions (18:17b, 21a, 25b). See Fokkelman, *Crossing Fates*, 228.

[21] See A. Graeme Auld, *I & II Samuel: A Commentary*, OTL (Louisville: Westminster John Knox, 2011), 219.

[22] See Joseph Kara's explanation of 18:19: *Commentaries of Rabbi Joseph Kara on the Former Prophets*, ed. Shimon Eppenstein (Jerusalem: Makor, 1973); and Shmuel Greenberg, *The Plain Meaning of the Text, Exegetical and Linguistic Studies* (in Hebrew; Tel Aviv: Tevunah, 1945), 30.

his refusal to his family's low status as compared to the royal family[23] and does so by means of self-deprecation.[24] The manner of David's refusal seems to define him as a humble person,[25] because the text does not state the real reason for his refusal and he may well have concealed ulterior motives.[26] David's response stands in sharp contrast to his reply to Saul's later offer of Michal (18:23). In this reply, David does not discuss his family's social class but only his economic status, in the realization that marriage would require him to pay a bride-price.

But while David vacillates, Merab has already been given to Adriel.

II. Why Did Saul Plan to Give His Daughter Merab to David?

And the men of Israel said, "Have you seen this man who has come up? Surely he has come up to defy Israel; and the man who kills him, the king will enrich with great riches, and will give him **his daughter**, and make his father's house free in Israel." (1 Sam 17:25)

According to this verse, Saul will give his daughter in marriage to the man who overcomes Goliath the Philistine in battle.[27] In the aftermath of the duel, however, the prize of the king's daughter and the promise to exempt the victor's family from taxes are not realized. Neither is the lucky princess identified; but it seems plausible that Merab, Saul's older daughter, is meant, given the ancient custom that

---

[23] For various types of marriages and marriages between people of different social strata, see Allen Guenther, "A Typology of Israelite Marriage: Kinship, Socio Economic and Religious Factors," *JSOT* 29 (2005): 387–407.

[24] His dismissal of his worth has two parts. The first part is a nominal clause that opens with the interrogative "who?" followed by the pronoun "I": "Who am I, and who are my kinsfolk, my father's family in Israel…?" The second part is linked to the first with the relative pronoun "that" followed by a verb in the counterfactual (future): "that I should be son-in-law to the king?" For formulas of self-denigration, see George W. Coats, "Self-Abasement and Insult Formulas," *JBL* 89 (1970): 14–26. On the self-abasement formula in the form of a rhetorical question introduced by the interrogative "who," along with a discussion of 1 Sam 18:18, see also *IBHS*, 322.

[25] See P. Kyle McCarter, *I Samuel: A New Translation with Introduction, Notes, and Commentary*, AB 8 (Garden City, NY: Doubleday, 1980), 307–8; Clines, "Michal Observed," 28; Fokkelman, *Crossing Fates*, 246; Brueggemann, *Power, Providence, and Personality*, 30.

[26] Keith Bodner asks whether David really expected Saul, his future father-in-law, to answer when he said, "Who am I?" (*I Samuel: A Narrative Commentary*, HBM 19 [Sheffield: Sheffield Phoenix, 2008], 197–98). Perhaps it was intended as a rhetorical question. David's reply is very similar to what Saul said to Samuel when the latter came to anoint him (1 Sam 9:21), and that does not seem to reflect true humility. Hence, we can assume that there is some hidden motive behind David's refusal, which Saul identified and therefore decided to marry Merab to Adriel and not to David.

[27] See Hans Wilhelm Hertzberg, *I & II Samuel: A Commentary*, OTL (London: SCM, 1967), 151.

younger daughters were not married off before their older sisters, as Laban tells Jacob: "It is not so done in our country, to give the younger before the firstborn" (Gen 29:26).

It is possible that Saul's subsequent proposal to David removes the anonymity of the daughter to be awarded to Goliath's victorious adversary (1 Sam 17:25): "Then Saul said to David, 'Here is *my daughter, the older one, Merab; I will give her to you for a wife;* only be valiant for me and fight the LORD's battles'" (1 Sam 18:17). Indeed, the question of the possible link between 17:25 and 18:17 has intrigued scholars and commentators, both traditional and modern.

Those who believe there is a connection between the two offers of a princess's hand advance several arguments:[28] (1) Saul's public promise (17:25) has to be kept.[29] It is plausible that, had Saul reneged on it, the people would have protested because of their love for David (18:6–7, 16).[30] (2) The condition set by Saul, that David prove himself as a warrior[31] in the LORD's battles, cannot be fulfilled immediately after his victory over Goliath because of David's youth and inexperience. (3) Even if David's victory over Goliath could be taken as a demonstration of his capacity as a

---

[28] Both marriage proposals are missing from Codex Vaticanus of the LXX. These lacunae support the mutual dependence of the two passages (1 Sam 17:25 and 18:17–19).

[29] Gersonides (Rabbi Levi ben Gershon [1288–1344]) argued that Saul was bound to keep his word and fulfill his vow. This view is shared by C. F. Keil and F. Delitzsch, *Biblical Commentary on the Books of Samuel* (1868; repr., Grand Rapids: Eerdmans, 1950), 191; M. Z. Segal, *The Books of Samuel* (in Hebrew; Jerusalem: Kiryat Sefer, 1976), 152; Yehuda Keel, *The Book of Samuel*, Da'at Mikra (in Hebrew; Jerusalem: Mossad Harav Kook, 1981), 191; D. F. Payne, *I & II Samuel*, Daily Study Bible (Philadelphia: Westminster, 1982), 97–98; McCarter, *1 Samuel*, 308; Peter D. Miscall, *1 Samuel: A Literary Reading*, ISBL (Bloomington: Indiana University Press, 1986), 86; Robert Polzin, *Samuel and the Deuteronomist*, Literary Study of the Deuteronomic History 2 (San Francisco: Harper & Row, 1989), 177; Diana Vikander Edelman, *King Saul in the Historiography of Judah*, JSOTSup 121 (Sheffield: Sheffield Academic, 1991), 139; Campbell, *1 Samuel*, 196; Robert Alter, *The David Story: A Translation with Commentary of 1 and 2 Samuel* (New York: Norton, 2000), 115.

[30] John Mauchline, *1 and 2 Samuel*, NCB (London: Oliphants, 1971), 139.

[31] According to Abravanel (1437–1508), the epithet בן חיל ("valiant [warrior]"—but literally "valiant son") is essential. Samuel Laniado (d. 1605), too, understood the phrase to mean that Saul was proposing to give David the status of a son and not only of a son-in-law (*Keli Yaqar* on the Former Prophets [Venice, 1603], on v. 17). Keel notes that Saul was telling David that he should act like a warrior (איש חיל) and a hero (גבור חיל), that is, a faithful retainer who will give his life for his lord (*Book of Samuel*, 191). Lillian R. Klein holds that there is nothing new in the condition that Saul sets David in 18:17—that he be a "valiant warrior," because David has already been recognized as such a man of valor (גבור חיל; 1 Sam 16:18) (*From Deborah to Esther: Sexual Politics in the Hebrew Bible* [Minneapolis: Fortress, 2003], 186). In any case, David's designation by this term really adds nothing, because the same epithet is attached to many of Saul's soldiers (1 Sam 14:52). See also David Toshio Tsumura, *The First Book of Samuel*, NICOT (Grand Rapids: Eerdmans, 2007), 482. We believe that the condition is so vague that it would be difficult for David to know when he would have been considered to have met it.

warrior in the LORD's wars, it might be a one-time fluke and not enough to satisfy the king.[32]

Those who claim there is no connection between the two proposals isolate them from each other.[33] Some even view the proposal in 18:17 as the first one made to David.[34] They make a number of assertions: (1) Saul did not make a public promise of his daughter's hand to the man who defeated Goliath; it was the people who floated this idea, a rumor that spread through the camp.[35] According to this, Saul did not discuss the matter with David, either before or after he went out to face Goliath. (2) Saul's proposal in 18:17 relates to the future—if and when David proves himself as a warrior and fights the LORD's wars—and has no connection to the reward that was to have been given for past victories.[36] (3) An additional facet is that only in 18:17 does Saul declare explicitly, and for the first time, that he intends to give his daughter Merab to David on his own initiative, and not to fulfill a promise.[37] (4) Saul's proposal in 17:25 appears to be sincere; that in 18:17 conceals his hope that David will be killed in battle, thereby releasing him from having to go through with the marriage.[38] (5) There is a difference in the climate in which the two proposals are made. The first of them was made in a sympathetic environment that linked the war with the alliance with the king's family: "and the man who kills him, the king will … give him his daughter" (17:25). But the second proposal is cold and distant, with an unnatural link between marriage and war created by the word אך ("only").[39]

We believe that the two marriage proposals are linked, for a number of reasons:

1. Linguistic considerations: The repetition of the elements "his/my daughter" and "him/you,"[40] along with the root נתן, which appear in the same order in both proposals:

   … and the man who kills him, the king will enrich with great riches, and will give him his daughter [lit., *his daughter will give to him*], and make his father's house free in Israel. (17:25)

---

[32] Hertzberg, *I & II Samuel*, 160.

[33] See Abravanel there and Laniado, *Keli Yaqar*, 216b.

[34] See Barbara Green, *How Are the Mighty Fallen? A Dialogical Study of King Saul in 1 Samuel*, JSOTSup 365 (London: Sheffield Academic, 2003), 304.

[35] Thus, e.g., Laniado, *Keli Yaqar*, 216b.

[36] Steven L. McKenzie, *King David: A Biography* (Oxford: Oxford University Press, 2000), 78.

[37] Shmuel Yerushalmi, *The Book of Samuel I*, Me'am Lo'ez (New York: Moznaim, 1991), 287. Bar-Efrat notes that 18:17 adds something new to the demand that Saul made of David in 17:25 (Shimon Bar-Efrat, *1 Samuel*, Mikra le-Yisrael [in Hebrew; Jerusalem: Magnes, 1996], 242).

[38] Greenberg, *Plain Meaning of the Text*, 30; Clines, "Michal Observed," 28.

[39] Fokkelman, *Crossing Fates*, 228.

[40] The variation *his daughter to him/my daughter to you* is because of the change of speaker—in the first case (1 Sam 17:25), an Israelite referring to the king in third person; in the second (18:17), Saul addressing David.

Here is *my elder daughter* Merab; *I will give her to you* for a wife [lit., *her I will give to you*]; only be valiant for me and fight the Lord's battles. (18:17)

2. Both offers end with an alliterative repetition of the verb and a cognate accusative: עשר ... יעשרנו, "enrich with great riches" (17:25), and הלחם מלחמות, "fight (the Lord's) battles" (18:17).

3. It is possible that the motive behind or the cause of the proposal in 18:17 is David's dialogue with the men who "stood near him": "What shall be done for the man who kills this Philistine, and takes away the reproach from Israel…? And the people answered him in the same way, 'So shall it be done to the man who kills him'" (1 Sam 17:26–27); namely, "the man who kills him, the king will enrich with great riches, and will give him his daughter" (17:25).

4. The two proposals are complementary—the second clarifies and expands the first. What began as a rumor turns out to be true, and the combination of the two proposals creates a single complete offer: "his daughter (17:25), [the] *older one, Merab* (18:17) he … will give him (17:25) *for a wife* (18:17)."

5. An additional link can be seen in the structure of the two proposals, each of which is accompanied by two supplementary clauses. The first promise of marriage is sandwiched between two additional rewards:

"the king will enrich [him] with great riches, and will *give him his daughter* and make his father's house free in Israel."

In the second proposal, it is the marriage that is emphasized, followed by two conditions:[41]

"Here is *my daughter,* the older one, Merab; I will *give* her to you for a wife; only be valiant for me and fight the Lord's battles."

Thus it appears that the offer of the princess's hand in marriage, whether to the man who defeats Goliath or to David, is part of the deal in both cases.[42] The first proposal includes financial benefits to the warrior and his family; the second proposal—that David become a warrior who fights the Lord's wars—is meant to benefit both parties.

III. Why Was David's Marriage to Merab Called Off?

The expectation that David would marry the king's daughter began during the confrontation with Goliath, when Saul promised his daughter to the victor in their

---

[41] See Auld, *I & II Samuel*, 219.

[42] Fokkelman views this bargain as a sort of partnership between Saul and David, on two levels: first, fighting Saul's battles ("be valiant *for me*"); second, being a partner *with* Saul in the "Lord's battles" (*Crossing Fates*, 228).

duel (1 Sam 17:25). Saul seemed to be ready to fulfill his promise when he offered his daughter Merab to David (18:17), but this expectation was frustrated by Merab's marriage to Adriel the Meholathite (18:19).[43]

Nothing in the biblical narrative can explain why Saul married Merab to Adriel or when the marriage took place. The verse is vague and inscrutable,[44] providing no information as to why the match with David was canceled or who initiated its cancellation. The text, as noted, does not provide the answer.

This issue has engaged many commentators and scholars from the Middle Ages to the present.[45] Most of them focused on the questions of who called off the marriage and why. Those who assert that Saul was responsible offer extremely varied reasons for his action: (1) The marriage was never meant to take place because it did not coincide with the divine plan.[46] (2) Saul never had any intention of allowing Merab to marry David and make David his son-in-law, and certainly not to have him marry his older daughter.[47] (3) The cancellation of the match is a sign of

---

[43] Peter R. Ackroyd notes that Merab's marriage to another fits with the biblical motif of a father's promising his daughter's hand in marriage and then breaking the promise. This is the case with Laban and his daughter Rachel (Gen 29:15) and again with Samson (Judg 14:1–15:2). See Ackroyd, *The First Book of Samuel*, CBC (London: Cambridge University Press, 1971), 153. Bodner (*1 Samuel*, 198) wonders about the match between Merab and Adriel the Meholathite. Did Saul not think about the implications of marrying his daughter to a man of low status (even lower than David, who had proven his bravery), who would then enter the royal palace as the king's son-in-law?

[44] How should we understand the syntactically difficult ויהי בעת תת, "at the time when … is/was [or, with the translations, *should have been*] given [to David]" (1 Sam 18:19)? See Laniado (*Keli Yaqar*, on v. 19), Rashi, Kimchi, Gersonides, Segal (*Books of Samuel*, 152), and Keel (*Book of Samuel*, 192). But these explanations do not answer the question of *when* Saul was supposed to give Merab to David. This is why Greenberg writes, "The modern commentators saw themselves forced to make various emendations in the text that have no basis" (*Plain Meaning of the Text*, 30). Clines understands the collocation בעת תת as a temporal reference indicating that Merab was to be given to David immediately after his victory in battle against the Philistines. Only then would he be worthy of marrying the princess ("Michal Observed," 27). See also GKC §§115e, 354, and Joüon and Muraoka's observation that the absolute infinitive תת is atemporal (Joüon, 439).

[45] The remarks by Rashi, Kimchi, Gersonides, and Joseph Kara appear in their comments on 1 Sam 18:19, with regard to the difficult phrase two verses later, which has been rendered variously: "Saul said to David a second time, 'You shall now be my son-in-law'" (RSV); "So Saul said to David, 'You can become my son-in-law even now through the second one'" (NJPS); "… be my son-in-law in the one of the twain" (Authorized Version); "my son-in-law in two things" (Vulg.); and can also be understood to mean, "through two [women] you will became related to me by marriage today." See also Greenberg, *Plain Meaning of the Text*, 28.

[46] Brueggemann, "Narrative Coherence and Theological Intentionality," 235.

[47] Keel states that the royal son-in-law married to the older princess outranked the son-in-law married to the younger daughter (*Book of Samuel*, 191). See also Klein, *From Deborah to Esther*, 186; and Diana V. Edelman, "Merab," in *Women in Scripture: A Dictionary of Named and Unnamed Women in the Hebrew Bible, the Apocryphal/Deuterocanonical Books, and the New Testament*, ed. Carol Meyers (Grand Rapids: Eerdmans, 2000), 124–25.

Saul's instability; he seems to be inconsistent and unable to carry through even his own strategies.[48] (4) The marriage was called off in order to infuriate David and drive him to violence, so that Saul could punish him as he saw fit.[49] (5) Saul did not want to enhance David's status, as marriage to the king's daughter would have done; calling off the match distances David from the palace.[50] (6) The additional indication "she was afraid," found in the Lucianic recension of the LXX after "But at the time when Merab ... should have been given," raises the possibility that Saul called off Merab's marriage to David in consideration of her feelings.[51] (7) Saul was angered by David's response to the marriage offer (1 Sam 18:18), which he felt was hypocritical, deficient in humility, and concealing ulterior motives.[52]

Can we hypothesize that it was Merab who canceled her betrothal to David? Some commentators believe that Merab arranged her own marriage to Adriel the Meholathite and wed him without her father's consent.[53] This possibility can be inferred from the case of her sister Michal. If Saul was sensitive to the feelings of Michal, who loved David, and permitted them to marry, he might have been similarly responsive to the feelings of Merab,[54] who did not love David but did love Adriel the Meholathite.[55] In the end, it was Merab's wishes that determined whom she wed.[56]

---

[48] Mayer I. Gruber, *The Women of Israel by Grace Aguilar*, Jewish Studies Classics 11 (Piscataway, NJ: Gorgias, 2011), 481. See also Brueggemann, *Power, Providence, and Personality*, 31; idem, "Narrative Coherence and Theological Intentionality," 234; Edelman, "Merab," 124–25; Nehama Aschkenasy, *Eve's Journey: Feminine Images in Hebraic Literary Tradition* (Philadelphia: University of Pennsylvania Press, 1986), 140–45; Garsiel, "David and Michal," 117–18; Roland de Vaux, *Ancient Israel*, 2 vols. (New York: McGraw-Hill, 1961), 1:26–29.

[49] Jo Ann Hackett, "1 and 2 Samuel," in *WBC*, 90; Brueggemann, "Narrative Coherence and Theological Intentionality," 135; Mauchlin, *1 and 2 Samuel*, 14·.

[50] Payne, *I & II Samuel*, 97–98.

[51] We do not know where the Lucianic recension found the motif of fear. According to Auld (*I & II Samuel*, 219), the only suggestion that Saul was afraid of David appears in this chapter (1 Sam 18:12, 29), so it is possible that this emotion has been transferred here from father to daughter. It may be an attempt by the Lucianic recensor to solve the inherent difficulty in the Hebrew text, which fails to say why the betrothal was broken off. According to Hertzberg (*1 and 2 Samuel*, 160), however, we cannot see Merab's fear (excessive sensitivity) as a reason for calling off the marriage. Hertzberg does not explain why, later in the story, Saul is described as taking account of the feelings of his daughter Michal, who is in love with David (1 Sam 18:20).

[52] Bodner, *I Samuel*, 198.

[53] Thus David Altschuler (eighteenth century; Metzudat David commentary), the Malbim (1809–1879), Yerushalmi (*Book of Samuel I*, 289), and Abravanel, 224.

[54] As we learn from the addition in the Lucianic recension; see n. 51 above.

[55] Laniado (*Keli Yaqar*, 216b) connects the phrases "when Merab should have been given" with "she was given": she was given to Adriel secretly, and only the two of them knew about it.

[56] Miscall, *1 Samuel*, 248. According to Tikva Frymer-Kensky, this possibility does not fit the reality of the period (*In the Wake of the Goddesses: Women, Culture and the Biblical Transformation of Pagan Myth* [New York: Free Press, 1992], 122). We know that daughters were entirely under their father's control in all matters related to life and death, and certainly marriage. From a stylistic perspective, Aschkenasy (*Eve's Journey*, 140–41) and Fuchs (*Sexual Politics in the Biblical*

Did David cancel the match with Merab? The possibility that David refused the princess's hand is right there in the text. Some claim that David's demurral was motivated by his humility[57] or by reasons that are not obvious.[58] But is this logical? What spurred his refusal? Saul proposes to make David his son-in-law, which would mean an intimate relationship with the royal family, money, power, and status. Saul's reason is to get David to proclaim full allegiance to the king; but David, too, has an interest in marrying into the royal family.[59] Entrée to the palace and power inside it are invaluable for him, because, as the king's son-in-law, he might eventually find himself Saul's legitimate heir.[60] Hence, there is no logic and no obvious reason for David's reticence to marry the princess. This is proven later, when David, after ascending the throne, demands that Saul's daughter Michal be returned to him (2 Sam 3:14–15). David is moved not by his love for Michal[61] but rather by the practical political consideration of the advantage he would reap from renewed intimacy with Saul's daughter. His marriage to the king's daughters legitimizes his own succession.

It is possible that Michal was pulling the strings behind the scene. Michal had to suppress her feelings and watch how David, whom she loved, was matched with her older sister, who may not have cared for him.[62] Is it possible that she was the one who prevented David from marrying Merab? This idea rests on the concatenation of the verses: "But at the time when Merab, Saul's daughter, should have been given to David, she was given to Adriel the Meholathite for a wife. Now Saul's daughter Michal loved David…" (1 Sam 18:19–20). As soon as Merab has married another, we are immediately informed that it is actually Michal who loves David.[63] This option assigns Princess Michal a standing that enabled her to influence her father about both marriages. Michal's love for David is mentioned twice (18:20, 28). This seems to be the only case in Scripture where a woman chooses her own husband, rather than the familiar pattern in which the man selects his wife, with her

---

Narrative, 112) suggest that the root נתן, used in connection with the father's relationship to his daughters, signifies his control over her. This is in contrast to Fokkelman (*Crossing Fates*, 233), who suggests that the passive form "was given" is used to avoid stating explicitly that Saul was responsible for this marriage. The phrase "when Merab … should have been given" (1 Sam 18:19) indicates that she was married without her consent. Brueggemann ("Narrative Coherence and Theological Intentionality," 233) suggests that neither the breaking of the betrothal nor the marriage proposal sheds any light on Merab's character.

[57] Thus Gersonides in his commentary on 1 Sam 18:19.
[58] See Polak, *Biblical Narrative*, 295.
[59] Thus Garsiel, "David and Michal," 119; Guenther, "Typology of Israelite Marriage," 388.
[60] McCarter, *I Samuel*, 318.
[61] Just as he is not motivated by love for Merab when he turns down the proposal. According to Fokkelman (*Crossing Fates*, 228), this is why Saul proposes that David marry Merab. But in his reply, David does not refer to Merab herself, but only to the marriage proposal. The word "love" is conspicuous by its absence.
[62] Gruber, *Women of Israel*, 482.
[63] Clines, "Michal Observed," 28.

father's assent.[64] In fact, we read that Michal, too, is "given" to David: "And Saul gave him his daughter Michal for a wife" (18:27). Later, she is "given" to Palti son of Laish: "Saul **had given** Michal his daughter, David's wife, to Palti the son of Laish" (1 Sam 25:44). Finally she is taken from Palti and returned to David, whether she wishes it or not: "**Give me** my wife Michal.... And Ish-bosheth sent, and **took her** from her husband Palti-el the son of Laish" (2 Sam 3:14–15). In the end, Michal, too is passed from one man to another like an object.[65] The Michal who was active (1 Sam 19:11–14, 17) and initiating is "replaced" by a passive Michal, just like her older sister Merab.

IV. Merab: A Vanishing Act?

The books of Samuel and Chronicles leave the impression that Saul's family lost its historical importance after his death. As R. J. Coggins puts it, "An outline sketch of the history of Israel normally gives the impression that the significance of the family of Saul virtually ended with his death."[66]

Two items allow us to assume that the book of Samuel has a negative attitude toward the house of Saul: (1) The Saulide genealogy ends at 1 Sam 31:6 with the mention of the death of Saul and his sons; in 2 Sam 9:12, two more generations are added and the line is extended to Jonathan's grandson, Mica[h]. In contrast, 1 Chr 8:33–40 lists ten generations after Micah,[67] indicating that, though Saul's descendants did not wear the crown, the family remained prominent for many generations, certainly in the tribe of Benjamin[68] and even in the tribe of Judah.[69] (2) The names Ish-Bosheth and Mephibosheth (2 Sam 2:8 and 9:6, respectively) are replaced in Chronicles by Eshbaal (1 Chr 8:33, 9:39) and Merib-baal (8:34, 9:40). The use of the derogatory element *bosheth* ("disgrace") is meant to disparage the house of Saul; the Chronicler's use of what were apparently the original names emphasizes his more favorable attitude toward it.

The genealogies of Saul's family in Chronicles (1 Chr 8:33–39, 9:39–40) omit

---

[64] Adele Berlin, "Characterization in Biblical Narrative: David's Wives," *JSOT* 23 (1982): 70.

[65] There are echoes of such a custom in an inscription on the pyramid of the pharaoh Unas: "'Then he took the women from their husbands—whomever he wanted, when he lusted for them" (Hugo Gressmann, *Die älteste Geschichtsschreibung und Prophetie Israels: Von Samuel bis Amos und Hosea*, Die Schriften des Alten Testaments 2.1 [Göttingen: Vandenhoeck & Ruprecht, 1921], 157).

[66] R. J. Coggins, *The First and the Second Books of the Chronicles*, CBC (Cambridge: Cambridge University Press, 1976), 55.

[67] See Yair Zakovitch, *Inner-Biblical and Extra-Biblical Midrash and the Relationship between Them* (in Hebrew; Tel Aviv: Am Oved, 2009), 166 n. 12.

[68] Coggins, *First and the Second Books of the Chronicles*.

[69] Paul K. Hooker, *First and Second Chronicles*, WeBC (Louisville: Westminster John Knox, 2001), 43.

his daughters. Why should this be, given that women are included in other genealogical lists?[70] (1) The omission of Saul's daughters may reflect a desire to conceal Michal and Merab, whose ties to David cast him in a negative light. (2) The reference to Merib-Baal/Meri-Baal and Micah in the genealogy in Chronicles parallels the list in 1 Sam 14:49 in terms of the order in which the individuals are listed:

> Now the sons of **Saul** were **Jonathan**, Ishvi, and Malchishua; and the names of his two daughters were these: the name of the firstborn was **Merab**, and the name of the younger **Michal**. (1 Sam 14:49).

> Saul [was the father] of **Jonathan**, Malchishua, Abinadab, and Esh-baal; and the son of Jonathan was **Merib-baal**; and Merib-baal was the father of **Micah**. (1 Chr 8:33–34)[71]

It is possible that the author of Chronicles adopted a strategy of phonetic similarity that implicitly includes Merab and Michal in the family tree, through the names of their nephew and great-nephew, with מְרִי(ב) בָּעַל[72] hinting at מרב, and מִיכָה at מיכל. Eberhard Nestle, followed by Scott C. Layton, notes a possible connection between the names Merab and Meri-Baal.[73] Nestle sees Merab as a truncated form of the name Merib-Baal, which appears in the genealogies in 1 Chr 8 and 9. He conjectures that מרב is a faulty abridgement of מריבבעל.[74] The difference between the two genealogical lists of the house of Saul found in consecutive

---

[70] See Gen 36:2–6, 12–15; 1 Chr 7:1–19:24 et passim.

[71] Umberto [M. D.] Cassuto notes the appearance of the names of Zerah and Perez, Judah's sons/grandsons, among those who descended to Egypt (Gen 46:12), "in place of his dead sons, Er and Onan, though they should not have been mentioned, so that the total will not be fewer than seventy" ("The Episode of Tamar and Judah," in Cassuto, *Biblical and Canaanite Literatures*, 2 vols. [in Hebrew; Jerusalem: Magnes, 1983], 1:113). Similarly, in our story, Merib-Baal and Micah are mentioned alongside Merab and Michal in order to preserve the dynastic structure of the house of Saul as recorded in 1 Sam 14:49.

[72] Samuel David Luzzatto (1800–1865) suggests that the name Meri-Baal is the result of haplography from Merib-Baal. This means that the name "Merab," with all its consonants, is preserved in the genealogy.

[73] Ebernard Nestle, "Some Contributions to Hebrew Onomatology," *AJSL* 13 (1896–97): 174–75; Layton, "Hebrew Personal Name," 194. Nestle rightly notes the similarity between the names, but his explanation is reasonable only if we accept his assumption that Merib-baal (1 Chr 8:34, 9:40a), rather than Meri-Baal (1 Chr 9:40a) is the original form. According to Layton (p. 195), this assumption is doubtful, because the same name appears in an ostracon from Samaria with the spelling מרבעל. See Samuel Ahituv, *Handbook of Ancient Hebrew Inscriptions* (Jerusalem: Bialik Institute, 1993), 165, ostracon 2 (Hebrew). It is difficult to determine from this spelling whether the *bet* is geminated. What is clear is that in Western Semitic orthography, doubled consonants are never written twice in the text. Hence, the spelling Merib-Baal is a secondary form. Moreover, it appears that the "difficult" form of the name is the more ancient of the two and that the author of Chronicles (or his sources) reinterpreted the name in order to make it more comprehensible.

[74] Nestle ("Hebrew Onomatology, 175") adds that it was common practice among Semites

chapters of Chronicles (8:33–40 and 9:35–44) may reflect an additional reason for camouflaging Saul's daughters in the names of Jonathan's descendants. After the Chronicler completed his list of the heads of the houses of the tribe of Levi, the servitors of the Lord, the royal family came next. But in order to reach the Davidic dynasty he first had to mention the line of Saul,[75] if only to provide historical continuity to the genealogical list of the Israelite monarchy.[76]

We do not think it mere coincidence that the names Merab and Michal resound in the names of Saul's descendants—Merab in his grandson Merib-Baal and Michal in his great-grandson, Micah. The indirect presence of their names may actually reflect the importance of the king's daughters, their essential role in the narrative of the house of Saul, and their relationship with David, their father's successor if not his biological heir. It is clear to us, therefore, that this is an attempt to continue the genealogy of Saul through his daughters as well as his sons.

V. Why Is Merab Mentioned?

> The human beings in the Biblical stories have greater depths of time, fate, and consciousness than do the human beings in Homer; … their thoughts and feelings have more layers, are more entangled.[77]

Merab is on stage for a brief moment and vanishes just as quickly. What purpose is served by her appearance? Is she essential? Is she a secondary character? If so, she must "move the plot forward" or "endow the narrative with greater meaning and depth."[78] Is her role merely to cast additional light on the protagonist, an example of the subordination of secondary characters to the main character? Does she do this?[79] Is she a marginal character in the political game? Does her appearance have some hidden significance? Is it a cultural requirement?

---

for members of the same family to bear similar names. He notes, too, that women's names are often shortened forms of men's names.

[75] Thus according to Hooker, *First and Second Chronicles*, 43.

[76] See Keel (*Book of Samuel*, 168–69), who maintains that the list in ch. 9 draws on a different source than the list in ch. 8. The latter is more complete because the genealogy of the house of Saul in ch. 8 not only presents the ruling dynasty but is interwoven within the families in the tribe of Benjamin.

[77] Erich Auerbach, *Mimesis: The Representation of Reality in Western Literature*, trans. Willard R. Trask (Princeton: Princeton University Press, 1953), 12.

[78] Simon, *Reading Prophetic Narratives*, 266.

[79] Even if Merab does not play these roles, as expected of her as a secondary character, the narrator's treatment of her as a secondary character stands out. The biblical narrator has the freedom to follow secondary characters or ignore them. See Simon, *Reading Prophetic Narratives*, 265.

In fact, many reasons for Merab's appearance come to mind.

1. Perhaps her story is part of the biblical narrative fabric in which fixed patterns must be repeated in various stories. In our case, this is the motif of two wives,[80] one dominant and active and the second entirely passive: Hannah and Peninah, Abigail and Ahinoam, and here Merab and Michal.[81]

2. It is possible that Merab is mentioned in order to create a mirror story.[82] The episode of Merab reminds readers of the triangle of Jacob, Leah, and Rachel.[83] This is a literary paradigm that can be gleaned from the many similarities between the two stories. Just as there is a third party, Leah, intervening between Jacob and Rachel, Merab is a third party in our story. Both Michal and Rachel are younger sisters. Laban tricked Jacob on his wedding night (Gen 29:25); Saul tricked David in that, after offering him Merab, when the time for their marriage arrived he gave her to someone else (1 Sam 18:19). Another link is the presence of *teraphim* in both stories. Michal uses them to help David escape her father (1 Sam 19:13); Rachel steals them when she and her husband are running away from her father (Gen 31:31–35). Both Rachel and Leah prefer their husband to their father; Jacob married two sisters just as David had his pick of two sisters (some think that David did marry both of them[84]). There are also strong contrasts: Leah fails in her efforts to

---

[80] David Jobling believes that this motif appears primarily in the book of Samuel (*1 Samuel* [Berit Olam; Collegeville, MN: Liturgical Press, 1998], 181); but it can also be found in Genesis, in the story of Leah and Rachel, also sisters. Fokkelman believes that the number 2 is a repeated motif in our story: two princesses mentioned by name, two stages in the negotiations, two speeches by Saul, and two hundred Philistine foreskins (*Crossing Fates*, 242).

[81] Jobling (*1 Samuel*, 183) adds that Merab in our story is even more featureless than Peninah (1 Sam 1), since the only thing we learn about her is that she was promised to David but given to Adriel.

[82] Yair Zakovitch, "A Mirror Story: An Additional Level for Evaluating Characters in Biblical Stories" (in Hebrew), *Tarbiz* 54 (1985): 166.

[83] See Garsiel, "David and Michal," 120.

[84] Giving two daughters in diplomatic marriage was a familiar practice in the ancient Near East. In both the Bible and Mari we find that in diplomatic matches of the greatest importance, it was not enough for the overlord to give one of his daughters to the vassal king; he often gave him two daughters. In a letter from Yam-Zum, one of the two commanders of the Mari garrison in Ilan-Zura, to Zimri-Lim, he recounts what he said to Haya-Sumu in a conversation that took place in the ninth year of the reign of Zimri-Lim. Yam-Zum mentions to Haya-Sumu the special favor that Zimri-Lim showed him by giving him the hands of two of his daughters, Shima-Tum and Ki-Rum. Thus Yam-Zum wrote to Zimri-Lim: "Depuis que Samši-Addu est mort, il y a quatre rois puissant {Hammurabi, Rīm-Sin, Amūd-pī-El et Yarīm-Lim]. Mais ils n'ont pas épousé deux filles de (la race de) Yahdun-Lim. Présentement, des filles de mon seigneur, tu en as épousé deux" (ARM 26: 303,20′–24′). See Moshé Anbar, "La critique biblique à la lumière des Archives royales de Mari II: 1S18, 21b," *Bib* 78 (1997): 247–51. There is support for the hypothesis that David married two sisters in what Saul says to him later (1 Sam 18:21): בשתים תתחתן בי היום—a translation crux that can be understood to mean, "through two [women] you will became related to me by marriage today" (which the Peshitta renders, בתרתיהן תהוא לי חתנא יומנא). The talmudic

get Jacob to pay attention to her (Gen 30:16), whereas Michal is successful in turning David's head (1 Sam 18:20). Jacob married Leah, but Merab was given to another man. Michal lacked something essential that Rachel possessed—her husband's love. Jacob loves Rachel, and Michal loves David; but nowhere do we read that David loves her.[85] All these elements show that the Merab episode mirrors that of Rachel and Leah.

3. Could the motive for Merab's appearance be political—an attempt to make David's accession to the throne legitimate and natural as the king's son-in-law?[86] The first attempt, with Merab, was abortive, so a new and successful try is made with Michal.[87]

4. Merab appears in the story in order to create a contrast with her sister Michal: Merab does not love David, but Michal does.[88] David insists that Michal be returned to him (2 Sam 3:14) after Saul has given her to Paltiel son of Laish (1 Sam 25:44), but he does not seek the restoration of Merab after her marriage to Adriel the Meholathite (1 Sam 18:19). An additional contrast is that Michal was childless (2 Sam 6:23), whereas Merab evidently had children.[89]

---

sages held that David married both of Saul's daughters, Merab and Michal. Their discussion also focuses on the question of how David could marry two sisters (Yalqut Shimoni, 1 Sam 18, §128), despite the biblical prohibition: "You shall not take a woman as a rival wife to her sister, uncovering her nakedness while her sister is yet alive" (Lev 18:18). Nahmanides (ad loc.) explains that "it is improper for a husband to take a woman and her sister to pit them against each another, because they should love one another and not be rivals."

[85] Garsiel ("David and Michal," 120) cites additional details that emphasize the differences between the stories.

[86] According to Elna Solvang, this is not a good reason for Merab's inclusion in the story (*A Woman's Place Is in the House: Royal Women of Judah and Their Involvement in the House of David*, JSOTSup 349 [London: Sheffield Academic, 2003], 89). Clearly the king's son-in-law is not his heir. Nor is there any report of the crown's passing directly to the king's daughter—neither in the kingdom of Judah nor in the kingdom of Israel. The same was true of other kingdoms in the region. The king could adopt his brother's children as his heirs or marry his own daughter. For example, the Hittite king Hattusili nominated his brother's son as his heir and later disinherited him. From this we learn that even the king's nephew could not succeed him directly. Another case is that of the pharaoh Amenhotep III, who married his daughter in addition to her mother. In Egypt, the king's daughter could succeed her father only if her brother was dead. Her husband acquired status and power but could not inherit the throne. Saul had four sons and it is reasonable to assume that they too would have had sons and heirs. Thus, David's prospects of inheriting the throne as the king's son-in-law were negligible.

[87] McCarter, *I Samuel*, 318.

[88] Jobling, *1 Samuel*, 183. Merab's feelings are not described in the text, so is difficult to see the contrast between the two sisters, though the text states explicitly that Michal loved David (1 Sam 18:20).

[89] We must assume that "the five sons of Michal" (2 Sam 21:8) are in fact Merab's children. Many scholars and commentators maintain that the text here is corrupt and should read "Merab" instead of "Michal." These include Kimchi and Gersonides, who believe that Merab, not Michal, was married to Adriel, and that Michal was the childless sister (2 Sam 6:23), not Merab. So too

5. The mention of Merab reflects positively on David's character. David shows humility in his response to Saul, as if he does not believe he is worthy of being the king's son-in-law.[90]

6. Michal's marriage to David requires a prior effort to marry off the elder daughter Merab, according to the cultural norm, just as in the story of Jacob: "Laban said, 'It is not so done in our country, to give the **younger** before the **firstborn**'" (Gen 29:26).[91]

7. Merab is a secondary character who appears in the story to permit a moral evaluation of the main character.[92] Though she is granted minimal space in the story, as Uriel Simon notes regarding secondary characters, "It is precisely the option of saying so little about them that makes them such an effective means for accenting the main issue."[93] The Merab episode creates a situation that sullies Saul's name.[94] Saul's Machiavellian plan to eliminate David can come to fruition only through the marriage.[95]

Even though Merab is both present and absent in the stories of the house of Saul, her inclusion in the narrative is essential. She is the one who creates the ties formed among the characters around her, even though no real links are forged between her and them.

---

among modern commentators: J. Cheryl Exum, *Tragedy and Biblical Narrative: Arrows of the Almighty* (Cambridge: Cambridge University Press, 1992), 91, 171; Stanley D. Walters, "The Childless Michal, Mother of Five," in *The Tablet and the Scroll: Near Eastern Studies in Honor of William W. Hallo*, ed. Marl E. Cohen, Daniel C. Snell, and David B. Weisberg (Bethesda, MD: CDL, 1993), 290. Rashi, drawing on b. Sanh. 19b, states that Merab bore the children and Michal raised them; consequently they were referred to as Michal's. We see the irony of the two sisters' relationship: they go their separate ways but are always brought back together, almost to the point of fusing into one: when David hands over Merab's children to the Gibeonites (2 Sam 21:8), the circle is closed and Merab, like Michal, is childless. The nebulous personal identification of Saul's daughters, as in "with two [women] you will became related to me by marriage today" (1 Sam 18:21), strengthens this contention.

[90] Thus Robert B. Lawton, "1 Samuel 18: David, Merob, and Michal," *CBQ* 51 (1989): 424–25. The Merab episode is not essential because David could have made his humble answer with regard to Michal as well.

[91] See Gersonides on 1 Sam 18:19.

[92] On one of the functions of secondary characters, see Simon, *Reading Prophetic Narratives*, 268.

[93] Ibid., 269.

[94] Campbell (*1 Samuel*, 197) notes that Merab is mentioned in order to add another story that displays Saul's negative character, violent behavior, and failure to keep his promises. Jobling (*1 Samuel*, 183) believes that the notion that Merab appears in the story in order to highlight Saul's violent side is unfounded. The next scene (18:20–29), as well as the other episodes in which Saul and David appear, do much more to demonstrate Saul's illness or violent tendencies.

[95] It can be argued against this idea that Saul could marry his younger daughter Michal to David and achieve the same goal.

NEW FROM B&H ACADEMIC

CONVICTIONAL CIVILITY: Engaging the Culture in the 21st Century
Edited by C. Ben Mitchell, Carla D. Sanderson, and Gregory A. Thornbury

"David Dockery is one of America's most outstanding college presidents. His transformational leadership has been characterized by the rare combination of virtues that this volume celebrates and promotes: Christian charity, theological orthodoxy, and moral integrity."

—Philip Ryken, President, Wheaton College

978-1-4336-8508-8 • 208 pgs • hard cover • $29.99

PERSPECTIVES ON THE EXTENT OF THE ATONEMENT: Three Views
Edited by Andrew David Naselli and Mark A. Snoeberger

"The quality of the discussion throughout is simply superb.... I strongly recommend a careful reading of [this book], in light of the continued controversy surrounding this doctrine."

—Bruce A. Ware, Professor of Christian Theology, The Southern Baptist Theological Seminary

978-1-4336-6971-2 • 240 pgs • paperback • $24.99

A HISTORY OF CHRISTIANITY: An Introductory Survey
Joseph Early Jr.

"I welcome this new, comprehensive account of the Christian story written with clarity, grace, and understanding."

—Timothy George, founding Dean, Beeson Divinity School

978-1-4336-7221-7 • 520 pgs • paperback • $39.99

PERSPECTIVES ON ISRAEL AND THE CHURCH: Four Views
Edited by Chad Brand

"The issue of the relation of Israel and the church is crucial in New Testament interpretation for soteriology, ecclesiology, and eschatology. [This book] affords scholarly, well-articulated accounts of how [these four views] address these crucial issues from their distinctive perspectives."

—Steve W. Lemke, Provost, New Orleans Baptist Theological Seminary

978-0-8054-4526-8 • 336 pgs • paperback • $29.99

bhacademic.com
bhacademicBLOG.com

See our new catalog at
bhacademic.com/catalog

The Legal Blend in Biblical Narrative (Joshua 20:1–9, Judges 6:25–31, 1 Samuel 15:2, 28:3–25, 2 Kings 4:1–7, Jeremiah 34:12–17, Nehemiah 5:1–12)

JOSHUA BERMAN
Joshua.berman@biu.ac.il
Bar-Ilan University, Ramat Gan 52900, Israel

In the 1980s scholars identified the "legal blend"—the phenomenon in Ezra-Nehemiah and Chronicles whereby the practice of a law is expressed as a conflation of two earlier iterations of the law as found in the legal corpora of the Pentateuch. The phenomenon is thought to reflect upheaval in Israel's history and the need to reach a great compromise between competing strands of legal tradition. Discussions have identified legal blends in the books of Ezra-Nehemiah and Chronicles in descriptions of normative practice. This study claims that we also find the legal blend employed toward "haggadic" or rhetorical ends, whereby the law is extracted from its original focus and emerges within a new configuration of meaning. This study identifies seven narratives that blend iterations of the same law from across what are normally construed as distinct legal corpora. These examples are found in a broad range of narrative texts, most from the so-called Deuteronomic History. Trends that emerge from these examples are identified. The findings complicate the claim that the legal blend was exclusively a postexilic phenomenon.

In the 1980s scholars delineated the dynamics of what Michael Fishbane termed the "legal blend" in postexilic biblical literature.[1] This referred to the oft-found phenomenon in Ezra-Nehemiah and Chronicles whereby the practice of a law is expressed as a conflation of two earlier iterations of the law as found in the

My thanks to David Rothstein for his comments on an earlier draft of this article.
[1] Michael Fishbane, *Biblical Interpretation in Ancient Israel* (Oxford: Clarendon, 1985), 110–19, 134–36; D. J. A. Clines, "Nehemiah 10 as an Example of Early Jewish Biblical Exegesis," *JSOT* 21 (1981): 113; H. G. M. Williamson, "History," in *It Is Written: Scripture Citing Scripture. Essays in Honour of Barnabas Lindars, SSF*, ed. D. A. Carson and H. G. M. Williamson (Cambridge: Cambridge University Press, 1988), 26.

legal corpora of the Pentateuch. Perhaps the most heralded of these has been the Chronicler's description of the paschal sacrifice in the time of Josiah. Exodus 12:9 is explicit that the paschal sacrifice is to be roasted in fire (צלי אש) and may not be boiled in water. The author of Deut 16:7, however, sought to align the paschal sacrifice with other cultic offerings, and prescribed boiling (ובשלת). The Chronicler created a legal blend of these two received traditions by conflating lexical elements of each statement of the law in his description of the paschal offering in the time of Josiah (2 Chr 35:13): ויבשלו הפסח באש כמשפט.[2] Another well-known example is Nehemiah's description of the Sabbatical Year. The Covenant Code had prescribed that during the Sabbatical Year Israel was to refrain from agricultural activity (Exod 23:11): והשביעית תשמטנה ונטשתה, "but in the seventh you shall let it rest and lie fallow." Deuteronomy, however, spoke of the Sabbatical Year solely in terms of economic activity. In this year (15:1), "each creditor [בעל משה ידו] shall remit the due that he claims from his neighbor." Nehemiah conflates language from each iteration of Sabbatical Year legislation (10:32 [Eng. 31]): ונטש את השנה השביעית ומשא כל יד, "we will forgo the produce of the seventh year and every outstanding debt." The first phrase draws from the verse in the Covenant Code the language of השביעית and the root נטש and with it the idea of a year in which the land lies fallow. The second clause of the verse in Nehemiah invokes the language of Deut 15:1, משה בעל ידו, calling for the cancellation of debts.[3] In some instances the author of Ezra-Nehemiah weaves as many as three sources in his description of legal practice. Consider the note in Ezra 3:4: "They made the festival of Sukkot as is written, with its daily burnt offerings in the proper quantities, on each day as is prescribed for it." Close scrutiny of the Hebrew shows how the author drew eclectically from the sources nominally referred to as the Priestly, Holiness, and Deuteronomic prescriptions concerning the Festival of Tabernacles:

חג הסכת תעשה לך (Deut 16:13)	ויעשו את חג הסכת
	ככתוב
	ועלת יום ביום
במספר(ם) כמשפט (Num 29 [7x])	במספר כמשפט
עלה זבח ונסכים דבר יום ביומו (Lev 23:36)	דבר יום ביומו

In each of the borrowed phrases, the language is distinct to one particular law source; "making" the festival (root עשי) is found only in Deut 16:13; the description

---

[2] I refrain here from providing a translation as the translation itself is a subject of great debate. For our purposes, however, it is sufficient to note that all expositors see the Chronicler's work as an attempt to blend the two earlier traditions. For an overview, see Ehud Ben Zvi, "Revisiting 'Boiling in Fire' in 2 Chronicles 35:13 and Related Passover Questions: Text, Exegetical Needs and Concerns, and General Implications," in *Biblical Interpretation in Judaism and Christianity*, ed. Isaac Kalimi and Peter J. Haas, LHBOTS 439 (New York: T&T Clark, 2006), 238–50.

[3] Fishbane, *Biblical Interpretation*, 134.

of sacrifices described as "in the proper quantity as prescribed" (במספרם כמשפט) is found only in Num 29 [7x]; the epithet "on each day" (דבר יום ביומו) is distinct to the language of Lev 23:37.

Fishbane offers a narrative to account for how and why the legal blend became such a prominent feature of the literature of the period. In the preexilic period, Israel's legal traditions were diverse and contradictory, having stemmed from a variety of priestly and lay communities. The exigencies of exile and return created an urgent need to create a vehicle that would grant legitimacy to these various communities and their attendant legal traditions. Their composition into a single text represented a great historical compromise. A new exegetical agenda developed that allowed the disparate laws to be contained within a single authoritative text. This agenda placed a premium on the scholarly study and comparison of texts and reflected the growing text culture that was Achaemenid Judea. Rational modes of exegesis were developed to harmonize and correlate all the different legal corpora. The literary phenomenon of the legal blend was an outgrowth of this process.[4]

Scholarly discussions have identified legal blends in the books of Ezra-Nehemiah and Chronicles in descriptions of normative practice. I will demonstrate here that we also find the legal blend employed toward "haggadic" or rhetorical ends. Fishbane demonstrated how prophetic literature utilized legal material in this fashion.[5] In their hortatory use of preexisting legal materials, the prophets often had no intention of reinterpreting law or of portraying their normative application as part of a *corpus juris*. Thus, the injunctions concerning the Day of Atonement (Lev 16 and 23:26–32) serve as an ideological matrix for their inversion and reapplication about fasting in Isaiah's discourse concerning asceticism (58:1–12).[6] The haggadic exegesis exists in such instances solely for its own rhetorical sake.[7] The law is extracted from its original focus and emerges within a new configuration of meaning.[8] I will demonstrate here that a wide range of biblical texts use not only a single law source toward such rhetorical ends but, indeed, blend iterations of the same law from across what are normally construed as distinct legal corpora.

In what follows, I examine seven narratives that invoke legal terminology known to us from the pentateuchal law corpora. In each, however, the law invoked is expressed in differing ways in at least two of the four legal corpora—the Covenant Code, the Priestly laws, the Holiness Code, and the Deuteronomic Code. The seven examples I examine demonstrate that the legal blend was employed toward three rhetorical ends: to enhance sermonic preaching, to mark compliance with normative practice, and to serve as a literary template for a narrative's plot structure. I will conclude that the broad array of books in which the legal blend is found mandates

---

[4] Ibid., 264–65; cf. 153; Clines, "Nehemiah 10," 111–17.
[5] Fishbane, *Biblical Interpretation*, 282–317.
[6] Ibid., 305.
[7] Ibid., 300.
[8] Ibid., 283.

us to question whether indeed the legal blend is strictly a literary phenomenon of the postexilic period.

I. The Legal Blend as a Tool of Sermonic Preaching

As Fishbane showed, the prophets of Israel utilized legal material to underscore their theological messages. I show here that the authors of Nehemiah and Jeremiah, respectively, report that their protagonists chastised the people by employing legal blends in their hortatory.

Blended Debt-Legislation Laws in the Sermon of Nehemiah 5:1–12

As several scholars note, the account of the debt-servitude crisis in Neh 5 invokes several phrases from the Jubilee legislation of Lev 25. They note in particular Nehemiah's reproach to the elites in vv. 7–8: "Are you pressing claims on loans made to your brothers [איש־באחיו]? Then I raised a large crowd against them (8) and said to them, 'We have done our best to buy back our Jewish brothers who were sold [הנמכרים] to the nations; will you now sell [תמכרו] your brothers so that they must be sold [back] [ונמכרו] to us?'" Nehemiah's charge that the nobles are pressing claims on "loans made to your brothers" (איש־באחיו), seems to invoke the language of Lev 25:46: "You shall not rule ruthlessly, one over his brother" (איש־באחיו). The references to Judeans being bought and sold back into servitude in Neh 5:8 invoke Lev 25:42: "For they are My servants, whom I freed from the land of Egypt, they may not be sold in a slave-sale" (ממכרת עבד).[9]

While scholars have identified lexical similarities between the narrative of Nehemiah and debt-relief terminology in the Jubilee laws of Leviticus, other phrases in Neh 5 resonate with distinct terms of debt-relief legislation from the Covenant Code and from the Deuteronomic Code.

Exodus 22:24–26 reads:

אִם־כֶּסֶף תַּלְוֶה אֶת־עַמִּי אֶת־הֶעָנִי עִמָּךְ לֹא־תִהְיֶה לוֹ כְּנֹשֶׁה לֹא־תְשִׂימוּן עָלָיו נֶשֶׁךְ.
אִם־חָבֹל תַּחְבֹּל שַׂלְמַת רֵעֶךָ עַד־בֹּא הַשֶּׁמֶשׁ תְּשִׁיבֶנּוּ לוֹ. כִּי הִוא כְסוּתֹה לְבַדָּהּ הִוא
שִׂמְלָתוֹ לְעֹרוֹ בַּמֶּה יִשְׁכָּב וְהָיָה כִּי־יִצְעַק אֵלַי וְשָׁמַעְתִּי כִּי־חַנּוּן אָנִי.

If you lend money to my people, to the poor who is in your power, do not act toward him as a creditor; exact no interest from him. (25) if you take your neighbor's garment in pledge, you must return it to him before the sun sets; (26) it is his only clothing, the sole covering for his skin. In what else shall he sleep? Therefore, if he cries out to me, I will pay heed, for I am compassionate.

---

[9] H. G. M. Williamson, *Ezra, Nehemiah*, WBC 16 (Waco, TX: Word, 1985), 238–40; Joseph Blenkinsopp, *Ezra-Nehemiah: A Commentary*, OTL (London: SCM, 1988), 258–59.

The author of Neh 5 creatively employs this passage in his narrative. Under the strain of debt, the people "cry out" (v. 1: ותהי צעקת העם), and Nehemiah, looking to act in accordance with the Lord's teachings, "pays heed" when he hears their plea (v. 6: שמעתי). Their plea, it turns out, borrows from the opening phrase of Exod 22:24, אם כסף תלוה את עמי, "We have borrowed money [לוינו כסף] to pay our taxes to the king." In v. 11, Nehemiah instructs the nobles to return (השיבו נא) the fields they had taken as pledges, drawing from the language of Exod 22:25, תשיבנו לו. In each text there are the semantic fields of (1) "borrowing money"; (2) "crying out" under duress; (3) "returning" the pledge; (4) "heeding" the cry. The resonances may be summarized in tabular form:

Neh 5:1–11	Exod 22:24–26
(1) ותהי צעקת העם...	(24) אם כסף תלוה את עמי...
(4) ויש אמרים לוינו כסף...	(25) שלמת רעך ... תשיבנו לו...
(6) ויחר לי מאד כאשר שמעתי...	(26) והיה כי יצעק אלי
(11) השיבו נא להם היום שדתיהם...	ושמעתי

Additionally, the author of Neh 5 incorporates language from the debt-relief legislation of Deuteronomy. Deuteronomy 24:10 reads, "When you lend your neighbor any kind of loan [כי־תשה ברעך משאת מאומה], you shall not go into his house to get his pledge." Nehemiah castigates the nobles with this verse in mind (Neh 5:7): "Are you pressing claims on loans made to your brothers?" (משא איש באחיו אתם נשים).

Juha Pakkala has argued that the exercise of tracing legal language in Ezra-Nehemiah back to the legal corpora of the Pentateuch is founded in error. He notes that in no single case does the purported quotation correspond exactly to a known pentateuchal text. Rather he sees it likely that the author(s) of Ezra-Nehemiah drew from a version of the Pentateuch dramatically different from the one known to us from the MT and the various Second Temple era witnesses.[10] We cannot rule out the possibility that other highly variant traditions were in play at this time. However, I am inclined to argue with H. G. M. Williamson that it is difficult to believe that a document that was purportedly a major formative influence in the development of postexilic Judaism should have been lost without a trace, while the Pentateuch should have risen silently to its position of supreme authority.[11] Indeed, as Pakkala himself notes, many late Second Temple texts such as the Temple Scroll and Jubilees made similarly substantial changes to source texts they saw as authoritative when adopting them into the new composition.[12]

---

[10] Juha Pakkala, "The Quotations and References of the Pentateuchal Laws in Ezra-Nehemiah," in *Changes in Scripture: Rewriting and Interpreting Authoritative Traditions in the Second Temple Period*, ed. Hanne von Weissenberg et al., BZAW 419 (Berlin: de Gruyter, 2011), 157.

[11] Williamson, "History," 26.

[12] Pakkala, "Quotations and References," 214 n. 48.

One could argue from a second angle that the author of Nehemiah does not allude to any of the verses cited here. The language of Nehemiah resonates with the various passages cited because they address common subject matter—debts, pledges, and the like—and these are the terms that a biblical author would most naturally employ to discuss economic duress. I would counter, however, that Nehemiah makes use of terms that are highly distinct. Nowhere in the Hebrew Bible, for example, do we find the word "money" (כסף) juxtaposed with the word "lending" outside of Exod 22:24 and Neh 5:4. The language of being sold in and out of bondage via the root מכר is distinct to the Jubilee legislation. Jeremiah 34:8–12 addresses very similar issues and yet discusses being sold in and out of bondage with different verbs.

The strongest case, though, for an intentional legal blend here stems from the legal exegesis that Nehemiah executed, mentioned earlier. There is a consensus that the author of Nehemiah blended differing iterations of particular pentateuchal laws to inform the legal practice of his day. When we see, then, that narrative sections of Nehemiah resonate with a variety of pentateuchal legal prescriptions, we should assume that the same act of blending and adaptation is at work, now toward rhetorical and hortatory ends.

Blended Debt-Servitude Laws in the Sermon of Jeremiah 34:12–17

We find a legal blend employed toward similar rhetorical ends in Jer 34:12–17. Here, as in Neh 5:1–12, we read that economic instability led to widespread debt servitude. Jeremiah chastises the nobles, imploring them to release the debtors from bondage. The prophet's words here draw from an array of debt-servitude passages. In v. 14, the prophet reminds King Zedekiah of the biblical injunction, "Every seventh year each of you must set free any Hebrew brother who has been sold to you and has served you for six years; you must set him free from you" (תשלחו איש את אחיו העברי אשר ימכר לך ועבדך שש שנים ושלחתו חפשי מעמך). The call closely echoes the language of Deut 15:12: "When your fellow Hebrew, man or woman, is sold to you, and serves you for six years, in the seventh year you shall set him free from you" (כי ימכר לך אחיך העברי או העבריה ועבדך שש שנים ובשנה השביעית תשלחנו חפשי מעמך). In v. 15, however, the prophet invokes the Jubilee section of Lev 25 and its call (Lev 25:10), "and you shall proclaim liberty" (וקראתם דרור). He claims that the elites had behaved correctly "by granting release to one another" (לקרא דרור איש לרעהו), and later castigates them for reversing their policy (v. 17): "You have not obeyed me by granting a release to your friends" (לקרא דרור איש לאחיו ואיש לרעהו).[13] In the sermons of both Neh 5 and Jer 34, the protagonist

---

[13] The resonance of two law codes in this passage has drawn a wide spectrum of interpretation. For a survey, see Mark Leuchter, "The Manumission Laws in Leviticus and Deuteronomy: The Jeremiah Connection," *JBL* 127 (2008): 635–53. Many scholars accept the account as one that

marshals a range of pentateuchal legal resources on a given aspect of debt relief to buttress the call for social justice.

II. The Legal Blend as a Marker of Compliance with Normative Practice

As we noted, scholars first identified the legal blend as distinct in passages that describe the execution of legal practice in Ezra-Nehemiah and Chronicles, such as the paschal sacrifice in 2 Chr 35:13 and the observance of the Sabbatical Year in Neh 10:32 [Eng. 31]. Similar employment of the legal blend, however, is attested in several books of the so-called Deuteronomic history.

Blended City-of-Refuge Legislation in Joshua 20:1–9

Consider the case of Josh 20:1–9, in which Joshua establishes six cities of refuge. Scholars have long recognized this passage as a textual weave of terms found in city-of-refuge legislation from Deut 19:1–13 and from Num 35:9–28. Scholars have also noted that significant parts of MT Josh 20:1–6 emerge as a plus when compared to the LXX, particularly vv. 4–6 of the MT. These materials themselves represent a weave of terms from Deut 19 and Num 35. The overall tone of the plus resonates with the passage in Deuteronomy. At the same time, we see in these additions usage of the term עָרֵי מִקְלָט ("cities of refuge"; Josh 20:2) and the stipulation that the offender may move with impunity following the death of the high priest (Josh 20:6), both elements distinct to Num 35. The disparity between the MT and the LXX has led many scholars to suspect that the weave of texts exhibited in the MT is a late development.[14]

---

chronicles an authentic event from the life of the prophet and accept the wording of these verses as inherent in the original text of Jeremiah. See Michael LeFebvre, *Collections, Codes, and Torah: The Re-characterization of Israel's Written Law*, LHBOTS 451 (New York: T&T Clark, 2006), 86–87; John Sietze Bergsma, *The Jubilee from Leviticus to Qumran: A History of Interpretation*, VTSup 115 (Leiden: Brill, 2007), 164–70; John Bright, *Jeremiah: Introduction, Translation, and Notes*, AB 21 (Garden City, NY: Doubleday, 1965), 223–24; William L. Holladay, *Jeremiah: A Commentary on the Book of the Prophet Jeremiah*, 2 vols., Hermeneia (vol. 1, Philadelphia: Fortress, 1986; vol. 2, Minneapolis: Fortress, 1989), 2:238–41; Artur Weiser *Das Buch Jeremia*, 2 vols., ATD 20, 21 (Göttingen: Vandenhoeck & Ruprecht, 1969), 2:313. Older source critics saw the style in these verses as reflective of heavy prose, typical of the Deuteronomic style. See the discussion in Jack R. Lundbom, *Jeremiah: A New Translation with Introduction and Commentary*, 3 vols., AB 21A, 21B, 21C (New York: Doubleday, 1999–2004), 2:558.

[14] See Alexander Rofé, "Joshua 20: Historico-Literary Criticism Illustrated," in *Empirical Models for Biblical Criticism*, ed. Jeffrey H. Tigay (Philadelphia: University of Pennsylvania Press, 1985), 131–47; Richard D. Nelson, *Joshua: A Commentary*, OTL (Louisville: Westminster John Knox, 1997), 228–30.

Blended Amalek Prescriptions in 1 Samuel 15:2

Pentateuchal literature addresses the future struggle against Amalek in two passages, Exod 17:14–16 and Deut 25:17–19. Most expositors see the passage in Deuteronomy as dependent on the passage in Exodus. In Exodus, God declares that he will engage in a struggle against Amalek, stating (17:14), "I will utterly erase the memory of Amalek from under the heavens" (מחה אמחה את זכר עמלק מתחת השמים). By contrast, these expositors claim, Deuteronomy transforms God's own battle into a mandate for action by Israel (25:19): "*You shall erase the memory of Amalek from under the heaven*" (תמחה את זכר עמלק מתחת השמים).[15]

The author of 1 Sam 15 invokes both passages in his introduction to Saul's campaign against Amalek (15:2): "I am exacting the penalty for what Amalek did to Israel, for the assault he made upon them on the journey, on their way up from Egypt." The verse invokes the language of Deut 25:17–18: "Remember what Amalek did to you on the journey, upon your exodus from Egypt, how he surprised you on the journey." The language of the Hebrew is close:

1 Sam 15:2	Deut 25:17–18
פקדתי	זכור
את אשר עשה עמלק לישראל	את אשר עשה לך עמלק בדרך
אשר שם לו בדרך בעלתו ממצרים	בצאתכם ממצרים אשר קרך בדרך

Yet at the same time as the author of the verse invokes the language of Deuteronomy he also incorporates a central element of the passage from Exodus: the divine initiative. In Deuteronomy, the campaign against Amalek is left to Israel to wage. In Exodus, Israel is nowhere charged with the campaign against Amalek. Rather, it is God who will wage the battle. To be sure, in 1 Sam 15 it is Israel that wages the battle, but the initiative is divine. As Moshe Garsiel notes, the divine command in 1 Sam 15:2 is introduced in a way that underscores that God is enjoining the battle

---

[15] Gerhard von Rad, *Deuteronomy: A Commentary*, trans. Dorothea Barton, OTL (London: SCM, 1966), 155; Jeffrey H. Tigay, *Deuteronomy* דברים: *The Traditional Hebrew Text with the New JPS Translation*, JPS Torah Commentary (Philadelphia: Jewish Publication Society, 1996), 237; David Toshio Tsumura, *The First Book of Samuel*, NICOT (Grand Rapids: Eerdmans, 2007), 388–89. By contrast, Ed Noort sees Deuteronomic influence in the Exodus passage ("Josua und Amalek: Exodus 17:8–16," in *The Interpretation of Exodus: Studies in Honour of Cornelis Houtman*, ed. Riemer Roukema et al., CBET 44 [Leuven: Peeters, 2006], 155–70). Some scholars have argued for a preexilic date of the tale. See Philip D. Stern, "1 Samuel 15: Towards an Ancient View of the War-Herem," *UF* 21 (1989): 413–20; and Meindert Dijkstra, "The Geography of the Story of Balaam: Synchronic Reading as Help to Date a Biblical Text," in *Synchronic or Diachronic? A Debate on Method in Old Testament Exegesis*, ed. Johannes C. de Moor, OtSt 34 (Leiden: Brill, 1995), 72–97. Other scholars have proposed a postexilic date. See Fabrizio Foresti, *The Rejection of Saul in the Perspective of the Deuteronomistic School: A Study of 1 Sm 15 and Related Texts*, Studia Theologica Teresianum 5 (Rome: Teresianum, 1984).

himself: "Thus said *the Lord of Hosts* [כה אמר יהוה צבאות]: 'I am exacting the penalty'" and so on.[16]

The author of this verse may have seen no contradiction between the passage in Exod 17 and the passage in Deut 25. He may have creatively interpreted the call to war in Deuteronomy as an expression of God's eternal battle against Amalek. What is important to note is that the Samuel narrative conflates two iterations of a given issue that are often seen as stemming from different sources with mutually exclusive viewpoints.

Blended Prescriptions for Cultic Desecration in Judges 6:25–31

Three passages of biblical law call for the obliteration of Canaanite cultic sites, invoking variations on a common formula:

Exod 34:13	כִּי אֶת־מִזְבְּחֹתָם תִּתֹּצוּן וְאֶת־מַצֵּבֹתָם תְּשַׁבֵּרוּן וְאֶת־אֲשֵׁרָיו תִּכְרֹתוּן	For their altars you shall tear down, and their pillars you shall break, and their Asherim you shall cut down.
Deut 7:5	מִזְבְּחֹתֵיהֶם תִּתֹּצוּ וּמַצֵּבֹתָם תְּשַׁבֵּרוּ וַאֲשֵׁירֵהֶם תְּגַדֵּעוּן וּפְסִילֵיהֶם תִּשְׂרְפוּן בָּאֵשׁ	Their altars you shall tear down, and their pillars you shall break, and their Asherim you shall chop down, and their images you shall burn in fire.
Deut 12:3	וְנִתַּצְתֶּם אֶת־מִזְבְּחֹתָם וְשִׁבַּרְתֶּם אֶת־מַצֵּבֹתָם וַאֲשֵׁרֵיהֶם תִּשְׂרְפוּן בָּאֵשׁ וּפְסִילֵי אֱלֹהֵיהֶם תְּגַדֵּעוּן	You shall tear down their altars, and you shall break their pillars, and their Asherim you shall burn in fire and the images of their gods you shall chop down.

Scholars have considered the diachronic development between these passages. Richard D. Nelson sees the passage in Deut 7 as an amplification of the earlier passage in Exod 34. Deuteronomy 7:5, he says, adds the distinctive call to burn images, and with regard to the Asherah, replaces the root כרת ("cut down"), found in Exodus, with the more intensive root, גדע ("to chop down").[17] Moshe Weinfeld likewise sees the passages in Deuteronomy as chronologically later. For Weinfeld, the passage in Exodus reflects an early stage of the law, as it omits reference to images. This, he says, is because cultic practices at the time consisted mainly of an

---

[16] Moshe Garsiel *1 Samuel*, Olam Ha-Tanakh (in Hebrew; Tel Aviv: Davidzon Etti, 1985), 140. Shimon Bar-Efrat likewise sees the blending here of Exodus and Deuteronomic passages concerning Amalek (*1 Samuel*, Miqra Le-Yisrael [Tel Aviv: Am Oved, 1996], 197). He also notices that the text of 1 Sam 14:47, וילחם סביב בכל איביו, which immediately precedes the call for battle against Amalek, satisfies the condition of Deut 25:19 that war is to be engaged against Amalek בהניח יהוה אלהיך לך מכל איביך מסביב.

[17] Richard D. Nelson, *Deuteronomy*, OTL (Louisville: Westminster John Knox, 2002), 100.

altar, a pillar, and a sacred tree. Deuteronomy took the law a step further and included idols in each of the two passages.[18] Conversely, Brevard S. Childs, following Martin Noth, sees the list in Exodus as reflecting Deuteronomic influence.[19]

I would add that at least some of the differences in formulation stem from the rhetorical needs of each writer in view of the wider hortatory context of his respective passage. In all likelihood, the author of Deut 7 wished to reserve the phrase תשרפון באש, "you shall burn with fire," for idols, to conform with his call in v. 25: "the idols of their gods you shall burn with fire [תשרפון באש]; you shall not covet the silver and gold upon them, lest you become ensnared by them, for it is an abomination to the LORD." To merely "chop down" (גדע) the idols, as per Deut 12:3, would still leave the silver and gold intact and for the taking, and thus the need to reserve the phrase "you shall burn with fire" (תשרפון באש) for the graven images. The author of Exod 34:13, as Weinfeld noted, omits mention of pagan images altogether. This, too, may have stemmed from rhetorical needs. The root כרת in that passage is a *Leitwort*. The Lord "cuts" (כרת) a covenant with Israel (34:10). Israel, therefore, must not "cut" (כרת) a covenant with the indigenous nations (34:12). "Cutting" a covenant with them (פן תכרת ברית) will result in cultural corruption (34:15–16). As opposed to cutting a covenant with the nations, Israel is commanded in 34:13 to "cut" down their Asherim (ואשריהם תכרתון). By omitting reference to treatment of pagan idols—which, no doubt, this author surely abhorred, the sentence of 34:13 rises to a climax that creates the apposition between proscribed "cutting" with the indigenous nations—cutting of a covenant—and mandated "cutting"—of their Asherim.

I would suggest that the author of Judg 6 was familiar with these three traditions and, in spite of their differences, saw each of them as a source of inspiration for his composition of the episode in 6:25–32, where Gideon is called upon to desecrate his father's cultic site. In this section, I highlight the various and several ways through which the author of Judg 6 achieves this.[20] No single resonance by itself is sufficient to make the case for intentional allusion to these formulae. Rather, it is the aggregate of all the allusions that creates this connection.

A reference to the desecration formulae may be detected in the words of the townsfolk whose verbal response to the desecration closely paraphrases the language of the formulae (6:28): "The townsfolk arose the next morning, and behold the altar to Baal had been demolished and the Asherah upon it had been cut down,"

---

[18] Moshe Weinfeld, *Deuteronomy: A New Translation with Introduction and Commentary*, AB 5 (New York: Doubleday, 1991), 366.

[19] Brevard S. Childs, *Exodus: A Commentary*, OTL (London: SCM, 1974), 613.

[20] Some scholars maintain that the stories of the saviors in Judges had already been formed into an edited cycle before coming to the hands of the Deuteronomic Historian. Others prefer to see these stories as part of a late revision of a basic Deuteronomic History. See the recent and thorough overview of the history of this scholarship in Barry G. Webb, *The Book of Judges*, NICOT (Grand Rapids, Eerdmans, 2012), 20–32.

והנה נתץ מזבח הבעל והאשרה אשר עליו כרתה. They repeat the formula in their accusation against Gideon in v. 30: "The townsfolk said to Joash, 'hand over your son that he may die, for he has demolished the altar of the Baal, and has cut down the Asherah upon it,'" כי נתץ את מזבח הבעל וכי כרת האשרה אשר עליו. One could counter that there is no deliberate invocation of the formula, and that this is the only way for a biblical writer to express these actions. Yet we should take careful note of the author's use of language in this passage. When the Lord instructs Gideon to destroy the altar, he does not use the verb נתץ, but rather הרס (6:25). The tight juxtaposition created in the exclamations of the townsfolk between tearing down the altar and the cutting down of the Asherah strengthens the case that the author has invoked the pentateuchal call for cultic desecration. Through the adroit hand of the author of Judg 6, Gideon obeys not only the word of the Lord as spoken in v. 25 but also the law as recorded in the legal prescriptions concerning the Asherah.

Indeed, the account as a whole seems to have been scripted with Deuteronomy 12:1–6 in mind. There, Israel is called upon to desecrate the cultic centers of the local inhabitants (vv. 2–3) and to replace them with a sanctioned center from which Israel will sacrifice offerings (vv. 5–6). The narrative of Judg 6:25–31 reports a highly similar tale. At the Lord's behest, Gideon destroys his father's pagan cultic center. The townsfolk are made to mimic the formula that calls for this desecration. After desecrating the cultic sites according to the prescription of Deut 12:2–3, Gideon erects an alternative and sanctioned cultic site to YHWH, from which he offers burnt offerings, just as the Israelites are commanded to do in Deut 12:6.

The instruction to cut down the Asherah is consistently expressed in this narrative through the verb כרת (6:25, 26[2x], 28, 30), the language found exclusively in Exod 34:13. In v. 26, though, the Lord further instructs Gideon to use the Asherah as firewood to offer the sacrifice on the rebuilt altar. The implication seems to be more than a mere suggestion to Gideon as to how he may procure fuel wood to offer the burnt offering. Rather, it seems that the Lord instructs Gideon to incinerate the Asherah in order to magnify the audacity of the act and the totality of the desecration. Not only will the Asherah be rendered nonfunctional by cutting it down, it will be obliterated by incineration. Not only will it be incinerated, it will serve in the establishment and consecration of a renewed cultic site, now dedicated to YHWH, as the firewood used in the first sacrifice to YHWH. By having Gideon not only cut down the Asherah but also burn it in fire, the author has Gideon fulfill the textual tradition preserved in Deut 12:3.[21]

We have seen, therefore, how the account of Judg 6 hews to the cultic desecration formulae of Exod 34:13 (through the language of כרת with regard to the Asherah) and of Deut 12:1–6 generally (in the overall plot of the story) and of 12:3

---

[21] As noted in Judith M. Hadley, *The Cult of Asherah in Ancient Israel and Judah: Evidence for a Hebrew Goddess*, UCOP 57 (Cambridge: Cambridge University Press, 2000), 54.

in particular (through the incineration of the Asherah), and through the towns-folk's mimicking of the general form of the formula with regard to altars and Asherim. Our author, however, has also woven a reference to the cultic desecration formula of Deut 7:5 through the name of the protagonist himself, Gideon. Several commentators have noted that the name Gideon stems from the root גדע ("to chop down"). Moreover, the orthography of Gideon's name itself hews closely to the language of Deut 7:5 ואשריהם תגדעון.[22] To be sure, other explanations can be offered to account for the etymology of the name Gideon, such as the cutting down of the horn of an enemy (Jer 48:25, Ps 75:11), or the cutting down of a staff (Zech 11:7–14). Such etymologies however, could befit virtually any biblical hero, yet no other such figure in the Hebrew Bible bears a name with this etymology. It seems more likely that the author of Judg 6 has named his hero Gideon to mark this seminal act in his career as a warrior for the Lord of Israel.

Finally, I invoke one more piece of lexical data from the account of Judg 6 to buttress my claim that its author is making deliberate use of the various legal passages concerning the Asherah. In v. 26, YHWH instructs Gideon to erect "an altar to the Lord your God" (מזבח ליהוה אלהיך). Outside of this reference in Judg 6, the phrase מזבח יהוה אלהיך is found only four times, all in Deuteronomy. Two of those references (12:9 and 27:5) speak of erecting "an altar for the Lord your God" in order to offer burnt offerings, as Gideon is instructed here in Judg 6:26. A third reference addresses the altar and the Asherah (Deut 16:21): "You shall not plant an Asherah near the altar of the Lord your God" (מזבח יהוה אלהיך). It would seem that the author of Judg 6 has deliberately reached to employ the Deuteronomic phrase to invoke tropes of proper cultic worship as Gideon destroys his father's cultic site. In accordance with Deuteronomic prescription, Gideon will erect an altar "to the Lord your God," where he will offer burnt offerings. Moreover, in accordance with the spirit of Deut 16:21, there will be no Asherah present at this new site; the Asherah that had been there will be immediately consumed upon the new altar that is a מזבח ליהוה אלהיך. It is worth underscoring again that no single resonance by itself is sufficient to make the case for intentional allusion to these formulae. Rather, it is the aggregate of all the allusions within the space of five verses that creates this connection. It is more reasonable to assume that the author of Judg 6 drew from legal traditions known to him, rather than to assume that three different legal draftsmen each drew from a different element of this narrative in the formulation of their respective laws of cultic desecration.

---

[22] Moshe Garsiel, "Homiletic Name-Derivations as a Literary Device in the Gideon Narrative: Judges 6–8," VT 43 (1993): 302–17; F. Zimmerman, "Folk Etymology of Biblical Names," in Volume du Congrès: Genève 1965, VTSup 15 (Leiden: Brill, 1966), 315–16; Yair Zakovitch, "The Synonymous Word and the Synonymous Name in Name Midrashim" (in Hebrew), Shnaton 2 (1977): 105–6.

III. The Legal Blend as a Literary Template for Plot Structure in Biblical Narrative

In the previous example, we saw that the account of Gideon's assault on his father's cultic center closely follows the sequence of commands to Israel found in Deut 12:1–6. Gideon seemed to be following what Israel had been called upon to do: to desecrate cultic centers in the land and to replace them with a sanctioned center from which to sacrifice burnt offerings. In this section I note two examples of narrative where the characters seem to follow a plot whose lines closely follow two separate iterations of a pentateuchal law.

Blended Necromancy Laws in 1 Samuel 28:3–25

Biblical law proscribes divination via the אוֹב/אֹב (ʾōb/ʾôb) in four passages: Lev 19:31; 20:6, 27; and Deut 18:11. Bill Arnold notes that the account of King Saul's visit to the woman of Ein-dor in 1 Sam 28 intentionally invokes the language of pentateuchal law, drawing out the intertextual implications that produce a critical reading of Saul's activities.[23] Arnold focuses on the references the Saul story makes to Deut 18. The language of inquiring of the dead, דרש אל המתים (Deut 18:11) is echoed in Saul's call to his servants to find a woman of אב, "that I may inquire of her," ואדרשה בה (1 Sam 28:7). I would add that in 1 Sam 28:8 Saul entreats her again using the language of Deuteronomy, "divine for me [קסמי נא] through the אב," invoking the language of divination in Deut 18:10, קסם קסמים.

However, the narrative of 1 Samuel 28 also borrows divinatory language from Leviticus. The plural form אֹבוֹת employed in 1 Sam 28:3 and 9 is found only in Leviticus (19:31, 20:6). When Saul charges his servants with "seeking" a woman necromancer (בקשו לי אשת אוב) in 1 Sam 28:7, the request invokes the language of prohibition in Lev 19:31 concerning the אבות and the ידענים (yiddĕʿōnîm), "do not seek out [תבקשו] to be defiled through them." Simply, then, on the level of language, we see how the Saul narrative resonates with more than one tradition of אב legislation.

---

[23] Bill T. Arnold, "Necromancy and Cleromancy in 1 and 2 Samuel," *CBQ* 66 (2004): 207. Christophe Nihan likewise emphasizes the role of Deuteronomic language in this story, but suggests a post-Deuteronomistic origin for the story ("1 Samuel 28 and the Condemnation of Necromancy in Persian Yehud," in *Magic in the Biblical World: From the Rod of Aaron to the Ring of Solomon*, ed. Todd E. Klutz, JSNTSup 245 [London: T&T Clark, 2003], 39–54). On the basis of ancient Near Eastern parallels, others suggest an early date. See Mordecai Cogan, "The Road to En-dor," in *Pomegranates and Golden Bells: Studies in Biblical, Jewish, and Near Eastern Ritual, Law, and Literature in Honor of Jacob Milgrom*, ed. David P. Wright et al. (Winona Lake, IN: Eisenbrauns, 1995), 319–26.

Moreover, however, the narrative of 1 Sam 28 invokes divination legislation from Leviticus and Deuteronomy in a far more profound way. The structure of the respective legal passages from Leviticus and Deuteronomy each contributes to the plot structure of the Ein-dor narrative. To appreciate how this works we need to understand the respective אב passages in their legal, pentateuchal contexts and then examine how they are employed in the narrative of 1 Samuel 28.

As many scholars have pointed out, the divination passage of Deut 18:9–22 paints a contrastive picture: rather than turning to various forms of divination—here proscribed in vv. 9–14—Israel is to turn to the prophets of YHWH, as outlined in vv. 15–22.[24] The contrast set up in this text is twofold. The first contrast is established concerning the appropriate resources through which to divine the future. To learn the future one must not turn to heathen divinatory practices but instead to a prophet of YHWH. Indeed, the hallmark of a true prophet according to this passage is his proven capacity to predict future events accurately (18:21–22). Jeffrey Tigay emphasizes, however, that the more dominant contrast at stake in this passage concerns the question of *authority*. To whom shall the Israelite turn for instruction? Deuteronomy 18:14 states that the heathens "listen to" or "obey" (ישמעו) the proscribed instruments of divination. By contrast, YHWH will raise up a true prophet and "to *him* you shall listen" (תשמעון) (18:15).[25] The root דבר as "word" and "speech" serves as a *Leitwort* in this section. In the space of only five verses, vv. 18–22, the root appears fourteen times. The word of the prophet is the word that he has received from the Lord, and it is that word that must be obeyed (vv. 18–19). To summarize, the section rejects the appeal to oracular sources such as the אב for either instruction or for clairvoyance as to the direction of future events. Instead, Israel is to turn to the prophets.

The author of 1 Sam 28 has employed both the language and the structure of Deut 18 in his construction of the encounter between Saul and Samuel in 1 Sam 28:15–19. Upon turning to the אב, Saul receives the rebuke of the prophet. The rebuke he receives is a paraphrase of the lessons of Deut 18:9–22. Saul admits that he turned to the אב to receive *instruction* (28:15): "So I called upon you that you should tell me what to do!" The author of the passage has Samuel carefully invoke the language of Deut 18 (see next page). The author of 1 Sam 28 continues to hew to the contours of Deut 18 as the plot continues. Samuel never does provide Saul with what he sought, namely, instruction, a course of action. Instead, Samuel proceeds to give Saul a highly detailed oracle of what awaits him; he predicts the future (28:19): "The Lord will also deliver Israel together with you into the hands of the Philistines and tomorrow you and your sons will be with me." Put differently, the author of 1 Sam 28 continues to script Samuel's rebuke straight out of the play book of Deut 18. The ultimate test of a true prophet, according to that chapter, is his capacity to predict future events accurately. Samuel's prediction, of course, is fully

---

[24] Tigay, *Deuteronomy*, 172; Nelson, *Deuteronomy*, 232.
[25] Tigay, *Deuteronomy*, 175.

Deut 18:19	1 Sam 28:17–18
והיה האיש אשר לא ישמע אל דברי	ויעש יהוה לו
אשר ידבר בשמי	כאשר דבר בידי
אנכי אדרש מעמו	ויקרע יהוה את הממלכה מידך
	ויתנה לרעך לדוד
	כאשר לא שמעת בקול יהוה
	ולא עשית חרון אפו בעמלק
	על־כן הדבר הזה עשה לך יהוה
	היום הזה
And the man who shall not heed my words	The Lord has done
Which [the prophet] shall speak in my name,	As He has spoken through Me
I shall call him to account.	And he has torn the kingdom from your hands
	And given it to your fellow, to David
	Because you did not heed the voice of the Lord,
	And did not visit His great anger upon Amalek.
	Therefore, this thing has God done to you this day.

realized in 1 Sam 31. The contrast that Deut 18 wishes to draw between the אב and the prophet of YHWH is fully replicated here. Saul sought the אב to gain instruction. He receives no instruction whatever. Instead, he receives rebuke for having failed to heed the instruction of the prophet earlier in his career at the battle with Amalek.[26] He is likewise given a demonstration of the clairvoyance of a true prophet of YHWH, who now, with great precision, presages his demise. These findings may be summarized in tabular form:

Motif	Deuteronomy 18:8–22	1 Samuel 28:7–19
Turning to the אב for instruction	Prohibition of turning to oracles for instruction (vv. 8–14)	Saul turns to the אב for instruction (vv. 7–14)
Heeding the prophet of YHWH	Rules guiding heeding the prophet (vv. 15–20)	Saul is rebuked for not heeding the prophet (vv. 15–18)
Clairvoyance of the prophet	True prophet predicts events (vv. 21–22)	Samuel foretells outcome of the battle (v. 19)

[26] My reading places a premium on Saul's failure to heed Samuel's voice in that episode as central to the contrast the author wishes to draw between reliance on the אב versus reliance on the prophets of YHWH. This stands in stark contrast to the view of P. Kyle McCarter, for whom the reference to the battle with Amalek here is "entirely superfluous and out of place" (*I Samuel: A New Translation with Introduction, Notes & Commentary*, AB 8 [Garden City, NY: Doubleday, 1980], 423).

While the encounter between Saul and Samuel in 1 Sam 28 follows the contours of אב legislation in Deuteronomy, the encounter between Saul and the woman of Ein-dor in vv. 8–14 follows the contours of the אב legislation in Lev 19. Here, too, we must examine that passage in its own context as a prelude to exploring how the author of 1 Sam 28 uses it in his present narrative. Leviticus 19:31–32 reads,

אל־תפנו אל־האבת ואל־הידענים אל־תבקשו לטמאה בהם אני ה׳ אלהיכם. מפני שיבה תקום והדרת פני זקן, ויראת מאלהיך אני ה׳.

(31) Do not turn to the אבות and the ידענים; do not seek out to become defiled by them; I am the Lord your God. (32) Before the aged you shall rise and show deference to the old, and you shall fear your God, I am the Lord.

The passage establishes an apposition around the lexeme "face" (פן). One should not turn toward or, literally, face (תפנו) the אבות and the ידענים. To "turn toward" or to "face" is to show deference and esteem. Rather, one should reserve esteem for its proper recipients. Verse 32 twice gives the instruction to show esteem when "faced" with the aged. Verse 32a directs, "Before the aged," or, literally, "In the face of the aged rise," מפני שיבה תקום. Verse 32b continues likewise, "you shall honor the face of the elderly," והדרת פני זקן. Leviticus 19:14 had safeguarded proper treatment of the weak—the deaf and the blind—with the injunction "and you shall fear your God, I am the Lord," and that same injunction is invoked here again, this time with regard to the proper treatment of another weak segment of society, the aged.[27] The structure of the passage forms an *inclusio* with vv. 3–4, which address honoring parents and refraining from "turning towards" (אל תפנו) idolatrous practices.[28]

Moving now to the narrative of 1 Sam 28, we may see how the author has crafted the meeting between Saul and the sorceress with this passage in mind. I earlier noted that Saul orders his servants (28:7), "seek for me a woman of אב" (בקשו לי אשת בעלת אוב), directly contradicting, in lexical terms, the call "do not seek [אל תבקשו] to be defiled by them" in Lev 19:31. One might counter that Saul's call "seek for me a woman of אב" is simply best expressed through the root בקש, and no connection to Lev 19:31 should be adduced. I also noted, however, that the plural form, אבות, found in vv. 3 and 9, is also distinct to the language of Lev 19–20. The reference to "seeking" in the Saul narrative as a deliberate reference to Lev 19:31 is buttressed when we identify other lexical cues in the Saul narrative. The woman reports that she saw אלהים rising from the ground (28:13). Although most commonly the word for "god," אלהים may also connote here a godlike being or a "celestial spirit."[29] Alternatively, the dead could be termed אלהים, as attested by appellations for the dead in Ugaritic and elsewhere.[30] Faced with אלהים—whatever the sorceress

---

[27] Jacob Milgrom, *Leviticus: A New Translation with Introduction and Commentary*, 3 vols., AB 3 (New York: Doubleday, 1991), 1703.

[28] Ibid., 1701–2.

[29] See discussion in Arnold, "Necromancy and Cleromancy," 202.

[30] Ibid., 203; Milgrom, *Leviticus*, 1773–74.

meant by that—she experienced dread (28:12–13). The semantic field of אלהים in Lev 19:32 mandates fear—ויראת מאלהיך. Yet here we see that Saul acts counter to that; he calls upon her *not* to be afraid of the אלהים she sees (28:13): "And the king said to her, 'do not fear—what have you seen?'" Saul himself demonstrates that he has no fear of God here, as he swears in vain, vowing to the woman in God's name that she will be guilty of no sin by summoning the dead (28:10). The woman describes the apparition she has seen as "an old man" (איש זקן). Saul, desiring to show deference, again gets it wrong; he prostrates himself on the ground. He surely meant to show deference. But in the skillful hand of the author of 1 Sam 28, Saul does exactly the opposite of what is called for—"Before the aged you shall *rise*" (Lev 19:32). Finally, and most significantly, the narrative of 1 Sam 28 proves that Saul has flagrantly violated the command of Lev 19:32. Israelites there are called to show "deference" to the old—והדרת פני זקן. Samuel—described here as איש זקן—reproaches Saul (28:15) for having "disturbed" him (הרגזתני), quite the opposite of showing deference. We can see therefore, that the author not only has borrowed language of necromancy from both Leviticus and Deuteronomy but, indeed, has crafted his story to form a homiletic tale. The exchange between Saul and the woman necromancer follows the structure of the אב passage of Lev 19:31–32. It incorporates the terms אבות, "seeking" (בקש), אלהים, "fear" (יראה), and "aged" (זקן).[31] Here, too, it is highly unlikely that the author of Lev 19 happened to pick up on the first half of the story and the author of Deut 18 the second half, as each formulated his proscription concerning the אב. It is more likely that the author of 1 Sam 28 conflated traditions that were available to him.

Blended Debt-Legislation Laws in 2 Kings 4:1–7

Second Kings 4:1–7 tells of the plight of a widow faced with the threat of default on her debt to a creditor poised to possess her two children.[32] The narrative resonates with the same legal texts employed in the legal blend of Neh 5: both the collateral law of the Covenant Code in Exod 22:22–26 and the revised version of the law in Deut 24:10–11.

The woman cries out (צעקה) to Elisha to save her children from the creditor, here referred to as the נשה (4:1). As Yael Shemesh notes, the woman's circumstances represent a conflation of cases described in two consecutive Covenant Code laws,

---

[31] Elsewhere I demonstrate how the structure of the book of Ruth hews to the order of laws registered in Deut 24:16–25:10 ("Ancient Hermeneutics and the Legal Structure of the Book of Ruth," *ZAW* 119 [2007]: 22–38). See also my "Law Code as Plot Template in Biblical Narrative (1 Kings 9.26–11.13; Joshua 2.9–13)," forthcoming in *JSOT*.

[32] On the basis of syntactic analysis, Frank Polak dates this story to the eighth century ("Development and Periodization of Biblical Prose Narrative [Second Part]" [in Hebrew], *Beit Mikra* 153 [1998]: 143–60). Thomas Römer argues for a Persian-period origin ("La fin de l'historiographie deutéronomiste et le retour de l'Hexateuque?" *TZ* 57 [2001]: 269–80).

one concerning a widow and the next concerning a debtor. Exodus 22:21–22 warns, "You shall not mistreat any widow or any orphan. If you do mistreat them, I will heed their outcry [כי אם צעק יצעק אלי] as soon as they cry out to Me." The next law states (22:24), "If you lend money to my people, to the poor who is in your power, do not act toward him as a creditor [כנשה] … (26) if he cries out to me [והיה כי יצעק אלי], I will pay heed, for I am compassionate." The poor woman of 2 Kgs 4:1–7 is a widow and her children orphans, as is the case of Exod 22:21–22. Yet she is also a debtor who owes money to a נשה, a creditor (cf. vv. 1, 7), which is the case found in Exod 22:24–26.[33] In this homiletic tale, the author of 2 Kgs 4 has her cry out to the "man of God" (cf. v. 7) as the Lord's representative, calling upon him to make good upon the promise of the two laws in the Covenant Code, that her cry will be heard. Note that the opening verse of the passage (v. 1) does not employ the form ותצעק, which would be followed by the subject, namely, the widowed woman. Rather, the syntax is varied so that the subject is the first word of the verse. The result is that the verb, צעקה, is now followed by the preposition אל, followed by the object, the Lord's representative, Elisha. The verb צע followed by the preposition אל matches the syntax of the legislation of Exod 22:22, 26, צעק אלי.

The passage also resonates with the Deuteronomic revision of the collateral law, found in Deut 24:10–11. That law extends the protection to the debtor stipulating that the creditor (נשה) may not enter the debtor's home (ביתו) to take the pledge. Instead, the creditor must wait outside the domicile for the debtor to bring it to him. The structure of v. 11 stresses the exterritorial nature of the debtor's home by bracketing the verse with the word "outside": "Outside [בחוץ] you shall stand, and the man to whom you made the loan shall bring the pledge out to you [החוצה]." As Nelson aptly puts it, "the domestic threshold" in this law "is a boundary not to be transgressed."[34]

The destitute widow cries out to Elisha (4:1), "The creditor [הנשה] has come to take my two children for himself as servants." The situation is urgent, as the creditor is poised to enter her home to take her children as pledge. As Mordechai Cogan and Hayim Tadmor note, Elisha's query (4:2), "What can I do for you?" is nearly rhetorical in nature. It expresses the prophet's acknowledgment of the legal right of the creditor to receive his pledge. Concern for the widow and the orphan is commonplace in the wisdom literature and in the prologues and epilogues of ancient Near Eastern legal literature.[35] Yet nowhere in that literature, not even in the Pentateuch, is there legislation that saves someone from debt servitude when they have defaulted on their debt (cf. Isa 50:1, Amos 2:6, 8:6).[36] Following the spirit

---

[33] Yael Shemesh, "Elisha and the Miraculous Jug of Oil (2 Kgs 4:1–7)," *JHebS* 8 (2008): 10, http://www.jhsonline.org/cocoon/JHS/a081.html.

[34] Nelson, *Deuteronomy*, 290.

[35] F. Charles Fensham, "Widow, Orphan, and the Poor in Ancient Near Eastern Legal and Wisdom Literature," *JNES* 21 (1962): 129–39.

[36] Mordechai Cogan and Hayim Tadmor, *II Kings: A New Translation with Introduction and Commentary*, AB 11 (Garden City, NY: Doubleday, 1988), 56.

of the law, though not its letter, Elisha seeks to prevent the creditor from violating her domain. The law of Deut 24:11 is extracted from its original focus and emerges within a new configuration of meaning. He instructs her to establish a clear boundary setting off the abode (בית) (twice in v. 3), where she is to shut the door behind her (vv. 4 and 5) after she has gone to bring vessels from "the outside" (החוץ). Her domicile is transformed into a secure zone in which her children assist her to produce the necessary oil with which she may go out and pay her creditor (v. 7). Following Yehuda Keel, we note that the bifurcation between בית ("home") and חוץ ("outside")—where the נשה must remain—invokes images of the revised law of collateral, as expressed in Deut 24:10–11.[37] When the woman exits from the house and proceeds to the man of God (v. 7) he explains how she may now extricate herself from the threat of debt, demonstrating, indeed, in the language of the laws of the Covenant Code, that the Lord hears the cries of the widow, the orphan, and the debtor. The core of the plot—the exterritorial status of the woman's house in the face of the creditor's threat—revolves around the imagery invoked from that law. The account emerges as a homiletic tale that draws from a conflation of the sensus plenior of the collateral laws of Exod 22:22–26 and Deut 24:10–11.

Were this narrative to resonate with only a single iteration of the law of collateral we could rightly question which text had chronological priority. Since the passage resonates with two versions of the law, it seems more reasonable to assume that they are both prior to the text in 2 Kgs 4, rather than assuming that the author of the Covenant Code picked up on part of the story in crafting his law, while the author of the Deuteronomic Code coincidentally picked up on other parts in crafting his version.[38]

IV. Conclusions

The legal blend is more widely employed in the Hebrew Bible than has been understood until now. At times it is employed to blend civil laws concerning issues of social justice (in the examples from Josh 20, 2 Kgs 4, Jer 34, and Neh 5), and at others to blend theological or cultic laws (in the examples from Judg 6, 1 Sam 15

---

[37] Yehuda Keel, *Kings*, 2 vols., Da'at Miqra (in Hebrew; Jerusalem: Mossad Harav Kook, 1988), 2:490.

[38] Calum Carmichael has proposed over a number of his works that the laws of the Pentateuch represent the crystallization of lessons drafted on the basis of the tales told in biblical narrative. See, e.g., Calum M. Carmichael, *Law and Narrative in the Bible: The Evidence of the Deuteronomic Laws and the Decalogue* (Ithaca, NY: Cornell University Press, 1985). For Carmichael's contention to stand, however, we would need to posit that time and again, authors of the various law corpora conveniently divvied up the narratives studied here, with each taking a separate phrase to formulate his respective legislation. For a critique of Carmichael's approach, see Bernard M. Levinson, *"The Right Chorale": Studies in Biblical Law and Interpretation*, FAT 54 (Tübingen: Mohr Siebeck, 2008), 224–55.

and 1 Sam 28). Laws from all four of the Pentateuch's law corpora contributed to the examples adduced here. The textual weaves present in Josh 20:1–9 and Jer 34:1–17 have been noted in the scholarship for some time. In this article I identified five more examples on the basis of what I took to be strong motivic and lexical connections between the respective narratives and the various laws with which they resonate. I am unaware of any other instances of the legal blend outside of Ezra-Nehemiah and Chronicles. Sensitive readers, it is hoped, will identify further examples of this phenomenon in the future.

The legal blend as a rhetorical device may be distinguished from the legal blend as a mere report of practice, as in the report of the paschal sacrifice in 2 Chr 35:12–13. The legal blend as rhetorical device incorporates motifs and images alongside lexical markers. By contrast, mere reports of legal practice in Ezra-Nehemiah and Chronicles achieve blending almost exclusively by melding together the language of disparate passages of legislation to the same issue. The legal blends identified here, which invoke biblical law for hortatory and rhetorical purposes, employ a wider range of blending techniques. All will invoke language. Yet alongside that, some, like 1 Sam 28, will adopt the order of a series of laws to structure the plot of the narrative. Others, still, will narrate an episode that touches on the law without explicitly reporting that the legal prescription is being followed. In fact, the opposite is true. The invocation of the laws is usually done with reference to a case that lies outside the purview of the strict letter of the pentateuchal law. Pentateuchal law prescribed actions to be taken against cultic sites of the heathen nations. The author of Judg 6, however, applies those laws to an Israelite heterodox site. Deuteronomy 24:11–12 states that the creditor must wait outside the debtor's home, and that the debtor must bring him the pledge. The author of 2 Kgs 4:1–7, however, never does have the debtor—the impoverished widow—bring out the pledge. Instead, she "brings out" oil, which she sells to pay off her debt. Nehemiah 5:1–12 invoked laws concerning pledges (Exod 22:24–26, Deut 24:10), yet Nehemiah does not enforce compliance with the literal letter of those laws, which seem not to be at issue there. Rather, he marshals the spirit of those laws to call for a general release from debt.

My findings here allow us to speculate anew concerning the origins of the literary practice of combining Israel's disparate laws. Scholars had long identified this phenomenon with the books of Ezra-Nehemiah and Chronicles, which strongly suggested that the phenomenon was postexilic in origin. As we saw at the outset, scholars theorized that the legal blend was part of a new exegetical agenda that allowed disparate laws to be contained within a single authoritative text, in response to the exigencies of exile and return to the land.

Here, however, we have seen the legal blend attested in the prophetic book of Jeremiah, and in each of the books of the so-called Deuteronomic History, where the events narrated are preexilic. With the dearth of epigraphic finds at our disposal, the dating and growth of these—indeed, most—biblical texts remains a vexing issue. Nor can we be certain that the versions of these legal traditions that were available to these authors were identical to what we find in the MT today. The origins of the legal blend, therefore, can no longer automatically be assumed to be a postexilic phenomenon, though, no doubt, many of the texts that employ it do stem from that period. The range of biblical texts employing this convention raises the possibility that ancient Israelites were adducing exegetical tools to combine their disparate legal traditions already at an earlier stage as well.

What, however, would have occasioned the blending of these disparate traditions, if not the exigencies of displacement and the need for unity? The question, I would submit, stems from an erroneous premise, namely, that the various law corpora of the Pentateuch are mutually exclusive and that the reformulation of a law in one is a rejection and concealment of the earlier iteration of that law in another. As I have written elsewhere, this view wrongly interprets biblical law as statutory law.[39] By this view, law exists in a written code. The law code supersedes all other sources of law that preceded the formulation of the code, and no other sources of authority have validity other than the code itself. The precise formulation of the written law is autonomous and exhaustive. This approach to norms and legal texts, however, is entirely foreign to the ancient Near East, where what we implicitly think of as statutory "laws" were actually records of judgments or examples of judicial wisdom. When later generations rewrote and interpreted these examples, the earlier texts still retained high regard and were kept on record as a datum from which to reason. It is in this spirit, I would claim, that ancient Israelites sought to blend their legal writings. This view sees the legal blend as an inherent part of the legal tradition of the biblical writings from their inception and not as the by-product of calamity and putative attempts at unity between formerly competing normative communities.

---

[39] See my "History of Legal Theory and the Modern Study of Biblical Law," *CBQ* 76 (2014): 19–38.

THE ANCHOR YALE BIBLE

A tradition of excellence in biblical scholarship and a commitment to advancing biblical understanding in the 21st century

The Anchor Yale Bible Commentary Series, a book-by-book translation and exegesis of the Hebrew Bible, the New Testament, and the Apocrypha

The Anchor Yale Bible Dictionary, with more than 6,000 entries from 800 international scholars

The Anchor Yale Bible Reference Library, currently consisting of 34 volumes by foremost scholars from a variety of religious backgrounds who focus on broad biblical themes.

Widely recognized as the flagship of American biblical scholarship, the **Anchor Yale Bible Series** is comprised of:

- Contributions from distinguished authors around the world, representing Protestant, Catholic, Jewish, and Muslim traditions;
- New translations, reflecting the latest knowledge of ancient languages;
- Extensive annotations, including alternative translations;
- Objective treatment of competing theories;
- Commentary to explain texts and clarify difficult passages;
- Historical background as well as up-to-date research;
- Helpful organizing tools including detailed introductions, overviews, and outlines;
- Relevant visual features such as maps, photographs, diagrams, and more.

For more information please visit YaleBooks.com/AnchorYaleBible

Yale UNIVERSITY PRESS

עיפה in Amos 4:13: New Evidence for the Yahwistic Incorporation of Ancient Near Eastern Solar Imagery

JOHN B. WHITLEY
john.b.whitley78@gmail.com
428 School Street, Belmont, MA 02478

In this article I argue that the term עיפה in Amos 4:13 is related to the West Semitic term for "winged sun disk" found, inter alia, in the Phoenician Yeḥawmilk stele (*KAI* 10), and in the Late Egyptian Semitic loanword ʿpy. This proposal, as I will show, suggests a new understanding of the balanced poetic structure of Amos 4:13 (the first of the so-called doxologies in Amos) and, furthermore, allows one to perceive its unique refraction of the motif "deity–mountain–winged sun disk"—a juxtaposition of images that is widely attested in ancient Near Eastern texts and iconography. In the final part of the article, I discuss how this new evidence comports with the use of solar imagery elsewhere in the Hebrew Bible and show that the usage in Amos 4:13 is particularly close to that found in wisdom writings.

The phrase עֹשֵׂה שַׁחַר עֵיפָה in Amos 4:13 has posed difficulties for commentators ancient and modern. Its rare vocabulary and terse, poetic style have allowed disagreement to persist over what exactly is being described in this short line and particularly over the syntactic problem of which of the two terms שחר and עיפה is to be understood as the material and which the rendered product, and over the interpretive issue of whether the phrase presents an ominous image or a creative and hopeful one like those in the surrounding text. Complicating matters further, Amos 4:13 forms the first of three so-called doxologies in the book of Amos that

---

All biblical translations in this article are, unless otherwise noted, adapted from the NRSV, and all drawings are by the author. A version of this article was presented at the New England and Eastern Canada regional meeting of the SBL and at the Ancient Near Eastern Iconography and the Bible session of the SBL annual meeting in 2013, and I am grateful to the participants for their feedback. I would like to extend a special thanks to Peter Machinist, Jeremy Hutton, Janling Fu, and Julie Faith Parker for their helpful suggestions on earlier drafts of this article.

are widely regarded as secondary insertions in their current contexts, and opinions about their date and original relationship to one another vary widely.¹ In this short essay, I argue for a new interpretation of עשה שחר עיפה that finds the phrase to contain a previously unrecognized reference to a common ancient Near Eastern solar icon—the winged sun disk—and therefore offers additional evidence for the way in which such imagery was recovered in ancient Yahwistic circles.² In section I, I briefly review previous interpretations of our phrase; in section II, I propose a new translation in light of Phoenician parallels and discuss its implications for understanding Amos 4:13; finally, in section III, I offer some final reflections on how the image comports with other known instances of ancient Yahwistic solar imagery.

I

I begin with a brief discussion of previous translations of עשה שחר עיפה. The vast majority of these follow one of two main trajectories, each understanding the term עיפה to mean "darkness." Perhaps the most frequently adopted translation of our phrase regards it as containing an ominous image, that is, "the one who makes dawn into darkness."³ According to this view, the phrase comprises syntactically a

---

¹ The doxologies in Amos include Amos 4:13, 5:8–9, and 9:5–6, and nearly every commentary since the early twentieth century has devoted an excursus to them. It is worth noting at the outset that not every commentator regards the doxologies as secondary; for example, Shalom M. Paul argues that the first and third "are related to their respective contexts and that therefore there is no need to assume that they are later interpolations" (*Amos: A Commentary on the Book of Amos*, Hermeneia [Minneapolis: Fortress, 1991], 153). For the more typical view that the doxologies are later interpolations—either composed by a later redactor or inserted from an earlier source—the following studies are especially worthy of mention: Friedrich Horst, "Die Doxologien im Amosbuch," *ZAW* 47 (1929): 45–54; Klaus Koch, "Die Rolle der hymnischen Abschnitte in der Komposition des Amos-Buches," *ZAW* 86 (1974): 504–37; Werner Berg, *Die sogenannten Hymnenfragmente im Amosbuch*, Europäische Hochschulschriften 23 (Bern: Lang, 1974); James L. Crenshaw, *Hymnic Affirmation of Divine Justice: The Doxologies of Amos and Related Texts in the Old Testament*, SBLDS 24 (Missoula, MT: Scholars Press, 1975). Critics frequently note formal comparison with other so-called participial hymns such as Job 9:5–10, for a discussion of which see Frank Crüsemann, *Studien zur Formgeschichte von Hymnus und Danklied in Israel*, WMANT 32 (Neukirchen-Vluyn: Neukirchener Verlag, 1969), 81–154. Though I tend toward the view that the doxologies are secondary insertions (though not necessarily unrelated to their current context in the mind of the scribe who inserted them), I do not see that any of these compositional determinations are substantially affected by the thesis that will be proffered in this article.

² It is not my intention here to suggest that solar imagery in general or the winged disk in particular was a foreign loan into Yahwism, but rather to show how that image, as part of a broader ancient Near Eastern heritage, was received by certain Yahwists.

³ So Jörg Jeremias, *The Book of Amos: A Commentary*, trans. Douglas W. Stott, OTL (Louisville: Westminster John Knox, 1998), 66; James Luther Mays, *Amos: A Commentary*, OTL (Philadelphia: Westminster, 1969), 77; Hans Walter Wolff, *Joel and Amos: A Commentary on the Books of the Prophets Joel and Amos*, trans. Waldemar Janzen, S. Dean McBride Jr., and Charles A.

construct chain with an objective genitive (שחר) followed by an accusative (עיפה) designating the final rendered product.⁴ Moreover, the term עיפה is understood to be related to a root *עיף ("to be dark"), so that we must understand the product (darkness) to be something that utterly negates dawn, doing away with it altogether, and therefore as a quasi-apocalyptic description.⁵ While this explanation of the phrase is syntactically plausible, the resulting image of YHWH's threatening (indeed, creation-destroying) power seems especially out of place in a hymnic moment that is otherwise devoted to positive descriptions of YHWH's role as the creator (e.g., "the one who forms the mountains / the one who creates the wind") and as one who maintains an amicable relationship with the created order (e.g., "the one who tells to humankind what his thoughts are").⁶ Those who support this interpretation argue that the doxologies are, in fact, focused on judgment or otherwise seek to balance the theme of YHWH's sovereignty over creation with his ability to overthrow it.⁷ However, while punishment of the wicked is briefly mentioned elsewhere in the doxologies (i.e., Amos 5:9, 9:5a), there is nothing in them that amounts to the undoing of creation, as the darkening of the dawn would seem to imply.⁸ In fact, in both Amos 5:9 and 9:5, YHWH punishes humanity as part of the

---

Muenchow, Hermeneia (Philadelphia: Fortress, 1977), 211; William Rainey Harper, *A Critical and Exegetical Commentary on Amos and Hosea*, ICC (Edinburgh: T&T Clark, 1905), 104–5.

⁴Note that עשה with *tsere* is diagnostically construct and, therefore, resists any analysis that seeks to understand שחר as an accusative, for which see below. The objective genitive is common following the participle of עשה (e.g., Exod 20:4, 31:15, Pss 77:15, 86:10, 103:6, 106:21), and especially in hymnic expressions magnifying YHWH's role in creation (e.g., Isa 45:18; 51:13; Jer 51:15; Pss 18:51; 115:15; 104:2b, 14; 146:6; Job 9:10). The fact that these are objective genitives and not accusatives is clearly marked in, e.g., Ps 104:2a, 3b, and Job 9:9 by the presence of *maqqep*. Hermann Gunkel referred to participles of the latter type as "hymnic participles" and noted that they are often found in close proximity to the divine name, which ultimately stands behind these references (*An Introduction to the Psalms: The Genres of the Religious Lyric in Israel*, completed by Joachim Begrich, trans. James D. Nogalski from the 4th German ed., 1933, Mercer Library of Biblical Studies (Macon, GA: Mercer University Press, 1998], 31). An exact parallel to the construction being described here (i.e., participle + objective genitive of material + accusative describing the final product) can be found in Ps 104:3b.

⁵A root *עיף ("to be dark") is clearly found in ארץ עיפתה (Job 10:22), where it is parallel to צלמות ("shade"), as well as in מעוף (Isa 8:22) and תעפה (Job 11:17), which is often emended to a verb (תעפה). The term מועף (Isa 8:23), however, is less certain, and some relate it to a root *עיף ("to gleam"); see, e.g., the entry for this term in *HALOT*. This understanding of עיפה as being related to the root "to be dark" is reflected also in the LXX (ὁμίχλη), Symmachus (ἑσπέρα), Vulg. (*nebula*), Syr. (ʿmtnʾ), Syro-Hexapla (*rmšʾ*), and also seems to lie behind the moralizing paraphrase in the Targum ("in order to bring darkness [חשוך] upon the wicked to destroy the wicked of the earth").

⁶More on this below.

⁷For the former position, see Horst, "Die Doxologien im Amosbuch," 50–53. For the latter, see the discussion in Jeremias, *Book of Amos*, 77.

⁸It is also not clearly the case, as many who argue for this understanding hold, that "the one who treads upon the high places of the earth" (Amos 4:13) and "the one who darkens day into night" (5:8) are also threatening images, especially as the latter is paired with "the one who turns

maintenance of the created order. Moreover, this sense also goes well beyond what is found in Amos 4:1–12 (the *Unheilsgeschichte* leading up to this doxological refrain), where punishments in Israel's past are explicitly understood to be didactic[9] and the future punishment is envisioned, somewhat concretely, in terms of exile (vv. 2–3) rather than apocalypse.[10]

Those who interpret the phrase as a creative and hopeful image—that is, as "the one who makes dawn out of darkness"—understand its syntax differently. They view it as a hyperbolic (or literal?) description in which עיפה is the material out of which the dawn (שחר) is made, implying one of the following assessments of the phrase's syntax: (1) a double construct chain with an objective genitive (שחר) followed by a genitive of material (עיפה);[11] or (2) a verb followed by a double accusative in which the first denotes the final, rendered product, and the second, the material.[12] Understood in this way, the image is essentially equivalent to that found in 5:8b, though perhaps with more emphasis on YHWH's beneficent creative activity than what is intended there.[13] Richard S. Cripps and Theodore H. Robinson, following the Greek, go a step further in finding here an image of YHWH creating both dawn and darkness—a translation that requires that darkness be understood

---

deep darkness into morning," emphasizing a more general control over creation. For a discussion of the former reference as positive, see below in section II.

[9] This is made especially clear by the repeated refrain "yet you did not return to me" in vv. 6, 8, 9, 10, and 11.

[10] Depending on how one understands the referent of כה ("thus") in 4:12, the punishment that is envisioned there may be akin either to the didactic punishments described in vv. 6–11 or to the exile described in vv. 2–3. In either case, our phrase in 4:13 goes beyond these by this translation.

[11] This view seems especially to inform the translation of Francis I. Andersen and David Noel Freedman, *Amos: A New Translation with Introduction and Commentary*, AB 24A (New York: Doubleday, 1988; repr., New Haven: Yale University Press, 2008), 453 ("the Maker of dawn out of darkness."). A possible parallel to this use might be found in Ps 104:4a. For the genitive of material, see GKC §128o.

[12] So apparently Julius Wellhausen, *Die kleinen Propheten übersetzt und erklärt*, 4th ed., Skizzen und Vorarbeiten 5 (Berlin: Reimer, 1963; orig. 1898), 5 ("der Dunkel zu Morgenrot macht"); Wilhelm Rudolph, *Joel-Amos-Obadiah-Jonah*, KAT 13.2 (Gütersloh: Mohn, 1971), 170 ("der zum Morgenlicht die Dunkelheit macht"). Examples of this construction are found in *IBHS*, 174 (§10.2.3c, examples 11–14), where it is described as being composed of a verb of creation with "*thing made + materials.*" The examples they cite, however, are not, strictly speaking, of the type supposed here in Amos (i.e., participle + accusative 1 + accusative 2); rather, two of the examples (Exod 38:3, Cant 3:10) are of the type accusative 1 (= thing made) + finite verb + accusative 2 (= material), one (Deut 27:6) is of the type accusative 1 (= material) + finite verb + accusative 2 (= thing made), and one (Gen 2:7) of the type finite verb + accusative 1 (= thing made) + accusative 2 (= material). It is precisely the participial form in our phrase in Amos 4:13 that casts doubt on this explanation, since the participle, functioning here as a gerund in reference to YHWH as the agent of creation, more likely forms part of a construct chain, as discussed above in n. 4. Clearer examples of this construction in Hebrew mark the thing made with the *lamed* of the product (as, e.g., Amos 5:8b), which is not present here.

[13] See n. 8 above.

as part of the created order.¹⁴ Although this latter notion is not absent from ancient Israelite creation theology, it appears to be a fairly late development.¹⁵ In any case, this reading is not well established in the manuscript tradition and is likely to be a late interpretive gloss.

One presupposition of all of the translations discussed above is that the term עיפה means "darkness." This translation has been revised at least twice by modern critics—first by Harry Torczyner, who understood it as a female "night-demon" on the basis of a proposed Aramaic cognate (עפתא) found in an incantation plaque from Arslan Tash,¹⁶ and second by Shalom Paul, who has completely reanalyzed our entire phrase. Following Ibn Janaḥ (ca. 990–ca. 1050), Paul argues that עיפה should be connected to a root *עיף ("brightness"), and he analyzes שַׁחַר as being related to *שחר ("blackness").¹⁷ Thus, Paul ultimately understands the phrase as a positive one ("Who turns blackness [שחר] into glimmering dawn [עיפה]"), corresponding to the praises of God the creator in the surrounding cola, while also preferring a syntactic explanation that is, as we have seen, typically relied upon by those advancing the opposite interpretation. While Paul has certainly made positive strides toward explaining how this phrase is in accord with the sense of those surrounding it and has offered an ingenious philological reanalysis of its terms, nevertheless, his attempt to understand שחר, which is clearly pointed in the MT as "dawn," as an otherwise unattested derivative of the Hebrew root *שחר ("blackness") is not very convincing.¹⁸ Thus, we leave our overview having established that Hebrew syntax is less of a deciding factor in the interpretation of our phrase than it is sometimes held to be. While the vast majority of previous interpretations are premised on the connection of עיפה to the root *עיף ("to be dark"), as we shall see further in the following section, this connection is far more tenuous than the

---

¹⁴ Richard S. Cripps, *A Critical and Exegetical Commentary on the Book of Amos*, rev. ed. (London: SPCK, 1969), 177; Theodore H. Robinson and Friedrich Horst, *Die Zwölf kleinen Propheten*, HAT 14 (Tübingen: Mohr Siebeck, 1964), 86. Although somewhat rare, explicit mention of YHWH creating darkness is found in Isa 45:7 and Job 38:9.

¹⁵ So, with reference to Isa 45:7, see, e.g., Jon D. Levenson, *Creation and the Persistence of Evil: The Jewish Drama of Divine Omnipotence* (Princeton: Princeton University Press, 1998), 124.

¹⁶ Harry Torczyner [Naphtali H. Tur-Sinai], "A Hebrew Incantation against Night-Demons from Biblical Times" *JNES* 6 (1947): 20. Torczyner, who clearly relates עפתא here to a root *עיף ("to be dark"), translates Amos 4:13 as, "He turns into morning the ʿEpha(ta)-demon(s) of the darkness." For a similar view, see André Dupont-Sommer, "L'inscription de l'amulette d'Arslan-Tash," *RHR* 120 (1939): 135 ("à la nuit"). This term עפתא and its potential relationship to עיפה will be discussed further in section II below.

¹⁷ Paul, *Amos*, 155.

¹⁸ As a comparable example he cites שַׁחַר in Joel 2:2, translating it there as "soot," but it is not clear that this translation is valid either. This latter instance is understood as another occurrence of שַׁחַר ("dawn") in *HALOT*, BDB, and by the majority of commentators. Other known nominal and adjectival patterns in Hebrew that are related to the concept of "blackness," are of the *qatul* (e.g., שָׁחֹר, Lev 13:31, 37; Cant 1:5; 5:11; Zech 6:2, 6) or *qutāl* (e.g., שְׁחוֹר, Lam 4:8) types (assuming that the latter is not an Aramaic loanword, which it may be). A *qatl* root is entirely hypothetical.

overwhelming scholarly support would seem to suggest. I move now to offer an alternative understanding of the phrase.

II

Contrary to the opinions surveyed above, I suggest that the term עֵיפָה is related to the root עוּף ("to fly") and has close cognates in the Phoenician term עפת, found in the famous stele of king Yeḥawmilk of Byblos from the fifth century BCE, and in the Aramaic term עפתא, found in the amulet from Arslan Tash mentioned briefly above. This new understanding of עֵיפָה, I suggest, has interesting consequences for the understanding of Amos 4:13 and its relationship to Israelite religious conceptions. The Yeḥawmilk stele[19] contains a relief in its upper portion that depicts King Yeḥawmilk making an offering to the "Lady of Byblos," and above this scene is found an image of the winged sun disk (see figure 1).[20] What is especially remarkable about this stele for our purposes is that it most likely attests to the Semitic term that was given to the winged sun disk: עפת.[21]

Figure 1. Yeḥawmilk Relief

---

[19] The Yeḥawmilk stele was originally discovered in 1869 and exists in two pieces, which are currently kept in the Louvre (AO 22368) and in the Beirut Museum. Photographs can be found in Josette Elayi, *Byblos, Cité Sacrée (8ᵉ-4ᵉ s. av. J.-C.)*, Transeuphratène Supplement 15 (Paris: Gabalda, 2009), plate VII, and at the Louvre website, http://www.louvre.fr/en/node/38534.

[20] A comparable scene can be found in the plaque numbered AO 27197, for which see Eric Gubel, "Une nouvelle représentation du culte de la Baalat Gebal?" in *Religio Phoenicia: Acta coloquii Namurcensis habiti diebus 14 et 15 mensis Decembris anni 1984*, ed. Corine Bonnet, Edward Lipiński, and Patrick Marchetti, Studia Phoenicia 4 (Namur: Société des études classiques, 1986), 263–76.

[21] The winged disk icon was especially prominent in ancient Egypt but is also found throughout ancient Near Eastern iconography. For a discussion of the significance of the winged disk in the twenty-first Egyptian dynasty, see Beatrice L. Goff, *Symbols of Ancient Egypt in the Late Period: The Twenty-First Dynasty*, Religion and Society 13 (The Hague: Mouton, 1979), 249–55. For its wider use throughout the ancient Near East, see Otto Eissfeldt, "Die Flügelsonne als

The relevant portion of the text reads as follows:

ופעל אנך לרבתי בעלת גבל המזבח נחשת זן אש בח[ן] [ז] ז והפתח חרץ זן
אש על פן פתחי ז והעפֿת חרץ אש בתכת אבן אש על פתח חרץ זן

> And I made for my lady, the Mistress of Byblos, this bronze altar that is in this [ ] and this carved[22] engraving that is on top of this, my engraving, and the winged disk of gold that is in the midst of the stone above this carved engraving. (*KAI* 10.3b–5)

What is being described here, as many others have pointed out before, is an offering by Yeḥawmilk that consists, in part, of this very stele. The stele was made to be ornate and, therefore, suitable both as an offering to the goddess and as an appropriate fixture in the religious space of which it was a part.[23] The description of the winged disk as an עפת, a reading first offered by Maurice Dunand,[24] likely reflects an attempt to name this ubiquitous image in a way that made sense to the Semitic-speaking people that encountered it. This term is likely cognate with Egyptian ʿpy, which was applied to the winged sun disk in the Late Period of Egyptian history (664–332 BCE) and commonly held to be Semitic.[25] It is certain, therefore, that this description of the winged sun disk as "the flying thing" had wider currency in the ancient Near East—especially, as we see, in the mid-first millennium—and was commonly used to designate the winged solar disk.

A second cognate may be found in the Arslan Tash amulet mentioned briefly above (*KAI* 27), which dates to the seventh century BCE.[26] The amulet is addressed

---

künstlerisches Motiv und als religiöses Symbol," in *Kleine Schriften*, 6 vols. (Tübingen: Mohr Siebeck, 1963), 2:416–19; Tallay Ornan, "A Complex System of Religious Symbols: The Case of the Winged Disc in Near Eastern Imagery of the First Millennium BCE," in *Crafts and Images in Contact: Studies on Eastern Mediterranean Art of the First Millennium BCE*, ed. Claudia E. Suter and Christoph Uehlinger, OBO 210 (Fribourg: Academic Press; Göttingen: Vandenhoeck & Ruprecht, 2005), 207–41.

[22] I follow the majority of scholars in finding two separate lexemes among the three occurrences of חרץ in these lines, for which see *DNWSI* 1:406–7 (s.v. חרץ$_4$ and חרץ$_5$).

[23] For a discussion of the archaeology and iconography of Phoenician religious spaces, including some discussion of Byblos and this stele, see Nicholas C. Vella, "Defining Phoenician Religious Space: Oumm el-ʿAmed Reconsidered," *ANES* 37 (2000): 27–55.

[24] Maurice Dunand, "Encore la stele de Yehavmilk roi de Byblos," *Bulletin du Musée de Beyrouth* 5 (1941): 74. This reading is followed by André Dupont-Sommer, "L'inscription de Yehawmilk, Roi de Byblos," *Sem* 3 (1950): 6; *KAI* 1:2 (#10); John C. L. Gibson, *Textbook of Syrian Semitic Inscriptions*, vol. 3, *Phoenician Inscriptions Including Inscriptions in the Mixed Dialect of Arslan Tash* (Oxford: Clarendon, 1982), 94; and Stanislav Segert, *COS* 2:151. Although he agrees that the term refers to the winged disk depicted in the relief, Shmuel Yeiven argues that the term should be read as והעדת, "decoration" ("'Ēdūth," *IEJ* 24 [1974]: 18–19). This is similar to the understanding of Franz Rosenthal in *ANET*, 656 ("engraved object of gold"). The reading והערת, "uraeus," is found in *NE*, 416; and *CIS* 1:6–8.

[25] See *WÄS* 1:179, s.v. ʿpj; and Dieter Wildung, "Flügelsonne," in *LÄ* 2:278–79.

[26] The plaque in question, commonly designated AT1, was written in Phoenician (occasionally incorrectly described in the literature as Hebrew) with occasional frozen Aramaic forms

to a series of intercessory figures, one of which is given the designation עפתא.[27] W. F. Albright's translation of this term as "O Flyers," has been widely adopted by many scholars,[28] and it seems to be the most plausible since it is clearly correlated with the winged cherub with human head on the upper obverse portion of the amulet (figure 2).[29] Taken together, these two cognates from *KAI* 10 and 27, with their associated (though admittedly different) images of winged figures, attest to concrete conceptual and iconographical associations with nouns derived from עוף ("to fly") in the ancient West Semitic world. Considering that the term עיפה in Amos 4:13 may reflect similar associations, particularly with the image of the winged sun disk, which is alluded to elsewhere in the Hebrew Bible in Mal 3:20 (Eng. 4:2) and attested iconographically in the *lmlk* seals, it remains for us to show how this new proposal adds to our understanding of that verse.[30]

(as with our עפתא) and was originally published by Le Comte du Mesnil du Buisson, "Une tablette magique de la région du moyen Euphrate," in *Mélanges Syriens offerts a Monsieur René Dussaud*, 2 vols. (Paris: Geuthner, 1939), 1:421–34. Subsequent to this initial publication, many readings were substantially revised by William Foxwell Albright, "An Aramaean Magical Text in Hebrew from the Seventh Century B.C.," *BASOR* 76 (1939): 5–11. For a response affirming the authenticity of the amulets in light of the more recent suspicion that they were forgeries, see the discussion in Dennis Pardee, "Les documents d'Arslan Tash: Authentiques ou faux?" *Syria* 75 (1988): 15–54.

[27] Critics differ as to whether this designation appears once or twice on the obverse of this amulet. That לעפתא appears on the winged sphinx/cherub is universally held. Disagreement centers on whether this term also appears in the first line of the main text on this side of the amulet. The reading לעתא was initially offered by du Mesnil du Buisson, which he understood as a proper noun ("Une tablette magique," 422), and he has since been followed by Dupont-Sommer, "L'inscription de Yeḥawmilk," 134–35; Javier Teixidor, "Les tablettes d'Arslan Tash au Musée d'Alep," *AuOr* 48 (1971): 106; André Caquot, "Observations sur la première tablette magique d'Arslan Tash," *JANES* 5 (1973): 46; and Pardee, "Les documents d'Arslan Tash," 18. The reading לעפתא was proposed as an alternative by Albright ("Aramaean Magical Text," 7), and he has since been followed by Frank Moore Cross and Richard J. Saley, "Phoenician Incantations on a Plaque of the Seventh Century BCE from Arslan Tash in Upper Syria," in Cross, *Leaves from an Epigrapher's Notebook: Collected Papers in Hebrew and West Semitic Palaeography and Epigraphy*, HSS 51 (Winona Lake, IN: Eisenbrauns, 2003), 265–69; and Wolfgang Röllig, "Die Amulette von Arslan Taş," in *Neue Ephemeris für Semitische Epigraphik*, ed. Rainer Degen, Walter W. Müller, and Wolfgang Röllig, 3 vols. (Weisbaden: Harrassowitz, 1974), 2:18–19.

[28] Torczyner, as we have seen above, translates "night-demon," deriving it from עוף, "to be dark" ("Hebrew Incantation," 19–20). This understanding seems to be affected, to some degree, by the designation for another of the intercessory figures as ללין—a moniker that is itself often translated "night-demon" but that is certainly related to the *lilû* and *lilītu* demons known from Akkadian texts.

[29] This translation is followed by Cross and Saley, "Phoenician Incantations," 267–68; P. Kyle McCarter, *COS* 2:223; Röllig, "Die Amulette von Arslan Taş," 18–19; Donner and Röllig, *KAI* 2:44. It was emended slightly by Rosenthal in *ANET*, 658 ("female flying demon").

[30] The phrase "the one who makes the Pleiades and Orion," which is found in the second doxology (Amos 5:8), supports the contention that the doxologies are more broadly concerned with astrological phenomena. For the following couplet in Amos 5:8b, compare Ps 104:19–23.

Figure 2. Arslan Tash Amulet 1

Understanding עיפה as a designation for the winged sun disk, we may now either translate the phrase as "the one who makes of dawn the winged disk" or perhaps "the one who makes at dawn the winged disk." The latter translation understands שחר as an adverbial accusative with temporal force. Viewed in light of its immediate context in Amos 4:13, this interpretation avoids the pitfalls, discussed above, of introducing an ominous image at this point in the doxology and makes the logic behind its balanced structure more readily perceptible. We may now recognize Amos 4:13 to contain the following chiastic structure:

A Behold! The one who forms *mountains*/
   B the one who <u>creates</u> wind/
      C and the one who tells to mankind what his thoughts are/
   B´ the one who <u>makes</u> the winged disk at dawn /
A´ the one who treads upon the *high places* of the earth

—YHWH, God of the hosts is his name.

The thematic balancing in this verse, which I have indicated in the translation above, is now rather obvious. A and A´ contain balanced references to mountains and high places respectively, and B and B´ contain references to YHWH as the creator of wind, on the one hand, and of the winged disk, on the other. C contains the climactic statement of this doxology, declaring YHWH to be the one who reveals his thoughts to humanity. B and B´ may be compared further in their subject matter, for neither seems to restrict its gaze to YHWH's original creation of the cosmos; rather, both have in view YHWH's role as the agent behind recurring events in the created order.[31]

In explaining this verse as an entirely positive description of YHWH's role in creation, as I have, I come finally to the line I have designated here as A´, which is also occasionally understood as an image of destruction. Here we may ask further if there is any connection between lines B´ and A´ of this doxology as there is formally, if not conceptually, between lines A and B.[32] To help us to understand the way in which B´ and A´ together may be construed positively, we turn to a Phoenician bulla from Acco that, like these two lines, unites a divine image with the winged sun disk and a mountain (figure 3).[33] Here we find an image of two caprids and a palmette—a common way of depicting the goddess in the West Semitic world[34]—on top of a mountain or hill with the sun disk above. This image and others like it have come to be understood as having overtones of creation, and especially of the goddess's role in sustaining creation, reflected in the tree providing nourishment for the animals but also in the natural setting and in the presence of the stars and rising sun.[35] Moreover, the connection between solar deities and hills is well known in various different religious environments in the ancient Near East, especially in the Heliopolite mythology in Egypt and in Mesopotamian hymns to Shamash.[36] Although it cannot be proven definitively, it appears that Amos 4:13

---

[31] Jeremias (*Book of Amos*, 79) and others have concluded that the second line in this verse (my C) is a secondary insertion. This need not be the case, though, since the verse, as I have explained, is not solely focused on YHWH's role as the *original author* of creation but also on YHWH's creative role in sustaining it, and divine communication with humanity may be seen through this lens as a necessary part of that process.

[32] Formally, A and B are two-stress units in Hebrew, whereas B´ and A´ are three-stress units.

[33] This bulla was first published in Raphael Giveon and Trude Kertesz, *Egyptian Scarabs and Seals from Acco: From the Collection of the Israel Department of Antiquities and Museums* (Freiburg, Switzerland: Universitätsverlag, 1986), 44–45 (#173). They call it an "Achaemian mixed style" and describe its content as follows: "Two goats crowned by stars, on a 'sacred mountain,' ending in a column, decorated with the Phoenician palmette, above this scene: the winged disk. Stars on back of both animals." This bulla is also discussed briefly by Othmar Keel and Christoph Uehlinger, *Gods, Goddesses, and Images of God in Ancient Israel*, trans. Thomas H. Trapp (Minneapolis: Fortress, 1998), 377–78 (#362), who cite it as a rare example of the Phoenician attempt in the Iron Age III to maintain cultural and artistic continuity with the Canaanite tradition. See also Othmar Keel, *Corpus der Stempelsiegel-Amulette aus Palästina/Israel: Von den Anfängen bis zur Perserzeit*, Katalog Band 1, *Von Tell Abu Farağ bis ʿAtlit*, with Daphna Ben-Tor, Bertrand Jaeger, Andrea Jäkle, et al., OBO 13 (Freiburg, Switzerland: Universitätsverlag; Göttingen: Vandenhoeck & Ruprecht, 1997), 580–81 (#144).

[34] For the close association of such an image with goddesses in the ancient Near East (including Israel), see Othmar Keel, *Goddesses and Trees, New Moon and Yahweh: Ancient Near Eastern Art and the Hebrew Bible*, JSOTSup 261 (Sheffield: Sheffield Academic, 1998), 20–48.

[35] Keel and Uehlinger, *Gods, Goddesses, and Images of God*, 72–74.

[36] For this connection in Egyptian literature (i.e., between the rising of the sun god and the primeval hill), see, e.g., *ANET*, 3 (Heliopolis), 8 (Thebes), and, somewhat differently, *ANET*, 12.

B′ and A′ may be drawing upon such associations, which are, of course, substantially demythologized here.

Figure 3. Acco Bulla[37]

Finally, the doxology in Amos 4:13, though not necessarily originally bound to that context, has, nevertheless, been inserted here to serve a particular function in the book of Amos.[38] Viewing this doxology in the way I have explained it here—that is, as a true praise of YHWH with its image of his daily sponsoring of the winged disk's rise into the heavens—this function would seem to be in (1) magnifying YHWH's ability to bring the previously mentioned judgment about, (2) proclaiming his right to do so, and, perhaps more to the point, (3) affirming that *in doing so* YHWH is performing a necessary part of his role as the sustainer of creation. Israel's sin, after all, is always a threat to holiness, as the earlier part of this chapter makes abundantly clear, and the particular sins described there—oppression of the poor and excessive financial aggrandizement—particularly threaten to unravel society. YHWH, whose final threat against Israel had been pronounced in 4:12, not only will act but, according to 4:13, must act.

For Mesopotamia, I call attention to several lines in the hymn (or compendium of hymns) to the sun god Shamash. The following are excerpted from the translation of Ferris J. Stephens in *ANET*, 387: "The mighty mountains are covered with thy brightness" (i.19); "When thou art risen over the mountains thou dost scan the earth" (i.21); "Which are the mountains that have not clothed themselves with thy brilliance?" (iv.6). Moreover, we may cite a more general comparison with Babylonian cosmology, wherein Shamash was thought to make his daily entrance into the upper world through the "eastern gate" located in the Hashur mountains, for a discussion of which see Piotr Steinkeller, "Of Stars and Men: The Conceptual and Mythological Setup of Babylonian Extispicy," in *Biblical and Oriental Essays in Memory of William L. Moran*, ed. Agustinus Gianto, BibOr 48 (Rome: Pontifical Biblical Institute, 2005), 18–21.

[37] Compare also the scene on the eighth-century BCE Phoenician bowl from Praeneste, Italy, cited by Vella, "Defining Phoenician Religious Space," 53 (fig. 6).

[38] For the possible lateness of the doxologies, see the sources cited above in n. 1.

III

In concluding the discussion, it remains for me to state where Amos 4:13 fits in the broader repertoire of Yahwistic solar imagery found in the Hebrew Bible. As I have explained it above, we are not dealing here with further evidence of solar language or imagery applied to YHWH himself.[39] Rather, the winged sun disk in Amos is something over which YHWH has full control and which he daily causes to rise as part of his ongoing and benevolent maintenance of the universe. We have seen above how this image is paired with the creation of the wind in the chiastic structuring of this verse. A parallel may be found, for example, in Ps 19:5b–7 [Eng. 4b–6]:[40]

> He has set a tent for the sun in [the heavens];/
> it comes out like a bridegroom from his wedding canopy,/
> and like a strong man runs its course with joy.
> Its rising is from the end of the heavens,/
> and its circuit to the end of them;/
> and nothing is hid from its heat.

Thus, the author of Amos 4:13 viewed the winged sun disk as something that ultimately signaled YHWH's total control over a well-ordered creation, a control that ideally redounds to the benefit of a faithful people. We, therefore, have in this image of YHWH daily forming the winged disk something of an *interpretatio Hebraica* of a widespread ancient Near Eastern icon.

---

[39] For discussion of this phenomenon, see Hans-Peter Stähli, *Solare Elemente im Jahweglauben des Alten Testaments*, OBO 66 (Freiburg, Switzerland: Universitätsverlag; Göttingen: Vandenhoeck & Ruprecht, 1985); J. Glen Taylor, *Yahweh and the Sun: Biblical and Archaeological Evidence for Sun Worship in Ancient Israel*, JSOTSup 111 (Sheffield: JSOT Press, 1993); Mark S. Smith, *The Early History of God: Yahweh and the Other Deities in Ancient Israel*, 2nd ed. (Grand Rapids: Eerdmans, 2002), 148–59. In addition to the direct application of solar appellations, the imagery in the Psalms related to seeing the divine face and to wings also has some relationship to solar metaphors, for which see Mark S. Smith, "'Seeing God' in the Psalms: The Background to the Beatific Vision in the Hebrew Scriptures," *CBQ* 50 (1988): 171–83; Joel LeMon, *Yahweh's Winged Form in the Psalms: Exploring Congruent Iconography and Texts*, OBO 242 (Fribourg: Academic Press; Göttingen: Vandenhoeck & Ruprecht, 2010).

[40] Rudolph, *Joel–Amos–Obadiah–Jonah*, 182. For a discussion of this section of Ps 19 and its relation to ancient Near Eastern solar imagery, see Nahum Sarna, "Psalm XIX and the Near Eastern Sun-God Literature," in *Fourth World Congress of Jewish Studies* (Jerusalem: World Union of Jewish Studies, 1965), 1:171–75. Compare also Job 38:12–13, Sir 43:1–5.

Cross-Gendered Romans and Mark's Jesus: Legion Enters the Pigs (Mark 5:1–20)

WARREN CARTER
warren.carter@tcu.edu
Brite Divinity School, Texas Christian University, Fort Worth, TX 76129

This reading engages two important and related dimensions of Mark's scene of Legion entering the pigs. First, is the name Legion to be understood as signifying numbers (Gundry), or as a largely nonintegrated or secondary military detail (Marcus, Collins), or, as will be argued here, a military reference that is, along with other military terms and motifs, central to the scene? Second, how might we understand the demon's unusual request to enter the pigs? Seeking to integrate a military meaning for the name "Legion" with an explanation for the demon's request to enter the pigs, and employing imperial-critical, masculinity, and sociopolitical-narrative approaches, this paper highlights the scene's polyvalent gendered and military-imperial language that has often been neglected since Derrett's brief but undeveloped 1979 reference to it. My argument is that the scene inscribes Jesus's hegemonic masculinity even while it mocks Roman power as an out-of-control, demonic, militaristic, and (self-)destructive masculinity, and fantasizes Rome's defeat as womanly weakness at Jesus's superior, commanding, masculine hands. Attention to the scene's cross-gendering, which draws from imperial-critical and gendered perspectives, has been ignored in previous work.

This article engages two matters of significance for reading Mark's "exorcism-of-Legion" scene (5:1–20). The first concerns the contribution of the nomenclature of "Legion." Is the term about numbers,[1] or a largely nonintegrated or secondary military detail,[2] or is it a military reference that is, along with others, central to the scene?[3] This reading develops the third approach.

[1] Robert Gundry, *Mark: A Commentary on His Apology for the Cross* (Grand Rapids: Eerdmans, 1993), 260.

[2] Joel Marcus, *Mark 1–8: A New Translation with Introduction and Commentary*, AB 27 (New York: Doubleday, 2000), 351–52; Adela Yarbro Collins, *Mark: A Commentary*, Hermeneia (Minneapolis: Fortress, 2007), 269–70. I will contest Marcus's view that Mark has no "anti-Roman sentiments" (pp. 351–52), and Collins's claim that there is "no theme of opposition to Rome in Mark" (p. 269).

[3] Walter Wink, *Unmasking the Powers: The Invisible Forces That Determine Human Existence* (Philadelphia: Fortress, 1986), 43–48; Ched Myers, *Binding the Strong Man: A Political Reading of*

The second matter concerns how we read the unusual request of the demon named Legion to enter into the pigs (Mark 5:12). Earlier twentieth-century interpreters regularly offered theological explanations for this request:[4] God defeats Satan and Jesus tricks the demons—at least partially though not yet fully; or, much less commonly, the demons trick Jesus; or the drowned pigs display Jesus's miraculous exorcistic powers. More recent twentieth- and twenty-first-century studies— even those with more historical-critical interests—tend to take the request in their narrative stride, seeing it as a win-win bargaining situation for exorcist and demons, though claims of Jesus's victory do not seem far away.[5]

This article builds on this narrative turn but finds the frequent spiritualized/ theological approaches neglectful of important dimensions of the scene. Seeking to integrate the name "Legion" with an explanation for the demon's request to enter the pigs, I attend to the scene's polyvalent gendered and military-imperial language. My argument is that the scene inscribes Jesus's hegemonic masculinity even while it mocks Roman power as an out-of-control, demonic, militaristic, and (self-) destructive masculinity and fantasizes Rome's defeat as womanly weakness at Jesus's superior, commanding, masculine hands. Attention to the scene's cross-gendering, which draws from imperial-critical and gendered perspectives, has been ignored in previous work.[6]

Important to this reading are the scene's military language and motifs, which have received little attention in interpretations of the scene. In a sometime-quoted

---

Mark's Story of Jesus (Maryknoll, NY: Orbis Books, 1988), 190–94; Richard A. Horsley, *Hearing the Whole Story: The Politics of Plot in Mark's Gospel* (Louisville: Westminster John Knox, 2001), 140–48; Stephen D. Moore, "'My Name Is Legion, for We Are Many': Representing Empire in Mark," in Moore, *Empire and Apocalypse: Postcolonialism and the New Testament*, Bible in the Modern World 12 (Sheffield: Sheffield Phoenix, 2006), 24–44; Hans Leander, *Discourses of Empire: The Gospel of Mark from a Postcolonial Perspective*, SemeiaSt 71 (Atlanta: Society of Biblical Literature, 2013), 201–19.

[4] For reviews, see Hermann Ridderbos, *The Coming of the Kingdom* (Philadelphia: Presbyterian and Reformed, 1962), 113–15; H. van der Loos, *The Miracles of Jesus*, NovTSup 9 (Leiden: Brill, 1968), 389–93.

[5] Gerd Theissen, *The Miracle Stories of the Early Christian Tradition* (Philadelphia: Fortress, 1983), 57; Marcus, *Mark 1–8*, 352; Collins, *Mark: A Commentary*, 270–71; R. Alan Culpepper, *Mark*, SHBC (Macon GA; Smyth & Helwys, 2007), 168.

[6] Three excellent discussions of masculinity and Mark give the scene minimal attention. Tat-siong Benny Liew, "Re-Mark-able Masculinities: Jesus, the Son of Man, and the (Sad) Sum of Manhood?" in *New Testament Masculinities*, ed. Stephen D. Moore and Janice Capel Anderson, SemeiaSt 45 (Atlanta: Society of Biblical Literature, 2003), 93–135, esp. 113–14, briefly noting Jesus's masculinity in relation to foreigners (Romans, Gerasenes); and, in the same volume, Eric Thurman, "Looking for a Few Good Men: Mark and Masculinity," 137–61, esp. 148, briefly highlighting military dimensions, as does (with a little more detail) Colleen Conway, *Behold the Man: Jesus and Greco-Roman Masculinity* (Oxford: Oxford University Press, 2008), 94–95, emphasizing Jesus's strength as a military conqueror. None explores the gendered dimensions of the scene as in the following argument.

but rarely engaged 1979 article, J. Duncan M. Derrett briefly asserted the "military overtones" of several terms,[7] though they played little part in his analysis, and his support for several items, notably ἀγέλη (5:11) and ἐπιτρέπειν (5:13), was dubious. Graham Twelftree certainly does not find Derrett convincing, dismissing any military significance for "Legion" and finding Derrett's other claims "of little consequence for ἀποστέλλω, ἐπιτρέπω, ὁρμάω, and ἀγέλη have wide varieties of meanings that do not, of themselves, suggest a military motif."[8] Twelftree is correct to notice that language has multiple uses, yet, as I will demonstrate, his dismissal of this multivalence seems unsustainable when the scene's cluster of military motifs and vocabulary is given attention.

Accordingly, this reading employs imperial-military, gender (especially masculinity), and sociopolitical-narrative approaches. Imperial (critical) approaches foreground the interactions of NT texts with the diverse structures, personnel, practices, and ideologies of Roman power; military dimensions are to the fore in this reading. Gender approaches employ interrelated notions of gender, sex, and hegemonic masculinity (explicated in the next section), here with a focus on gender performance that involves the genitals.[9] A sociopolitical-narrative approach concerns itself with the Gospel's narrative as "rhetorical in character" involving "discursive or communicative interactions between the author of a text and its readers, both past and present."[10] It does not claim any representation of an actual event but recognizes that the narrative is embedded in, assumes, and inscribes cultural, ideological, social, and political structures from the world in which it originates.

I

My starting point is to observe the presentation of Jesus in the chapters preceding 5:1–20. I employ R. W. Connell's notion of "hegemonic masculinity" to identify what forms the basis for Jesus's gendered roles in this scene. Connell, drawing on Antonio Gramsci's analysis of class relations in terms of social dominance, defines hegemonic masculinity as a "pattern of masculinity" comprising "configurations of practice generated in particular situations and in a changing structure of relationships" that guarantee "the dominant position of men and the subordination

---

[7] J. Duncan M. Derrett, "Contributions to the Study of the Gerasene Demoniac," *JSNT* 3 (1979): 2–17, esp. 5–6.

[8] Graham H. Twelftree, *Jesus the Exorcist: A Contribution to the Study of the Historical Jesus*, WUNT 2/54 (Tübingen: Mohr, 1993), 76–77.

[9] Gender concerns "the performative aspect of being a 'man' or a 'woman,' the cultural role models one adopts to act as one or the other." Sex refers "to the physical aspects of being identified as 'male' or 'female.'" So Caroline Vander Stichele and Todd Penner, *Contextualizing Gender in Early Christian Discourse: Thinking beyond Thecla* (New York: T&T Clark, 2009), 4.

[10] Ibid.

of women."[11] This societal and gendered domination is both a societally and "historically mobile relation" that can be contested and destabilized by both women and men in changing cultural patterns. Connell notes a paradox within hegemonic masculinity involving both complicity and marginalizing subordination. While dominance is achievable by only some men, is agonistic, and needs to be maintained through constant performance, other men are complicit in benefitting from it without assuming the risk of dominance. This means that societal dominance is exerted not only over women but also over men who do not necessarily seek or actively support dominance. And given these gender hierarchies, not only are some men excluded from the ranks of the culturally dominant, some are disadvantaged and marginalized by dominant males in contexts, for example, of imperial structures, where a very small percentage of elite males exert power at the expense of others. Male identity is therefore polyvalent and contested. Connell recognizes that gender dynamics are not isolated from other structures such as class and race.

Jesus enters ch. 5 with his hegemonic masculinity well in place. In Mark 1–4, Jesus's imperially imitative and contestive masculine identity as "God's son"[12] (1:1, 11) is expressed in dominant practices of gendered power authorized by God. He continually achieves and maintains masculinity through the performance of public rhetoric, providing teaching and instruction (1:15, 35–39; 4:3–9), as well as competing with and besting the male leaders through challenge and riposte interactions that separate the men from the boys and the men from the women (2:1–12).[13] He exercises authority over other men's lives in summoning them to follow him; they sustain his power by submitting to him (1:16–20, 2:14, 3:13–19). He exercises power over the lives of men and women by ridding them of diseases, physical impediments, and demons (1:21–28, 29–34, 39; 2:1–12; 3:1–6, 10–12). He challenges the ruling power of male, Galilean, imperially allied officials[14] in asserting control over matters such as access to God's forgiveness (2:1–12), Sabbath observance (2:1–12, 23–28), meal companions (2:15–17), and the legitimacy of his authority (3:22–30). He claims and demonstrates power over land (4:3–9, 13–20, 26–29) and sea (4:35–41), asserting God's sovereignty (Ps 24:1, Gen 1:6–10), imitating yet contesting the imperial sovereignty over "land and sea" associated with

---

[11] On hegemonic masculinity and notions of subordination, complicity, and marginalization, see Robert W. Connell, *Masculinities* (Berkeley: University of California Press, 1995), 76–81; for discussion, see Toby Miller, "Masculinity," in *A Companion to Gender Studies*, ed. Philomena Essed, David Theo Goldberg, and Aubrey Kobayashi (Oxford: Blackwell, 2005), 114–31, esp. 116–18.

[12] Simon Samuel, *A Postcolonial Reading of Mark's Story of Jesus*, LNTS 340 (London: T&T Clark, 2007), 89–97; Michael Peppard, *The Son of God in the Roman World: Divine Sonship in Its Social and Political Context* (Oxford: Oxford University Press, 2011).

[13] Maud Gleason, *Making Men: Sophists and Self-Presentation in Ancient Rome* (Princeton: Princeton University Press, 1995); Conway, *Behold the Man*, 30–34.

[14] Anthony J. Saldarini, *Pharisees, Scribes and Sadducees in Palestinian Society* (1988; repr., Grand Rapids: Eerdmans, 2001), 35–49, 144–73.

elite males and Roman emperors.[15] In all of these activities, Jesus demonstrates the repertoire of masculine characteristics or virtues that Colleen Conway highlights as constituting Roman manliness: piety toward God, self-control and control over others, public moderation, courage, wisdom, and justice. One virtue, though, is missing, that of military dominance.[16]

This manly man, Jesus, comes into "the country of the Gerasenes" (5:1).[17] Of what significance is the location? Commonly, interpreters emphasize that the region is inhabited by gentiles, especially interpreters who read the story in terms of the transformations of a demon-possessed wild man into an apostle to the gentiles.[18] Adela Yarbro Collins, however, argues correctly that "the gentile character of Gerasa ... should not be overemphasized" with "Jewish remains from the Roman period ... well known from Gerasa."[19] Josephus also presents (somewhat irenic) interactions between gentiles and Jews in Gerasa (*J.W.* 2.480). A reading centered on ethnicity is not adequate.

With other scholars, Stephen Moore highlights the exorcism by arguing that the Hebrew root of the name Gerasa (*grš*) means "banish," "drive out," "cast out." The name thereby signifies "the land in need of exorcism" and indicates Jesus's arrival in a place whose very name "constitutes a preexisting appeal to ... his (now) manifest destiny to drive out the powers that possess them."[20] Moore's reading of the scene draws together demon possession, exorcism, and Roman occupation.[21]

Hans Leander helpfully develops the suggestion made by several interpreters concerning military-imperial associations with Gerasa.[22] He points to a scene

---

[15] For example, the Seleucid Antiochus IV Epiphanes (2 Macc 9:8), and the Roman emperors Augustus (Philo, *Flacc.* 1.104; *Legat.* 1.309), Tiberius (Philo, *Legat.* 1.141), Gaius Caligula (*Legat.* 1.44; Josephus, *Ant.* 19.81), Vespasian (Josephus, *J.W.* 3.401–402), Titus (*J.W.* 6.43), Domitian (Juvenal, *Sat* 4.83; Philostratus, *Vit. Apoll.* 7.3), and Trajan (Pliny, *Pan.* 4.4). See Rick Strelan, "A Greater than Caesar: Storm Stories in Lucan and Mark," *ZNW* 91 (2000): 166–79, esp. 167–76.

[16] Conway, *Behold the Man*, 22–30.

[17] The textual traditions locate the scene variously in the district or country of the Gerasenes, of the Gergesenes, or of the Gadarenes. The first option, "Gerasenes" (5:1), has the best manuscript attestation in Alexandrian (Sinaiticus and Vaticanus) and Western (Bezae) manuscript traditions. It is also the most difficult reading because the town of Gerasa is today some thirty-five or so miles southeast of the Sea of Galilee, a rather lengthy run for the pigs (5:13). See Bruce Metzger, *A Textual Commentary on the Greek New Testament: A Companion Volume to the United Bible Societies' Greek New Testament (3d ed.)* (London: United Bible Societies, 1971), 23–24, 84; Collins, *Mark: A Commentary*, 263–64.

[18] John F. Craghan, "The Gerasene Demoniac," *CBQ* 30 (1968): 522–36, esp. 524, 534.

[19] Collins, *Mark: A Commentary*, 267, quoting Eric Meyers, "Jesus and His Galilean Context," in *Archaeology and the Galilee: Texts and Contexts in the Graeco-Roman and Byzantine Periods*, ed. Douglas R. Edwards and C. Thomas McCollough, SFSHJ 143 (Atlanta: Scholars Press, 1997), 57–66, esp. 62.

[20] Moore, "'My Name Is Legion,'" 28.

[21] Ibid., 26.

[22] Leander, *Discourses of Empire*, 212–15.

narrated by Josephus in which, during the 66–70 war, General Vespasian sends a force of cavalry and infantry under Lucius Annius to attack Gerasa (*J.W.* 4.487–489). According to Josephus, the military force displayed its overwhelming power in killing a thousand young men, taking their families captive, plundering the town, burning houses, and attacking surrounding villages. Leander recognizes that scholars have raised questions about the historical accuracy, motivation, and placement of Josephus's report in his account. What matters more, Leander rightly argues, are the "painful poetics of Gerasa" that associate Gerasa with a vicious and murderous assertion of Rome's military power at the instigation of the now emperor Vespasian. In gender terms, these military actions performed Rome's hegemonic masculinity in Gerasa to devastating effect. Jesus's interactions in this place with forces designated by a military term *Legion* create an important contestive and imitative intertextuality with Roman military and masculine power.

II

In Mark's narrative, Roman power dominates the area not only by these "painful poetics" but also by means of the man possessed by a demon named Legion. This domination is established through the inability to bind the man with chains (5:3–4a), by the numerous futile attempts to do so (πολλάκις), and by the absence of anyone to match—let alone exceed—his strength (5:4b). The narrative accounts for this power in terms of an unclean spirit whose name is Legion (5:2, 9).

There has been much debate as to whether the name should be read with military dimensions.[23] As is well known, the name Legion refers to the central unit of the Roman army comprising in the late first century around fifty-four hundred troops divided into ten cohorts. There were twenty-eight legions at the end of the first century CE.[24] Is this military structure of any relevance here? Those who resist the link point to the explanation in 5:9b, "for we are many," to claim that the name signifies numerical, not military, power.[25] But the antithesis is a false one. The attention in 5:9b to numerical power in no way obliterates the military source and nature of this power. High numbers of military resources are not antithetical to, but expressions of, military might. And as I detail below, this name occurs in a passage that employs a significant number of terms capable of military interpretation. Reading "Legion," then, as a term denoting military power involves recognizing both the importance of numbers and the common cultural knowledge of Rome's military effectiveness. Significantly, the use of the name Legion immediately links

---

[23] For a summary and convincing argument concerning its military referent, see Joshua Garroway, "The Invasion of a Mustard Seed: A Reading of Mark 5:1–20," *JSNT* 32 (2009): 57–75, esp. 60–66. Garroway's analogy with Marines in Iraq is helpful.

[24] John Campbell, "Legion," *OCD* (3rd ed.), 839–42.

[25] See nn. 1 and 8 above.

the demon possession of this man with a central technique of Roman imperial control of local subjects, namely, its military might, both actual and threatened. As Conway demonstrates, military success constitutes a primary component of Roman (hegemonic) masculinity.[26]

By linking the man with the name Legion, the narrative constructs him as an embodiment of Roman power. But what sort of embodiment? Moore argues that we should read allegorically, following Jesus's example of 4:13–20, whereby "literary representations of individual colonial subjects stand in allegorically for the histories and destinies of entire colonized peoples."[27] Allegorically, then, the deranged man depicts a person subjected to Roman power. Maud Gleason similarly speaks of "images of the body as synecdoche for society" in which human bodies function as "metaphors of the body politic" and bodily actions—body language—communicate something about the constructions and experiences of a society's power structures.[28] In these terms, the man as metaphor for society subdued and dominated by militarily based Roman dominance communicates in vv. 2–5 the experience of that power in terms of death (among the tombs), social alienation, overwhelming power, lack of control, self-destruction, demonic control, and antithesis to God's empire/rule manifested by the manly man Jesus (1:15). This is a scathing indictment of Roman power, but we must not miss its important gendered texture. Integral to the characterization of the man in these terms in vv. 2–5 is the lack of self-control. A lack of self-control "calls into question one's masculinity" and creates a process of "sliding down the scale from man to unman."[29] Lack of self-control was womanish. The presentation of this unruly unman in vv. 2–5 constructs Roman power as effeminately out-of-control.

Accordingly, the confrontation between Jesus and the out-of-control unman/demon in vv. 6–13 positions Jesus on top. The unman/demon immediately yields to Jesus's authority in v. 6 (running to Jesus, bowing down) while simultaneously, as often happens in contexts of assertions of power, contesting Jesus's authority. The unman/demon attempts to ward off Jesus first by crying out a question ("what have you to do with me?"), then, ironically, by using an exorcist's formula for casting out a demon ("I adjure you by God"; cf. Acts 19:13). The demon ironically invokes God's authority in an attempt to circumscribe Jesus's power, which comes from God! The demon further protests that Jesus is "torment(ing) me," a verb associated with eschatological judgment, including of the devil in Rev 20:10. While contending with Jesus, the unman/demon names Jesus's identity as "son of the Most High"

---

[26] Conway, *Behold the Man*, 23–24, 29–30, 39–47.

[27] Moore, "'My Name Is Legion,'" 27, 29.

[28] Maud Gleason, "Mutilated Messengers: Body Language in Josephus," in *Being Greek under Rome: Cultural Identity, the Second Sophistic and the Development of Empire*, ed. Simon Goldhill (Cambridge: Cambridge University Press, 2001), 50–85, esp. 52.

[29] Conway, *Behold the Man*, 21–25. On "masculinity and self-control," see Craig A. Williams, *Roman Homosexuality*, 2nd ed. (Oxford: Oxford University Press, 2010), 151–56.

(5:7). The demon's designation of God as "Most High," can refer to both Zeus and Israel's God (Deut 32:8, Isa 14:14); the latter use is particularly associated with gentiles in diaspora contexts (Dan 3:26, 4:2, 2 Macc 3:31, 3 Macc 7:9, Acts 16:17).

More especially, the demon's use of the term "Most High God" identifies God (whom Jesus represents) as the most powerful—hegemonic—being in the scene. The title in the Hebrew Bible presents God as exercising power over the whole earth (Deut 32:8, Dan 4:17) and as the one who allocates the guardianship of other nations to lower gods while Israel was "the Lord's own portion" (Deut 32:7–9). God exercises this power as the all-conquering warrior God who subdues nations and enemies (Pss 9:3–5, 47:1–9), especially in battle with Israel's enemies (Ps 83:1–18). By addressing Jesus in relation to the "Most High God," the unman/demon links Jesus and him/itself with this larger narrative of God the warrior, victorious over the nations, empires, and their armies, whether Egyptian (Exod 14–15), Babylonian-Persian (Isa 40–55; e.g., 44:28–45:1), or Greek (Dan 7:2–28). By evoking this warrior tradition of God as "Most High," the unman/demon, as the embodiment of Rome's power, positions Rome as the next in line to experience God's (hegemonic) subduing warrior power. In so doing, the demon continues the destructive behavior of vv. 3–5, ironically threatening his own imperial embodiment of Rome and the emperor's assertion of mastery over land and sea.

In this context, how are we to make sense of the exchange between the unman/demon and Jesus as the demon requests first not to be expelled from the country and then to enter into some nearby pigs (5:10–12)? Clearly the request positions the unman/demon as the inferior and Jesus as the superior in this deployment of power. But beyond this, what else is in play? Attention to the military and gender dimensions of imperial power opens up an interesting and frequently ignored vista.

Jesus embodies the threat and power of the Most High, all-conquering, warrior God who, like Rome's rulers, claims sovereignty over the earth and nations. In the face of this claim and true to its name Legion, the occupying demon tries in v. 10 to maintain its imperial grip over land that is not its own but that it has claimed through invasion. We might think of Rome's fresh taking of land in Galilee (Josephus, *J.W.* 4.120) and Judea, parts of which Vespasian gives as gifts to allies such as Josephus (*Life* 1.425). In begging Jesus "not to send them out of the country" (5:10; cf. 12:7), the demon continues to locate himself in a subordinate position to Jesus even while it tries to control and limit Jesus's power and defend its occupied land. Legion employs the verb "send" (ἀποστείλῃ) in the request to Jesus. The verb appears in military contexts with meanings such as "dispatch" as when a commanding officer dispatches military spies (Josh 2:1, 6:24) or military forces (Josh 8:3, 9; Judg 4:6; 2 Kgs 6:14; Isa 20:1), or when God wages war in "sending out arrows" (2 Sam 22:15). Josephus similarly uses the verb for the exercise of imperial and military authority: the Syrian governor Cestius (*J.W.* 2.510), the emperor Vespasian (*J.W.* 3.8, 4.658), and his son the future emperor Titus (*J.W.* 7:18, 117) "send" troops into battle. The use of this verb with such meanings thus contributes to a scene in which the demon Legion addresses Jesus as a superior military officer and urges him to use his imperial-military authority, even while it presents itself as subject to Jesus's command and seeks to secure its own interests, power, and territory (χώρα).

We need look no further than Herod's efforts to secure his land and rule over Judea as he switches allegiances from Cassius, then to Antony, then to Octavian (Josephus, *J.W.* 1.242–244, 386–400; *Ant.* 14.301–303; 15.187–201, 217), or Josephus's change of allegiance during the war against Rome (*J.W.* 3.137–408) to understand the subordinate demon's self-interested negotiation of a superior commander as he seeks to secure his own position and interests.

III

The demon continues to construct the manly man Jesus as a military commander. Jesus does not respond to the demon's initial begging to stay in the land (5:10–11). The demon tries again with a double request, "Send us into the pigs, let us enter them" (5:12, πέμψον ἡμᾶς εἰς τοὺς χοίρους, ἵνα εἰς αὐτοὺς εἰσέλθωμεν). Legion's request is expressed in an aorist imperative using not ἀποστέλλω, as in 5:10, but πέμπω. This latter verb repeats the dynamics of ἀποστέλλω in expressing both imperial authority, as when emperors send or dispatch governors to Judea,[30] and military commands, as when a commander such as the governor of Syria Varrus (Josephus, *J.W.* 2.68, 75), the emperor Gaius (*J.W.* 2.185), the governor of Judea Felix (*J.W.* 2.260, 270), the emperor Vespasian (*J.W.* 3.446, 486; 4.57, 419, 487), and the general and later emperor Titus (*J.W.* 5.96-97, 446; 6.135-136) send or dispatch troops into battle. The demon's language places Jesus in such company, continuing to construct him as an imperial and/or military commander.

While the "demonstrative departure of the demon" is a feature of exorcism scenes, the specific request to be sent into a herd of pigs is most unusual.[31] How might we make sense of it? Most discussions of the scene do little with the detail except to conclude (erroneously) for a setting in gentile territory.[32] Eric Thurman suggests that it reenacts Pharaoh's defeat.[33] More aptly, Conway highlights a witty dimension—the "comic demise" of Rome's army—but without elaborating (as I will

---

[30] E.g., Josephus, *J.W.* 2.169 (Tiberius sent Pilate); 2.220 (Claudius sent Fadus); *Ant.* 20.137 (Claudius sent Felix); 20.182 (Nero sent Festus); 20.197 (Nero sent Albinus); 20.252 (Nero sent Florus). For sending an official or embassy, see Philo, *Flacc.* 109; *Legat.* 239, 369.

[31] Rudolf Bultmann, *The History of the Synoptic Tradition* (New York: Harper & Row, 1963); Twelftree, *Jesus the Exorcist*, 74–76, 86; the technique is absent from Theissen's summary, *Miracle Stories*, 85–90. See also nn. 4–5 above.

[32] E.g., Ezra P. Gould, *A Critical and Exegetical Commentary on the Gospel according to St. Mark*, ICC (New York: Scribner's Sons, 1905), 91; Eduard Schweizer, *The Good News according to Mark* (Richmond: John Knox, 1970), 112;

[33] Thurman, "Looking for a Few Good Men," 148.

do below) the wit.³⁴ Attention to numerous imperial-military-gender dimensions of the scene provides some elaboration and offers compelling alternative explanations.

For instance, Legion's request to be sent into the pigs expresses his submission to Jesus and imminent defeat even as it seeks to maintain domination not only over land but over what the land supports and what belongs to local inhabitants (5:11–12). Along with control of the land, the demon has, with impeccable imperial logic, sought to preserve control over the land's production, particularly animals. Rome exercised such control in various ways, the most obvious of which was through payment of taxes and tribute, paid often in kind. Peter Garnsey and Richard Saller argue that every province, whether willingly or by requisition, contributed wheat to feed Rome, supplies for the army, and money-taxes for army pay.³⁵ Tacitus, for example, offers a glimpse of this control of production in noting the revolt of the Frisii, a nation beyond the Rhine, over the imposition of an annual levy of ox hides for Roman military use. Tacitus comments, "First it was their herds, next their lands, last, the persons of their wives and children, which they gave up to bondage" (Tacitus, *Ann.* 4.72).

The display and subjugation of wild and exotic animals in the arena communicated the same message of Rome's control over land and living creatures. Even the procurement of beasts for the arena demonstrated Rome's military control and subjugation of the natural world. Christopher Epplett collects epigraphic and papyrological evidence to argue that capturing and supervising wild animals for *venationes* or wild beast hunts in arenas "formed an important part of a soldier's duty."³⁶ The arena, according to Thomas Wiedemann, confronted the chaos of nature (wild beasts), people (criminals), and death (both) with "the ordered world, the cosmos; it was the place where the civilised [Roman imperial] world confronted lawless nature."³⁷ So in his poems "On the Spectacles" concerning the games that marked the opening of the Colosseum in 80 CE, Martial celebrates Rome's sovereignty over people and over the many wild beasts of the subjugated nations, sovereignty

---

³⁴ Conway, *Behold the Man*, 94.

³⁵ Peter Garnsey and Richard Saller, *The Roman Empire: Economy, Society and Culture* (Berkeley: University of California Press, 1987), 95–97. E.g., Tacitus, *Ann.* 1.71 (supplies of weapons, horses, and gold offered); *Ann.* 2.5 (horses from Gaul); Josephus, *J.W.* 2.528 (wheat seized from local farms to feed an army). See *Feeding the Roman Army: The Archaeology of Production and Supply in NW Europe*, ed. Sue Stallibrass and Richard Thomas (Oxford: Oxbow, 2008), 4–5: pig bones were prominent at many military sites and pigs were important in soldiers' diets.

³⁶ Christopher Epplett, "The Capture of Animals by the Roman Military," *GR* 48 (2001): 210–22; Roger Dunkle, "A Brief History of the Arena Hunt," in idem, *Gladiators: Violence and Spectacle in Ancient Rome* (Harlow: Pearson/Longman, 2008), 207–44; Ingvild Saelid Gilhus, *Animals, Gods and Humans: Changing Attitudes to Animals in Greek, Roman and Early Christian Ideas* (London: Routledge, 2006), 31–35.

³⁷ Thomas Wiedemann, *Emperors and Gladiators* (London: Routledge, 1992), 180.

exercised justly and mercifully by the emperor Titus (poems 23 and 31).[38] Three poems concern the death of a pregnant sow, "pierced" by a spear, enacting the spectacle of death and rebirth (14–16). A *bestiarius* kills a boar, a bear, a lion, and a leopard exemplifying Roman control over wild beasts (17). J. P. Sullivan comments that "over 50,000 [animals] by some accounts, often of exotic provenance fell to the weapons."[39] The spectacle of subjugated animals contributed to normative Roman identity as conquerors of the world, the triumph of the civilized over the barbaric other.[40] The request of the demon Legion that Jesus "send us into the pigs," I am suggesting, similarly enacts this imperial control over the animals and the land that sustains them.

IV

But such generic imperializing practice can contextualize, but must not divert attention from, the specific involvement of pigs. The languaging of Legion's request in terms of "enter(ing) into" (εἰσέρχομαι) the pigs adds military and gender dimensions to the scene.

First, this verb, "enter into," is commonly used to denote imperial-military scenarios of entering, occupying, and defeating an enemy space and military force in battle.[41] Such "entering into" expresses military power exercised by male commanders and troops. Legion's use of the verb in Mark 5:12 constructs Jesus as a military commander authorizing an invasion. Conquest is what a legion does, on command.

---

[38] I follow the numbering in "On the Spectacles," in D. R. Shackleton Bailey, *Martial: Epigrams*, vol. 1, LCL (Cambridge: Harvard University Press, 1993).

[39] J. P. Sullivan, *Martial, the Unexpected Classic: A Literary and Historical Study* (Cambridge: Cambridge University Press, 1991), 7–9. Through Martial's eyes, a rhinoceros displays great power (p. 11). A "treacherous lion" is justly killed for "harming his master with his ingrate mouth, daring to violate the hands he knew so well," the slaughtered lion embodying the potential fate of all "ingrate" subjugated people (p. 12). A tigress gains power by being "among us" (p. 21), while a bull is killed (p. 22). A suppliant elephant (p. 20) and a mercy-seeking hind (p. 33) yield directly to the emperor Titus, who presides with courage, justice, clemency, and piety over all proceedings (pp. 23, 31).

[40] This perspective has affinity with the argument of Erik Gunderson, "Ideology of the Arena," *ClAnt* 15 (1996): 113–51, arguing against Carlin A. Barton, "The Scandal of the Arena," *Representations* 27 (1989): 1–36.

[41] Babylon invaded or entered into Jerusalem's sanctuary (Lam 1:10); Antiochus Epiphanes "enters into" or invades Egypt (1 Macc 1:17); Ptolemy tries to enter Jerusalem (Josephus, *J.W.* 1.55); Vespasian sends troops to enter Joppa (*J.W.* 3.417); Titus enters Taricheae (*J.W.* 3.497); Roman troops enter Jerusalem (*J.W.* 5.336). See also Judg 9:5; 18:9; 1 Sam 26:6; 30:1–2; 2 Sam 5:6–9; 10:14; 1 Kgs 12:21; 22:30; 2 Kgs 3:24; 7:4, 10, 12; 10:17, 25; Isa 20:1; 37:33; Jer 4:5; 8:14; Lam 1:10; Dan 11:9, 10, 40; 1 Macc 1:17; 12:48; 2 Macc 9:2; 11:5; Josephus, *J.W.* 1.55; 4.70, 575; *Ant.* 5.28; etc.

Yet, second, with the military language come gender and sexual dimensions. The demon's request to be sent into the pigs reads literally: "so that we might enter into them" (5:12 [my translation]: ἵνα εἰς αὐτοὺς εἰσέλθωμεν). The language of "enter into" employs, as Joel Marcus notes, though without elaboration, a sexual innuendo for sexual intercourse.[42] While Derrett reads this innuendo in terms of bestiality,[43] rape seems the more appropriate category, given a conventionally close connection between language of military power, sexual violence, and imperial claims.

The sexual overtones of the verb "enter into" (along with its previously discussed military meanings) cannot be contested. Liddell and Scott define the non-prefixed verb ἔρχομαι as "sexual intercourse ... *go in to* her, *to* him" referencing Herodotus 2.11.5 and 6.68.[44] The prefixed form εἰσέρχομαι commonly references sexual intercourse in the LXX.[45] More significant, the verb εἰσέρχομαι appears in contexts of forcible sexual penetration, situations that contemporary readers would identify as "rape" in which a woman's consent is absent.[46] Forcible penetration (rape) is, of course, a long-practiced tactic of occupying armies in humiliating woman and subjugating an enemy.[47]

Language of sexual violence, military actions, and imperial claims frequently intersect in constructing scenes of victory. In discussing Rome's sacking of cities, the *urbs direpta*, Adam Ziolkowski argues that central to this act of *direptio* is the loss of all control in "the soldiers' freedom to slaughter, rape, and plunder."[48] Ziolkowski's analysis brings together motifs of military action, taking property, taking life, and sexual violence, all of which are evident in this scene involving Legion's entering the pigs. Josephus mentions rape in the contexts of military campaigns (*J.W.* 4.560), though he denies any such activity himself (*Vita* 80, 259). The Hebrew Bible instructs warriors to "take as your booty the women, the children, the livestock" of a conquered town and "enjoy these spoils" (Deut 20:14 NRSV). Attentive only to male desires and knowing only a male gaze, it sanctions—not

---

[42] Marcus, *Mark*, 345, 352 referencing J. Duncan M. Derrett, "Spirit-Possession and the Gerasene Demoniac," *Man* NS 14 (1979): 286–93, esp. 290.

[43] Derrett, "Spirit Possession," 290.

[44] LSJ, 695, s.v. ἔρχομαι, no. 7; italics original.

[45] Jacob's intercourse with Leah (Gen 29:23; 30:16), Rachel (Gen 29:21, 30), Bilhah (Gen 30:3–4), Zilpah (Gen 30:9), Shua (Gen 38:2); Onan's intercourse with his brother Er's widow Tamar (Gen 38:8–9); Judah's intercourse with Tamar (Gen 38:16, 18); Samson with a prostitute (Judg 16:1); David with Bathsheba (2 Sam 12:24); a brother with the wife of a husband who has died in levirate marriage (Deut 25:5).

[46] Hagar (Gen 16:2, 4), Rizpah (2 Sam 3:7), and David's concubines or mistresses (2 Sam 16:21–22).

[47] The classic discussion is Susan Brownmiller, *Against Our Will: Men, Women, and Rape* (New York: Fawcett Columbine, 1993), 31–113.

[48] Adam Ziolkowski, "*Urbs Direpta*, or How the Romans Sacked Cities," in *War and Society in the Roman World*, ed. John Rich and Graham Shipley, Leicester-Nottingham Studies in Ancient Society 5 (London: Routledge, 1993), 69–91, esp. 86; Williams, *Roman Homosexuality*, 112–16.

forbids—a male warrior "entering into" (εἰσελεύσῃ πρὸς αὐτήν; Deut 21:13) a foreign "beautiful" woman taken captive in battle, though after one month has passed to allow her to mourn the loss of her family (Deut 21:10–14)![49] Her rape is appallingly re-languaged as marriage. Also from the perspective of a male gaze, the Hebrew Bible presents scenarios of cities overrun in battle as the rape of a woman.[50] Several such passages use the sexual language of "enter into" or "go into" to image military action against cities as rape (Isa 47:1–4, εἴσελθε; Lam 1:8–10, εἰσελθόντα εἰς).

Third, gender and sexual overtones pervade the request's multivalent language of Legion's desire to enter into the pigs. The term "pig" has well-established sexual associations with female genitalia. Liddell and Scott in their entry (!) on χοῖρος identify its first meaning as "pig" as a synonym for ὗς in referring to the literal animal. Their second definition does not include an English translation, employing only the Latin phrase *pudenda muliebria*. While the phrase remains untranslated and without English synonyms, they offer an explanation, "frequently in Comedy Poets who are always puning on the word and its compounds."[51] The untranslated phrase means literally "shameful womanly things" and refers to female genitalia; perhaps modesty prevents the editors from translating χοῖρος as "vulva."

Modesty, though, does not seem to have influenced Aristophanes's use of χοῖρος. In his play *Acharnians* (lines 765–815), the main character Dicaeopolis, who opposes Athens's involvement in the Peloponnesian War with Sparta and its allies, sets up a rural market in which only Athens's enemies (Spartans, Megarians, Boiotians) might trade. A hungry Megarian brings his two young starving daughters to sell for food. Throughout the exchange with Dicaeopolis, the father refers to them as "piggies" and has them make pig noises. The movement between food and sex, animal and female genitalia through a series of double entendres directed to a (mainly?) male audience is constant. For example, lines 781–796:[52]

---

[49] Carolyn Pressler, *The View of Women Found in the Deuteronomic Family Laws*, BZAW 216 (Berlin: de Gruyter, 1993), 9–15.

[50] Pamela Gordon and Harold Washington, "Rape as a Military Metaphor in the Hebrew Bible," in *A Feminist Companion to the Latter Prophets*, ed. Athalya Brenner, Feminist Companion to the Bible 8 (Sheffield: Sheffield Academic, 1995), 308–25, identifying Lam 1–2, Micah 4:11, Jer 6:1–4 (in which the attackers "go into her"; 6:3), Jer 13:20–27 (all referring to Jerusalem); Isa 47:1–3 (Babylon); and Nahum 3:5–6 (Nineveh).

[51] LSJ, 1996, s.v. χοῖρος.

[52] Jeffrey Henderson, *Aristophanes: Acharnians, Knights*, LCL (Cambridge: Harvard University Press, 1998), 153–55. Various editions note the link in this passage between χοῖρος (pig) and female genitalia. So Alan H. Sommerstein (*Acharnians* [Warminster: Aris & Phillips, 1980], 194–95) notes that the term means both "young pig" and "vulva"; Henderson (*The Maculate Muse: Obscene Language in Attic Comedy* [New Haven: Yale University Press, 1975]) observes that "χοῖρος, piggy, is the land animal to which the cunt is more frequently compared in double entendres; this word seems to have been a most popular slang expression.... [It] indicates the pink, hairless cunt of young girls as opposed to that of mature women" though "a pink hairless state

MEGARIAN. Is that a piggy?
DICAEOPOLIS. It looks like a piggy now but all grown up it'll be a pussy!
MEGARIAN. Rest assured, in five years she'll be just like her mother.
DICAEOPOLIS. But this one isn't even suitable for sacrifice.
MEGARIAN. Indeed? In what way unsuitable for sacrifice?
DICAEOPOLIS. It's got no tail! [glossed as, "Also a slang term for penis"]
MEGARIAN. She's still young but when she's grown to sowhood she'll get a big fat pink one....
DICAEOPOLIS, *looking at the other girl.* Why, this one's pussy is the twin of the other one's!
MEGARIAN. Sure, she's got the same mother and father. If she fills out and gets downy with hair, she'll be a very fine piggy to sacrifice to Aphrodite [glossed as "Goddess of sexual enjoyment"].... What's more, the meat of these piggies is absolutely delicious when it's skewered on a spit.[53]

This exchange in *Acharnians* is but one example of the double entendre involving "pig" as a euphemism for "female genitalia" in Aristophanes and in other examples from Old Comedy.[54] Aristophanes's use of "obscene language" is extensive, as Henderson's 115-page cataloging of words for male and female sexual organs, intercourse, and scatological humor demonstrates.[55] Within this range, Henderson notes that "animals ... often symbolize strong and unrestrained passion" and commonly "indicate the genitalia of both sexes." The penis is imaged by a horse, a ram, a bull, and a dog, while female genitalia are imaged by a pig, a dog, a bull, and perhaps a horse. The link between genitalia and animal is made, he argues, because generally "these metaphors emphasize the power and passion of animals rather than their physical resemblance to the organs themselves," though he recognizes "some degree of physical comparison" in some of the metaphors "as in the case of 'piggy' which emphasizes the warm, pink hairless member of a young girl" or of an older physically mature but depilated female.[56]

---

could, however, also be achieved even for grown-up cunts by depilation" (p. 131). The term is used for depilated slave girls; a derivative χοιροπῶλαι refers to prostitutes, while a man using prostitutes is a χοιρόθλιψ, which Henderson translates as "piggy-squeezer" (p. 132). Compare the translation of Michael Ewans, which uses "pussy" not "piggies" (*Aristophanes: Acharians, Knights, and Peace* [Norman: University of Oklahoma Press, 2012]). Ewans explains that "Aristophanes embarks on an extended sequence of puns (Greek *choiros* = both 'pig' and 'cunt').... I believe the only effective choice in English is to change the animal" (p. 69). For analysis of the scene, see Kenneth James Dover, *Aristophanic Comedy* (Berkeley: University of California Press, 1972), 63–65.

[53] The spit refers to a male penis, and meat being eaten refers to female genitalia; so Henderson, *Maculate Muse*, 123, 144.

[54] E.g., Aristophanes, *Thesm.* 538: "Singe the hair off this woman's pussy; that'll teach her never again to badmouth her fellow women."

[55] Henderson, *Maculate Muse*, 108–222.

[56] Ibid., 48, 131.

Henderson notes that Aristophanes did not invent the association between "pig" and female genitalia but employs popular slang.[57] And certainly the association continued for centuries long after Aristophanes, including through the performance of his plays.[58] James Adams notes in his study of Latin sexual vocabulary that the term *porcus* ("pig") is "a nursery word used by women, especially nurses, of the pudenda of girls," listing Varro, *Rust.* 2.4.10.[59]

I have argued that Legion's double request, "Send us into the pigs so that we might enter into them" (Mark 5:12 [my translation]) employs multivalent language embracing imperial, military, gender, and sexual dimensions. The request seeks to maintain imperial control over land and its production. The verb "enter into" denotes military violence and occupation, as well as sexual intercourse, particularly the weapon of war, rape. The noun *pig* denotes both literal animals and female genitalia. The request to enter the pigs made by the demon Legion draws together these various dimensions of gendered, imperial, military violence.

V

But to what end? Identifying this mix is quite predictable once we identify the cluster of imperial context and military language that pervades the scene. Yet there is a witty surprise involving the pigs. A further link between pigs and empire, I suggest, stages Jesus as a masculine military commander and Rome's conquered army as unmanned, womanly, boarish and/or piggy.

Some commentators have noted that one of the emblems of a Roman legion, the Tenth Fretensis legion, was the boar. Given that wild boars were one of the animals used in the arena to attack human victims, the boar probably symbolized ferocity and lethal attack,[60] along of course with male power and aggression. The Tenth Fretensis legion played a leading role in the capture of besieged Jerusalem in 70 and occupied the city after the war, when Mark was written (Josephus, *J.W.* 3.8, 64–65; 5.69–70, 135; 7.5, 17).

---

[57] Ibid., 131.

[58] Sommerstein (*Acharnians*, 16–17, 28–29) indicates that Aristophanes's plays, along with other representatives of Old Comedy such as Cratrinus and Eupolis, were well known through "the first three centuries of the Christian era." The late-first-century CE authors Horace (*Sat.*1.4.1) and Quintilian (10.1.65–66) mention Aristophanes.

[59] James N. Adams, *The Latin Sexual Vocabulary* (Baltimore: Johns Hopkins University Press, 1990), 82. The *Oxford Latin Dictionary* (ed. P. G. W. Glare [Oxford: Clarendon, 1977], 1405) similarly shares Liddell and Scott's preference for circumlocution, listing three meanings for *porcus* and providing English definitions for the first and third. For the second, they quote Varro in Latin without any English explanation or translation.

[60] Dunkle, *Gladiators*, 84–85, 225, 238, 242.

The demon Legion's entering into the pigs allies demons and pigs. They become one. If the pigs evoke the emblem of the Tenth legion, the link between demons and Roman power established by naming the demon as Legion in 5:9 continues as the demon enters the pig.

This link, of course, is not neutral. Most obviously, it constructs Roman power as demonic; the legion is controlled by Legion. Further, it evokes the depiction of Rome's out-of-control and (self-)destructive power in 5:2–8 in the unman's behavior. And it subjects the demonic power Legion to the command of the commander Jesus. Moreover, and with considerable wit, Legion entering into pigs crosses genders. If the pigs are read as boars (masculine, τοὺς χοίρους), the emblem of the Tenth legion, Legion "enters into" or penetrates other males, shaming Rome's finest fighting force, the boarish and now unmanned/effeminate, and dominated Tenth legion.[61] If, with the Tenth legion's emblem in mind, the pigs are read in terms of female genitalia, Legion "enters into" or penetrates females, an act that frames Rome's military might, the piggy Tenth legion, as womanly. The multivalent language requires no decision between the options. Either way, this fantasy scene cross-genders Rome and its military might, mocked and shamed by male humor that trades in imperial-military, gendered, and sexual innuendo.

Military and gender language, therefore, frames this exorcistic exchange in vv. 9–13, presenting the scene in masculine terms and military perspective. Jesus emerges as a military commander dispatching and commanding[62] the subordinate demon Legion into the pigs. The demons "enter into" the herd of some two thousand pigs (the strength of less than half a legion[63]) and "ride" them (another sexual image[64]) into the sea as into battle (5:13b). The verb "rushed" (ὁρμάω) is commonly associated with military action and troops rushing into battle.[65] And, as other commentators have noted, the drowning evokes Pharaoh's armies similarly destroyed in the sea (Exod 15:1–21), layering Egyptian and Roman forces.[66] Demons and pigs, Legion and the Tenth legion, are united in the destruction they bring upon themselves, depicting Rome's military power as self-destructive. Jesus's military victory is emphasized in that not only is the demon "dispatched out of the country" contrary to its wishes but, in entering the pigs as it requests, it disappears into the sea, over which—including its stormy demons—Jesus has demonstrated his

---

[61] Williams, *Roman Homosexuality*, 17–19, 112–16, esp. 114, 137–76.

[62] The verb ἐπιτρέπω, usually translated in v. 13 "so he gave them permission," is better rendered as "so he commanded them" (Esth 9:14; 1 Clem. 1.3).

[63] Varro (*Rust.* 2.4.22) says that 150 sows constitute a large herd.

[64] Henderson, *Maculate Muse*, 155, 165.

[65] Xenophon, *Anab.* 1.8.25; Thucydides 7.34.4 (a naval battle); 2 Macc 12:32; and very commonly in Josephus, *Ant* 12.270, etc.; *J.W.* 1.23, 32, 39, 62; 2.296, 345; 3.9, 61, 111; 4.518, etc.

[66] Thurman, "Looking for a Few Good Men," 148. Henderson (*Maculate Muse*, 166) notes that nautical terminology (sailing, oars, swimming, and so on) is common for intercourse. Drowning is the ultimate negation.

command in the preceding scene (4:35–41). The manly Jesus has accomplished a military victory.[67]

Such a fantasy of destruction of course co-opts and reinscribes imperial values of overwhelming power and destruction of the enemy. The scene constructs Jesus as the victorious military commander, his now-enhanced hegemonic masculinity imitative of, yet established at the expense of, unmanned boarish/piggy Rome. Any victory celebration, though, would be precipitous. The empire always strikes back. Ten chapters later, in crucifixion, as an "emasculated victim," Jesus will be defeated, weak, womanly.[68]

[67] Conway, *Behold the Man*, 94.
[68] Ibid., 100–106.

Christ and Community: The Gospel Witness to Jesus
9781426793080

It turns out that the Gospels do more than simply affirm that Jesus is the Christ; they cast a vision of messianic community for those who would call him Lord.

"...fluidly-written, easy-to-understand, and important."
—**Joel Marcus,** Duke Divinity School

"...a fresh, illuminating, and accessible introduction to the New Testament gospels." —**John T. Carroll,** Union Presbyterian Seminary

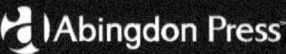

Pacifist Jesus? The (Mis)Translation of ἐᾶτε ἕως τούτου in Luke 22:51

DAVID LERTIS MATSON
dlmatson@hiu.edu
Hope International University, Fullerton, CA 92831

Jesus's refusal to be defended by the sword at his arrest plays a significant role in popular and scholarly understandings of Jesus as a committed pacifist. Of the four NT accounts, the Gospel of Luke offers Jesus's most forceful and unequivocal rebuke: "No more of this!" (Luke 22:51 NRSV), translating ἐᾶτε ἕως τούτου. Such a translation, however, is tendentious and misleading, seemingly the result of a twentieth-century translational bias that has exerted enormous influence on subsequent biblical translation and interpretation. An analysis of Luke's lexical usage, grammar, and context rather suggests that, instead of rebuking his disciples, Jesus is reminding them of the divine plan to which Jesus must not only submit, but which he must actively carry out. In Luke's narrative framework, Satan has received permission to sift the disciples in the present hour of darkness, and the disciples must not interfere with the divine *permissio*. This apocalyptic reading allows the words ἐᾶτε ἕως τούτου their more natural force: "permit until this," or, more pointedly, "allow the arrest to continue." The subsequent healing of the high priest's slave guarantees the continuation of the plan and expresses Jesus's control over the situation more than his presumed compassion or love. The implications for Christian ethics are considerable: Jesus may have been a "pacifist" but not in the way one might think.

The occasion of Jesus's arrest has figured prominently in pacifistic understandings of Jesus. Of the four accounts in the NT, the Gospel of Luke contains Jesus's seemingly most forceful rebuke to the use of the sword: "No more of this!" (22:51, NRSV), translating the enigmatic expression ἐᾶτε ἕως τούτου. The ambiguity of these words, however, demands much more attention than it has usually received by commentators, who simply assume that the words communicate a strong rebuke by Jesus, animated as he was by his own teaching of enemy-love.[1] An analysis of

---

[1] So most commentators, e.g., Donald Senior, *The Passion of Jesus in the Gospel of Luke* (Wilmington, DE: Glazier, 1989), 91; and Jerome H. Neyrey, *The Passion according to Luke: A Redaction Study of Luke's Soteriology*, Theological Inquiries (New York: Paulist, 1985), 41.

the Lukan text and a history of translation will show that this rendering of Jesus's words is questionable at best, tendentious at worst.

In understanding the meaning of these words in their Lukan context, a number of intriguing and interlocking exegetical questions confront the interpreter: To whom is Jesus speaking—the disciples or the crowd that has come out to arrest him? What is the meaning of ἐᾶτε? Does it mean to "permit" or, seemingly its opposite, to "stop"? What is the grammatical object of ἐᾶτε? Is it Jesus himself, the disciples, or the crowd that has come out to arrest him? What is the meaning of the ambiguous phrase ἕως τούτου? Does it modify ἐᾶτε, or is it part of an elliptical expression to be interpreted solely on its own? Answers to these questions are much more than answers to a grammatical jigsaw puzzle; they provide the stated rationale in Luke for why Jesus refuses to be defended by the sword.

I. Analysis of the Lukan Text

The question of Jesus's precise audience on this occasion is perhaps the best place to begin. Some commentators and translators, taking ἐάω in its basic meaning of "allow" or "permit," construe it with Jesus's healing of the slave of the high priest that immediately follows (22:51b). This interpretation assumes a με ("me") as the implied object of ἐᾶτε, which first appears in the Twentieth Century Version around 1900 and somewhat frequently thereafter.[2] In some translations, the sentence is punctuated with a comma, making permission to heal the content of Jesus's request. Moffatt (1913), for example, translates, "Jesus said, 'Let *me* do this at least,' and cured him by touching his ear." More recently, the Complete Jewish Bible (trans. David H. Stern, 1998) follows suit: "But Yeshua answered, 'Just let *me* do this,' and, touching the man's ear, he healed him."[3] Yet this rather creative construal of the Greek grammar makes sense only if Jesus is speaking to the crowd that has come out to arrest Jesus, led by Judas (22:47), in effect making the crowd responsible for granting Jesus's request. If Jesus was speaking to his disciples, it is difficult to imagine why he would be asking *them* for permission to perform this act of healing.[4]

Three features in the narrative, however, strongly suggest that Jesus is in fact here speaking directly to his disciples, making such a translation unlikely. First, Jesus does not explicitly address the crowd until v. 52, when he speaks directly

---

[2] So Weymouth (1903), Moffatt (1913), Goodspeed (1923), Ballantine (1923), Williams (1952), and Wuest (1961).

[3] Italics mine. This view receives support from R. C. H. Lenski, commenting not too long after this interpretation was coming into vogue (*The Interpretation of St. Luke's Gospel* [Minneapolis: Augsburg, 1946], 1082).

[4] Why would they stand in his way? Such a view implies the unthinkable notion that the disciples represented a physical threat to Jesus in some way—as if there was a possibility that they would turn the sword on him!

Matson: (Mis)Translation in Luke 22:51   159

(λέγω) to the chief priests, officers of the temple, and elders who had come out to arrest him.⁵ Second, in the Lukan sequence of events, Jesus is not actually apprehended (συλλαμβάνω) until v. 54, and thus there is no reason at this point for Jesus to be seeking his arresters' permission.⁶ Only a homogenized reading of Luke's narrative that imports the Markan sequence into Luke can account for the plausibility of such a request.⁷ Third, Luke uses ἀποκριθείς ("answered") as a preface to Jesus's response in v. 51a, a point obscured in many English translations that leave the word untranslated, presumably combining it with the corresponding εἶπεν as a pleonasm.⁸ This circumstantial participle occurs with a verb of speaking forty-five times in Luke and Acts, and in all but two of those instances the speaker is responding directly to a statement or question.⁹ This pattern is certainly present here as Jesus responds in the immediate vicinity to a question put forward by the disciples: "Lord, should we strike with the sword?" (22:49), a question posed only in Luke. Jesus's "answer" is thus most naturally a response to this question and not a request to the arresting party for permission to heal.

If, then, Jesus is speaking to his disciples in Luke 22:51, what exactly does he say? It scarcely needs documenting in scholarly and popular literature just how prevalent the assumption is that Jesus is here rebuking his disciples for their use of the sword and thus instructing his disciples in the way of nonviolence. Yet one wonders why, if Luke is intending a decisive rebuke in this crucial scene, he is so ambiguous on this occasion; he could well have used his favored term ἐπιτιμάω and

---

⁵ It is possible grammatically that the group to whom Jesus speaks in 22:52 is different from the crowd mentioned in 22:47, being a second group of late arrivers suggested by the aorist παραγενομένους.

⁶ Noted by Alfred Plummer, *A Critical and Exegetical Commentary on the Gospel according to St. Luke*, 5th ed., ICC (Edinburgh: T&T Clark, 1922), 512.

⁷ Interestingly, Matthew follows Mark's sequence (Mark 14:46–47) by placing the sword-wielding after the arrest (Matt 26:50–51), while John, like Luke, places the sword-wielding before the arrest (John18:10–12).

⁸ See, e.g., the RSV, NRSV, ESV, NAB, and CEB. The construction owes to Semitic influence. J. H. Moulton and W. F. Howard point out the frequency of this expression in the Synoptics but note that it is hardly ever redundant "in the sense that nothing has been said to which an answer is needed," citing only Mark 9:5, 11:14, 12:35, Matt 11:25, 12:38, 15:15 [?], 17:4, and 28:5 as exceptions (J. H. Moulton and W. F. Howard, *Accidence and Word-Formation with an Appendix on Semitisms in the New Testament*, vol. 4 of *A Grammar of New Testament Greek*, ed. J. H. Moulton, 4 vols. [Edinburgh: T&T Clark, 1929], 453). Daniel B. Wallace considers the participle a subset of the participle of means, defining the action of the main verb (*Greek Grammar beyond the Basics: An Exegetical Syntax of the New Testament* [Grand Rapids: Zondervan, 1996], 649–50). In the present case Jesus spoke by answering.

⁹ This statistic includes the probable reading of ἀποκριθεὶς δὲ Πέτρος καὶ οἱ ἀπόστολοι εἶπαν in Acts 5:29. It does not include the textually more uncertain variant in Acts 21:13. The only two places in my mind where Luke uses a purely pleonastic construction are Luke 13:14 and 14:3. Slight variation occurs in Luke 17:20, where the indicative ἀπεκρίθη is used with εἶπεν, and in Acts 15:13, where the indicative ἀπεκρίθη appears with a participial verb of speaking (λέγων).

removed all doubt.[10] In fact, on one previous occasion Jesus explicitly "rebuked" (ἐπετίμησεν) the disciples for their violent proclivities (9:55), a passage not wholly unrelated to the present one in tone and content. Instead, Luke utilizes the rather puzzling ἐᾶτε ἕως τούτου, which most modern English Bibles translate as a rebuke and punctuate accordingly. Like a fisherman's tale, a survey of twentieth-century English translations shows the rebuke only growing with time, with many adding an exclamatory "Stop!" to Jesus's clear and forceful prohibition, "No more of this."[11]

But whether ἐάω means anything as forceful and abrupt as "stop" in this passage is highly questionable.[12] Certainly no English translation prior to modern times, at least that I have found, thought that it did. Translations up to the mid-twentieth century are rather impressive in their uniform rendering of the verb as allowance or permission (Middle English "suffer").[13]

Luke 22:51 in English Translation: Permission

Wycliffe (1388)	"Suffer ye till hither."
Tyndale (1526)	"Soffre ye thus farre forthe."
Coverdale (1535)	"Suffre the thus farre forth."
Great Bible (1538)	"Soffre ye thus farre forthe."
Geneva (1560)	"Suffre *them* thus farre:"
Bishops' (1568])	"Suffer ye thus farre forth."
King James (1611)	"Suffer ye thus farre."
Campbell (1826)	"let this suffice;"
Webster (1833)	"Suffer ye thus far."
Young (1862)	"Suffer ye thus far,"
Anderson (1866)	"Let this matter proceed thus far."
Rotherham (1872)	"Let be,—as long as this!"
Darby (1884)	"Suffer thus far;"
English Revised (1885)	"Suffer ye thus far."
Douay-Rheims (1899)	"Suffer ye thus far."
Twentieth Century (1900)	"Let me at least do this;"

---

[10] This term appears twelve times in Luke (nine times in Mark, six times in Matthew, none in Acts), including instances of special Lukan redaction (4:39, 41; 19:39; 23:40; but cf. Lukan deletions in Mark 3:12//Matt 12:16; Mark 8:32–33//Matt 16:23). Even if Luke is using an independent source for his account of the arrest, one must still explain his curious lack of redaction if he wanted to make a rebuke clear to his audience. Had he so wanted, Luke was certainly capable of having Jesus express a rebuke.

[11] See also the NAB, NASB, NCB, REB, and, most recently, the CEB. The Simplified English Bible is particularly simplified with simply its forceful injunction, "Stop!"

[12] François Bovon rightly states, "It is difficult, if not impossible, to translate the imperative ἐάω with 'stop,' as some would like to do" (*Luke 3: A Commentary on the Gospel of Luke 19:28–24:53*, trans. James Crouch, Hermeneia [Minneapolis: Fortress, 2012], 216 n. 36).

[13] "Suffer" (suffren) in the sense of "permit" or "allow" first appears in English literature around 1300.

American Standard (1901)	"Suffer ye *them* thus far."
Godbey (1902)	"hold on until this:"
Weymouth (1903)	"Permit me thus far,"
Fenton (1908)	"Here let the matter rest;"
Moffatt (1913)	"Let me do this at least,"
Goodspeed (1923)	"Let me do this much!"
(W.) Ballantine (1923)	"Let me at least do this,"
Montgomery (1924)	"Permit me to do this at least,"
(C.B.) Williams (1937)	"Let them do it. No more of this!"
Basic English (1941)	"Put up with this, at least."
(C.K.) Williams (1952)	"Let me do this much;"
Simplified (1961)	"Allow them!"
New English Bible (1961)	"Let them have their way."
Wuest (1961)	"Be permitting me to do what I wish to do up to this point"
Beck (1963)	"Let them do it. No more of this!"
New King James (1982)	"Permit even this."

As impressive as this list is, one must be careful not to overstate the case since the Tyndale Bible exerted an enormous influence in the history of English translation.

The verb ἐάω can on occasion have the sense of "leave" and be used for putting a stop to an action, but even when it does so, the idea of permission is never far from view.[14] In keeping with the dominant history of English translation, a close analysis of Luke's lexical usage, grammatical syntax, and overall context strongly points in the direction of "let" and the primary sense of permission.[15]

---

[14] The idea behind the verb is often that of allowing something to remain in a specified state, hence "leave alone" or "let be"—not "leave off" (JB) in the primary sense of simply stopping an action. The permissive idea inherent in the verb explains why the same verb can seemingly mean two contradictory things. The idea of allowing something to remain as it is can be readily observed, for example, in the vision given to Nebuchadnezzar to cut down the tree but "leave" (ἐάσατε) its stump and roots in the ground (Dan 4:15, 23, 26 [Theodotion]) and in the Shepherd's exhortation to Hermas to "leave alone" (ἔασον) the crooked path (Herm. Mand. 6.1.2) and those things in his vision that he cannot understand (Herm. Sim. 9.2.7). This meaning occurs in the papyri (P.Tebt. 2.319–24), sometimes directly alongside "allow" (P.Fay. 122.6). So too ἐάω sometimes appears in the LXX with this meaning (Esth 3:8, Job 7:19, 9:28). See also Justin, *Dial*. 85.5. In one instance Josephus says that he "refrains" (ἐῶ) from further comment (*Ag. Ap*. 2.118), meaning that his original words must suffice. It is possible that the interjection ἔα ("let alone!" "away!" "alas!") may derive from the imperative form of ἐάω (Job 25:6 LXX; Luke 4:34; 1 Clem. 39.5). Since Luke shows that he is familiar with this word and its exclamatory function (4:34; cf. Mark 1:24 [v.l.]), one wonders why he has not chosen to use it in 22:51 to express Jesus's forceful exasperation at the disciples' use of the sword.

[15] BDAG cannot produce *any* textually certain NT passages with a prohibitive meaning apart from Luke 22:51. Even the one place in Homer that they cite (*Il*. 21.221) is questionable.

The usage of ἐάω in the NT is predominantly Lukan, with only two of the eleven occurrences found outside the Lukan corpus.[16] Excepting Luke 22:51 in the present case, all of Luke's usages carry a clear sense of allowance but possibly one, and in the one case Luke may well be reflecting a nautical *terminus technicus* in his narration of Paul's shipwreck voyage to Rome (Acts 27:40).[17] Yet even in this passage the permissive idea is not entirely absent. The passengers aboard the debilitated ship "left" (εἴων) the anchors in the sea, allowing them to remain where they were.

Moreover, Luke's syntax connects ἐᾶτε with a prepositional phrase (ἕως τούτου) whose meaning, although ambiguous, accords much more naturally with the idea of permission than with prohibition.[18] Only by grammatically divorcing ἕως τούτου from ἐᾶτε can one plausibly argue that Jesus is commanding his disciples to renounce the use of the sword. Even then, it simply strains translational credibility to think that ἕως τούτου in and of itself means something like "No more of that!" (REB) or "That will do!" (JB).[19]

That Jesus is distinctly *not* rebuking the disciples on this occasion becomes even clearer when one considers two additional textual features. First is Luke's use of ἀποκριθείς, mentioned earlier, which renders Jesus's words a statement, not a rebuke.[20] Second is the present plural form of ἐᾶτε, which grammatically conforms

---

Scamander is asking Achilles to let the river remain with the corpses that it has without adding any more (hence "let be" [Loeb]). Allowance is clearly the more common meaning in the LXX, a highly influential text on Luke (Gen 38:16, Exod 32:10, Deut 9:14, Josh 19:47, Judg 11:37, 2 Kgdms 15:34, Job 9:18, 10:20, 31:34, 1 Macc 12:40, 15:14, 2 Macc 12:2). Bovon (*Luke 3*, 216 n. 37) claims that Augustine was aware of a prohibitive meaning of the word in Luke 22:51 (which Augustine rejected), but the passage in Augustine cited by Bovon (*Cons.* 3.5.17) does not appear to bear out this contention.

[16] Luke 4:41, 22:51, Acts 14:16, 16:7, 19:30, 23:32, 27:32, 27:40, 28:4. Doubtful variants appear in Acts 5:38 and Rev 2:20. The only other two appearances of the term are in Matt 24:43 and 1 Cor 10:13, both with the meaning of allowance or permission.

[17] See BDAG, 269, s.v. ἐάω. I am aware of the danger of word-count fallacy, but I am still recognizing that context is paramount, enough to overrule Luke's decided lexical preference in Luke 22:51 if warranted.

[18] The word ἕως commonly means "up to" or "to the point of." When functioning as a preposition (and sometimes conjoined with other parts of speech), ἕως can denote both spatial ("as far as this") and temporal ("until") limits (Murray J. Harris, *Prepositions and Theology in the Greek New Testament: An Essential Reference Resource for Exegesis* [Grand Rapids: Zondervan, 2012], 246–47). Luke uses the term spatially (Luke 2:15; 4:29, 42; 10:15; 23:5; 24:50; Acts 1:8; 8:40; 9:38; 11:19, 22; 13:47; 17:14, 15; 21:5; 23:23; 26:11) as well as temporally (Luke 1:80, 2:37, 11:51, 23:44, Acts 1:22, 7:45, 13:20, 28:23). Understanding ἐᾶτε as "leave!" or "leave off!" would seem to demand an ablatival sense of ἕως of which the preposition is not capable.

[19] As suggested, for example, by Max Zerwick and Mary Grosvenor, with the assistance of John Welch, *A Grammatical Analysis of the Greek New Testament*, 5th ed. (Rome: Pontifical Biblical Institute, 1996), 273, without lexical justification.

[20] Augustine correctly perceived that Jesus's expressed answer constituted "a reply to the question which had been addressed by those who were about Him, and not a statement directed

to the question put forth collectively by the disciples in v. 49 and not to the sword blow of one singular disciple in v. 50.²¹ Thus, Luke's strong lexical preference as well as his grammatical syntax should caution the interpreter not to read rebuke into Luke 22:51 unless compelled by overriding contextual factors.

Those factors are not forthcoming. In fact, quite the opposite is the case. In Luke's understanding of salvation history, Jesus's one-year ministry is the year of Jubilee (4:19), the time when the kingdom was uniquely present on earth in Jesus and Satan was absent (4:43, 10:18, 11:20, 13:16, 17:20–21). After leaving Jesus for an "opportune time" (4:13), Satan returns at the end of the story when he enters the heart of Judas (22:3).²² Only in Luke does Satan expressly receive Joblike permission (ἐξαιτέω) to sift the disciples like wheat (22:31), which finds its most natural fulfillment at the scene of Jesus's arrest.²³ Satan's reappearance at the start of the

---

to Peter's act" (Cons. 3.5.17; trans. Salmond, NPNF¹). Only once does Luke use ἀποκριθείς in the context of a rebuke (23:40), and there only because of the all-important addition of ἐπιτιμάω. Rotherham ("Let be,—as long as this!") and Goodspeed ("Let me do this much!") anticipate the RSV (to be discussed below) by making Jesus's words a rebuke, punctuating as they do with an exclamation point (though retaining the permissive idea in the verb; so also the Simplified: "Allow them!"). C. K. Williams seems to want to have it both ways—"Let them do it. No more of this!"

²¹ In such a case we could have expected an aorist singular (ἔασον), not a present plural (ἐᾶτε), imperative to correspond to the εἷς τις and the singular strike of v. 50. By way of contrast, both Matthew (ἀπόστρεψον) and John (βάλε) use singular verbs when Jesus addresses the sword-wielder (Matt 26:52, John 18:11).

²² Though Luke mentions Satan in the context of his defeat (10:18, 11:18, 13:16), Satan does not explicitly reappear as a character in the story until 22:3 (the one possible exception being 8:12, but there it is difficult to know whether Luke is thinking of the period of Jesus or the period of the church). Moreover, the exorcistic activity of Jesus, rather than showing the continued presence of Satan, demonstrates that "the evil forces are dethroned and the new age has already begun" (A. J. Mattill Jr., *Luke and the Last Things: A Perspective for the Understanding of Lukan Thought* [Dillsboro: Western North Carolina Press, 1979], 164). The threefold schema of Lukan salvation history, with Jesus as the "middle" of time between the period of Israel and the period of the church, of course, owes to Hans Conzelmann (*The Theology of St. Luke*, trans. Geoffrey Buswell [Philadelphia: Fortress, 1982]). I find Conzelmann's proposal broadly persuasive but disagree on some of the particulars and the delayed apocalypticism of the *Fernerwartungsschule* (see also Joseph A. Fitzmyer, *Luke the Theologian: Aspects of His Teaching* [New York: Paulist, 1989], 61–63). Critical of Conzelmann's proposal is Susan R. Garrett, *The Demise of the Devil: Magic and the Demonic in Luke's Writings* (Minneapolis: Fortress, 1989), 41–43.

²³ The intriguing reference to Satan's permission does not indicate whether God or Jesus hears (and grants) Satan's request, but the fact that Jesus prays for Peter's faith not to fail (22:32) suggests that God is granting the permission. The use of the aorist (ἐξῃτήσατο) may further imply that the request was successful (Plummer, *Gospel according to St. Luke*, 503). The compound form ἐξαιτέω is a *hapax legomenon* that seems to carry a particularly strong sense of asking for something to which one is entitled (BDAG, 44, s.v. ἐξαιτέω). If so, it underscores the inevitability of Jesus's arrest as Satan's "hour" (22:53). An allusion to Job is tempting: "Just as in Job's case, God allowed Satan this liberty, but always within bounds—the Evil One has no free and unlimited right to act against the faithful, but must always submit to the overruling and permissive authority of the Lord" (Norval Geldenhuys, *A Commentary on the Gospel of Luke*, NICNT [Grand Rapids: Eerdmans, 1951], 566).

passion narrative suggests that all of the subsequent events, including the arrest, are part of the plan of God, which has accorded Judas (and Satan) a pivotal role (22:22).[24] Here Luke's apocalyptic dualism comes to the fore; as Susan R. Garrett observes, "Luke believed that visible human events often have an invisible spiritual dimension."[25] As in apocalyptic thought generally, evil is allowed its time under the guiding and controlling hand of God, who will bring it to a climactic and fitting end. Hence, the present "hour" belongs to Jesus's adversaries precisely because it is the time when the "power of darkness" is exercising its divinely granted ἐξουσία (22:53b).[26]

This contextual emphasis on the divine *permissio* makes Jesus's words to the disciples in Luke 22:51 readily intelligible. Instead of *rebuking* his disciples, Jesus is *reminding* his disciples of the divine plan to which both he and they must submit. A complex of terms appears in Luke to depict that plan: it is "necessary" (δεῖ) that Jesus undergo great suffering (9:22) in accordance with what is "written" (γράφω) in the Scriptures (γραφή) of Israel (18:31; 24:25–27, 44–47; Acts 13:29);[27] his death is "ordained" (ὁρίζω/προορίζω) by God as part of the "plan" (βουλή) of God (22:22, Acts 2:23, 4:28) and thus something that Jesus must "carry out" or "accomplish" (πληρόω) in his life (9:31, Acts 3:18) as part of the divine "goal" (τελέω/τελειόω/τέλος) toward which he strives (12:50, 13:32, 18:31, 22:37).[28] Not even Herod

---

[24] Despite the weight Conzelmann gives to Satan's reentry in 22:3, he is careful to point out that God, not Satan, is responsible for the passion. Satan's request to sift the disciples (22:31) indicates that God is still sovereign (*Theology of St. Luke*, 156–57).

[25] Garrett, *Demise of the Devil*, 55. She further points out that Luke "has given many strategically placed indications that the earthly events of Jesus's suffering, death, and resurrection had spiritual or cosmic causes and consequences (22:3,31,35–38,43–44; 23:44–45) ."

[26] "It is as if Jesus gives permission for his own arrest" (Frank J. Matera, *Passion Narratives and Gospel Theologies: Interpreting the Synoptics through Their Passion Stories* [New York: Paulist, 1986], 169). In Lukan theology, "darkness" is practically synonymous with Satan, as the parallelism in Acts 26:18 indicates. It is possible that the καί in Luke 22:53b is epexegetical, suggesting that the human opponents of Jesus are acting as representatives of Satan.

[27] While Luke does not often cite Scripture directly or use a scriptural fulfillment formula à la Matthew, Luke nevertheless makes use of summary references, strategic placements, and scriptural echoes to make clear that "what is happening in and through Jesus is not only the unfolding but indeed the fulfillment of God's design, witnessed in the Scriptures" (Joel B. Green, *The Theology of the Gospel of Luke*, New Testament Theology [Cambridge: Cambridge University Press, 1995], 26). Luke's use of δεῖ (eighteen times in Luke, twenty-two times in Acts) far surpasses that of Matthew (eight times) and Mark (six times).

[28] In my judgment, πληρόω and τελέω are better translated "accomplish" or "carry out" since they imply that some initiative is required on the part of Jesus to carry out the plan. As Green notes, the Lukan Jesus deliberately embraces his divine mission, "exercising his own volition and acting in ways that advance God's aim. Luke portrays Jesus as one actively engaged in discerning the will of God so as to take steps toward its consummation" (*Theology of the Gospel of Luke*, 29). In Lukan theology, the plan of God can be served, à la David (Acts 13:36), or thwarted, à la the Pharisees (Luke 7:30). Jesus ensures that he does the former. Hence, Jesus prays on the Mount of Olives for courage "to face the destiny that is his" (Fitzmyer, *Luke the Theologian*, 164).

Antipas can terminate Jesus's life prematurely since the divine plan necessitates (δεῖ) that Jesus die in Jerusalem (13:33) and be counted among transgressors (22:37).[29]

This strong divine determinacy in Luke allows the words ἐᾶτε ἕως τούτου to retain their more natural force, as all major English translations prior to the mid-twentieth century so translate (as well as the Vulgate and Luther).[30] While somewhat obscure, the words more plausibly mean something like, "permit them as far as this," "permit them up to this point," or, more contextually, "allow them to continue with the arrest," which the continuous aspect of the present-tense verb (ἐᾶτε) certainly underscores.[31] In this grammatical rendering, the object of ἐᾶτε is an implied αὐτούς ("them") and refers to the arresting party led by Judas.[32] The referent of τούτου is the arrest itself, or perhaps the entire passion event, beginning with the arrest.[33] John Nolland accepts the latter and notes that "the whole development is to be accepted as the will of God."[34]

---

[29] Noted by Lenski, *Interpretation of St. Luke's Gospel*, 757–58. Green observes the "dual causation" characteristic of Luke and the larger biblical witness that refuses "to collapse the tension between divine sovereignty and human responsibility" (*The Gospel of Luke*, NICNT [Grand Rapids: Eerdmans, 1997], 765).

[30] Contemporary German translations follow the same linguistic trajectory as the English, with Jesus becoming more and more forceful in his "denunciation" of the sword (compare "Aber Jesus befahl: 'Hort auf damit!'" [Hoffnung fur Alle, 1983] or "Aber Jesus rief: 'Halt! Hort auf'" [Neue Genfer Übersetzung, 2000] with Luther's, "Jesus aber antwortete und sprach: Lasset sie doch so machen!"). The use of *rufen* in the NGÜ is certainly questionable, while the use of *befehlen* in the HfA seems particularly unjustified in translating ἀποκριθεὶς δὲ ... εἶπεν. The Vulgate reads, respondens autem Iesus ait sinite usque huc et cum tetigisset auriculam eius sanavit eum.

[31] Buist M. Fanning, *Verbal Aspect in New Testament Greek*, Oxford Theological Monographs (Oxford: Clarendon, 1990), 353. J. M. Creed similarly translates, "Let events take their course—even to my arrest" (cited in I. Howard Marshall, *The Gospel of Luke: A Commentary on the Greek Text*, NIGTC [Grand Rapids: Eerdmans, 1978], 837). Most recently, Bovon, *Luke 3*, 217. This interpretation is at least as old as Augustine: "For it is more correct to suppose that when they put the question to Him, 'Lord, shall we smite with the sword?' He replied then, 'Suffer ye thus far'; His meaning being this: 'Let not what is about to take place agitate you. These men are to be suffered to go thus far; that is to say, so far as to apprehend me" (*Cons.* 3.5.17; trans. Salmond, *NPNF¹*).

[32] Preferred by Marshall, *Gospel of Luke*, 837. Plummer thinks it at least possible that the implied αὐτούς could be referring to the disciples, in which case Jesus is speaking to the crowd to tolerate "them" (the disciples) and their ill-advised use of force, which Jesus then rectifies (*Gospel according to St. Luke*, 512). The ἀποκριθείς of v. 51 militates against this view.

[33] The arrest was something "about to happen" (τὸ ἐσόμενον, 22:49a), prompting the sword stroke (so also Bovon, *Luke 3*, 217). Only Luke credits the disciples with this anticipation, making the action of the sword-wielder preemptive. Grammatically, the genitive form of τούτου is required by ἕως, and thus no "of" is necessary in English translation. Forty of the forty-two improper prepositions in the NT take the genitive object (see the discussion in Harris, *Prepositions and Theology*, 239–51).

[34] John Nolland, *Luke 18:35–24:53*, WBC 35C (Dallas: Word, 1993), 1088. It is doubtful that τούτου refers to the sword stroke. Paul W. Walaskay appears to accept this referent ("You may go

Narratively, Luke has been slowly preparing for Jesus's eventual arrest. Earlier in the Gospel, Jesus gives a cryptic answer to the question of paying taxes to the emperor precisely to avoid a premature arrest (20:20–26). Upon his arrival in Jerusalem, Jesus taught regularly and openly in the temple precincts but was not apprehended because it was not yet his "hour" (22:53; cf. 20:19). At Passover, when his "hour" had indeed come (22:14, 53), Jesus instructs his disciples to procure swords.[35] This acquisition would guard against his being attacked by priestly authorities or their henchmen on the way out of the city to the Mount of Olives (22:35–38; cf. 19:47; 20:19, 20; 22:2).[36] Once on the Mount of Olives and at his designated "place" (τοῦ τόπου, 22:40), Jesus begins prayerfully to fortify himself in his Father's will (22:41–46) and to ready himself to carry out the plan that God has determined for him to do (22:22).[37] The disciples must not interfere with that plan! Unlike Forrest Gump, who thwarted Lieutenant Dan's destiny by saving him from death on the battlefield, the disciples must not interfere with Jesus's arrest by seeking to save him.

In keeping with this theme of divine purpose, Luke's portrait of Jesus at the passion is one of confidence and control. As Paul S. Minear recognizes, Jesus "remains in full control of the developing situation" as events run their course.[38]

---

thus far, but no farther") and gives it a decided political slant: Jesus is limiting the disciples' defensive use of the sword to "the Jewish pawns of Rome"; "Rome itself must not be confronted" (*"And So We Came to Rome": The Political Perspective of St. Luke*, SNTSMS 49 [Cambridge: Cambridge University Press, 1983], 17).

[35] Only Luke introduces the theme of the "hour" at the Passover meal (22:14). According to Raymond E. Brown, "hour" is one of Luke's terms for the divine plan (*The Death of the Messiah: From Gethsemane to the Grave. A Commentary on the Passion Narratives in the Four Gospels*, 2 vols., ABRL [New York: Doubleday, 1994], 1:293). In Luke, the "hour" begins when Satan enters the heart of Judas (22:3); it is thus the "hour" of Jesus and Satan simultaneously, a theological tension that Luke makes no attempt to resolve (Acts 2:23).

[36] That Jesus deemed only two swords sufficient suggests a more limited scope to his directive. Plummer thinks that the swords were intended on this occasion to guard against possible attack in the city (*Gospel according to St. Luke*, 506). Like the Essenes, historically Jesus's disciples may well have carried a small sword (μάχαιρα) for protection against brigands on the highways. One at least must explain how it is that the disciples could so quickly produce swords. In a subsequent paper, I will argue that the explanatory γάρ in Luke 22:37 establishes an often overlooked rationale for Jesus's directive to procure swords, a rationale not altogether unlike his directive in Luke 22:51, albeit from another direction. Both directives ensure that God's plan will be carried out to the smallest detail.

[37] Brown observes that Luke likes to portray Jesus as praying in a certain τόπος, such as in Luke 4:42 and 11:1 (*Death of the Messiah*, 1:148). Brown considers τοῦ τόπου not a technical designation but a term of familiarity, the place where Jesus lodged at night (Luke 21:37). Interestingly, the Gospel of John also calls the same location τὸν τόπον (18:2). Luke never calls the location of Jesus's arrest "Gethsemane" (cf. Mark 14:32, Matt 26:36), avoiding "exotic Semitic names and expressions" (Brown, 1:148–49).

[38] Paul S. Minear, "A Note on Luke 22:36," *NovT* 7 (1964–65): 131. I disagree with the upshot that Minear wants to make of this point, but his point remains valid for my purposes nevertheless.

Jesus prearranges the logistics of the Passover meal (22:10–13). He knows he is about to suffer (22:15), pouring out his life in an act of covenantal sacrifice (22:20, accepting the longer ending). He is aware of the betrayal and the identity of his betrayer (22:21, 48). He assigns the apostles a special place of ruling in his kingdom, which no events on earth can annul (22:28–30). He prays for Peter's faith (22:31) and predicts Peter's threefold denial (22:34) and eventual restoration (22:32). He proactively demands that the disciples procure swords (22:35–38).

Now on the Mount of Olives at the pivotal moment in the divine drama, Jesus calmly anticipates and permits his arrest, confident in the divine δεῖ that governs his life. In a stunning act of divine reversal, Jesus heals the slave of the high priest (22:51b), allowing the arrest to proceed and God's plan to continue. Luke alone of the four evangelists narrates this healing.[39] Contrary to the view of most commentators, Luke does not attribute this healing to Jesus's love of enemies, and it is sloppy (or else wishful) reading to see its thematic presence here.[40] References to love are not as numerous in Luke as one might think.[41] Assuming enemy-love as the

---

[39] From a historical perspective, singular attestation as well as the presence of Lukan vocabulary in Luke 22:49–51 compels John P. Meier to consider the passage a Lukan creation (*A Marginal Jew: Rethinking the Historical Jesus*, vol. 2, *Mentor, Message, and Miracles*, ABRL [New York: Doubleday, 1994], 716–18). Contra Plummer, who thinks that the very obscurity of the saying in v. 51a lends credence to its historical veracity (*Gospel according to St. Luke*, 512). Marion L. Soards more precisely assigns the "rebuke" in the first half of v. 51 to a Lukan composition stemming from an oral tradition, and the healing in the second half to a Lukan composition stemming from Luke's own personal reflection (*The Passion according to Luke: The Special Material of Luke 22*, JSNTSup 14 [Sheffield: JSOT Press, 1987], 99–100).

[40] Typical is Richard J. Cassidy: "Jesus had previously stressed love for enemies as an alternative to responding toward them with violence, and Luke now shows him observing this teaching in the breach. Responding with love and forgiveness, rather than with violence, Jesus heals the wound of one who had come out against him as an enemy" (*Jesus, Politics, and Society: A Study of Luke's Gospel* [Maryknoll, NY: Orbis Books, 1978], 46). Cassidy's comments are surprising, given that he himself exhorts his reader to pay attention to "what Luke's description actually states" (p. 44). Admittedly, the love interpretation is ancient, going back at least to Ephrem the Syrian in the fourth century: "He whose ear had been healed expressed his gratitude for this love with hatred" (Arthur A. Just Jr., *Ancient Christian Commentary on Scripture: Luke* [Downers Grove, IL: InterVarsity, 2003], 347).

[41] This point is admitted by Richard B. Hays, *The Moral Vision of the New Testament: Community, Cross, New Creation. A Contemporary Introduction to New Testament Ethics* (San Francisco: HarperSanFrancisco, 1996), 201–2. Jack T. Sanders is correct to say that love constitutes only a "minor" theme in Luke (*Ethics in the New Testament: Change and Development* [Philadelphia: Fortress, 1975], 38). See the sobering statistics in Meier, *A Marginal Jew: Rethinking the Historical Jesus*, vol. 4, *Law and Love*, AYBRL (New Haven: Yale University Press, 2009), 581 n. 6. Source-critically, enemy-love appears only in a single Q saying (Matt 5:44//Luke 6:27, 35) and in "L" material brought into redactional relationship with the Markan Jesus's love command (Luke 10:25–37; cf. Mark 12:29–31). Meier further notes that no single form of Jesus's love command is multiply attested (p. 480). Enemy-love as an explicit theme is absent from Mark, John, Paul, the Catholic Epistles, and Revelation and strikingly from Acts, meaning that the sermons of Acts

motivation for the healing of the slave of the high priest only underscores this problematic hermeneutical move.[42] Despite the widespread view that Jesus is demonstrating enemy-love toward the slave of the high priest, ironically the only "love" (φιλέω) expressly shown on this occasion is that of Judas, who seeks to betray the Son of Man with a kiss (22:47b–48).[43] Rather, the healing of the slave of the high priest could well express Jesus's control of the situation and the inevitability of God's plan. As Minear recognizes, "His knowledge of the disciples and God's design enables him not only to anticipate the impending events but also to halt those events when the divine purpose has been accomplished."[44]

The preceding grammatical and contextual analysis of Jesus's words in Luke 22:51 offers compelling grounds for challenging the prevailing and nearly ubiquitous view that Jesus was rebuking the disciples for their use of the sword. It is astonishing, therefore, to read that Luke's "denunciation of the use of the sword is unambiguous and emphatic" and that "more emphatically Luke could hardly have stated his case."[45] It is equally surprising to read, "The fact that Jesus replied so

---

(whether penned or edited by Luke) manage to articulate the gospel without recourse to this (for us) much-overused word. The closest one comes to a repetition of Jesus's teaching is Rom 12:14 and 1 Pet 3:9, but even in those places neither Paul nor the Petrine author can bring himself to say "love your enemy" despite having enjoined believers to mutual love in the immediate context (Rom 12:9, 10; 1 Pet 3:8). The paucity of NT material discussed by Victor Paul Furnish (*The Love Command in the New Testament*, NTL [Nashville: Abingdon, 1972], 45–58) and Pheme Perkins (*Love Commands in the New Testament* [New York: Paulist, 1982], 38–40) is telling.

[42] Luke 22:51b provides an excellent "test case" in this regard: Is Jesus's healing of the slave an act of love or perhaps control, or both? While we must guard against the word-concept fallacy here, we must also be careful not to read love too easily into Jesus's acts of healing and forgiveness so as to expand the semantic field quite considerably (contra Furnish, *Love Command in the New Testament*, 20–21). As Paul reminds us, good and noble deeds do not necessarily stem from love (1 Cor 13:1–3). D. A. Carson's incisive comments are instructive in this regard (*The Difficult Doctrine of the Love of God* [Wheaton, IL: Crossway, 2000], 28). Other motivations could stand behind many of Jesus's actions. Soards observes, for example, that Jesus's act of healing demonstrates that "Jesus was not powerless at the time of his arrest," possessing the "same authority he has exercised throughout the course of his ministry" (*Passion according to Luke*, 94).

[43] Meier's observation is to the point: "Most believers take for granted that what lies at the heart of Jesus's message and what is repeated incessantly throughout his preaching is love, both of neighbor and love of enemies. This is the received 'gospel' of generations who have grown up believing that all you need is love. However, if we restrict ourselves for the moment to the Synoptic Gospels, one would not get such an impression from the sayings of Jesus. Love as a verb or noun occurs relatively rarely on the lips of Jesus. When it does occur, Jesus is often citing a text from the Jewish Scriptures or commenting on it" (*Law and Love*, 480–81).

[44] Minear, "Note on Luke 22:36," 131.

[45] Eben Scheffler, "Compassionate Action: Living according to Luke's Gospel," in *Identity, Ethics, and Ethos in the New Testament*, ed. Jan G. van der Watt, BZNW 141 (Berlin: de Gruyter, 2006), 95–96.

emphatically to the disciples' question and the action that one of them took is in itself sufficient to indicate that his position against violence was firm."[46]

If Jesus is not condemning the use of the sword per se, the implications for Christian ethics, at least from a Lukan perspective, are considerable and far-reaching. Granted, even if the idea of permission is paramount in Luke 22:51, it is still necessary for the disciples to put away their swords, but now the command is indirect, decidedly not a rebuke, and subservient to the larger eschatological purposes of God. Michel Desjardins is honest enough to admit that in Luke's account of the arrest "violence *per se* does not appear to be condemned, only violence not in accord with God's plan."[47] In other words, there is no "principled" stand against violence on the part of the Lukan Jesus in a manner reminiscent for us of a Tolstoy, a Gandhi, or a King, just as the witness of the Third Gospel itself is not completely consistent on the question of violence.[48] Jesus may have been a pacifist, but not for the reasons one might think. To put it starkly but quite anachronistically: atonement, not "Anabaptism," lies behind the pacifism of Jesus.

II. LUKE 22:51 AND THE REVISED STANDARD VERSION

So, who or what has led us along a path of potential mistranslation and misunderstanding? The root of the problem appears to lie at the feet of the Standard Bible Committee of the Revised Standard Version, whose formative work in revising the American Standard Version of 1901 both before and during the years of the Second World War makes one at least wonder if the effects of the war may have unduly influenced their translation of Luke 22:51.[49] The problematic history of the reception of the RSV, of course, is well known, being suspected as it was of ideological bias.[50] While much of the criticism in hindsight was unjustified, the translation could perhaps be more justifiably criticized here.[51] In a war-torn Europe and

---

[46] Cassidy, *Jesus, Politics, and Society*, 46. He considers Jesus's statement in Luke 22:51 a "clear and explicit response" indicating Jesus's principled stand against violence (154 n. 34).

[47] Michel Desjardins, *Peace, Violence and the New Testament*, BibSem 46 (Sheffield: Sheffield Academic, 1997), 23.

[48] Cassidy is willing to concede that Luke's presentation of Jesus is so aggressive at times (e.g., 12:51–52) that "some scholars have concluded that Luke actually presents him as sanctioning the use of violence" (*Jesus, Politics, and Society*, 41).

[49] The translation work began in 1930 but ran out of funds in 1932. The work would not resume until 1937 with the financial backing of the publisher Thomas Nelson and Sons.

[50] Some of the charges leveled against the RSV included the denial of the virgin birth, Christ's deity, blood atonement, and the avowal of communism! See Bruce M. Metzger, *The Bible in Translation: Ancient and English Versions* (Grand Rapids: Baker Academic, 2001), 119–20, as well as his comments in Bruce M. Metzger, Robert C. Dentan, and Walter Harrelson, *The Making of the New Revised Standard Version of the Bible* (Grand Rapids: Eerdmans, 1991), 51.

[51] For an appreciative and fair critique of the RSV from a conservative direction, see F. F. Bruce, *History of the Bible in English: From the Earliest Versions*, 3rd ed. (New York: Oxford

a weary America fighting in both the European and Pacific theaters, Jesus's words could not be more prophetic, poignant, or pointed: "No more of this!"[52] With this exclamation, Jesus's words suddenly jump off the Lukan page and into the headlines of World War II.

Actually, one can pinpoint the exact date that a fundamental change in translation occurred. A check of the RSV Committee Papers housed in the Special Collections of the Yale Divinity School reveals a shift in the translation of Luke 22:51 between 1940 and 1942.[53] The third draft of the Gospel of Luke, dated to August 1940 and edited by James Moffatt acting as executive secretary of the New Testament revision committee, shows the committee's original revision of the passage ("Let this go no further"), itself problematic, crossed out in pencil and a handwritten translation written directly above it: "No more of this!"[54] The date of the change inscribed in the margin of the draft is May 28, 1942[55] (see next page).

This new rendering of Luke 22:51 constitutes a radical departure from the ASV's nonexclamatory "suffer ye *them* thus far."[56] Is it possible that America's entry into World War II on 7 December 1941 at least partially (or subconsciously) accounts for a more vociferous Jesus? With this translation, of course, the RSV would set a precedent in the English translation of Luke 22:51 for years to come.[57] The RSV thus appears truly to mark a watershed moment in the history of the English translation of the passage in contrast to the dominant English translation of the passage beginning with Tyndale.

University Press, 1978), 186–203, as well as Jack P. Lewis, *The English Bible from KJV to NIV: A History and Evaluation* (Grand Rapids: Baker, 1982), 107–28. While recognizing the harmful and excessive rhetoric of the RSV's detractors, Bruce registers the concern that the "relative freedom which the revisers permitted themselves has at times led to inaccurate renderings" (p. 191), particularly in their blurring of finer distinctions in the Greek (p. 194). I would contend that Luke 22:51 is one of those instances.

[52] The second edition (1935) of the French Louis Segond version appears to anticipate this rendering somewhat with its "Laissez, arretez!" ("Leave off! Stop!"), noted by Bovon, *Luke 3*, 217 n. 38. It is probably impossible to know if any of the RSV translators were aware of this version or influenced by it. The setting of the 1930s for both translations is telling.

[53] I wish to thank my former student and Yale Divinity School graduate Craig Canfield for his invaluable assistance in locating these collections.

[54] I take the word "this" here to refer to the sword stroke, a rather doubtful interpretation, as pointed out earlier. Moreover, the translation mistakenly assumes that ἕως carries implications about a future course of action ("no further") when in fact the preposition presages no such meaning. The word means "up" to this point, not "beyond" this point.

[55] For a firsthand account of the working procedures of the committee, see Luther A. Weigle, "The Making of the RSV of the New Testament," *Religion in Life* 15 (1946): 163–73.

[56] Even today the ASV is not completely passé. One contemporary scholar who bases his work on it is Mattill, who calls the ASV "that rock of biblical honesty" (*Luke and the Last Things*, iii).

[57] One notable exception was the New English Bible ("let them have their way"), which later changed to a rebuke in the Revised English Bible ("Stop! No more of that!").

Luke 8-24
Moffatt Edited
August 1940

Chapter Twenty-Two

50 with the sword?" And one of them ~~did strike~~ struck the servant
51 of the high priest, and cut off his right ear. But
Jesus said, ~~"Let this go no further!~~ "No more of this!" And he touched
52 his ear and healed him. Then Jesus said to the chief
priests and captains of the temple and elders, who had
come out against him, "Have you come out as against
53 a robber, with swords and clubs? When I was with you
~~daily~~ day after day in the temple, you did not lay hands on me. But
this is your hour, and the power of darkness."

54 Then they seized him and led him away, bringing
him into the high priest's house. Peter followed at a
55 distance; And when they had kindled a fire in the
middle of the courtyard and sat down together, Peter
56 sat among them. Then a maid-servant, seeing him as he
sat in the light and gazing at him, said, "This man also
57 was with him." But he denied it, saying, "Woman, I do
58 not know him." And a little later another servant saw
him and said, "You also are one of them." But Peter
59 said, "Man, I am not." And after an interval of about
an hour still another insisted, saying, "Certainly this
60 man also was with him; for he is a Galilean." But
Peter said, "Man, I do not know what you are saying."
And immediately, while he was still speaking, the cock
61 crowed. And the Lord turned and looked at Peter. And
Peter remembered the word of the Lord, how he had said

Luke 22:51 in English Translation: Prohibition

Revised Standard Version (1946)	"No more of this!"
Phillips (1952)	"That will do!"
Jerusalem Bible (1966)	"Leave off! That will do!"
New American Bible (1970)	"Stop, no more of this!"
New American Standard (1971)	"Stop! No more of this."
Translator's (1973)	"Stop! No more!"
Today's English Version (1976)	"Enough of this!"
Simplified English (1978)	"Stop!"
New International Version (1984, 2011)	"No more of this!"
New Jerusalem Bible (1985)	"That is enough."
New Century Version (1987)	"Stop! No more of this."
Revised English Bible (1989)	"Stop! No more of that!"
New Revised Standard (1989)	"No more of this!"
Scholars Version (1993)	"Stop! That will do!"
New Living Translation (1966)	"No more of this."
NET Bible (1998)	"Enough of this!"
Holman Christian Standard (1999)	"No more of this!"
Today's New International Version (2001)	"No more of this!"
English Standard Version (2001)	"No more of this!"
Common English Bible (2010)	"Stop! No more of this!"
Kingdom New Testament (2011)	"Enough of that!"

One must certainly exercise great caution, as F. F. Bruce reminds us, before accusing a translation of theological or ideological bias.[58] Theological or ideological "biases" are often in the eye of the religious and political beholder, and it remains an open question the extent to which pacifist inclinations or commitments may have influenced the translators of the RSV. Nevertheless, though ecumenical in nature, the RSV translation committee remained "resolutely mainline Protestant in affiliation."[59] Moreover, while the members of the committee prided themselves on offering impartial renderings of biblical phraseology, many of the members spoke of translation less as a science and more as an art.[60] Edgar J. Goodspeed was a particularly forceful advocate for colloquial renderings of the NT, informed and inspired as he was by the discovery of the Greek papyri in the last decades of the nineteenth century and opening decades of the twentieth.[61]

---

[58] Bruce, *History of the Bible in English*, 200.

[59] Metzger, Dentan, and Harrelson, *Making of the New Revised Standard Version*, 9. This particular observation is that of Dentan regarding the RSV, the predecessor to the NRSV.

[60] Peter J. Thuesen, *In Discordance with the Scriptures: American Protestant Battles over Translating the Bible* (New York: Oxford University Press, 1999), 82.

[61] On the impact of the Greek papyrological finds on the vernacular character of NT Greek, see Edgar J. Goodspeed, *How Came the Bible* (Nashville: Abingdon, 1940), 120–31.

One member of the Standard Bible Committee was the devoted pacifist and Quaker Henry J. Cadbury, widely regarded in his day as the foremost authority on the writings of Luke. Cadbury's work on behalf of peace was extensive and thoroughgoing. For example, he worked to help Quakers and conscientious objectors find alternative avenues of service in wartime, helping to organize in 1917 the American Friends Service Committee (AFSC), on whose behalf he would later accept the Nobel Peace Prize (1947).[62] It is difficult to imagine that the author of such groundbreaking works as *The Style and Literary Method of Luke* and *The Making of Luke-Acts* did not exert a considerable influence on the RSV's translation of Luke, either as principal translator or in subsequent committee discussions.[63] Cadbury had the reputation of being a fastidious translator, often reversing his own philological judgments when it came time for a vote.[64] Complicating matters somewhat is the fact that Cadbury took some time off from committee translation work in 1941–42 due to a depression brought on partly by the effects of the war.[65] The extent of Cadbury's influence on the particular translation of Luke 22:51 remains

---

[62] For a full account of Cadbury as Quaker and pacifist, see Margaret Hope Bacon, *Let This Life Speak: The Legacy of Henry Joel Cadbury* (Philadelphia: University of Pennsylvania Press, 1987).

[63] In a pamphlet entitled *Translating the Bible for Today* put out by the RSV translation committee in 1947 (and housed in the Yale Divinity School Special Collections), Clarence T. Craig described the committee's translation procedures as follows: "A book would be assigned to an individual or a pair to produce the first draft.... Copies would be made of these drafts and circulated for study, and we would write into the margin the changes we intended to propose. When the committee came together, Dr. Moffatt, as executive secretary, would read a paragraph; and then the group around the table would start in. By the time they were through, it would be difficult to tell who had made the first draft, so carefully had it been gone over by the committee as a whole. This was then mimeographed, and given further study; it was revised again, and then a third time." Any proposed change to the ASV required a two-thirds approval of the entire thirty-two member committee (Weigle, "Making of the RSV of the New Testament," 166). I have not as of yet been able to determine whether Cadbury was assigned the Gospel of Luke. Given his reputation as the foremost living Lukan scholar, it would only make sense that he was. Since the principal translation change occurred during the third draft, this question may be less important than first appears.

[64] Thuesen, *In Discordance with the Scriptures*, 84. For a firsthand anecdote, see Edgar J. Goodspeed, *As I Remember: The Autobiography of Edgar J. Goodspeed* (New York: Harper & Brothers, 1953), 75–76. Cadbury had the reputation of being a tough negotiator more than a team player (Richard I. Pervo, "'On Perilous Things': A Response to Beverly R. Gaventa," in *Cadbury, Knox, and Talbert: American Contributions to the Study of Acts*, ed. Mikeal C. Parsons and Joseph B. Tyson, BSNA [Atlanta: Scholars Press, 1992], 42 n. 21, apparently relying on the personal observation of Amos N. Wilder).

[65] Bacon, *Let This Life Speak*, 129–34. Unfortunately, Bacon's chronology at the point of Cadbury's depression is not entirely clear.

an open question.⁶⁶ If he was a leading influence behind the translation, Cadbury himself came dangerously close to the "peril" of modernizing Jesus.⁶⁷

While not all mainline Protestants of the time were strict pacifists or remained so (Reinhold Niebuhr certainly comes to mind!), the era in which the RSV committee both began (1930) and resumed (1937) its work represented a high point for liberal pacifism and its confidence in the abolition of war. The growing pacifism between the two World Wars received regular reinforcement on the pages of *The Christian Century*, the leading mainline Protestant magazine of the time to which Cadbury often contributed, and from its pacifist editor, Charles Clayton Morrison. As Martin E. Marty recounts, "Between the wars a broad pacifist sentiment had developed. Protestant clergy, often coached or rallied by this most influential mainline and liberal magazine, leaned toward the peacemaking side."⁶⁸ Despite the looming threat of Hitler, pacifism was in the air.

---

⁶⁶ To be fair, Cadbury did not base his pacifism on any one saying or deed of Jesus but looked to "the whole tenor of his life and death" (Bacon, *Let This Life Speak*, 47). Nevertheless, Jesus's actions (or lack thereof) at his arrest are pivotal for that pacifistic "sounding." As to the leading influence on the translation of Luke 22:51, it may be possible to narrow it down somewhat. Of the original members of the NT translation committee, James Hardy Ropes resigned in 1932, A. T. Roberston died in 1934, and both William P. Armstrong and Andrew Sledd departed in 1937. Of the surviving members, Millar Burrows was a specialist in Aramaic, F. C. Grant specialized in the history of English translation, and Luther A. Weigle served as chair. As a Scotsman, James Moffatt refused to vote on any colloquial English phraseology and did not insist on the propriety of his own published translation. In a game of historical detective work, that leaves Walter Russell Bowie, Craig, Abdel R. Wentz, Goodspeed, and Cadbury (for a listing of the entire Standard Bible Committee, see Thuesen, *In Discordance with the Scriptures*, 74–75). My best guess is a combination of Cadbury and Goodspeed. Goodspeed once recounted that he and Cadbury often teamed up in their RSV translation work—but often in a losing cause! (Goodspeed, *As I Remember*, 76). If the collaboration was successful on this occasion, was Cadbury largely responsible for the initial change ("let this go no further"), which Goodspeed then put into the "vernacular"? The ultimate translation that found its way into the RSV would appear to need this penultimate rendering as a transitional stage. The final version is simply too radical a departure from the Tyndale tradition reflected in the ASV.

⁶⁷ See Cadbury, *The Peril of Modernizing Jesus* (New York: Macmillan, 1937). Despite strong circumstantial evidence, we would still be wise to heed Beverly R. Gaventa's caution "to be careful lest we impute to him a view he did not actually have." This, in her view, is the peril of modernizing Henry J. Cadbury ("The Peril of Modernizing Henry Joel Cadbury," in Parsons and Tyson, *Cadbury, Knox, and Talbert*, 8). Cadbury, for example, fully recognized the apocalyptic character of Jesus's life and work but appears to understate the problem of eschatological imminence for Christian ethics (see his "Social Translation of the Gospel," *HTR* 15 [1922]: 1–13). Cadbury liked to say that he was always trying to "translate" the NT.

⁶⁸ Martin E. Marty, "War's Dilemmas: The *Century* 1938–1945," *ChrCent* 101, no. 28 (September 1984): 867.

The Apocrypha Committee in session, (l. to r. around the table) Drs. Clarence T. Craig, Bruce M. Metzger, Henry J. Cadbury, Luther A. Weigle, Floyd V. Filson, Robert H. Pfeiffer and Allen P. Wikgren.

Special Collections, Yale Divinity School

Whether the RSV's translation committee breathed in too much of that air so as to affect their translation unnecessarily may be impossible to say. But as Lawrence Venuti reminds us of translations in general, "we do not need to attribute a deliberate intention to the translator in order to perceive the skewed representation in the translation."[69] All translations, in Venuti's view, cannot help but rewrite foreign texts in a way that makes them more congenial to the dominant culture receiving the translation.[70] If, for example, as Abraham Smith observes, "translations of Mark could re-present or reshape the cultural identities of Mark's world and characters in ways palatable and ideologically meaningful to translators and their audiences,"

---

[69] Lawrence Venuti, *The Scandals of Translation: Towards an Ethics of Difference* (New York: Routledge, 1998), 3. Venuti himself is relying on the work of I. Mason here (Mason, "Discourse, Ideology, and Translation," in *Language, Discourse and Translation in the West and Middle East*, ed. R. de Beaugrande, A. Shunneq, and M. Helmy Heliel [Amsterdam: Benjamins, 1994]).

[70] While recognizing the inevitability of ethnocentrism in translation, Venuti believes that an "ethics of difference" can take place in translation by restoring formerly neglected elements, taking into account the interests of not simply the domestic culture but the originating culture, decentering domestic terms by an openness to foreign cultural values and not seeing the work of translation as a finished task (*Scandals of Translation*, 81–87).

the same could certainly be said of the RSV translation of Luke.[71] As one reviewer observed at the time, the RSV "not only represents the best of modern scholarship but fits the habits and feelings of the churches which are expected to use it."[72]

Applying Venuti's insights to the translation of Luke, a pacifist Jesus who rebukes his disciples' use of the sword certainly takes on a more domesticated cultural identity for many contemporary liberal Protestants than a Jesus who acts in concert with a predetermined plan of God that grants the figure of Satan a decisive role in an apocalyptic drama involving heaven and earth. A pacifist Jesus who says, "No more of this violence!" feels much more theologically comfortable and politically tenable to us than an apocalyptic Jesus who says, "Permit them to proceed with the arrest because it is Satan's hour."[73] To domesticate Jesus in this way, to use Venuti's term, involves one in the "scandal" of translation that constantly calls for attentiveness to the originating culture and a willingness to reassess the evidence.

[71] Abraham Smith, "Cultural Studies: Making Mark," in *Mark and Method: New Approaches in Biblical Studies*, ed. Janice Capel Anderson and Stephen D. Moore, 2nd ed. (Minneapolis: Fortress, 2008), 188.

[72] W. E. Garrison, "A New New Testament—Coming," *ChrCent* 53, no. 6 (1946): 172.

[73] Ironically, conservative evangelical translations more theologically in line with apocalyptic eschatology (NASB, NIV, ESV, HCSB) perpetuate the RSV's misleading translation of Luke 22:51.

Interrupted Speech in Luke-Acts

DANIEL LYNWOOD SMITH
dsmit133@slu.edu
Saint Louis University, St. Louis, MO 63108

Although past scholarly attention has centered on the interruptions of Acts, the Gospel of Luke and Acts each include several instances of interrupted speech. While some interruptions by external events function simply to increase the drama of a scene (e.g., Luke 9:34; 22:47, 60; 24:36; Acts 10:44), I argue that Luke also deploys interruption as a powerful literary and rhetorical device. By setting Luke's use of interruption alongside the use of interruption in other ancient Greek narratives, I demonstrate the unique form of Lukan interruption, which focuses on the effect of a speaker's message on the hearers. From Jesus's interruption by his hearers in the Nazareth synagogue in Luke 4 to Paul's interruption by Festus in Acts 26, Luke portrays Jesus and his followers as being interrupted frequently by emotional audiences (Luke 4:28; 11:27; Acts 4:1; 7:54, 57; 13:48; 22:22; 24:25; and 26:24). The emotional and often violent character of these interruptions serves to underscore the powerful impact of early Christian preaching about the resurrection and exaltation of Jesus and about the subsequent availability of salvation to all nations.

As they heard these things [ἀκούοντες ταῦτα], all in the synagogue were filled with rage, and they rose up, drove [Jesus] out of the city, and led him to the edge of the hill on which their city was built, so that they might throw him down. (Luke 4:28–29)

But while [Paul] was making his defense [ταῦτα δὲ αὐτοῦ ἀπολογουμένου], Festus said in a loud voice, "Paul, you've gone mad! Your great learning is driving you crazy!" (Acts 26:24)[1]

In both Luke and Acts, speakers are interrupted by their audiences. Scholars, however, have focused their attention almost exclusively on the interruptions in Luke's second volume. For example, in his major study of the speeches of Acts, Marion L. Soards observes a "pattern of interruption" that "occurs repeatedly."[2]

I would like to thank Geoffrey Miller, Matthew Thiessen, and Jeffrey Wickes for their helpful comments on an earlier version of this article.

[1] All translations are my own, unless otherwise noted.
[2] Marion L. Soards, *The Speeches in Acts: Their Content, Context, and Concerns* (Louisville: Westminster John Knox, 1994), 114.

Soards here echoes the conclusion of several other studies of the speeches of Acts.[3] Yet, even though he recognizes that Luke and Acts form a "two-part account," Soards makes no mention of interrupted speech in the Gospel of Luke.[4] Perhaps this myopia should not surprise those who are familiar with long-established scholarly opinions about the relative literary merits of the Gospel and Acts. In Acts, we find speeches; in Luke, only sermons and teaching material. Or so claimed Martin Dibelius: "Luke has not ascribed one single speech to Jesus."[5] This preoccupation with the "speeches" in Acts has stunted scholarly exploration of interrupted speech across both Luke and Acts. To understand interrupted speech in Luke-Acts, these two Lukan volumes must be read together.

I. "Apostolic Irresistibility" or Kerygmatic Volatility?

In a recent article, Joshua D. Garroway has taken a step forward by arguing that a fuller understanding of the interrupted speeches of Acts is possible only by attending to Luke's Gospel. Garroway identifies a theory of "apostolic irresistibility" outlined in Luke 21:12–15.[6] In this passage, Jesus foretells the trials that his followers will face, balancing the warnings with a promise in v. 15 that they will receive "eloquence and wisdom [στόμα καὶ σοφίαν] that all your adversaries will be unable to resist or contradict [ἀντιστῆναι ἢ ἀντειπεῖν]." For Garroway, this promise "holds the key for unlocking the mystery of Luke's use of interruption in Acts."[7] Garroway goes on to argue that the "interrupted speeches" of Acts are a product of Luke's

---

[3] Henry J. Cadbury, "The Speeches in Acts," in *The Beginnings of Christianity*, part 1, *The Acts of the Apostles*, ed. F. J. Foakes Jackson and Kirsopp Lake, 5 vols. (London: Macmillan, 1920–33), 5:402–27, esp. 425–26; Martin Dibelius, *Studies in the Acts of the Apostles*, ed. Heinrich Greeven (London: SCM, 1956), 160; Fred Veltman, "The Defense Speeches of Paul in Acts," in *Perspectives on Luke-Acts*, ed. Charles H. Talbert (Edinburgh: T&T Clark, 1978), 243–56, esp. 254–55; George A. Kennedy, *New Testament Interpretation through Rhetorical Criticism* (Chapel Hill: University of North Carolina Press, 1984), 134, 137; G. H. R. Horsley, "Speeches and Dialogue in Acts," *NTS* 32 (1986): 609–14, esp. 610–11; Richard I. Pervo, *Profit with Delight: The Literary Genre of the Acts of the Apostles* (Philadelphia: Fortress, 1987), 76.

[4] Soards, *Speeches in Acts*, 194. My argument both assumes the unity of Luke-Acts and serves as further support for reading these two volumes together.

[5] Dibelius, *Studies in the Acts of the Apostles*, 184. Luke 4:17–27 might be raised as a counterexample, but, for Dibelius, this discourse is simply an instance of "collating traditional material" (p. 185). Ironically, Dibelius claims earlier in his essay that the characteristic feature of speeches is that "they are addressed to, or are known to have claimed the attention of a large number of people in some other way" (p. 150). Surely Luke 4:17–27 "claimed the attention" of those in the Nazareth synagogue!

[6] Joshua D. Garroway, "'Apostolic Irresistibility' and the Interrupted Speeches in Acts," *CBQ* 74 (2012): 738–52.

[7] Ibid., 740.

literary attempt to balance the *theological* affirmation of apostolic irresistibility with the *historical* fact that Jesus's followers were indeed resisted by many Jews and gentiles. Following this line of thought, if the apostles had been permitted to finish their speeches, their audiences would have been won over; this inevitable fate is avoided only by the repeated cutting short of the apostolic preaching.

Garroway is correct to search for a literary solution to the question at hand, and he draws helpful connections between Luke 21:15 and the apostles' discourses in Acts. However, his attempt to explain the phenomenon of interrupted speech in Acts on the basis of apostolic irresistibility does not adequately account for all the instances of interruption in Acts. Furthermore, his argument is too limited, focusing only on interruption in Acts; David E. Aune has pointed out that interrupted speech appears in Luke's Gospel as well as in Acts.[8] While Garroway is certainly not alone in identifying seven "interrupted speeches" in Acts 3, 7, 10, 17, 22, 24, and 26, I would argue that attending to the narrative in which the discourses in Luke-Acts are embedded offers a more defensible list of at least six interruptions in the Gospel of Luke (4:28; 9:34; 11:27; 22:47, 60; 24:36) and eight interruptions in Acts, with clear evidence of interruption in Acts 4:1; 7:54, 57; 10:44; 13:48; 22:22; 24:25; and 26:24.[9]

By examining interruption in other ancient Greek narratives, including Luke's Gospel, we can arrive at a more satisfactory explanation of interruption in Acts. First, a survey of other ancient Greek narratives reveals a common understanding that people should take turns when speaking. There are rules for taking turns, and interruption can be described as the violation of these turn-taking rules. With a more contextual understanding of interruption in other Greek narratives, we will be able to appreciate the ways in which the interrupted discourses of Luke-Acts are unique in their form, frequency, and function. Upon closer examination, we can see that, in both volumes, interrupted speech has a range of literary and rhetorical functions. Still, a general pattern emerges. Close attention to the details of each rhetorical situation reveals that the intentional interruption of a speaker by an emotional audience repeatedly directs the reader's attention to the powerful impact of early Christian preaching about the resurrection of Jesus and the subsequent availability of salvation to all nations. Whether the audience accepts this preaching varies, but the potency of these dynamic discourses remains constant. The frequency of intentional interruption in Luke-Acts is thus a result not of apostolic irresistibility but of kerygmatic volatility.

---

[8] David E. Aune, *The New Testament in Its Literary Environment*, LEC 8 (Philadelphia: Westminster, 1987), 127.

[9] For reasons explained below, I do not consider Paul to be interrupted at the end of the Areopagus speech (Acts 17:22–31), nor do I find evidence that his defense speech before Felix in 24:10–21 is interrupted. A stronger case can be made for considering Luke 15:21 as an interrupted discourse, based on 15:18–19.

II. Discerning Interrupted Speech in Ancient Greek Narratives

To achieve any clarity, a discussion of the "interrupted speeches in Acts" requires a treatment of nomenclature. Garroway readily admits that "interruption" is an imprecise term. He summarizes the scholarly inconsistency that pervades discussions of the interrupted speeches of Acts as follows: "Precisely how many speeches are interrupted varies according to the interpreter, just as does the total number of speeches in Acts. Because there is so much spoken dialogue in Acts, identifying which discourse counts as a 'speech' is a messy, and ultimately arbitrary, affair."[10] Garroway is correct: when scholars tally the speeches—or the "interrupted speeches"—of Acts, the widely divergent totals demonstrate the arbitrary nature of the methods employed. One could also argue that the widely divergent totals demonstrate the problem of discussing "interrupted speeches" without defining what is meant by "interruption" or "speech." The following discussion, which seeks to elucidate interruption in an ancient Greek narrative context, will demonstrate the value of discussing "interruption" in relation to "speaking turns," rather than "speeches."

The concept of "interrupting" a speaker makes sense only if there are some recognized ground rules in place for turn-taking. These rules can vary from culture to culture, but both modern American political debates and ancient Greco-Roman assemblies were generally governed by a simple (yet often broken) rule: "*not more than one party should speak at a time.*"[11] Consequently, speakers should take turns, and they should follow the written or unwritten rules for beginning and relinquishing their speaking turns. An attempt to gain a speaking turn prematurely, or to bring another person's turn to an involuntary end, violates this practice of turn-taking, and these attempts, whether successful or not, can be construed as interruptions.[12]

Ancient texts offer both evidence of respect for turn-taking rules and multiple examples of speaking turns being violated. For instance, numerous ancient authors

---

[10] Garroway, "'Apostolic Irresistibility,'" 739 n. 3. Garroway contributes to this problem by later referring to his own preferred list of "the thirteen major speeches delivered in Acts" (p. 745).

[11] Harvey Sacks, *Lectures on Conversation*, ed. Gail Jefferson, 2 vols. (Oxford: Blackwell, 1992), 1:633 (Sacks's emphasis). For a sampling of different cultural practices, see Deborah Tannen, "Turn-Taking and Intercultural Discourse and Communication," in *The Handbook of Intercultural Discourse and Communication*, ed. Christina Bratt Paulston, Scott F. Kiesling, and Elizabeth S. Rangel, Blackwell Handbooks in Linguistics (Chichester: Wiley-Blackwell, 2012), 135–57, esp. 143–45.

[12] Jack Bilmes describes interruption more formally as the "violation of the interrupted party's speaking rights, or at least an attempt at such violation" ("Being Interrupted," *Language in Society* 26 [1997]: 508).

describe the various practices adopted by speakers in assemblies, such as standing to take the floor.[13] Often, a speaker claimed a turn by standing in the middle of the assembly: "Peter stood in the midst [ἐν μέσῳ] of the brothers and said…" (Acts 1:15).[14] In larger or more formal assemblies, the speaker might stand on a raised platform (βῆμα) to mark a speaking turn (e.g., 2 Macc 13:26; Diodorus Siculus, *Bibl. hist.* 13.19.6; Arrian, *Anab.* 7.8.3). As these common practices show, the concept of speaking turns was widespread.

Further evidence for common understandings of turn-taking can be found in legislation and exhortation against the violation of speaking turns. For example, in *Ant. rom.* 7.17.5, Dionysius of Halicarnassus records an incident when a Roman assembly was so disorderly that the tribunes introduced a law against interrupting the tribunes: "When a tribune is declaring his opinion to the people, let no one say anything against him, and let no one interrupt his speech [μηδὲ μεσολαβείτω τὸν λόγον]." Plutarch warns would-be students against acting like "those who instantly interrupt with contradictions, neither hearing nor being heard, but talking while others talk" (*Rect. rat. aud.* 4 [LCL]).[15] From the Roman assembly to the lecture hall and beyond, turn-taking rules were known and enforced.[16]

That is not to say that these rules stood inviolate. The very existence of such rules suggests that interruption was not uncommon in the ancient world.[17] However, we must distinguish between ancient reality and ancient narrative. As normal as interruption may have been in the agora, interruption appears less frequently in ancient Greek narratives.[18] Still, examples are ready to hand.[19] In his *Roman*

---

[13] These practices go back at least as far as Homer's time. For examples of standing to take the floor, see Homer, *Il.* 1.68, 101; 2.76; 7.354, 365; *Od.* 2.224; Dionysius of Halicarnassus, *Ant. rom.* 11.4.4; Josephus, *B.J.* 2.26, 34; Appian of Alexandria, *Bell. civ.* 9.3.4. See also Craig S. Keener, *Acts: An Exegetical Commentary*, 3 vols. (Grand Rapids: Baker Academic, 2012–14), 1:754.

[14] See also Acts 17:22, 27:21; cf. Diodorus Siculus, *Bibl. hist.* 13.102.1–2. Josephus often uses a version of παρέρχομαι εἰς μέσην τὴν ἐκκλησίαν to describe speakers who "come into the midst of the assembly." See *B.J.* 4.216; *A.J.* 9.10; 19.261; *Vita* 134, 251, 255. For a discussion of this usage, see Steve Mason, *Life of Josephus: Translation and Commentary*, vol. 9 of *Flavius Josephus: Translation and Commentary*, ed. Steve Mason (Leiden: Brill, 2001), 43 n. 220.

[15] I am grateful to Jeremy Hultin for drawing this reference to my attention.

[16] For a discussion of turn-taking rules and the prohibition on interruption at Qumran (1QS VI, 10–11), see Tzvi Novick, "Tradition and Truth: The Ethics of Lawmaking in Tannaitic Literature," *JQR* 100 (2010): 223–43, esp. 225 n. 7.

[17] For a discussion of interruptive speech in Athenian courts, see Victor Bers, "Dikastic Thorubos," *History of Political Thought* 6 (1985): 1–15.

[18] For this reason, Dibelius could make the claim that interruption is "peculiar" to Luke and "rarely to be observed elsewhere in the work of the ancient historians" (*Studies in the Acts of the Apostles*, 161). For a critique of this claim, see Daniel Lynwood Smith, *The Rhetoric of Interruption: Speech-Making, Turn-Taking, and Rule-Breaking in Luke-Acts and Ancient Greek Narrative*, BZNW 193 (Berlin: de Gruyter, 2012), 112–13.

[19] For a catalogue of interruptions in ancient Greek narratives, see the appendixes in Smith, *Rhetoric of Interruption*, 252–99.

Antiquities, Dionysius of Halicarnassus offers one clear example of awareness of turn-taking rules and their violation. In book 11, Appius Claudius Sabinus, chief of the *decemviri*, addresses the Roman senate. As he is speaking, Lucius Valerius Potitus stands up (ἀνίσταται) to take the floor, presumably to voice his opposition to the *decemvir*'s address (11.4.4). Appius Claudius treats this movement as an interruption, and his response to Lucius Valerius is revealing: "O Valerius, it is not … your turn [οὐχ οὗτος ὁ τόπος … σός], nor is it fitting for you to speak now; but when these men who are older and more honored than you have declared their opinions, then you too will be called on, and you will say what seems right to you" (11.4.5). In an (unsuccessful) effort to turn back Valerius, Appius Claudius rebukes the senator and attempts to silence him by invoking the customary turn-taking rules.

This example of an explicit rebuke reported in direct discourse is rare. Few characters in ancient narratives draw explicit attention to interruptions. No characters in Luke-Acts, for example, ever claim that they are interrupted. Thus, those who seek to discern the presence of interruption in ancient Greek narratives must look beyond the speech of the characters to the narrative surrounding the discourse—what might be called the "narrative framework" around the discourse. In the example above, we can see evidence of interruption both in the speech of Appius Claudius ("it is not … your turn") and in the narrative framework, when Lucius Valerius stands to take the floor from Appius Claudius. More typically, character speech offers little help in discerning the presence of interruption; one must pay careful attention instead to the narrative framework in which the speaker's discourse is embedded.

To illustrate, we can briefly examine Homer's *Iliad*, where the entire plot revolves around the central conflict between King Agamemnon and the warrior Achilles. In book 1, these two figures engage in a fierce argument, which culminates in an interruption of the king by the angry warrior: "Then, interrupting [ὑποβλήδην], noble Achilles answered him" (1.292). This introduction to Achilles's words makes the interruptive nature of his discourse clear, by using the *hapax legomenon* ὑποβλήδην. Achilles then vents his wrath on the king and abandons the Greek camp, striking a severe blow to the Greeks' hopes of victory. For eighteen books, Achilles keeps to himself; only in book 19 does he return. When Achilles returns, he is met with a reproachful King Agamemnon, who quickly points out that "it is not fitting to interrupt [ὑββάλλειν]" (19.79–80). This remark suggests that the king remembers Achilles's interruptive discourse from book 1.[20] However, we can only make this connection based on the narrative framework of Achilles's words in book 1. A reader cannot deduce from the earlier words of Agamemnon

---

[20] This connection between the ὑποβλήδην of 1.292 and the ὑββάλλειν of 19.80 is defended in Mark W. Edwards, *The Iliad: A Commentary*, ed. G. S. Kirk, 6 vols. (Cambridge: Cambridge University Press, 1985–93), 5:243–45.

that the king was going to continue speaking. As in many other cases, the interruption is marked in the narrative framework.

Aside from pointing out the importance of narrative frameworks for discerning the presence of interruption in ancient texts, we can also use this Homeric example to showcase the potency of interruption as a literary device. In the *Iliad*, Greek ambassadors argue with Achilles, gods rage at each other, and dueling spearmen take turns delivering death threats. Yet the only intentional interruption in the entire epic occurs when Achilles violates Agamemnon's speaking turn in the midst of their heated quarrel in book 1—an interruption that is also referenced later in book 19. Thus, interruption is involved both in bringing that conflict to a head and in bringing that conflict to an end.[21]

From this survey of turn-taking and interruption in ancient Greek narratives, we can draw several lessons that can helpfully be applied to the study of interruption in Luke-Acts. First, we can import an understanding of interruption as the violation of a speaking turn. Second, we can look primarily to narrative frameworks to find evidence that a speaking turn is being violated. Ideally, this attention to what the narrator actually says can serve to reduce scholarly confusion over what is or is not an interrupted discourse in Luke-Acts. Third, our reliance on the concept of speaking turns obviates the need to determine whether a given discourse deserves to be classified as a "speech." Regardless of whether a speaker's words are reported in direct or indirect discourse, the speaker can be interrupted; hence, we should discuss "interrupted speech" in Luke-Acts rather than "interrupted speeches." And finally, given the plot-framing significance of a single interruption in Homer's *Iliad*, we have reason to suspect that interruption can be more than an innocuous literary device.

Consequently, although interruption may have been common in the streets and courts of ancient Athens or Corinth, interruption gains potency when used in ancient narratives like the *Iliad*. As I have argued elsewhere, the intentional interruption of a speaker by an audience is a literary device that tends to be clustered around key conflicts and key narrative turning points.[22] As shown above, in Homer's *Iliad*, intentional interruption occurs only during the quarrel between Achilles and Agamemnon (1.292). In Herodotus's *Histories*, interruptions crop up near narrative turning points in the decisive books 8 and 9 (8.26.3, 8.59.1, 8.61.1, 9.11.2). Xenophon's *Anabasis* features a trio of interruptions in book 3, immediately following the climactic capture of the Greek generals through Persian treachery (3.1.27, 3.1.31, 3.2.9). Moreover, later works, such as the *Roman Antiquities* of Dionysius of Halicarnassus and the *Roman History* of Appian of Alexandria, also

---

[21] For discussion of the role of interruption in the *Iliad*, see Smith, *Rhetoric of Interruption*, 30–36; see also Elizabeth Minchin, *Homeric Voices: Discourse, Memory, Gender* (New York: Oxford University Press, 2007), 222–44.

[22] For further discussion, see Smith, *Rhetoric of Interruption*, 112–20.

tie interruption to key conflicts that drive the larger plot of the works.[23] This focused use of interruption in other ancient Greek narratives should inform our analysis of interrupted speech in Luke-Acts. Where interruption is used as a literary device, we can expect to find interruption connected to key conflicts in the narrative. The following discussion will demonstrate that this pattern holds in Luke-Acts: emotional audience reactions to the early Christian proclamation frequently generate interruptions.

III. Discerning Interrupted Speech in Luke-Acts

While others have limited their treatments of interruption to instances found in Acts, my analysis of interrupted speech spans both Lukan volumes. It is not difficult to demonstrate the relevance of the preceding examination of turn-taking and interruption to Luke-Acts. Luke is well aware of speaking turns, their transfer, and their violation. For example, the inauguration of Jesus's public ministry in Luke 4 begins with Jesus standing to read (ἀνέστη ἀναγνῶναι; 4:16). Similarly, in Acts 13:16, Paul "stood up, motioned with his hand, and said" (Ἀναστὰς δὲ Παῦλος καὶ κατασείσας τῇ χειρὶ εἶπεν). C. K. Barrett observes that Paul's gesture "suggests a Greek rhetor rather than a synagogue preacher."[24] Paul's speaking turn is clearly marked. Again, in Acts 18, Paul is accused before Gallio, and "When Paul was about to open his mouth [to speak], Gallio said to the Jews..." (18:14). Paul is about to start his speaking turn, but Gallio preemptively takes the floor and dismisses the charges. In contrast, Luke portrays the participants in the Council of Jerusalem taking clearly defined turns and even observing silence between speakers (15:12).

The Gospel of Luke shows attention not only to turn-taking but also to interruption. Whereas Garroway looked to Luke 21:12–15 to explain the many interrupted speeches of Acts, Luke 4 offers a superior starting point. Here, in the Nazareth synagogue, Jesus describes the ministries of Elijah and Elisha to gentiles (4:25–27). His words enrage his audience: "As they heard these things [ἀκούοντες ταῦτα], all in the synagogue were filled with rage" (Luke 4:28). Like Agamemnon's words in book 1 of the *Iliad*, Jesus's discourse gives no sign of being cut short. Creative readers can imagine how Jesus might have continued speaking, but conjectural continuation of Jesus's discourse does not seem to be the desired reader response. Rather, the narrative framework, with its present participle ἀκούοντες, highlights that the people were still hearing Jesus's words when they reacted.[25] The

---

[23] For further discussion of these two authors, see Smith, *Rhetoric of Interruption*, 81–95 (on Dionysius), and 100–112 (on Appian).

[24] C. K. Barrett, *A Critical and Exegetical Commentary on the Acts of the Apostles*, 2 vols., ICC (Edinburgh: T&T Clark, 1994–98), 1:629.

[25] The progressive aspect of the present participle ἀκούοντες implies ongoing, not completed, action that takes place *at the same time as* the action of the main verb ἐπλήσθησαν.

narrative thus reveals that the violent outburst of the audience in Nazareth occurred *while* the crowd was listening to Jesus speak; hence, Luke 4:28 should be considered an interruption of Jesus's discourse. This interruption anticipates future audience reactions to the incendiary proclamation of God's saving acts among the nations.

This identification of interrupted speech in Luke's Gospel, prior to Luke 21, could be taken as ancillary support for Garroway's hypothesis. On this reasoning, both the apostles and Jesus would be cut short, because their words would be otherwise irresistible. "Apostolic irresistibility" would simply be a later echo of "dominical irresistibility." However, the weakness of this line of argument quickly becomes clear. Jesus is interrupted by a hostile, emotional audience only here in Luke 4. Nowhere else are his challenging words interrupted.

On the other hand, we do find a different sort of interruption in Luke 11, as Jesus refutes charges that he casts out demons by Beelzebul and tells a story about an unclean spirit: "And it happened that, as he was saying these things [ἐν τῷ λέγειν αὐτὸν ταῦτα], a woman from the crowd raised her voice and said to him, 'Blessed is the womb that bore you, and the breasts that you sucked!'" (11:27). This interruption, again described as occurring during Jesus's speaking turn (ἐν τῷ λέγειν αὐτόν), is a positive response to the speaker. As we will discuss below in relation to Acts 10:44 and 13:48, interruptions are not always negative. Sometimes, interruptions function simply to add drama to a narrative.[26] In other cases, cooperative interruptions can reveal an audience's irrepressible affection or support for a speaker.[27]

Instead of reading the interruptions of Acts through the lens of Luke 21, we should read the interruptions of Acts through the lens of Luke 4. The interruptions are not a narrative defense of "apostolic irresistibility" but rather Lukan proofs of the volatility—or, to use a more Lukan word, δύναμις—of the gospel being preached. When Jesus preaches in Luke 4 that God is willing to work among the gentiles, the audience is immediately enraged. As we survey the interrupted discourses of Acts, we will find that emotional audiences repeatedly interrupt the followers of Jesus when they are speaking about one of the two core elements of the apostolic proclamation: the resurrection and exaltation of Jesus, and the availability of salvation to the gentiles.

Turning to Acts, I follow Garroway in beginning to treat interrupted speech in Acts 4.[28] Here, he is squarely aligned with an older tradition. Just over sixteen

---

[26] For examples of interruptions that function dramatically, see the interruption of Peter by a cloud (Luke 9:34), of Jesus by the arrival of Judas (22:47), of Peter by the rooster's crow (22:60), and of the disciples by the arrival of the resurrected Jesus (24:36).

[27] For examples of cooperative interruption, see Josephus, *Vita* 94, 244, 259. These examples are discussed in Smith, *Rhetoric of Interruption*, 159–63.

[28] While many scholars argue that Acts 2:37 is an interruption, Garroway affirms that Peter's Pentecost speech "is *not* interrupted" ("'Apostolic Irresistibility,'" 745; Garroway's emphasis). Jacob Jervell concurs in his assessment of v. 37: "Die Rede ist zu Ende, jetzt kommt die Wirkung auf die Zuhörer" (*Die Apostelgeschichte*, KEK [Göttingen: Vandenhoeck & Ruprecht, 1998], 150).

hundred years ago, John Chrysostom was apparently the first to notice the multiple interruptions in Acts, commenting on them in his extant homilies on Acts. In his tenth homily, which treats Acts 4:1–22, Chrysostom describes the reaction of the Jewish authorities to the preaching of Peter and John: "The miracles shut their mouths: they would not so much as let them [Peter and John] finish their speech, but cut them short in the middle, most insolently."[29] According to Acts 4:1, Peter and John were indeed still "speaking to the people [λαλούντων δὲ αὐτῶν πρὸς τὸν λαόν]" when the authorities arrived. The present participle in the narrative framework again reveals the ongoing nature of a speaking turn, as in Luke 4:28. Whereas the rationale behind the outburst in Luke 4 must be deduced by the reader, here the narrator adds the reasoning for the interruption: the leaders are "troubled on account of [Peter and John's] teaching the people and proclaiming in Jesus the resurrection of the dead" (Acts 4:2). Garroway looks beyond this explanation to Acts 4:4, which reports the increase in the total number of believers (from three thousand in 2:41) to five thousand. He claims that the interruption in Acts 4:1 helps to explain the "diminution in Peter's persuasiveness, one Luke possibly signals when he inventories the converts won: the Pentecost speech yields three thousand souls; the second brings in two thousand."[30] Any degree of resistance by the audience, anything short of unanimous consent, seems to Garroway a falsification of Jesus's words in 21:15. Thus, Luke must have introduced the interruption to spare this conception of "apostolic irresistibility."

Still, a speech that wins some two thousand converts hardly requires an apology, and the narrator seems to consider this mass conversion worthy of mention. A better explanation is offered by the narrative framework, which brings the concept of resurrection to the fore. The narrator attributes the interruption directly to the fact that Peter and John were teaching the people and proclaiming Jesus's resurrection from the dead (Acts 4:2). In Luke 4, Jesus's closing comments about God's grace to gentiles triggered a violent interruption; in Acts 3–4, Peter's (and John's) final words about Jesus's resurrection led to their arrest and imprisonment. Earlier scholars have already noted this connection between the final element of a speaker's message and a subsequent interruption, as Garroway mentions.[31] To his credit, Garroway grants that Dibelius and others "might represent Luke's intention in

---

[29] Translation from *NPNF¹* 11:65. For another example of Chrysostom's comments on interruption, see Chrysostom's forty-eighth homily on Acts 22, esp. *NPNF¹* 11:287.

[30] Garroway, "'Apostolic Irresistibility,'" 747. This simple arithmetic is problematic, as two variables are ignored. First, the "five thousand" in Acts 4:4 is restricted to the number of adult males (ἀριθμὸς τῶν ἀνδρῶν), whereas the "three thousand" in 2:41 refers to "souls" (ψυχαί). Second, Acts 2:41 reports three thousand converts; 4:4 reports only the total number of believers. There were already presumably more than three thousand—at least 120 are already present in 1:15. Finally, this entire line of inquiry likely presumes a degree of numerical precision that is foreign to ancient Greek narratives, as Keener explains (*Acts*, 1:995–96).

[31] Garroway ("'Apostolic Irresistibility,'" 740) attributes this view both to Dibelius (*Studies in the Acts of the Apostles*, 160) and to Cadbury ("Speeches in Acts," 425–26).

interrupting so many speeches."³² In this passage, the link between message and audience response supports a dual reading of interrupted speech in Luke-Acts: it is not only a literary device used at key points in a larger narrative but also a rhetorical device used to underscore the impact of a message on an audience.

Early on, from Luke 4 to Acts 7, interruptions of speakers by emotional audiences typically involve a Jewish audience that cuts short the speaking turn of either Jesus or one of his followers. While the woman in Luke 11 interrupts Jesus to pronounce a blessing, the interruptions in Luke 4, Acts 4, and Acts 7 are decidedly antagonistic, even violent. In Acts 7, Stephen becomes not only the first martyr but also the first follower of Jesus in Luke's narrative to be interrupted twice consecutively. In Acts 7:54, his lengthy speech is cut short by an audience "while they were hearing [ἀκούοντες] these things." Stephen then has a vision of the exalted Jesus, but his description of the vision is again interrupted: "they cried out in a loud voice, covered their ears [συνέσχον τὰ ὦτα], and together rushed at him" (7:57). In both verses, Luke marks the ongoing nature of the apostle's speaking turn by indicating the ongoing listening (or refusal to listen) of the audience.

For Garroway, this plugging of the ears should be "understood as part of Luke's effort to preserve the imperviousness of the apostolic preaching by attributing the failure of the apostles to their not being fully heard."³³ Garroway's suggestion, however, appears to assume that Luke's priority here is to show that the Jewish authorities would have accepted Stephen's preaching if only they had allowed him to continue. Yet this suggestion seems dubious. It is more likely that the interruption serves to highlight the Jewish authorities' resistance to Stephen's description of the exalted Jesus. As in Luke 4, Acts 7:54 emphasizes that the audience interrupts "while hearing" (ἀκούοντες). And in Acts 7:57, the audience refuses to hear at all, instead covering their ears. Pointing to Stephen's critique of his audience for their uncircumcised ears in 7:51, Garroway suggests that Luke is venturing yet another explanation for the failure of apostolic speech: "the audience is simply too dim to discern the unassailable logic."³⁴

Robert Tannehill offers a more convincing explanation that accords with our proposal of a rhetorical function of interruption in Luke-Acts. He describes Acts 2–7 as follows: "The speeches to the people of Jerusalem and their leaders produce emotional responses, either of repentance or of passionate opposition."³⁵ The narrative is designed to accentuate these responses to the apostolic preaching. The words of Jesus and his followers were powerful, and they were capable of eliciting powerful audience responses. Those who hear and accept the preaching are

---

³²Garroway continues irenically, "The goal of this essay is not to overturn or dispel these views but to complement them with an alternative approach" ("'Apostolic Irresistibility,'" 740).

³³Ibid., 748.

³⁴Ibid., 749.

³⁵Robert C. Tannehill, *The Narrative Unity of Luke-Acts: A Literary Interpretation*, 2 vols. (Philadelphia: Fortress, 1986–90), 2:97.

transformed through the dynamic outpouring of the Holy Spirit; those who refuse to hear—or hear and refuse—also give a forceful response, but this response often manifests itself in violence.

Acts 10:44 describes a different sort of interruption. Using his hermeneutic of apostolic irresistibility, Garroway finds the interruption in Acts 10:44 to be "anomalous," and he struggles to explain it in accordance with his theory.[36] However, we can avoid this problem by attending to the narrative description of this interruption. Earlier interruptions, such as the interruption of Stephen in Acts 7, are rightly classified by Dibelius as "intentional interruption of the speaker by the hearers."[37] But Dibelius also describes another type of interruption by "external events."[38] Here, in Acts 10:44, the descent of the Holy Spirit "while Peter was still speaking these words" should not be considered an intentional interruption of a speaker by his hearer. Rather, this interruption may be classified as an "external event."[39] Instead of reading this interruption rhetorically, we can simply note that the descent of the Holy Spirit functions within the narrative as a clear sign that God is willing to extend salvation even to the gentiles. The prophetic words of Simeon in Luke 2:30-32, the suggestive words of Jesus in Luke 4:25-27, and the programmatic outline of Acts 1:8 all point to the salvation of gentiles, and here in Acts 10, the interruption of Peter's preaching serves to dramatize this major event in salvation-history.

This link between interruption and gentile mission is found also in Acts 13, which features an interruption ignored by Garroway and many others. Acts 13 defies Garroway's theory of apostolic irresistibility on two counts. First, Paul's major speech in the synagogue in Pisidian Antioch is not interrupted, yet it is also not a clear success. There is no throng of converts, only a request for Paul to return on the following Sabbath. This request is surely a positive sign, yet, if they have already heard Paul's "irresistible" words, why do they not convert instantly? Garroway's theory falls short here. Second, when Paul and Barnabas return, they are opposed by "the Jews." The two men announce that they are turning to the gentiles, and they are interrupted by the delighted gentiles in their audience: "As they heard these things [ἀκούοντα], the gentiles began to rejoice and glorify the word of the Lord" (Acts 13:48). Again, we find the present participle (ἀκούοντα) marking the interruption of a follower of Jesus by an emotional audience. Again, we find the interruption closely following the mention of the gentile mission. But this time, the emotional response is one of praise and joy, rather than violence and threat.[40]

---

[36] Garroway, "'Apostolic Irresistibility,'" 750–51.
[37] Dibelius, *Studies in the Acts of the Apostles*, 160.
[38] Ibid., 161.
[39] For other Lukan interruptions by external events, see Luke 9:34; 22:47, 60; 24:36.
[40] Cf. the cooperative interruption of Luke 11:27.

The violence and threats return in the later chapters of Acts.[41] Paul once more announces his turn to the gentiles in Acts 22:21, and the audience response is immediate: "They listened to him up to this point [ἤκουον δὲ αὐτοῦ ἄχρι τούτου τοῦ λόγου], but then they raised their voice, saying, 'Remove such a man from the earth, for he is not fit to live!'" (22:22). This time Luke uses an imperfect verb, ἤκουον, still with a progressive aspect, to highlight the emotional response to the content of the apostolic preaching. The announcement that salvation will be made available to the gentiles draws a violent response from the hearers.

Again, we must note the Lukan emphasis on hearing. The rejections of Luke 4, Acts 7, and Acts 22 all arise while a Jewish audience is still hearing; in Acts 28, Paul's final speech will condemn his Jewish audience with the words of Isaiah, announcing that they will not "hear with their ears" (28:27). Moreover, Paul will announce with his final words in 28:28 that the gentiles "will listen" (ἀκούσονται). The recurring interruptions by emotional audiences throughout Luke-Acts dramatize this repeated failure to hear the twofold proclamation: Jesus is risen, and salvation is available even to the gentiles. Both Jews and gentiles are called upon to hear and to obey. The repeated interruptions by Jews who are "hearing" mark their rejection of the apostolic preaching.

Many gentiles also fail to hear. The last two interruptions showcase the unwillingness of gentile rulers to heed what might be called the "foolishness" preached by Paul. First, in Acts 24, we find an interruption of indirect discourse: "While [Paul] was discussing [διαλεγομένου] justice, self-control, and the coming judgment, Felix became afraid and answered, 'Go away for now; when I have time, I will summon you'" (24:25).[42] Acts 24:25 is never cataloged as one of the "speeches" of Acts; still, Paul is clearly speaking, and his discourse is still ongoing—note the progressive aspect of the present participle διαλεγομένου—when a frightened Felix interrupts. Another gentile ruler treats Paul similarly a few chapters later. When Paul addresses Festus, he proclaims the resurrection of Jesus and the availability of salvation to the gentiles in Acts 26:23. Festus is not swayed: "While [Paul] was defending himself [αὐτοῦ ἀπολογουμένου], Festus said in a loud voice, 'Paul, you've gone mad!'" (26:24). Again, there is no threat of violence, but Festus is sufficiently perturbed to question Paul's sanity while the latter is in the process of making his defense (ἀπολογουμένου). Luke here uses interruption "as the equivalent of a double underline" to accentuate his key theological themes of resurrection and gentile

---

[41] Garroway finds an interruption in Acts 17:32 ("'Apostolic Irresistibility,'" 746, 749). While the audience does respond to a mention of the resurrection of Jesus, the aorist participle ἀκούσαντες should be read as "after they heard" or "when they heard," not "as they were hearing." Consequently, there is no conclusive evidence of interruption in the speech itself or in the narrative framework.

[42] Garroway asserts that Paul is "clearly interrupted" in Acts 24:22 ("'Apostolic Irresistibility,'" 745). There is no evidence that the speech is unfinished, and nothing in the narrative framework suggests that Felix violates Paul's speaking turn.

mission once more.[43] From the Jews in the Nazareth synagogue to this gentile ruler in Caesarea, the discourses of Jesus and his followers repeatedly arouse immediate, emotional responses. Their words can be resisted, but they cannot be ignored.

IV. Conclusions

Looking at interruption in Luke-Acts as a whole offers the opportunity to draw helpful conclusions about its form, frequency, and function. The interruptions by external events have a primarily dramatic function; as a result, I have focused on the intentional interruptions of speakers by emotional audiences. First, while the interruptions are marked in a variety of ways, the most common marker is a form of ἀκούω as either a present participle (Luke 4:28, Acts 7:54, 13:48) or imperfect verb (Acts 22:22). Along with the covering of ears in Acts 7:57, Luke consistently emphasizes the hearing of the interruptive audience.[44] Not only is this form of interruption unusual, but so, too, is the overwhelming frequency of interrupted speech in Luke-Acts.[45] Finally, these interruptions consistently function rhetorically to draw attention to the enthusiastic acceptance (in Luke 11:27 and Acts 13:48) or the emotional rejection (in Luke 4:28; Acts 4:1; 7:54, 57; 22:22; 24:25; 26:24) of a message. Audiences might resist the message with anger and violence, or they might embrace the message with joy, but Luke wants to communicate the powerful dynamics between these speakers, their messages, and their hearers, from the beginning of Jesus's public ministry, to the final trial scenes of Acts.

In the end, Luke 21:15 and its message of apostolic irresistibility are best applied to passages in Acts that clearly portray the apostles as irresistible. While Garroway's thesis of "apostolic irresistibility" works extremely well to elucidate the silence of the Sanhedrin in Acts 4:14—where they are unable to "contradict" (ἀντειπεῖν) the apostles—and possibly even to explain the dearth of "paired speeches" in Acts, I have argued that close attention to each individual rhetorical situation can better explain the rhetorical function of interrupted discourses. A more modest reading of Luke 21:15 is in order, perhaps along the lines of Green's proposal:

> That this witness cannot be withstood or contradicted finds ready fulfillment in Acts 4:14; 6:10, as well. This, however, does not guarantee that the testimony of Jesus' witnesses will win the day, only that the resistance they attract and even

---

[43] Richard I. Pervo, *Acts: A Commentary*, Hermeneia (Minneapolis: Fortress, 2009), 635.

[44] I have noted only four ancient instances of marking interruption with a form of ἀκούω in non-Lukan texts: Polybius, *Hist.* 18.46.6; 38.12.3; Diodorus Siculus, *Bibl. hist.* 18.66.6; Dionysius of Halicarnassus, *Ant. rom.* 10.41.1 (Smith, *Rhetoric of Interruption*, 198 n. 56).

[45] Of the many Greek narratives surveyed in my earlier work, Luke-Acts features interrupted speech at the highest frequency—more often than in the histories of Herodotus and Dionysius of Halicarnassus, the works of Josephus, early Greek novels, or the other NT writings (Smith, *Rhetoric of Interruption*, 246).

the executions they undergo are not to be perceived as testimony against the truth or vitality of their witness or the authenticity of their understanding of God's purpose.[46]

Instead of reading Luke 21:15 as the hermeneutical key to the interruptions of Acts, it should be read as a more limited claim.

By adopting a simple definition of interruption as the violation of a speaking turn, and by looking at all the discourses of Luke and Acts, we have been able to gain a clearer view of the function of interruption in Luke's two volumes. From Luke 4:28 to Acts 26:24, Luke repeatedly uses intentional interruption to underscore the volatility of the apostolic (and dominical) message—especially its twin focus on the resurrection of Jesus and the availability of salvation to the gentiles— and to highlight the different audience responses. Attention to the use of interruption throughout Luke-Acts (and beyond) has enabled us to begin to grasp the rhetorical impact of Luke's literary technique. Luke harnessed a powerful rhetorical device found in other ancient narratives, and he put it to work in service of the proclamation of the gospel of salvation to all peoples.

---

[46] Joel B. Green, *The Gospel of Luke*, NICNT (Grand Rapids: Eerdmans, 1997), 737.

fortress press
scholarship that matters

new possibilities!

The Divine in Acts and in Ancient Historiography
SCOTT SHAUF

"Shauf compiles the relevant texts, examines them critically, and synthesizes his findings in masterly fashion. It will be a 'must-read' for students of Luke–Acts, for scholars. . . and for all who struggle to understand the relationship between history and theology."—CARL R. HOLLADAY
Emory University
9781451484779 224 pp pbk $49

Portrait of the Kings
The Davidic Prototype in Deuteronomistic Poetics
ALISON L. JOSEPH

"Joseph shows how and why the Deuteronomist turned David and Jeroboam into prototypes of good and bad kings and how these prototypes were mapped onto other kings."   —ADELE BERLIN
Emerita, University of Maryland
9781451465662 192 pp pbk $39

Genealogies of New Testament Rhetorical Criticism
TROY W. MARTIN

Martin gathers appreciations of five pioneers of rhetorical criticism—Hans Dieter Betz, George A. Kennedy, Wilhelm Wuellner, Elisabeth Schüssler Fiorenza, and Vernon K. Robbins—and highlights their approaches and legacies for interpretation.
9780800699741 288 pp hc $59

Rethinking Early Christian Identity
Affect, Violence, and Belonging
MAIA KOTROSITS

"A daring and subtle account of ancient Christian literature—and contemporary engagements with it—that is both incisive and deeply moving. . . . "
—JENNIFER KNUST, Boston University
9781451492651 208 pp pbk $39

Available wherever books are sold or
800-328-4648
fortresspress.com

The First Pauline Chronologist? Paul's Itinerary in the Letters and in Acts

RYAN S. SCHELLENBERG
ryan.schellenberg@fresno.edu
Fresno Pacific University, Fresno, CA 93702

Since the recent work of the Westar Institute's Acts Seminar, and especially the publication of Richard Pervo's *Dating Acts*, the possibility that Paul's letters served as a source for the book of Acts requires renewed examination. This article tests the hypothesis of Luke's dependence on the Pauline corpus by examining its credibility as an explanation for one particular feature of the narrative, namely, Paul's itinerary as reported in Acts 15:36–20:16. The basic geographical framework of these chapters is easily explicable as Lukan deduction from Paul's letters; differences in detail are convincingly explained as Lukan redaction, clearly in keeping with his theological and narrative interests and in accord with the editorial procedure that is evident, mutatis mutandis, in his Gospel. What is more, this hypothesis accounts for features of the narrative that other theories of the itinerary's source do not, specifically, the remarkable correspondence between those cities named in the Pauline corpus and those that serve as Luke's narrative settings for Paul's activity, as well as the intertextual resonances in Acts 19:21 and 20:22 of Paul's travel announcement in Rom 15:31. In short, an examination of Paul's itinerary in these chapters provides strong confirmation of the explanatory value of the hypothesis that Luke used Paul's letters as a primary source.

Since the recent work of the Westar Institute's Acts Seminar, and especially the publication of Richard Pervo's *Dating Acts*, the possibility that Paul's letters served as a source for the book of Acts requires renewed examination.[1] Pervo is not, of course, the first to put forward such an argument. No, as Morton Enslin reported in his 1938 article on the matter, "the Tübingen school took the dependence of Acts upon the Pauline letters for granted."[2] But for the past century, despite a slow but

---

[1] Dennis E. Smith and Joseph B. Tyson, eds., *Acts and Christian Beginnings: The Acts Seminar Report* (Salem, OR: Polebridge, 2013), 116–17, 206–7, and passim; Richard I. Pervo, *Dating Acts: Between the Evangelists and the Apologists* (Santa Rosa, CA: Polebridge, 2006), 51–147.

[2] Morton S. Enslin, "'Luke' and Paul," *JAOS* 58 (1938): 81.

193

insistent trickle of studies proposing its revival,[3] this theory has remained safely on the margins of Lukan scholarship.[4] It is not yet clear to what extent *Dating Acts* has changed this situation: outside of Finland, where the theory already had a strong foothold,[5] Pervo's proposal has met mostly with rather guarded approval,[6] and also some rather perfunctory rejection.[7]

It need hardly be said that the question is an important one, with profound implications both for our understanding of the compositional practice of Luke and for the ongoing debate concerning the role of Acts in the study of Paul. But my purpose here is not to probe the implications of the theory, nor to discuss its merit in general.[8] Rather, I propose to test the hypothesis of Luke's dependence on the Pauline corpus by examining its credibility as an explanation for one particular feature of the narrative, one that has been fertile ground for a number of

---

[3] In addition to Enslin's work, see William O. Walker, "Acts and the Pauline Corpus Reconsidered," *JSNT* 24 (1985): 3–23; idem, "Acts and the Pauline Corpus Revisited: Peter's Speech at the Jerusalem Conference," in *Literary Studies in Luke-Acts: Essays in Honor of Joseph B. Tyson*, ed. Richard P. Thompson and Thomas E. Phillips (Macon, GA: Mercer University Press, 1998), 77–86; Michael D. Goulder, "Did Luke Know Any of the Pauline Letters?" *PRSt* 13 (1986): 97–112; Lars Aejmelaeus, *Die Rezeption der Paulusbriefe in der Miletrede (Apg 20:18–35)* (Helsinki: Suomalainen Tiedeakatemia, 1987); Anthony J. Blasi, *Making Charisma: The Social Construction of Paul's Public Image* (New Brunswick, NJ: Transaction, 1991), 39–73; Heikki Leppä, "Luke's Critical Use of Galatians" (PhD diss., University of Helsinki, 2002). Cf. also Kirsopp Lake, "Paul's Route in Asia Minor," in *The Beginnings of Christianity*, part 1, *The Acts of the Apostles*, ed. F. J. Foakes-Jackson and Kirsopp Lake, 5 vols. (London: Macmillan, 1920–33), 5:239.

[4] Enslin—convinced, one suspects, that his work had been unjustly ignored—published essentially the same study again more than thirty years later, and to much the same fate ("Once Again, Luke and Paul," *ZNW* 61 [1970]: 253–71).

[5] See now Lars Aejmelaeus, "The Pauline Letters as Source Material in Luke-Acts," in *The Early Reception of Paul*, ed. Kenneth Liljeström, PFES 99 (Helsinki: Finnish Exegetical Society, 2011), 54–75; and, in the same volume, Heikki Leppä, "Luke's Selective Use of Gal 1 and 2: A Critical Proposal," 91–124.

[6] See, e.g., Mikeal C. Parsons, *Acts*, Paideia (Grand Rapids: Baker Academic, 2008), 15–16; Stanley E. Porter, "Was Paulinism a Thing When Luke-Acts Was Written?" in *Reception of Paulinism in Acts*, ed. Daniel Marguerat, BETL 229 (Leuven: Peeters, 2009), 11–12; Joseph B. Tyson, *Marcion and Luke-Acts: A Defining Struggle* (Columbia: University of South Carolina Press, 2006), 15–22; Tyson, "Source Criticism of Acts," in *Method and Meaning: Essays on New Testament Interpretation in Honor of Harold W. Attridge*, ed. Andrew B. McGowan and Kent Harold Richards, RBS 67 (Atlanta: Society of Biblical Literature, 2011), 41–57. See also the reviews by Robert C. Tannehill, *CBQ* 69 (2007): 827–28, and F. Scott Spencer, *Int* 62 (2008): 190–93.

[7] E.g., Craig S. Keener, *Acts: An Exegetical Commentary*, 4 vols. (Grand Rapids: Baker Academic, 2012–14), 1:233–37.

[8] Accordingly, I will refrain from comment here on many of the questions that have been at the forefront of this debate. For general discussion, see John Knox, "Acts and the Pauline Letter Corpus," in *Studies in Luke-Acts: Essays Presented in Honor of Paul Schubert*, ed. Leander E. Keck and J. Louis Martyn (Nashville: Abingdon, 1966), 279–87; C. K. Barrett, "Acts and the Pauline Corpus," *ExpTim* 88 (1976): 2–5; Pervo, *Dating Acts*, 51–58; Tyson, "Source Criticism of Acts," 52–56; Aejmelaeus, "Pauline Letters as Source Material."

source-critical theories—namely, Paul's itinerary as reported in Acts 16–20. My question here is twofold: First, to what extent can the itinerary of Acts 16–20—or, more precisely, 15:36–20:16—be explained as Luke's deduction from his reading of Paul's letters? And, second, are there features of the narrative that make this explanation preferable to other common proposals, specifically, that Luke had access to an independent "itinerary" source,[9] or was a traveling companion of Paul?[10]

Indeed, it is the proliferation of just such proposals that makes the itinerary of chs. 16–20 a particularly useful testing ground for the hypothesis of Lukan dependence on the Pauline corpus. If, as I will propose, it can be demonstrated that there are no significant barriers to viewing Paul's letters as a primary source of Luke's itinerary and, further, that this explanation mitigates difficulties inherent in other proposals, this would provide strong confirmation of the explanatory value of the hypothesis.

I. The Framework of Luke's Itinerary

It will be useful to begin by considering the basic geographical framework of Luke's account (see table 1). Following the council in Jerusalem (Acts 15:1–35), Luke has Paul reprise the journeys through Syria, Cilicia, and Lycaonia undertaken in chs. 13 and 14 (15:36–16:5), then narrates his evangelizing activity in Phrygia and Galatia (16:6),[11] and—via Troas (16:8)—Philippi (16:12), Thessalonica (17:1), Beroea (17:10), Athens (17:15), and Corinth (18:1). This is followed by a brief stopover in Ephesus (18:19) en route to Jerusalem and Antioch (18:22), a return to Ephesus (19:1) via Phrygia and Galatia (18:23), and then a second trip to Macedonia (20:1) and Greece (20:2). Finally, Paul makes his farewell journey to Jerusalem via Philippi (20:3, 5), Troas (20:6), and Miletus (20:14).

---

[9] So Martin Dibelius, *Studies in the Acts of the Apostles*, ed. Heinrich Greeven, trans. Mary Ling (New York: Scribner's Sons, 1956), 196–201; Gerd Lüdemann, *Early Christianity according to the Traditions in Acts: A Commentary* (Minneapolis: Fortress, 1989), 13–15. Cf. Stanley E. Porter, *Paul in Acts*, Library of Pauline Studies (Peabody, MA: Hendrickson, 2001), 10–46.

[10] So Adolf Harnack, *The Acts of the Apostles*, trans. J. R. Wilkinson, NTS 3 (London: Williams & Norgate, 1909), 162–63. And, more recently, Claus-Jürgen Thornton, *Der Zeuge des Zeugen: Lukas als Historiker der Paulusreisen*, WUNT 56 (Tübingen: Mohr Siebeck, 1991); Colin J. Hemer, *The Book of Acts in the Setting of Hellenistic History*, ed. Conrad H. Gempf, WUNT 49 (Tübingen: Mohr Siebeck, 1989), 308–64.

[11] The analogies provided by Acts 19:21 (τὴν Μακεδονίαν καὶ Ἀχαΐαν) and 27:5 (τὴν Κιλικίαν καὶ Παμφυλίαν), as well as Luke's varied usage (cf. 16:6; 18:23), tell against the notion that Luke intends by τὴν Φρυγίαν καὶ Γαλατικὴν χώραν to designate a single region ("Phrygia-Galatia"). Cf. Luke 3:1. So James Moffatt, *An Introduction to the Literature of the New Testament*, International Theological Library (New York: Scribner's Sons, 1922), 93; Ernst Haenchen, *The Acts of the Apostles: A Commentary*, trans. Bernard Noble and Gerald Shinn (Oxford: Blackwell, 1971), 483–84. Contra, e.g., Rainer Riesner, *Paul's Early Period: Chronology, Mission Strategy, Theology*, trans. Doug Stott (Grand Rapids: Eerdmans, 1998), 285.

Table 1. Paul's Itinerary in Acts 15:36–20:16, with Epistolary Cues

15:36–16:5	Dispute of Paul and Barnabas
	Syria and Cilicia
	Derbe*
	Lystra (and Iconium)
	   Timothy circumcised as concession to "the Jews"
	   "the cities" [of Lycaonia]
		cf. Gal 2:13
		Gal 1:22
		
		2 Tim 3:11
		cf. 2 Tim 1:5, Gal 2:3–5

16:6–10	**Phyrgia* and Galatia**
	(bypassing Asia, Bithynia*, Mysia*)
	   Hindered (κωλύω) by the Spirit
	Troas
	   Vision of Macedonian
		Gal 4:12–20
		
		cf. Rom 1:13
		cf. **2 Cor 2:12–13**

16:11–40	Samothrace*
	Neapolis*
	Philippi
	   Conversion of Lydia
	   Exorcism of slave girl; imprisonment; conversion of jailer
		1 Thess 2:1–2; cf. **2 Cor 11:9**
		cf. 1 Thess 2:1–2, 2 Cor 11:23

17:1–9	Amphipolis*
	Apollonia*
	Thessalonica
	   Proclamation in synagogue
	   Jewish opposition embroils Jason, who posts bail
		1 Thess 2:1–2, Phil 4:15–16

17:10–15	**Beroea***
	   Proclamation in synagogue
	   Thessalonian Jews renew opposition
	   Silas and Timothy remain behind
	Athens (Paul alone)
		cf. **1 Thess 3:6**
		1 Thess 3:1

17:16–34	Paul at Areopagus, converts Dionysius and Damaris	

18:1–17	**Corinth**
	   Encounters Aquila and Priscilla
	   Silas and Timothy rejoin Paul
	   Gives up on Jews
	   Converts Crispus in house of Titius Justus
	   Receives reassuring vision, and stays 18 months
	   Jews bring Paul before Gallio
	   Sosthenes beaten
		2 Cor 11:9
		cf. Rom 16:3
		2 Cor 1:19, 1 Thess 1:1, 3:6
		cf. 1 Cor 1:14
		
		cf. 1 Cor 1:1

Boldface = primary toponyms; * = toponym not attested in Pauline corpus

Table 1 (cont.)

18:18–23	Cenchreae *Hair cut; under a vow* **Ephesus** *Declines extended stay; leaves Priscilla and Aquila* Caesarea [Maritima]* [Jerusalem] **Antioch** **Galatia and Phrygia***	cf. Rom 16:1 1 Cor 16:8–9 cf. 1 Cor 16:19 Gal 4:13
18:24–19:20	*Priscilla and Aquila correct Apollos in Ephesus* *Apollos goes to Achaia with letters of recommendation* **Ephesus** *Paul rebaptizes [Apollos's?] deficient converts* *Preaches in synagogue, then Tyrannus's σχολή* *Miracle summary—handkerchiefs and aprons* *Sons of Sceva rebutted*	 cf. 1 Cor 1–4, 16:12; 2 Cor 3:1 1 Cor 16:8–9
19:21–41	*Resolves to go to Macedonia/Achaia en route to Jerusalem* *Sends Timothy and Erastus ahead of him to Macedonia* *Uproar in Ephesus led by Demetrius*	1 Cor 16:3–6, 2 Cor 1:16, Rom 15:22–25 cf. 1 Cor 16:10, 2 Cor 2:12–13 cf. 1 Cor 15:32, 2 Cor 1:8
20:1–12	**Macedonia** **"Greece" [Corinth]** *Aborts plan to sail for Syria due to Jewish plot* *Reroutes through Macedonia* **Macedonia/Philippi** *With Timothy/delegates from Beroea, Thessalonica, Derbe* **Troas** *Meet representatives from Asia* *Eutychus saved*	1 Cor 16:5–8 cf. 2 Cor 8–9 cf. 2 Cor 1:16–17 cf. 1 Cor 16:3–4, 2 Cor 8:19
20:13–16	Assos* Mitylene* Chios* Samos* **Miletus** (bypassing Ephesus; en route to **Jerusalem**)	 cf. 2 Tim 4:20

It should be immediately clear that, with the exception of Paul's visit to Jerusalem in Acts 18, this is an itinerary the framework of which could quite easily have been constructed from cues in the letters. The letter to the Galatians attests to Paul's evangelistic work in that region,[12] and perhaps to a subsequent visit also (4:12–20).[13] Although it is not easy to determine on the basis of his letters whether Paul was first in Galatia before or after his initial trip to Europe,[14] one can certainly imagine Luke deciding on an early visit simply on account of the geography. Paul will travel from east to west, thus providing Luke with an opportunity too good to miss. If he is to visit Galatia twice—and in Luke's scheme Paul must visit every place he evangelizes a second time, to strengthen and encourage the believers (cf. 14:22, 15:41, 16:5, 18:23, 20:1–3a)[15]—the most economical solution is to have Paul make his first pass through the region on his way to the Aegean.

From Troas[16] to Corinth Luke's task is a simple one. The sequence Philippi, Thessalonica, Athens, Corinth can quite easily be deduced from Paul's own remarks (1 Thess 2:1–2, 3:1–3, Phil 4:15–16, 2 Cor 11:9).[17] And one hardly has to imagine Luke going to the trouble of carefully collating the three or four relevant texts. He need only have considered that it was to Philippi, Thessalonica, and Corinth that Paul wrote letters, remembered Paul's comment about being "left alone in Athens" (1 Thess 3:1), and then connected the dots. Of course, the appearance of Beroea does present an additional problem here, and one to which we will return.

Things get somewhat more complicated henceforward. It is no surprise that Paul will end up in Ephesus. His letters clearly attest to his presence there (1 Cor 15:32, 16:8), and, indeed, 1 Cor 16:8–9 seems to reflect an initial evangelizing visit that took place only after the Corinthian community had been founded. But there is nothing in Paul's letters to indicate two separate visits to Ephesus bracketing a

---

[12] By Galatia, I refer to the traditional ethnic territory ("North Galatia") and not the Roman province. See n. 33 below.

[13] Paul's τὸ πρότερον in Gal 4:13 is often interpreted to mean "the first time [I visited]," thus implying a second visit. See Gerd Lüdemann, *Paul, Apostle to the Gentiles: Studies in Chronology* (Philadelphia: Fortress, 1984), 90–92; Moffatt, *Introduction to the Literature*, 84. Regardless of whether this was indeed Paul's meaning, Luke certainly could have interpreted the phrase in this way.

[14] See Lüdemann, *Studies in Chronology*, 109.

[15] Note that Luke's wording of these texts almost certainly betrays his familiarity with the letters. Although the words στηρίζω/ἐπιστηρίζω and παρακαλέω may be common enough, a *TLG* search demonstrates that, prior to the fourth century, they appear together only in 1 Thess 1:2, 2:7, Acts 14:22, 15:32, and texts clearly dependent thereon (e.g., Acts Andr. 28; Acts John 45).

[16] Paul's presence in Troas is attested in 2 Cor 2:12. On the city as a logical launching point for Paul's transition from Asia to Europe, see Dietrich-Alex Koch, "Kollektenbericht, 'Wir'-bericht und Itinerar: Neue (?) Überlegungen zu einem alten Problem," *NTS* 45 (1999): 386.

[17] See Thomas H. Campbell, "Paul's 'Missionary Journeys' as Reflected in His Letters," *JBL* 74 (1955): 82–83; Blasi, *Making Charisma*, 47–48.

trip to Jerusalem, Antioch, Phrygia, and Galatia. Here Luke is not taking direct cues from Paul's letters.[18]

Once back in Ephesus, however, matters clear up considerably. An extended stay in Ephesus is described in 1 Cor 16:8–9, and Paul's follow-up visit to Macedonia and then Greece could easily be inferred from vv. 5–7.[19] It is interesting that Luke refers only generally in 20:2 to "Greece" instead of naming Corinth, which is presumably what he means.[20] In what are perhaps related omissions, we hear nothing of Paul's protracted conflict with the Corinthian community, of his restless travels waiting to hear news from Titus (2 Cor 2:12–13, 7:5–6), or of his disastrous second visit to the city (2 Cor 12:21, 13:1–2). Given Luke's well-known preference for harmony among the believers, this would not be a surprising abbreviation of the story. Notice, though, that the motif of a mediating ambassador to Corinth does not disappear entirely. Certainly the controversy-stained Titus does not figure here—or anywhere else in Acts, for that matter[21]—but Luke does report that Paul sends his trusted helpers Timothy and Erastus ahead of him from Ephesus (19:22; cf. 1 Cor 16:10).

That Paul should travel from Corinth back to Jerusalem comes as no surprise.[22]

---

[18] Contra Bartosz Adamczewski, *Heirs of the Reunited Church: The History of the Pauline Mission in Paul's Letters, in the So-Called Pastoral Letters, and in the Pseudo-Titus Narrative of Acts* (Frankfurt am Main: Lang, 2010), 100–101.

[19] When Paul describes here his intention to remain in Ephesus prior to retracing his steps around the Aegean, he notes that there are "many adversaries" (1 Cor 16:9)—and this he describes not as a reason to leave the city but rather as a reason to stay. Perhaps we hear an echo of this remark when Luke, in narrating Paul's departure from Ephesus, emphasizes that he was not driven out of town by Demetrius's riot but left on his own accord, and only after the tumult had already died down (μετὰ δὲ τὸ παύσασθαι τὸν θόρυβον [Acts 20:1]).

[20] Haenchen, *Acts of the Apostles*, 581. Cf. 18:12, 27; 19:1, 21.

[21] On Luke's irenic motivations for eliminating Titus, see William O. Walker, "The Timothy-Titus Problem Reconsidered," *ExpTim* 92 (1981): 231–35; Enslin, "'Luke' and Paul," 89. And see already Matthias Schneckenburger, *Ueber den Zweck der Apostelgeschichte: Zugleich eine Ergänzung der neueren Commentare* (Bern: Fischer, 1841), 115. If Richard Fellows's suggestion that Titus *was* Timothy is correct, then Luke could have decided to refer to him exclusively as Timothy for precisely the same reason ("Was Titus Timothy?" *JSNT* 23 [2001]: 33–58).

[22] What has indeed proven surprising to Pauline scholars is the lack of any clear mention in Acts of what Paul describes as the purpose of the trip, namely, his delivery of the collection to "the poor among the saints at Jerusalem" (Rom 15:26–28). Luke's reticence cannot be taken as ignorance, since in Acts 24:17 we do get an oblique reference to the project (as perhaps also in Acts 20:4–7), though it has now been transformed into a general act of piety: ἐλεημοσύνας ποιήσων εἰς τὸ ἔθνος μου παρεγενόμην. Hence, this is no more of a difficulty for my hypothesis than for any other account of Luke's sources, each of which confronts the same basic problem: Why has Luke downplayed the collection if he or his sources knew about it? The most compelling solution is still that of John Knox, who suggests that Paul's motive would, from Luke's perspective, have been anachronistic: "This offering was essentially a peace offering, but according to Luke-Acts there

Indeed, Luke has already had Paul announce—in terms strikingly reminiscent of Rom 15, as we will see—that he is on his way to Jerusalem, after which he must see Rome (19:21; cf. 20:22–23). But Luke makes a point of noting that Paul changes his intended route. After learning of a Jewish plot—and here we have the sort of characteristic comment that should surely be attributed to Lukan redaction (cf. 9:24, 20:19, 23:30)[23]—Paul chooses to go overland through Macedonia instead of sailing directly for Syria (20:3).[24] The Paul of the letters too, remember, spoke of modified travel plans, also involving both Macedonia and Corinth, though in that text the change of mind did not take place in Corinth but on the way to it (2 Cor 1:15–17). Still, one might justifiably ask, as did Enslin, "whether Luke was led to his statement by words of Paul which he remembered, but not too exactly."[25]

In sum, then, it should be clear that with only one or two exceptions the basic framework of Paul's itinerary in these chapters can easily be explained as Luke's deduction from a few key passages in the letters. These need not have been open before our author, nor, for the most part, recalled with any great precision. In fact, a fairly general familiarity with what Paul had written, combined with a willingness creatively to connect the dots, could have sufficed to suggest these routes.

Of course, to observe that Luke could have constructed this itinerary on the basis of Paul's letters does not yet provide grounds for concluding that he did so. Indeed, a curious feature of this discussion is that scholars on each side have their own reasons for highlighting the striking similarities between the itinerary of Acts 16–20 and that suggested by Paul's own passing comments. So, when Anthony Blasi lists the correspondences that, to his mind, attest to Luke's knowledge of the letters,[26] he provides much the same data as that adduced by Thomas Campbell three decades earlier, for whom these correspondences represented instead just what "one would expect from two reliable, but independent sources."[27] So, how is one to decide which explanation of the data is preferable? Is Luke dependent on the Pauline corpus, or does he simply report reliably, and independently, the same itinerary to which Paul's letters attest?

---

had been peace in the church for many years—indeed ever since the apostolic council, early in Paul's ministry" (*Chapters in a Life of Paul*, rev. ed. [Macon, GA: Mercer University Press, 1987], 51). See also Morton S. Enslin, "Emphases and Silences," *HTR* 73 (1980): 223–25.

[23] See, e.g., Luke's modification of Paul's escape from the hands of King Aretas (2 Cor 11:32–33) into deliverance from a Jewish plot (Acts 9:23–25). See Richard I. Pervo, *Acts: A Commentary*, Hermeneia (Minneapolis: Fortress, 2009), 507.

[24] Against Enslin's tentative suggestion ("'Luke' and Paul," 90), which has been taken up by Adamczewski (*Heirs of the Reunited Church*, 101), I am not convinced that Acts 20:3 depends on Rom 15:31.

[25] Enslin, "Once Again, Luke and Paul," 255.

[26] Blasi, *Making Charisma*, 43–50, 64–65.

[27] T. H. Campbell, "Paul's 'Missionary Journeys,'" 86. And see now Keener, *Acts: An Exegetical Commentary*, 1:237–50.

We may begin, I suggest, with a question posed already in Enslin's programmatic article: "Is it simply coincidence," Enslin asked, "that the missionary journeys of Paul as sketched in Acts carry him to precisely those communities to which we have Pauline letters?"[28] The force of this question has not, I think, been adequately felt. It is evident from Paul's letters—and particularly his claim in Rom 15:19 to have "fulfilled the gospel" (πεπληρωκέναι τὸ εὐαγγέλιον) from Jerusalem clear around to Illyricum—that neither the letters nor Acts provides a complete account of the geographical scope of Paul's work (cf. 2 Cor 11:23-27). Indeed, it is common for even the most committed defenders of Acts' historicity to acknowledge that Luke's treatment of Paul's career is selective.[29] But why should it select just those parts of the story to which the letters themselves bear clearest witness?[30] If Luke were in fact working from an independent source, this would be an extremely unlikely result.

To be sure, Luke does name numerous other cities visited by Paul, cities not mentioned at all in the Pauline corpus. For some, this is clear evidence that he is utilizing an independent source. Said Martin Dibelius, "It is inconceivable that Luke should have included insignificant and unimportant stations in his account of the journey if he had not had a description of the route at his disposal."[31] But in fact these numerous station stops only sharpen the point of Enslin's question: Is it only a coincidence that, with the sole exception of Beroea, cities named in Acts 16–20 fall neatly into two categories: first, those that are absent from Paul's letters and regarding which Luke tells us nothing except that Paul came and went; and, second, those that do appear in Paul's letters and also provide the setting for extended Lukan narrative? Not once does Luke name a city that appears in Paul's letters and then neglect to provide his readers with an account of Paul's work there; only once does he name a city not mentioned by Paul and then use it as a narrative setting. Again, why should he choose to omit events that take place in just those cities about which the letters also leave us uninformed? To my mind, the fact that the list of Luke's "redundant toponyms"—that is, those places mentioned only in passing—is almost precisely coextensive with the list of those cities unique to Acts is most credibly explained as a result of Luke's dependence for his "primary toponyms" on his knowledge of the Pauline corpus.[32]

---

[28] Enslin, "'Luke' and Paul," 84; cf. Lake, "Paul's Route in Asia Minor," 228.

[29] E.g., Keener, *Acts: An Exegetical Commentary*, 1:228; Ben Witherington, *The Acts of the Apostles: A Socio-Rhetorical Commentary* (Grand Rapids: Eerdmans, 1998), 88.

[30] See Pervo, *Dating Acts*, 98–99.

[31] Dibelius, *Studies in the Acts of the Apostles*, 197.

[32] Loveday Alexander draws this useful vocabulary from the work of Tomas Hägg (Alexander, "The Pauline Itinerary and the Archive of Theophanes," in *The New Testament and Early Christian Literature in Greco-Roman Context: Studies in Honor of David E. Aune*, ed. John Fotopoulos, NovTSup 122 [Leiden: Brill, 2006], 153–54; Hägg, *Narrative Technique in Ancient Greek Romances*:

Luke's narration of Paul's travels through Galatia provides striking confirmation of this pattern of correspondence. Regardless of what Paul meant when he addressed αἱ ἐκκλησίαι τῆς Γαλατίας (Gal 1:2), it is quite clear that Luke understood the term to designate the region often referred to in scholarship as "North Galatia."[33] Uncharacteristically, he names not a single city in the region (cf. 16:6; 18:23). Can it be merely coincidence that this is the one missionary region that Paul too refers to only generically, failing to name the specific cities in which he labored?[34]

In sum, then, it is not only in his account of the geography that Luke corresponds to Paul but also in his description of that geography. In other words, these are not historical correspondences only, but also literary correspondences, and thus they are explained most credibly by positing literary dependence. What we have here is, in a word, intertextuality.

II. A Key Instance of Luke–Paul Intertextuality

If there is one aspect of Paul's itinerary in these chapters that most clearly reflects the influence of his letters, it is surely his announced intention to travel to Jerusalem and then Rome. What is particularly noteworthy here, we will see, is, again, that it is not merely with regard to geography that Luke agrees with Paul; his description of that geography too corresponds to Paul's.

In Acts 19:21 and again in 20:22, Luke has Paul speak determinedly and ominously about the journey to Jerusalem that will be narrated in ch. 21. Both texts contain numerous intertextual echoes,[35] not least echoes of each other. Both refer to the fact that the trip is undertaken under the impetus of the Spirit (ἐν τῷ πνεύματι / δεδεμένος ἐγὼ τῷ πνεύματι), and they use very similar language to describe Paul's

---

Studies of Chariton, Xenophon Ephesius, and Achilles Tatius, Skrifter Utgivna av Svenska Institutet i Athen 8/8 [Uppsala: Almqvist & Wiksell, 1971], 87–89).

[33] *Pace* Hemer, *Book of Acts*, 277–307. When discussing the so-called South Galatian cities of Antioch, Iconium, Lystra, and Derbe, Luke speaks not of Galatia but of Pisidia and Lycaonia (13:14, 14:7). Moreover, the aorist participle κωλυθέντες in Acts 16:6 most naturally indicates that Luke envisions Paul's traversal of τὴν Φρυγίαν καὶ Γαλατικὴν χώραν as explained by his abortive plan to enter Asia, and thus subsequent to his time in Derbe, Lystra, and Iconium. See Moffatt, *Introduction to the Literature*, 92–93n; Haenchen, *Acts of the Apostles*, 484 n. 1; Hans Conzelmann, *Acts of the Apostles: A Commentary on the Acts of the Apostles*, Hermeneia (Philadelphia: Fortress, 1987), 126; Joseph A. Fitzmyer, *The Acts of the Apostles: A New Translation with Introduction and Commentary*, AB 31 (New York: Doubleday, 1998), 578. Conzelmann is surely right that Luke's knowledge of the interior was vague (*Acts of the Apostles*, 126–27; cf. Koch, "Kollektenbericht, 'Wir'-bericht," 384–85; Acts 19:1), which renders Riesner's geographical objection to the North Galatian interpretation moot (*Paul's Early Period*, 282).

[34] Though note also "Arabia" in Gal 1:17, which Acts omits entirely.

[35] See further Aejmelaeus, *Die Rezeption der Paulusbriefe*, 112–19; Pervo, *Dating Acts*, 119–20.

destination: πορεύεσθαι εἰς Ἱεροσόλυμα / πορεύομαι εἰς Ἱερουσαλήμ. Clearly they are to be read in tandem.[36]

And when we do read them in tandem, the evidence for the influence of Rom 15 is compelling indeed.[37] Corresponding elements include the precise phrase πορεύομαι εἰς Ἱερουσαλήμ (Rom 15:25, Acts 20:22) as well as the temporal marker νῦν or νυνί, which, in each case, modifies just this phrase. More generally, both Rom 15:30-31 and Acts 20:22-23 refer to Paul's foreboding regarding his fate upon arrival (cf. 21:4, 12-14). And, tellingly, both Paul and Luke draw our attention all in the same breath both to Paul's final journey to Jerusalem and to his desire thereafter to "see" (θεάσασθαι/ἰδεῖν) Rome (Rom 15:23-25, Acts 19:21; cf. Rom 1:11). In short, it is not only the Achaia-Jerusalem-Rome itinerary that Luke shares with Paul but also the anticipatory mode and the foreboding mood in which that itinerary is first announced. Luke's knowledge of the itinerary itself could easily enough reflect independent historical memory, but such correspondence with Paul's anticipatory description of it is difficult to explain unless one acknowledges a literary relationship.

That Luke meanwhile can saturate this Pauline material with his own characteristic emphases,[38] and even cause it to resonate with his description of Jesus's own announcement of a fateful journey to Jerusalem,[39] attests to the nature of his literary art. There is no reason to doubt that he is capable of this. Studies of intertextuality in Luke's Gospel, the sources of which are somewhat less in doubt, attest to his ability to create what Joel Green aptly refers to as an "echo chamber" of intertextual resonances.[40] An author who can, as Green demonstrates, draw on the language of Genesis to make Zechariah resemble both Abraham and Sarah, and then go on to construct parallels between Zechariah and Cornelius,[41] cannot be said to be innocent of Romans simply because he is reiterating his gospel.

---

[36] See Robert C. Tannehill, *The Narrative Unity of Luke-Acts: A Literary Interpretation*, 2 vols., FF (Philadelphia: Fortress, 1986), 2:239. On Luke's propensity "to express himself independently but similarly on the same theme," particularly in summary material, and his tendency to paraphrase his sources in so doing, see Henry J. Cadbury, "The Summaries in Acts," in Foakes-Jackson and Lake, *Beginnings of Christianity*, part 1, *Acts of the Apostles*, 5:392-402.

[37] See Pervo, *Dating Acts*, 119; Adamczewski, *Heirs of the Reunited Church*, 101.

[38] Note esp. the role of the Spirit in guiding Paul's travels, here as in 13:24, 16:6-10. See further Koch, "Kollektenbericht, 'Wir'-bericht."

[39] See esp. Luke 9:51-52 ([συμ]πληρόω, πορεύεσθαι εἰς Ἱερουσαλήμ, ἀποστέλλω), but also 9:22; 13:33; 22:37; 24:7; 24:26, 44, in which Luke indicates the "divine necessity" of Jesus's suffering and death in Jerusalem by use of the impersonal verb δεῖ (cf. Acts 19:21, 23:11). See further Tannehill, *Narrative Unity of Luke-Acts*, 2:239-40; Armand Puig i Tàrrech, "Les voyages à Jérusalem (Lc 9,51; Ac 19,21)," in *The Unity of Luke-Acts*, ed. J. Verheyden, BETL 142 (Leuven: Leuven University Press, 1999), 493-505.

[40] Joel B. Green, *The Gospel of Luke*, NICNT (Grand Rapids: Eerdmans, 1997), 57.

[41] Joel B. Green, "Internal Repetition in Luke-Acts: Contemporary Narratology and Lucan

In fact, we need not speculate that Luke could take the words of his hero from his source material (Mark 8:31, 9:31, 10:32–33), reiterate them in a variety of permutations (Luke 9:22, 31, 44, 51; 13:22, 33; 17:11, 25; 18:31–34; 24:6–7, 25–27, 44–74), and then integrate this complex into both the thematic and geographical structure of his narrative.[42] We know with near certainty that he did so. And he appears to have done it again in Acts.

III. Addressing Objections: Luke's Use of Paul's Letters and the Gospel of Mark

In inviting consideration of Luke's redactional tendencies in his Gospel, I am following the methodological suggestion of Ben Witherington, who in a 1996 essay opined that "a study of how Luke handles Mark ... should give us some basic clues about the character, style, and tendencies of his editorial work in general," and therefore also his treatment of sources in Acts.[43] As we approach some potential objections to the hypothesis that the itinerary of Acts 16–20 is, in the main, derived from Luke's knowledge of Paul's letters, it will indeed be useful to bear in mind what we know from studying his Gospel about how Luke handles his sources.

A brief note is in order before we begin: As will already have been observed, I assume here Markan priority, and I take it to be at least approximately true that the Gospel of Luke and Acts were composed by the same author. Neither position is uncontested;[44] to defend either would take me well beyond the scope of this article. In any case, advocates of the revived Griesbach hypothesis and those who question the authorial unity of Luke and Acts will notice that the credibility of my

---

Historiography," in *History, Literature and Society in the Book of Acts*, ed. Ben Witherington III (Cambridge: Cambridge University Press, 1996), 291, 294.

[42] See John T. Squires, *The Plan of God in Luke-Acts*, SNTSMS 76 (Cambridge: Cambridge University Press, 1993), 140–41, 168–70.

[43] Ben Witherington, "Editing the Good News: Some Synoptic Lessons for the Study of Acts," in Witherington, *History, Literature and Society*, 326. Cf. Leppä, "Luke's Selective Use of Gal 1 and 2," 105–8. Still, in making such comparisons, we must be careful not to beg the question of the *nature* of the sources, as Witherington could be accused of doing. See also Haenchen, *Acts of the Apostles*, 81; Tyson, "Source Criticism of Acts," 42.

[44] The most significant recent challenge to Markan priority comes in the labor of William Farmer and his intellectual heirs. See, e.g., *One Gospel from Two: Mark's Use of Matthew and Luke. A Demonstration by the Research Team of the International Institute for Renewal of Gospel Studies*, ed. David B. Peabody (Harrisburg, PA: Trinity Press International, 2002). And, amid a larger debate regarding the relationship between Luke and Acts, it is Patricia Walters who has most forcefully called into question their common authorship: *The Assumed Authorial Unity of Luke and Acts: A Reassessment of the Evidence*, SNTSMS 145 (Cambridge: Cambridge University Press, 2009).

account of the use of sources in Acts is enhanced by but not dependent on these positions.

First, then, it is significant to our topic here that Luke, though he generally preserves the order of the Markan material, is demonstrably more concerned with the demands of his narrative than with fidelity to the chronology suggested by his sources. To give just one example, he is quite willing to delay the call of the disciples, which, according to Mark, occurs immediately upon Jesus's appearance in Galilee (1:16–20), until after the first remarkable incidents of the Galilean ministry (Luke 5:1–11).[45] Such a change occurs not, I would suggest, because Luke is uninterested in chronology but rather because chronological accuracy is not so important to him as chronological verisimilitude.[46] Or, better, it is precisely because he knows that narrative order (cf. 1:3) is meaningful that Luke is willing to improve on the chronology of his sources—in this case by providing Simon and the sons of Zebedee with a credible reason to drop everything and follow.[47]

Such flexibility pertains not only to the chronology of Luke's narration but also to his explicit chronological notices. Luke has no scruples about changing, for reasons that continue to elude commentators,[48] Mark's six-day pause prior to the transfiguration (9:2) into a period of "about eight days" (9:28). And he can treat Mark's geographical settings with equal plasticity: Mark specifies that the healing of Bartimaeus occurred after Jesus had passed through the city of Jericho and was on his way out of town (10:46). But Luke has another Jericho story he wants to tell, and thus his τυφλός τις meets Jesus not as he leaves the city, but as he approaches it (18:35).[49] Only a pedant would be troubled by such a modification, which clearly has no bearing on the import of the story. Luke is not one.

Evidently, then, it will not do to argue, as does Craig Keener, that the fact "that Luke appears to contradict [Paul's letters] on some points of detail (Acts 17:14–16, 1 Thess 3:1–2)[50] ... reinforces the likelihood ... that where his accounts agree with

---

[45] For additional examples, see Henry J. Cadbury, *The Style and Literary Method of Luke*, HTS 6 (Cambridge: Harvard University Press, 1920), 77–78; John Drury, *Tradition and Design in Luke's Gospel: A Study in Early Christian Historiography* (Atlanta: John Knox, 1976), 85–96; C. F. Evans, *Saint Luke*, TPINTC (London: SCM, 1990), 266–67.

[46] On the relationship between veracity and verisimilitude in Hellenistic historiographical narrative, see esp. Todd Penner's incisive reading of Polybius in his *In Praise of Christian Origins: Stephen and the Hellenists in Lukan Apologetic Historiography*, Emory Studies in Early Christianity (New York: T&T Clark, 2004), 153–62.

[47] See Drury, *Tradition and Design*, 84–87; Green, *Gospel of Luke*, 42–44.

[48] See François Bovon, *Luke: A Commentary on the Gospel of Luke*, 3 vols., Hermeneia (Minneapolis: Fortress, 2002–13), 1:373–74.

[49] For discussion, see I. Howard Marshall, *The Gospel of Luke: A Commentary on the Greek Text*, NIGTC 3 (Grand Rapids: Eerdmans, 1978), 692–93.

[50] What Keener refers to here is the apparent discrepancy between Timothy's dispatch from Athens to Thessalonica (per Paul) and his tarrying with Silas in Beroea (per Luke). Karl Paul

Paul's letters ... they do so independently of the letters."[51] By this logic, Luke should have had to narrate the story of Bartimeaus independently as well.

Second, it is clear from Luke's method in the Gospel that he finds travel thematically suggestive and is willing, if necessary, to generate more of it than his sources provide. Of course, Mark's Jesus too does indeed make the trip from Galilee to Jerusalem. But, in constructing the famous "travel narrative" of his central section, Luke elaborates considerably, albeit vaguely, on what he found in his source.[52] Most notably, Luke has Jesus pass through Samaria (9:52, 17:11), a deviation from the route presupposed by Mark,[53] and one that appears to be motivated by Luke's singular concern for Samaritans. This does, incidentally, result in some geographical imprecision (cf. 17:11)[54]—imprecision comparable, perhaps, to that which we noted above in Luke's description of Paul's travels through the Galatian hinterland.

Luke also feels free to omit travel. Missing entirely from his Gospel are the travels of Jesus to Bethsaida, Gennesaret, Tyre and Sidon, "the region of the Decapolis," "the district of Dalmanutha," then again Bethsaida, all of which occur during Luke's so-called great omission (Mark 6:45–8:26).[55] Clearly, then, the fact that this author neglected to report the details of Paul's second and third trips to Corinth cannot be taken as evidence that he lacked access to such sources as could have informed him of them. Likewise, though one might have expected to find Luke's Paul in Illyricum at some point (Rom 15:19), this omission cannot be construed as evidence that Luke had not seen Rom 15. Our author in fact omits very few places

---

Donfried has recently broken consensus by insisting that the discrepancy results only from an unnecessary reading of 1 Thess 3 ("Was Timothy in Athens? Some Exegetical Reflections on 1 Thess. 3:1–3," in *Paul, Thessalonica, and Early Christianity* [Grand Rapids: Eerdmans, 2002], 209–21). I will refrain from comment on the question here.

[51] Keener, *Acts: An Exegetical Commentary*, 1:235.

[52] For a general overview, see Evans, *Saint Luke*, 433–34.

[53] See C. C. McCown, "The Geography of Luke's Central Section," *JBL* 57 (1938): 59; John R. Donahue, *The Gospel of Mark*, SP 2 (Collegeville, MN: Liturgical Press, 2002), 292; Evans, *Saint Luke*, 657.

[54] Still a lucid discussion is that of McCown, "Geography of Luke's Central Section," 60; cf. Evans, *Saint Luke*, 624.

[55] Some, of course, have argued that Luke's copy of Mark was missing the section in question. But Frans Neirynck has noted reminiscences of this Markan material elsewhere in Luke's Gospel, thus providing compelling evidence that Luke had access to these pericopae ("Synoptic Problem," in *NJBC*, 589). For recent attempts to account for such redaction, see Michael Pettem, "Luke's Great Omission and His View of the Law," *NTS* 42 (1996): 35–54; Filip Noël, *De compositie van het Lucasevangelie in zijn relatie tot Marcus: Het probleem van de "grote weglating,"* Verhandelingen van de Koninklijke Academie voor Wetenschappen, Letteren en Schone Kunsten van België, Klasse der Letteren 56/150 (Brussels: AWLSK, 1994).

named by Paul—only Illyricum, Arabia, and Spain[56]—and these lacunae pale in comparison to the geographical data omitted from Mark.[57]

Of course, we must also account for the places Luke adds to the itinerary deducible from the letters. Here it is immediately striking that, as noted above, with the exception of Bereoa, all of the cities unique to this section of Acts are "redundant toponyms"—places in which nothing happens.[58] This in itself does not settle the question of their origin, but it does invite us to consider the possibility that at least some of this geography derives from Lukan invention. The fact that these are, for the most part, "natural stopping places" along Paul's route has often been taken as evidence that they come from authentic tradition.[59] But, as Pervo notes,[60] the argument just as easily cuts the other way: If Luke thought it would improve his narrative to provide additional geographical specificity—no strange notion in a narrative concerned precisely with the geographical advance of the gospel[61]—these are just the cities we should have expected him to name.

And it is clear from Luke's procedure in the Gospel that he is not averse to adding geographical specificity where it is lacking in his source. Note, for example, the appearance of Bethsaida in Luke 9:10, where Mark and Matthew have Jesus in an unnamed desert place (Mark 6:32, Matt 14:13).[62] One could argue that here Luke is preparing the soil for Jesus's condemnation in 10:13 of Bethsaida's otherwise unnarrated lack of repentance—though that would require considerable advance planning on Luke's part, not only anticipating the woe in the following chapter but also recalling in advance that he plans to omit upcoming Markan pericopae in

---

[56] To refer to Spain (Rom 15:24, 28) would, of course, have taken Luke beyond the scope of his narrative, the abrupt ending of which remains puzzling regardless of one's understanding of its sources. Such advance notices of Paul's geographical destiny as are provided in regard to Jerusalem (19:21, 20:22, 21:13) and Rome (19:21, 23:11, 27:24) are valuable to Luke because they attest to the "divine necessity" of this itinerary and, when that very itinerary is subsequently narrated, to the realization of God's plan (see esp. Charles H. Cosgrove, "The Divine ΔEI in Luke-Acts: Investigations into the Lukan Understanding of God's Providence," *NovT* 26 [1984]: 178–79). Advance mention of a trip to Spain would have served no such purpose and, if Luke or his audience suspected that Paul had never made it to Spain, would indeed have contradicted it. (On this latter question, see the various essays in Friedrich W. Horn, ed., *Das Ende des Paulus: Historische, theologische und literaturgeschichtliche Aspekte*, BZNW 106 [Berlin: de Gruyter, 2001].)

[57] See Cadbury, *Style and Literary Method*, 127–28.

[58] The pattern persists throughout the description of Paul's activities in Acts, with only a few additional exceptions: Cyprus (13:1–12), Caesarea (9:30; 21:8–14; 24), and Malta (28:1–10).

[59] So, regarding the station stops listed in 16:11, Lüdemann, *Traditions in Acts*, 183.

[60] Pervo, *Acts: A Commentary*, 401.

[61] See Daniel Marguerat, *The First Christian Historian: Writing the "Acts of the Apostles,"* SNTSMS 121 (Cambridge: Cambridge University Press, 2002), 231–56, esp. 254: "To travel is to claim a territory for the Word."

[62] For discussion, see Evans, *Saint Luke*, 402.

which Bethsaida will appear (6:45, 8:22). It may also simply provide, to use the happy phrases of Loveday Alexander, "topographical depth" and/or "geographical verisimilitude."[63] In any case, Luke feels free here to add geographical detail that is lacking in his source, and is even contradicted by it.[64]

But this is not, in fact, very common—certainly not so common as I am positing for Acts. More frequently in the Gospel we find Luke providing, as C. C. McCown long ago noted, "indefinite geographical settings where his sources had none."[65] Note, for example, the addition of the notice that Jesus's healing of a leper occurred ἐν μιᾷ τῶν πόλεων (5:12; cf. 8:1, 13:22). But this vagueness need not be interpreted as reticence on Luke's part to name speculative names. Perhaps he simply did not have a large supply of serviceable Galilean place-names at his disposal. In other words, it is at least possible that these vague notices should be considered structurally equivalent to the more specific information we get once we are in geographical territory with which our author is more familiar.[66]

Or perhaps once on the sea he is simply better informed.[67] Alexander once noted the affinity between the topographical descriptions in Acts and the *periplus* literature,[68] those guides to coasts and harbors that served "travellers and merchants," yes, but also "a growing public of armchair tourists."[69] Texts of this sort would have provided just such information as Luke needed to fill out Paul's itinerary—and he would by no means have been the first to incorporate *periplus* material into a narrative of another genre.[70] It comes as no surprise that the *Periplus* attributed to Scylax includes all four of the way stations that appear in Acts 16:11 and

---

[63] Loveday Alexander, "Narrative Maps: Reflections on the Toponymy of Acts," in *The Bible in Human Society: Essays in Honour of John Rogerson*, ed. M. Daniel Carroll R., David J. A. Clines, and Philip R. Davies, JSOTSup 200 (Sheffield: Sheffield Academic, 1995), 40–41.

[64] Likewise, Luke modifies Mark's notices that Jesus, after teaching in the temple, spent the night in Bethany (Mark 11:11), "outside the city" (Mark 11:19), by providing him with the "custom" (Luke 22:39) of sleeping at the Mount of Olives (Luke 21:37), where he was finally arrested. Here it is not easy to tell whether Luke is working toward narrative continuity, modifying Jesus's lodging place in order to give Judas reasonable grounds for anticipating his location on the night of the arrest, or whether the change results from his dependence on the association of Bethany with the Mount of Olives in Mark 11:1.

[65] McCown, "Geography of Luke's Central Section," 56.

[66] On Luke's knowledge of the Aegean region, and especially Ephesus, see esp. Pervo, *Acts: A Commentary*, 5–6. See also Loveday C. A. Alexander, "'In Journeyings Often': Voyaging in the Acts of the Apostles and in Greek Romance," in *Acts in Its Ancient Literary Context: A Classicist Looks at the Acts of the Apostles*, LNTS 298 (London: T&T Clark, 2006), 84.

[67] As Alexander has observed, Luke's focus on the coast "is one of the features that makes the mental map of Acts look so different from that of Paul, despite the fact that almost all Paul's toponyms are included in Acts" ("Narrative Maps," 44).

[68] Ibid., 41.

[69] Marguerat, *First Christian Historian*, 242.

[70] See Yuval Shahar, *Josephus Geographicus: The Classical Context of Geography in Josephus*, TSAJ 98 (Tübingen: Mohr Siebeck, 2004), 40–41.

17:1, and all in close proximity (66–67).[71] I am not proposing that Luke used this particular text as a source. My point is rather that for an author who was, like ours, at least modestly bookish, if not also well traveled, there were other ways to become informed of shipping routes than accompanying Paul or happening upon a copy of his itinerary.

Certainly this does not prove that Luke had no additional sources. But I would insist that, just as "local color" provides no guarantee of historicity,[72] so Luke's specific place-names are not in themselves evidence that he was following a source. Again, Luke is known from his Gospel to have added geographical notices as he found them useful. There is no reason he should not have done the same in Acts. Therefore, claims that he was using an independent source here will have to be made on other grounds. (In my judgment, with regard to the travel narrated in 16:11 and 17:1, no such grounds are apparent; the detailed accounts in 20:5–6 and 20:13–14 of the diverging routes of Paul and his companions may be a different matter.)

As noted above, however, Beroea does present a special problem: it is the only city that is absent from the Pauline corpus but which Luke nevertheless uses as a narrative setting. To be sure, the story itself contains nothing that is not easily attributable to Lukan variation on favorite themes.[73] But why should Luke have insisted on locating it just here, in a town that, according to Cicero, lies off the beaten track (*Pis.* 36.89)?[74] One answer is perhaps suggested by Cicero's remark itself, which is occasioned by that fact that Piso, the subject of Cicero's invective, had, like Paul, fled to Beroea from Thessalonica when he found the crowds in the latter city uncomfortably hostile. In other words, the geography is logical enough—and thus, again, equally likely to be either veracious or verisimilitudinous.

But perhaps we can still make some progress. Notably, Beroea appears again in 20:4 as the hometown of one of the delegates who accompany Paul on his way to Jerusalem. Despite a few arguments to the contrary,[75] most agree that in listing

---

[71] Text in Karl Müller, *Geographi Graeci minores*, 2 vols. (Paris: Didot, 1855), 1:15–96.

[72] So Koch, "Kollektenbericht, 'Wir'-bericht," 368. And note esp. Stephen J. Harrison, "Literary Topography in Apuleius' *Metamorphoses*," in *Space in the Ancient Novel*, ed. Michael Paschalis and Stavros A. Frangoulidis, Ancient Narrative Supplementum 1 (Groningen: Barkhuis, 2002), 40–57.

[73] A visit to the local synagogue (17:10b; cf. 13:14, 14:1, 17:1–2); an initial welcome (17:11; cf. 13:42); the conversion of some (17:12a; cf. 13:48, 14:1, 17:4), including Greeks and respectable women (17:12b; cf. 17:4); envious Jews who stir up the crowd (17:13; cf. 13:45, 50; 14:2; 17:5)—in this case from cities previously visited (17:13; cf. 14:19); and the flight of the apostle(s) (17:14; cf. 13:51; 14:5–6, 20; 17:10a).

[74] See Riesner, *Paul's Early Period*, 360.

[75] E.g., David J. Downs, *The Offering of the Gentiles: Paul's Collection for Jerusalem in Its Chronological, Cultural, and Cultic Contexts*, WUNT 2/248 (Tübingen: Mohr Siebeck, 2008), 64–65 n. 93.

these delegates Luke is dependent on source material that is no longer extant.[76] If so, it is not difficult to imagine Luke inferring from the appearance of a Beroean delegate that Paul had evangelized the town, and then finding a narrative home for the incident in his account of Paul's journey from Thessalonica to Athens. This procedure might also explain the summary narration in Acts 14 of the evangelization of Derbe (14:20b–21a; cf. 14:4, 16:1)—another city that fails to appear in the Pauline corpus but from which a delegate is named in 20:4.

One final difficulty demands explanation. If Luke derived Paul's itinerary in these chapters from the letters, how are we to account for the trip to Jerusalem, Antioch, and Galatia that interrupts Paul's stay in Ephesus (18:20–23), a journey of which those letters provide not a hint? Here two observations are in order.

First, it is worth pausing to consider the function of this journey in Luke's narrative. This is by all accounts an odd story.[77] Paul deposits Priscilla and Aquila in Ephesus,[78] yet, despite a successful visit to the synagogue, he refuses to stay in town himself. Then, in a mere two verses, Luke narrates his trip all the way to Jerusalem and most of the way back. No purpose for the trip is given. Finally, leaving Paul to traverse the inland roads of Galatia, our author returns our gaze to Ephesus, where the real action is taking place in Paul's absence (18:24–28). From a narrative perspective, it appears that the real purpose of Paul's trip is simply to remove him from the Ephesian stage until it can be prepared for his triumphant arrival.[79]

It is probably not coincidental that Paul's presence in Ephesus had been avoided earlier as well, when, close as he was, the Spirit would not allow him to proclaim the word in Asia (16:6). Thus, it was Apollos who was destined first to make converts in Ephesus (18:25); Paul's role would rather be to reeducate those who were, at least by implication, the former's deficient disciples—those possessing, as Apollos had been, only John's inadequate baptism (19:2–7). What is more, against 1 Cor 16:12, Luke explicitly avoids allowing the tenures of Paul and Apollos in Ephesus to overlap (19:1).[80] This makes it difficult to avoid the conclusion that what we have here is intentional dissociation of Paul from the earliest proclamation

---

[76] Rudolf Pesch, *Die Apostelgeschichte*, 2 vols., EKKNT 5 (Zurich: Benziger, 1986), 2:185; Pervo, *Acts: A Commentary*, 13–14, 508; Fitzmyer, *Acts of the Apostles*, 87, 665; A. J. M. Wedderburn, "Paul's Collection: Chronology and History," *NTS* 48 (2002): 103–4; Koch, "Kollektenbericht, 'Wir'-bericht," 375. Cf. Conzelmann, *Acts of the Apostles*, 167.

[77] See esp. Haenchen, *Acts of the Apostles*, 546–48.

[78] For an argument that the movements of Priscilla and Aquila here are deductions from the Pauline corpus, see William O. Walker, "The Portrayal of Aquila and Priscilla in Acts: The Question of Sources," *NTS* 54 (2008): 479–95.

[79] Thus Pervo, *Dating Acts*, 399 n. 251.

[80] See esp. Michael Wolter, "Apollos und die ephesinischen Johannesjünger (Act 18:24–19:7)," *ZNW* 78 (1987): 58–60.

of the gospel in Ephesus, which Luke apparently finds suspect.[81] His motivation here is not transparent. Ernst Haenchen proposed that this narrative strategy allowed Luke to depict Paul as one who "wins over the sects."[82] Or perhaps there persisted in Luke's time Asian believers who traced their origins to non-Pauline roots and thereby occasioned such narrative polemic.[83] Whatever Luke's precise motivation, he is clearly expending considerable effort in keeping Paul away from both Apollos and premature activity in Ephesus.

Second, it is evident even from his Gospel that Jerusalem plays a special role in Luke's vision, serving as "the necessary base from which the Christian movement is to proceed."[84] Relevant here is what is perhaps the most substantial change in geography that Luke makes to his Gospel sources, and one that we have not yet had occasion to mention—his transposition of the disciples' final encounter with Jesus from Galilee to Jerusalem.[85] Mark makes things perfectly clear: "He is going ahead of you to Galilee; there you will see him, just as he told you" (16:7; cf. Matt 28:7, 16–20). And so does Luke: "Stay here in the city" (24:48; cf. Acts 1:4).[86] For Luke, then, Jerusalem remains home base. Related to this, of course, is Luke's well-recognized emphasis on Paul's cooperation with, even subordination to, the Jerusalem apostles. Indeed, these twin Lukan *Tendenzen* almost certainly cooperated earlier in the narrative to generate an extra Pauline visit to Jerusalem (Acts 9:20–29; cf. Gal 1:17).[87] It should be no great surprise if they did likewise here, thus mitigating for Luke the inconvenience of having Paul remain in Ephesus.

IV. Conclusion

Pervo offers the methodological principle that we should prefer sources we know to those we do not.[88] Given the vagaries governing the survival of ancient

---

[81] Cf. Christopher N. Mount, *Pauline Christianity: Luke-Acts and the Legacy of Paul*, NovTSup 104 (Leiden: Brill, 2002), 113–20.

[82] Haenchen, *Acts of the Apostles*, 557; cf. Fitzmyer, *Acts of the Apostles*, 642.

[83] Note Tyson's similar attempt to explain Paul's avoidance of Bithynia as anti-Marcionite polemic (*Marcion and Luke-Acts*, 77).

[84] Evans, *Saint Luke*, 888. Cf. J. Bradley Chance, *Jerusalem, the Temple, and the New Age in Luke-Acts* (Macon, GA: Mercer University Press, 1988), 99–113; Drury, *Tradition and Design*, 52–53.

[85] See Chance, *Jerusalem, the Temple, and the New Age*, 65–66.

[86] Cf. Luke 24:6–8, where the dominical sayings to be recalled do not pertain to Galilee but instead were uttered there.

[87] The essential arguments are laid out by Ferdinand Christian Baur, *Paul the Apostle of Jesus Christ: His Life and Work, His Epistles and His Doctrine*, 2nd ed., ed. Eduard Zeller, trans. Allan Menzies, 2 vols. (London: Williams & Norgate, 1876), 1:110–20; Knox, *Chapters in a Life of Paul*, 35–40.

[88] Richard I. Pervo, "Acts in the Suburbs of the Apologists," in *Contemporary Studies in Acts*, ed. Thomas E. Phillips (Macon, GA: Mercer University Press, 2009), 32.

documents, perhaps this leaves rather too much to chance.[89] Still, it does seem clear that when extant texts explain the phenomena in question, there are no good grounds for inquiring into hypothetical ones.

In considering Paul's itinerary in Acts 15:36–20:16, I have found very little fuel for further source-critical speculation. The basic geographical framework is easily explicable as Lukan deduction from Paul's letters. With perhaps a single exception (Beroea; see below), differences in detail are convincingly explained as Luke's redaction, clearly in keeping with his theological and narrative interests and, moreover, in accord with the editorial procedure that is evident, mutatis mutandis, in the Gospel. This last point merits additional emphasis: it surely speaks to the credibility of the hypothesis that the authorial role it demands is one into which the author we know from the Gospel very comfortably steps.

Not only is Luke's use of Paul's letters a credible explanation for this itinerary, but there are also at least two considerations that make this explanation preferable both to alternative source theories and to the claim that the author drew on personal recollections. First, we noted the striking correspondence between Luke's "primary toponyms"—that is, the places in which the action happens—and those cities that appear in the Pauline corpus, as well as correspondence between Luke's "redundant toponyms" and those absent from it. Given that the scope of Paul's work was broader than that directly attested either in the letters or in Acts, this is difficult to explain except as literary dependence of Acts on Paul's letters. The failure of each author to name specific localities for Paul's work in Galatia further strengthens the case. Second, the twin announcements in Acts 19:21 and 20:22 of Paul's intention to make a perilous visit to Jerusalem and then to proceed to Rome evince not only knowledge of Paul's route but also knowledge of his anticipatory description of that route in Rom 15.

Of course, the conclusion that Paul's letters provided Luke with his primary source for the itinerary of these chapters does not necessarily preclude his use of other sources. But it does render hypothetical sources very difficult to detect, for, if the bulk of the itinerary has already been explained, there is little specific data to be attributed to them. Since attempts to identify sources solely on stylistic grounds—including the use of the first person plural—have famously floundered,[90] the scarcity of such data leaves very little scope for additional reconstruction.

In only one instance did I find it necessary to appeal to an additional source: Beroea is the only city in these chapters that both is absent from Paul's letters and is the setting for Lukan narrative. If Luke's report of the delegation in 20:4 derives from an independent source, the presence of a Beroean delegate there could easily

---

[89] See Tannehill, review of Pervo, *Dating Acts*, 828.

[90] See Harnack, *Acts of the Apostles*, 163; Dibelius, *Studies in the Acts of the Apostles*, 5, 104–5; Jacques Dupont, *The Sources of Acts: The Present Position*, trans. Kathleen Pond (New York: Herder & Herder, 1964), 166–67; William S. Campbell, *The "We" Passages in the Acts of the Apostles: The Narrator as Narrative Character*, SBLStBL 14 (Atlanta: Society of Biblical Literature, 2007), 4–5.

have provided the impetus for Luke to narrate the city's evangelization. Such a conclusion does not demand but does leave room for the hypothesis that the detailed travel narrative associated with the delegation (20:5–6, 13–14) derives from the same source.[91]

I have made no effort here to account for the stories that flesh out the itinerary I traced. In any case, these are more often ascribed to "tradition" than to specific sources. I might note, however, that compelling arguments have been made that certain of these narratives too derive from Luke's reading of Paul's letters.[92]

The foregoing analysis requires Luke to have accessed almost all of Paul's undisputed letters—Romans (including ch. 16), 1 Corinthians, 2 Corinthians (chs. 1–2 and perhaps 11), Galatians, 1 Thessalonians, and probably Philippians. Paul's itinerary in Lycaonia and Pisidia can also be accounted for if one adds to this list 2 Timothy.[93] Notably, for our purposes we need not attribute to Luke such conscientious collation of the data in the letters as we find in modern reconstructions of Pauline chronology—a procedure for which he would likely have lacked both motive and technological means.[94] He need only have possessed such familiarity as comes with careful and repeated reading. It is therefore only in a rather attenuated sense that we can indeed refer to Luke as the first Pauline chronologist.

---

[91] So Pervo, *Acts: A Commentary*, 13–14.

[92] E.g., Walker, "The Timothy-Titus Problem Reconsidered"; Enslin, "Once Again, Luke and Paul," 265.

[93] Note that Walker also finds it necessary, though on other grounds, to posit Luke's knowledge of 2 Timothy in addition to the undisputed letters ("Aquila and Priscilla," 495).

[94] See esp. F. Gerald Downing, "Compositional Conventions and the Synoptic Problem," *JBL* 107 (1988): 69–85; R. A. Derrenbacker, *Ancient Compositional Practices and the Synoptic Problem*, BETL 186 (Leuven: Leuven University Press, 2005).

RECENT BOOKS from EERDMANS

THE BOOK OF ISAIAH
Enduring Questions Answered Anew
*Essays Honoring Joseph Blenkinsopp
and His Contribution to the Study of Isaiah*
Richard J. Bautch and **J. Todd Hibbard,** editors
"This collection of cutting-edge essays by eminent scholars at once advances dialogue between European and American scholars and provides a fitting tribute to one of the most prolific interpreters of Isaiah in this generation." — JOHN J. COLLINS
ISBN 978-0-8028-6773-5 • 242 pages • paperback • $35.00

WISDOM'S WONDER
*Character, Creation, and Crisis in
the Bible's Wisdom Literature*
William P. Brown
"Bill Brown deftly juxtaposes the formation of character by Israel's sages with the awe-inspiring universe in which that frequently disorienting process of education took place. In this way, he explores in amazing detail the richness and diversity of Proverbs, the book of Job, and Ecclesiastes."
— JAMES L. CRENSHAW
ISBN 978-0-8028-6793-3 • 236 pages • paperback • $25.00

POETIC HEROES
*Literary Commemorations of Warriors and
Warrior Culture in the Early Biblical World*
Mark S. Smith
"Mark Smith takes us on a fascinating tour of the 'lost world' of early Israelite warrior culture.... At once erudite and engaging, this is a treat for discerning readers of the Bible."
— RONALD HENDEL
ISBN 978-0-8028-6792-6 • 660 pages • paperback • $55.00

THE PSALMS AS CHRISTIAN LAMENT
A Historical Commentary
Bruce K. Waltke, James M. Houston, and **Erika Moore**
"Masterful exegesis blends with luminous pre-critical theological perspectives to give the book special value." — J. I. PACKER
ISBN 978-0-8028-6809-1 • 328 pages • paperback • $28.00

At your bookstore,
or call 800-253-7521
www.eerdmans.com

**WM. B. EERDMANS
PUBLISHING CO.**
2140 Oak Industrial Drive NE
Grand Rapids, MI 49505

The Sexual Use of Slaves: A Response to Kyle Harper on Jewish and Christian *Porneia*

JENNIFER A. GLANCY
glancy@lemoyne.edu
Le Moyne College, Syracuse, NY 13214

Kyle Harper has argued that by the first century CE, *porneia* "was the chief vice in a [Jewish] system of sexual morality rooted in conjugal sexuality. For Hellenistic Jews, in a culture where sex with dishonored women, especially prostitutes and slaves, was legal and expected, the term condensed the cultural differences between the observers of the Torah and Gentile depravity" ("*Porneia*: The Making of a Christian Sexual Norm," *JBL* 131 [2012]: 374). Harper argues that for Paul, as for other first-century Jews, *porneia* encompassed "that wide subset of extramarital sexual activity that was tolerated in Greek culture, the sexual use of dishonored women" (p. 378). I demonstrate, however, that Hellenistic Jewish writers did not use the word *porneia* to refer to a man's exploitation of slaves he owned. Moreover, while Jewish writers promoted conjugal sexuality, they were tolerant of extramarital sexual relationships between slaveholders and enslaved women. We have no evidence that Paul challenged that sexual norm. This article thus (1) clarifies the parameters of the contested term *porneia*; (2) contributes to an understanding of the logic of Jewish sexual ethics during the Second Temple period; and (3) locates Paul's silence on the sexual exploitation in the context of first-century Jewish teaching.

Kyle Harper's "*Porneia*: The Making of a Christian Sexual Norm," which appeared in this journal in 2012, enriches our understanding of the sense of the word πορνεία as its use evolved from the sixth century BCE to the sixth century CE.[1] Harper shows, for example, that Jewish writers expanded usage of the word to encompass not only the activities of those who sell their bodies (or whose bodies are sold) in prostitution but also the activities of men who frequent prostitutes. He

---

I thank the Le Moyne College Faculty Senate Research and Development Committee for research funding and David R. Andrews and Virginia Burrus for reading drafts of the article.

[1] Kyle Harper, "*Porneia*: The Making of a Christian Sexual Norm," *JBL* 131 (2012): 363–83.

argues that accurate translation of the vocabulary of ancient Mediterranean sexualities—specifically, the word πορνεία—compels acknowledgment of the degree to which sexual norms were informed by the social status of participants in those acts, their honor or dishonor.[2]

However, one of Harper's central claims—a claim with implications both for translation of the debated term πορνεία and for histories of Jewish and Christian sexualities—is unsupported by evidence he adduces and challenged by evidence he does not consider. Harper concludes, "Jewish and Christian πορνεία could evoke the whole array of extramarital sex acts of which Greek and Roman culture approved."[3] Is this the case? Greek and Roman cultures unequivocally sanctioned the right of male slaveholders to use their slaves sexually. Harper argues that Jewish writers relied on the word πορνεία to express disapproval of behavior prominently featuring exercise of that right: "By the first century C.E., πορνεία was the chief vice in a [Jewish] system of sexual morality rooted in conjugal sexuality. But for Hellenistic Jews, in a culture where sex with dishonored women, especially prostitutes and slaves, was legal and expected, the term condensed the cultural differences between the observers of the Torah and Gentile depravity."[4] Given the Torah's tolerance for the sexual use of slaves, this is a surprising statement, and one at odds with Catherine Hezser's verdict in *Jewish Slavery in Antiquity*: "Slaves were sexually exploited in both Jewish and Graeco-Roman society. The phenomenon that masters would sleep with and produce children with their slaves is taken for granted by both Jewish and Roman writers."[5]

In two major monographs, *Slavery in the Late Roman World AD 275–425* and *From Shame to Sin: The Christian Transformation of Sexual Morality in Late Antiquity*, Harper argues that Christian sexual ethics dissolved distinctions based on status and honor.[6] Both works assume the findings of "*Porneia*: The Making of a

---

[2] Kathy L. Gaca defines πορνεία in terms of religious exogamy (*The Making of Fornication: Eros, Ethics, and Political Reform in Greek Philosophy and Early Christianity*, HCS 40 [Berkeley: University of California Press, 2003]). I share Harper's reservations about so limited a definition ("*Porneia*," 366 n. 8, 377 n. 63).

[3] Harper, "*Porneia*," 383.

[4] Ibid., 374.

[5] Catherine Hezser, *Jewish Slavery in Antiquity* (New York: Oxford University Press, 2005), 386. On the Torah's regulation of sex with slaves, see Exod 21:7–11, Lev 19:20–22, and Deut 21:10–14, texts discussed in Hezser, *Jewish Slavery in Antiquity*, 192–93; David P. Wright, "'She Shall Not Go Free as Male Slaves Do': Developing Views about Slavery and Gender in the Laws of the Hebrew Bible," in *Beyond Slavery: Overcoming Its Religious and Sexual Legacies*, ed. Bernadette J. Brooten with Jacqueline L. Hazelton, Black Religion/Womanist Thought/Social Justice (New York: Palgrave Macmillan, 2010), 125–42.

[6] Kyle Harper, *Slavery in the Late Roman World AD 275–425* (Cambridge: Cambridge University Press, 2011), 322, 322 n. 271; *From Shame to Sin: The Christian Transformation of Sexual Morality in Late Antiquity* (Cambridge: Harvard University Press, 2013), 11–12, 86–93. In his review of *From Shame to Sin*, Peter Brown characterizes the monograph as a "scintillating

Christian Sexual Norm." Assessment of Harper's findings is thus important not only for translation of a ubiquitous but vague term in Christian sexual ethics but also for understanding the contours of Jewish and Christian sexual norms and practices in antiquity.

Harper does not cite a single instance in which πορνεία refers to a man's sexual use of his own slave. However, the summary statements I have quoted and others throughout the article encompass such behavior. Relying on the *Thesaurus Linguae Graecae* (*TLG*), Harper bases his findings on a "comprehensive examination" of over fifty-three hundred iterations of πορνεία in Greek literature between the sixth century BCE and the sixth century CE.[7] One advantage of relying on a database is that others are able to replicate those searches in order to assess data for themselves.[8] I restricted my *TLG* search to instances of πορνεία in Jewish and Christian sources prior to 200 CE, under four hundred iterations of the term.[9] Sex involving prostitutes exemplifies πορνεία in a number of the sources. However, sources prior to 200 CE do not characterize sexual exploitation of household slaves as πορνεία. Indeed, it is worth noting that, although my argument focuses on Jewish writers, including Paul, no Christian source prior to 200 CE explicitly characterizes a man's sexual exploitation of his household slaves as πορνεία.[10]

Moreover, beyond the constraints of a word search, other evidence supports Hezser's contention that Jews shared the tolerance of surrounding cultures for the sexual use of domestic slaves. Tracing usage of the word πορνεία does not advance our understanding of whether and under what circumstances Jews and Christians

---

contribution" to investigations of sexual norms in Christian antiquity ("Rome: Sex and Freedom," *New York Review of Books*, 19 December 2013, http://www.nybooks.com/articles/archives/2013/dec/19/rome-sex-freedom/).

[7] Harper, "Porneia," 365, 365 n. 5.

[8] I recommend replication of a database search, including assessment of data, as a pedagogical exercise.

[9] Cf. Harper, "Porneia," 369. Christian use of the vaguely defined term πορνεία should be seen in the wider context of reliance on sexual invective in the self-definition of Christian communities, as Jennifer Wright Knust has convincingly argued (*Abandoned to Lust: Sexual Slander and Ancient Christianity*, GTR [New York: Columbia University Press, 2006]); her argument is broadly relevant to the earlier proliferation of πορνεία in Jewish sources, a discussion outside the scope of the present article.

[10] Commenting on a number of sources that pair general admonitions against μοιχεία with admonitions against πορνεία (Did. 2.2; Barn. 19.4; Herm. Mand. 4.29.1), Harper concludes, "For a married man, [extramarital] sex might be μοιχεία or πορνεία, depending on whether the female partner possessed sexual honor" ("*Porneia*," 380). A more careful assessment of dual injunctions against μοιχεία and πορνεία: blameworthy extramarital sex might be μοιχεία or πορνεία, a formulation leaving open the possibility that some extramarital sexual activities would not attract the censure from ancient readers that twenty-first-century readers infer, notably, a male slaveholder's sexual use of domestic slaves. I have not traced the evolution of the term in sources after 200 CE.

before 200 CE would have considered a male slaveholder's sexual use of his household slaves to be blameworthy.[11]

Rare in classical Greek sources, πορνεία is widely used both in the LXX and in Jewish writings of the Second Temple period, an expansion of meaning illuminated by Harper. However, use of the term to categorize sexual activity with slaves other than prostitutes is *at most* occasional—indeed, Harper marshals the only instances of πορνεία that might be construed as relevant, iterations of πορνεία in Sirach, Testaments of the Twelve Patriarchs, and Philo. Along with considering those texts, I ask what the Dead Sea Scrolls, Josephus, and rabbinic sources contribute to understanding Jewish attitudes toward the sexual use of slaves, before turning to πορνεία in 1 Cor 5–7.

Ben Sira/Sirach

Quoting the NRSV, Harper refers to Sirach's generalized admonition to be "ashamed of sexual immorality [περὶ πορνείας] before your father or mother" (41:17 NRSV). After listing a variety of other behaviors of which to be ashamed—leaning on one's elbows when eating, for example—Sirach returns to specific injunctions regarding sexual morality, again mixed with other kinds of advice. The (presumptively male) reader should be ashamed of looking at a prostitute (γυναικὸς ἑταίρας), of rejecting appeals from relatives, of looking at another man's wife (γυναικὸς ὑπάνδρου), and "of meddling with his servant girl" (41:22a NRSV). The text continues, "and do not approach her bed" (41:22a NRSV).[12] On this basis, Harper writes, "Sirach attests to the ascent of a conjugal sexual morality in late Second Temple Judaism; the injunctions again sex with slaves and prostitutes are a noteworthy development."[13]

However, the LXX—on which the NRSV translation is based—only enjoins the (male) reader to keep away from women belonging to another man's household, to keep his eyes off the matron of that household, and to avoid sexual contact with

---

[11] In the course of my argument I revisit conceptual terrain mapped by me in "Obstacles to Slaves' Participation in the Corinthian Church," *JBL* 117 (1998): 71–87; and *Slavery in Early Christianity* (New York: Oxford University Press, 2002), 50–53, 59–70; and by Sheila Briggs, "Paul on Bondage and Freedom in Imperial Roman Society," in *Paul and Politics: Ekklesia, Israel, Imperium, Interpretation. Essays in Honor of Krister Stendahl*, ed. Richard A. Horsley (Harrisburg, PA: Trinity Press International, 2000), 110–23, esp. 114–17; and Carolyn Osiek, "Female Slaves, *Porneia*, and the Limits of Obedience," in *Early Christian Families in Context: An Interdisciplinary Dialogue*, ed. David L. Balch and Carolyn Osiek, Religion, Marriage and Family (Grand Rapids: Eerdmans, 2003), 255–74. Systematic consideration of πορνεία in Jewish writings from the Second Temple period advances these earlier discussions, enabling me in some cases to extend and refine their findings and in other cases to dissent.

[12] καὶ ἀπὸ κατανοήσεως γυναικὸς ὑπάνδρου / ἀπὸ περιεργίας παιδίσκης αὐτοῦ / καὶ μὴ ἐπιστῇς ἐπὶ τὴν κοίτην αὐτῆς (Sir 41:23b–24).

[13] Harper, "*Porneia*," 371.

the enslaved females in that household. The presumed reader of Sirach is a slaveholder (see 7:20 and 33:25–33), but the Greek text does not warn him away from the beds of enslaved women in his own household. Discouraging men from violating other men's households, the passage promotes a domestic sexual morality without endorsing an exclusively conjugal sexual morality.[14]

The situation is more complex if one considers the only extant Hebrew manuscript of Ben Sira witnessing to the relevant passage, the Masada manuscript dating from the first century BCE, which Patrick W. Skehan and Alexander A. Di Lella take to represent the original Hebrew text.[15] Ben Sira admonishes his reader, in Skehan's reconstruction and translation, to be ashamed "of meddling [with a maidservant] of yours, and of coming upon her bed."[16] So far as I know, this is the clearest statement by a Jewish writer of the Second Temple period discouraging a slaveholder from sexual contact with his own slave.[17] It is therefore interesting that Ben Sira's translator, his Greek-speaking grandson, altered that instruction to a narrower warning against sexual contact with enslaved women belonging to another man, a change of pronoun implicitly conceding a man's right to use his own slaves sexually.[18] The grandson's studied silence on sexual use of household slaves is in keeping not only with the values of the wider Hellenistic world but also with the norms of Second Temple period Judaism; Ben Sira himself is an isolated voice daring to criticize a man who took sexual advantage of his slave, not unlike Musonius Rufus, whose criticism of the sexual use of slaves was not adopted by fellow moralists.[19]

---

[14] Regarding marital advice in Ben Sira, Ibolya Balla writes, "Ben Sira has an interesting mixture of comments on marital relationships. What is perhaps the most striking feature one observes by reading these passages, is that there is relatively little advice to husbands on how they should conduct themselves. There is much more on what effects a wife has on her husband's life. While there are concrete instructions to men concerning issues of sexuality, passions/desires, a number of them are not found in the context of discussing marriage" (*Ben Sira on Family, Gender, and Sexuality*, DCLS 8 [Berlin: de Gruyter, 2011], 222).

[15] Patrick W. Skehan and Alexander A. Di Lella, *The Wisdom of Ben Sira: A New Translation with Notes*, AB 39 (Garden City, NY: Doubleday, 1987), 51–53.

[16] מהתעשק ע[ם שפ[חה לך (MS M Sir 41:22a; for reconstruction of text, see Skehan, *Wisdom of Ben Sira*, 479; Ibolya Balla, *Ben Sira on Family*, 265).

[17] Balla floats (but stops short of endorsing) another possible reading of Ben Sira 41:22a: Lev 19:20–22 penalizes sexual contact with an enslaved woman who is betrothed; perhaps such a situation is implicitly in view here (*Ben Sira on Family*, 155).

[18] About this passage, Osiek writes, "Most interesting is a text that seems to have been altered from Hebrew to LXX in the direction of justifying sex with one's own slave" ("Female Slaves, *Porneia*," 265). Although Harper cites Osiek's "Female Slaves" in a footnote cataloging other scholars who have written about πορνεία (364 n. 2; see also n. 3), he does not refer to her verdict on translation of this passage in Ben Sira, a verdict that complicates his argument.

[19] Musonius Rufus, frag. 12. Bolla notes that the wording of the LXX is "in line with popular values of the time and values reflected in the law" (*Ben Sira on Family*, 155).

Testaments of the Twelve Patriarchs

Harper characterizes Testaments of the Twelve Patriarchs as the "most intriguing witness to the expansion of πορνεία and its ascent to the position of a chief vice." After noting that, in the Testaments of the Twelve Patriarchs, πορνεία is an "inclusive sexual category denoting illicit sexual activity, including incest, prostitution, exogamy, and unchastity," Harper comments, "For Jews living in a Hellenic culture that tolerated, even encouraged the sexual use of dishonored women, πορνεία was an ever-present temptation."[20] This is a misleading assessment of a text implicitly condoning the sexual use of one category of "dishonored women," enslaved females used sexually by their owners. On the subject of sexual use of slaves in the Testaments of the Twelve Patriarchs, Harper writes only, "Reuben was guilty of πορνεία for sleeping with Bilhah, Rachel's maid, because his father had been in the same bed (T. Reu. 1:6)."[21] In Testaments of the Twelve Patriarchs, Reuben's πορνεία consists of incest—but Jacob escapes criticism for his sexual liaisons with the enslaved Bilhah and Zilpah.[22]

Building up to his confession that he forced himself on (an inebriated and naked) Bilhah, Reuben admonishes his progeny not to be taken by a woman's appearance, not to be alone with a female subject to another man (μηδὲ ἰδιάζετε μετὰ θηλείας ὑπάνδρου) and not to interfere in affairs of women (T. Reu. 1:10).[23] Particularly interesting is the second warning, discouraging dalliance with a θηλείας ὑπάνδρου—not a married woman (γυναικὸς ὑπάνδρου) but a female (sexually) subject to another man, wording that would accurately describe an enslaved female sexually exploited by her male owner.

The Testaments of the Twelve Patriarchs could not discourage slaveholders from sexual contact with their own slaves without implicit criticism of the patriarch Jacob. More broadly, the patriarchs' sexual histories would have made it difficult for Jews (or Christians) to condemn men who confined their extramarital sexual activities to female slaves within their own households.[24]

---

[20] Harper, "*Porneia*," 372–73. Harper acknowledges debate over whether Testaments of the Twelve Patriarchs should be considered a product of Hellenistic Judaism or second-century Christianity, a question beyond the scope of my argument.

[21] Harper, "*Porneia*," 382.

[22] Although in one passage Judah refers to Bilhah as his father's wife (γυναικὸς πατρός μου [T. Jud. 4.13.3]), the text explicitly treats Bilhah as a slave—daughter of a παιδίσκη, property of Rachel (T. Naph. 8.1)

[23] Ishay Rosen-Zvi's otherwise helpful analysis does not consider the significance of servile status in the text's construction of Bilhah as temptress, naked and drunk ("Bilhah the Temptress: The Testament of Reuben and 'The Birth of Sexuality,'" *JQR* 96 [2006]: 66–94).

[24] In late antiquity, Christian theologians urging men to confine sexual activities to marriage likewise contended with examples set by the patriarchs. In *Slavery in the Late Roman World*, Harper mentions Ambrose of Milan, who argues that Christians should take the example of Abraham's liaison with Hagar as a caution against sexual entanglements with slaves (p. 425;

Damascus Document[25]

Although Harper claims that the Damascus Document characterizes as "fornication" "sex that falls outside of marriage according to the Jewish law," the text proscribes only the taking of two wives, a curious enough proscription in light of Torah's tolerance of polygamy (CD IV, 12b–V, 14a).[26] However, in a passage not mentioned by Harper, a fragmentary manuscript of the Damascus Document does refer to sex with a female slave. Given the damaged state of the text, Cecilia Wassen is appropriately cautious in her estimation: "Possibly the law in 4Q270 4 elaborates upon Lev 19:20–22, concerning a man taking a slave woman designated for someone else, and imposes some kind of purity restrictions on the slave woman for seven years. Apart from these prescriptions, the halakhic opinion on the matter of sexual relations with slave women is not preserved."[27]

Philo

Harper writes, "The most important witness to the development of πορνεία in Hellenistic Judaism is Philo."[28] Philo uses the word in two passages (according to the *TLG*), only one of which Harper discusses.[29] The more relevant instance is Philo's elaboration of a biblical story in which Israelites first become sexually entangled with the women of Moab and then begin to worship their gods (Num 25). On

---

Ambrose, *Abr.* 1.4). Harper does not comment on the continuation of Ambrose's discussion, counseling male Christian slaveholders who nonetheless choose to have sex with their slaves to make sure their enslaved sexual partners remain deferential to their mistresses (discussed in Jennifer A. Glancy, *Corporal Knowledge: Early Christian Bodies* [New York: Oxford University Press, 2010], 66).

[25] Citations of πορνεία that Harper culls from Jubilees and Tobit are not relevant to my argument.

[26] Harper, "*Porneia*," 373. Harper cites only Joseph A. Fitzmyer, "The Matthean Divorce Texts and Some New Palestinian Evidence," *TS* 37 (1976): 197–226, esp. 219–20. Fitzmyer argues that CD IV, 12b–V, 14a forbids remarriage after divorce; more recent scholars have argued convincingly that the passage forbids polygamy. See Cecilia Wassen, *Women in the Damascus Document*, AcBib 21 (Atlanta: Society of Biblical Literature, 2005), 114–18; Tal Ilan, "Women in Qumran and the Dead Sea Scrolls," in *The Oxford Handbook of the Dead Sea Scrolls*, ed. Timothy H. Lim and John J. Collins (Oxford: Oxford University Press, 2010), 123–47, 133–35.

[27] Wassen, *Women in the Damascus Document*, 71. Lawrence H. Schiffman discusses possible connections between 4Q270 4 and later halakic discussions ("Laws Pertaining to Women and Sexuality in the Early Stratum of the Damascus Document," in *The Dead Sea Scrolls and Contemporary Culture: Proceedings of the International Conference Held at the Israel Museum, Jerusalem [July 6–8, 2008]*, ed. Adolfo D. Roitman, Lawrence H. Schiffman, and Shani Tzoref, STDJ 93 [Leiden: Brill, 2011], 547–70, esp. 561–62).

[28] Harper, "*Porneia*," 373. Compare his assessment in *From Shame to Sin*: "In Philo's voluminous commentaries on sexual propriety, *porneia* never becomes a central term" (p. 90).

[29] Harper does not mention a passage in which incontinence is said to school the soul in a sexualized immorality (πορνεία), an instance irrelevant to his discussion (Philo, *Spec. Laws* 1.282).

Philo's telling, the incident involves a ploy engineered by Balaam and Balak, requiring Balak to abrogate laws on adultery, seduction, and πορνεία so that the women of Moab can indulge their lusts and thus entice Israelite men into idolatry (*Mos.* 1.300). Harper writes, "When Philo ... imagines the different classes of sexual conduct that had to be deregulated to allow this sexual ruse to succeed, there were three categories: μοιχεία, φθορά, and πορνεία. The violation of a wife or otherwise respectable girl was μοιχεία or φθορά; sexual use of other women was πορνεία."[30] Harper here assumes precisely what needs to be defined, the contours of πορνεία. The passage focuses on sexual behavior contravening normal laws. Philo was certainly aware that sexual use of household slaves was ordinarily licit; it is hard to imagine what ancient law might need to be rescinded to free a male slaveholder to pursue sexual relations with his own slave.

In Harper's assessment of what he terms a "tectonic shift in Jewish sexual ethics," Philo is "the most important witness to the sexual sensibilities of Hellenistic Judaism on the eve of the Pauline missions," a claim ultimately resting not on Philo's limited use of the term πορνεία but more broadly on his views on sexuality, especially conjugal sexuality (his ideal) and prostitution (which he understood to be forbidden by the law of Moses).[31] In *From Shame to Sin*, Harper summarizes his understanding of Philo's sexual ethics:

> The "polity of Moses," by its very nature, "excluded the prostitute from citizenship." As a "common *miasma*," she was worthy of stoning. Adultery was punishable by death, while the seduction of a free citizen girl was a damnable violation. In a community without prostitutes, where honorable women were available only as wives, the limitation of sex to marriage would be built into the very borders of sexual polity.[32]

Harper's claim that a (free) man's sexual choices were restricted to honorable marriage or consorting with prostitutes is at the crux of my disagreement with him, as it ignores the ready availability of enslaved women to men of means, an availability with which Philo was quite familiar.[33]

Philo favors restriction of sexual activity to marriage, and even within marriage urges temperance.[34] At the same time, however peculiar it may seem to

---

[30] Harper, "Porneia," 374.

[31] Harper, *From Shame to Sin*, 89–90.

[32] Ibid., 90; on Philo's exclusion of prostitutes from citizenship, see *Spec. Laws* 3.51.

[33] Indeed, it is difficult to reconcile Harper's reductive summary of a free man's sexual choices to free women or prostitutes with his recognition elsewhere of the ubiquity of sexual exploitation of domestic slaves: "The Roman slave system was a sex racket established by and for men of the higher classes. The power of free men over servile women was exercised in multifarious ways, from the use of brothels or transitory amours at the whim of the master to durable relations of companionship between partners of unequal status" (*Slavery in the Late Roman World*, 442).

[34] Harper quotes some relevant passages, including *Spec. Laws* 3.9 and *Joseph* 43 ("Porneia," 373–74). Mary Rose D'Angelo usefully locates Philo's family and sexual ethics in a wider political

twenty-first-century readers, Philo "assumes and never questions" a slaveholder's sexual access to enslaved women of his own household, as William Loader concludes after an extensive study of Philo's treatment of sexuality.[35] Philo does not directly address the morality of sexual use of slaves, but his allegorical readings of patriarchal narratives include frequent references to the patriarchs' enslaved sexual partners.[36] Along with many references to Hagar (and fewer to Bilhah and Zilpah) scattered throughout Philo's corpus, *On the Preliminary Studies* centers on the story of Abraham and Hagar read as an allegory for training the mind through preparatory study of lower subjects. *On the Preliminary Studies* neither promises nor delivers a coherent program of sexual ethics, of course. Its argument is nonetheless predicated on hierarchical dynamics of household slavery familiar to Philo both from his study of Genesis and from the cosmopolitan milieu of first-century Alexandria. He imagines, for example, a male slaveholder chastised by his wife for honoring his enslaved sexual partner as though she were a wife (152). Philo's implicit attitude toward female slaves is consistent with attitudes expressed in other writings of the era—he writes that Hagar is properly called a παιδίσκη, for example, because she is both a slave (δούλη) and childish (154).

Perhaps more telling are offhand remarks Philo makes about sexual relations with slaves. He demonstrates familiarity with (an elite male take on) emotional exchanges between slaveholders and their slaves when he refers to slaveholders effectively enslaved by their shapely slave girls (εὔμορφα παιδισκάρια; *Prob.* 38). More disturbingly, in a passage condemning the seduction of wellborn, unmarried females, Philo rails against treating free women as though they are (unfree) servants (ταῖς ἐλευθέραις ὡς θεραπαίναις), a tirade reflecting a double standard between treatment of respectable women, whose honor should be protected, and women of lower social status, who have no honor to protect (*Spec. Laws* 3.69.4).

For Philo, a male slaveholder's sexual exploitation of his female slave seems to belong to the category of licit behavior, neither praiseworthy nor blameworthy nor noteworthy. Because he addresses the sexual use of slaves directly, Plutarch, Philo's near contemporary, can help us understand how a moralist might reconcile advocacy of conjugal sexuality with sexual exploitation of slaves. In the paean to marriage concluding his dialogue on Eros, Plutarch promises that the generative desire expressed within marriages leads to the greatest of all pleasures (*Mor.* 769F–770A).

---

discourse ("Gender and Geopolitics in the Work of Philo of Alexandria: Jewish Piety and Imperial Family Values," in *Mapping Gender in Ancient Religious Discourses*, ed. Todd C. Penner and Caroline Vander Stichele, BibInt 84 [Leiden: Brill, 2007], 63–88).

[35] William Loader, *Philo, Josephus, and the Testaments on Sexuality*, Attitudes towards Sexuality in Judaism and Christianity in the Hellenistic Greco-Roman Era (Grand Rapids: Eerdmans, 2011), 257.

[36] As Loader observes, in all Philo's references to the patriarchs and their enslaved concubines, the "assumption appears to be that the household head has sexual access to slaves" (*Philo, Josephus, and the Textaments*, 128).

However, his *Instruction to a Bride and Groom* includes the suggestion that a slave would be a legitimate sexual outlet for a man so unable to control his appetites that he would otherwise use his wife coarsely, an ill-bred man incontinent in his pleasures (ἀκρατὴς δὲ περὶ τὰς ἡδονὰς καὶ ἀνάγωγος)—that is, a man deficient in self-control (*Mor.* 140B).[37] Plutarch's instruction is thus not meant to encourage men to pursue liaisons with slaves but to encourage women to interpret their husbands' dalliances in such a fashion. He recounts an anecdote about the orator Gorgias, mocked for speaking on a concord lacking in his own home, his infatuation with a female slave (θεράπαινα) having provoked his wife to jealousy (*Mor.* 144C). Continuing, Plutarch informs male readers that a wife knows when her husband has come from the bed of another. He thus urges men to be considerate of their wives' feelings, advice that may be taken to counsel either discretion or fidelity (*Mor.* 144D).[38] For Plutarch, trysts between male slaveholders and their slaves are tolerated, though not exemplary. Philo seems not far from such a view.

Josephus

Because πορνεία is not part of Josephus's vocabulary, his writings do not figure in the story Harper tells, but his comments on marital and extramarital relations are relevant to understanding Jewish sensibilities in the first century CE. Loader writes:

> Slavery laid one open to sexual exploitation. In this regard Josephus may well be very strict if his statement that husbands are to engage in sexual intercourse only with their wives (*Ap.* 201) also places household slaves among the forbidden partners, though concubines were an obvious exception. This is, however, unlikely (cf. *A.J.* 16.194; 18.40). He is quite clear, however, in disapproving marriage to slaves by freemen, citing the issue of "decorum and the proprieties of rank" (*A.J.* 4.244).[39]

---

[37] I include myself among NT scholars who have discussed this passage without adequate acknowledgment of its characterization of men who pursue such relations as intemperate (Glancy, *Slavery in Early Christianity*, 21; Osiek, "Female Slaves, *Porneia*," 264; Joseph A. Marchal, "The Usefulness of an Onesimus: The Sexual Use of Slaves and Paul's Letter to Philemon," *JBL* 13 [2011]: 749–70, esp. 756).

[38] Sarah B. Pomeroy takes the passage to commend discretion ("Reflections on Plutarch, Advice to the Bride and Groom: Something Old, Something New, Something Borrowed," in *Plutarch's Advice to the Bride and Groom and A Consolation to His Wife: English Translations, Commentary, Interpretive Essays, and Bibliography*, ed. Sarah B. Pomeroy [New York: Oxford University Press, 1999], 33–42, esp. 37); in the same volume, Cynthia Patterson takes the passage to commend fidelity ("Plutarch's Advice to the Bride and Groom: Traditional Wisdom through a Philosophic Lens," 128–37, esp. 130).

[39] Loader, *Philo, Josephus, and the Testaments*, 342 (but compare his more cryptic assessment in *Making Sense of Sex: Attitudes towards Sexuality in Early Jewish and Christian Literature* [Grand Rapids: Eerdmans, 2013], 47).

Josephus's assertion in *Against Apion* that Jewish law insists on conjugal fidelity is coupled with injunctions against sexual contact with women betrothed or married to other men (2.201). In *Jewish Antiquities*, he outlines sexual norms for young Jewish males—to marry freeborn virgins; to avoid sexual contact with other men's wives; not to marry slaves or prostitutes (4.244). Restriction of sexual activity outside marriage is not absolute, but rather predicated on the status of female partner. In narrating the story of the Parthian king Phraates, Josephus reports that Phraates accepted from Julius Caesar the gift of an Italian slave named Thermusa. At first, the king treated the woman as a concubine; trouble ensued, according to Josephus, only when Phraates unwisely decided that she should have the honorable status of wife (18.40).

To a twenty-first-century reader, it may seem obvious that a prescription for marital fidelity precludes sexual contact with enslaved women. Josephus, however, was able to pair such a prescription with tolerance for sexual relationships between free men and slaves (and even prostitutes). Disturbed that a free man might marry an enslaved woman, Josephus was not disturbed by the prospect of a free man having sex with a woman legally designated his property.

Rabbinic Sources

In his 2011 *JBL* article, Harper explores Jewish πορνεία in order to illuminate Paul's deployment of the term in 1 Corinthians, a deployment with signal impact on the rhetoric of Christian sexual ethics. He does not consider Jewish sources dating after Philo and Paul, nor could the *TLG* help him navigate the rabbinic corpus. Still, attention to rabbinic sexual norms complicates Harper's claim in "*Porneia*" that Jewish culture was distinctively set apart from surrounding cultures with their denial of sexual honor to women of low social status, including enslaved women. Quite simply, rabbinic sources take for granted that slaveholders—including Jewish slaveholders—enjoy unpenalized sexual access to enslaved women in their households whose routine vulnerability to sexual exploitation disqualified them from claims to sexual honor.[40]

---

[40] On rabbinic assumptions that (1) female slaves have no sexual honor to protect and (2) male slaveholders routinely have sex with household slaves, see, e.g., Judith Romney Wegner, *Chattel or Person? The Status of Women in the Mishnah* (New York: Oxford University Press, 1988), 21–23; Dina Stein, "A Maidservant and Her Master's Voice: Discourse, Identity, and Eros in Rabbinic Texts," *Journal of the History of Sexuality* 10 (2001): 375–97; Michael L. Satlow, *Jewish Marriage in Antiquity* (Princeton: Princeton University Press, 2001), 188, 315 n. 144; Hezser, *Jewish Slavery in Antiquity*, 198–99; Gail Labovitz, "The Purchase of His Money: Slavery and the Ethics of Jewish Marriage," in Brooten and Hazelton, *Beyond Slavery*, 91–106, esp. 98–99; and Labovitz, "More Slave Women, More Lewdness: Freedom and Honor in Rabbinic Constructions of Female Sexuality," *JFSR* 28 (2012): 69–87.

In *Slavery in the Late Roman World*, Harper writes, "the slave body in antiquity was an object, an object sexually available to its legal owner." In a footnote, he cites as warrant four classicists and—without comment—Hezser's *Jewish Slavery in Antiquity*.[41] Developing the theme of the sexual availability of slaves, Harper compiles a list of relevant illustrations from a variety of late ancient sources, including—again, without comment—three references to the Babylonian Talmud.[42] It is no secret, even to Harper, that rabbinic sources presuppose the sexual availability of domestic slaves, nor is there reason to doubt that in late antiquity Jewish slaveholders took advantage of the sexual availability of their slaves. I have argued that the situation was no different in the first century CE—our sources suggest that Jews shared the wider cultural assumption that legalized vulnerability to sexual exploitation stripped enslaved women of claims to sexual honor, including enslaved women belonging to Jewish slaveholders.[43]

Paul

After surveying other New Testament uses of the term, Harper notes that "Christian understandings of πορνεία develop out of Paul's letters, especially 1 Corinthians 5–7."[44] Harper's analysis of Paul's use of πορνεία in these chapters is predicated on his understanding that, as a first-century Jew, Paul would have categorized as πορνεία any extramarital sexual contact between a free man and a woman whose low social status denied her claims to sexual honor, an understanding of Jewish sexual norms I have shown to be inconsistent with available evidence. Harper refers to 1 Cor 6:12–20 as "the crux of any interpretation of Pauline πορνεία."[45] "The body is meant not for fornication [πορνεία], but for the Lord," Paul tells the reader before warning that anyone who has sex with a female prostitute becomes one flesh with her. Paul urges the reader to flee πορνεία.

---

[41] Harper, *Slavery in the Late Roman World*, 292, 292 n. 73.

[42] Ibid., 293, 293 nn. 78, 79, 84.

[43] Catherine Hezser notes that, although in biblical texts an enslaved concubine might be treated as a family member and her offspring with the slaveholder might be considered his "proper children," in Hellenistic and Roman times Jewish sources draw "clear boundaries between the freeborn members of the family and the slave *familia*." She writes, "Sexual relations between masters and their slaves were still tolerated (although not by all; cf. *Lev. R.* 9:5), but they did not have any repercussions as far as the family and inheritance structure was concerned" ("Slavery and the Jews," in *The Cambridge World History of Slavery*, vol. 1, *The Ancient Mediterranean World*, ed. Keith Bradley and Paul Cartledge [Cambridge: Cambridge University Press, 2011], 445–46).

[44] Harper, "Porneia," 376–77. In the interest of concision, I focus this discussion on Harper's reading of 1 Cor 5–7 rather than engaging the entirety of the scholarly discussion on πορνεία in these chapters, a literature discussed only as immediately relevant to my argument.

[45] Ibid., 378.

Harper comments:

> At issue is a category of sexual activity that some members of the Corinthian community believe is allowed but that Paul views as illicit. This category is most readily comprehensible as that wide subset of extramarital sexual activity that was tolerated in Greek culture, the sexual use of dishonored women. If there were any doubt that Paul had prostitution principally in mind, his immediate reference to the πόρνη makes it clear that for him, as for Philo, prostitution was the main venue of such pagan sexual license.[46]

But Jewish culture likewise tolerated the sexual use of slave women who had no claim to sexual honor. The passage only censures men who frequent prostitutes; there is no basis to infer that Paul has a broader category in mind, "that wide subset of extramarital sexual activity that was tolerated in Greek culture, the sexual use of dishonored women."[47] For Paul and Philo, sex with prostitutes—one category of low-status women lacking claims to sexual honor—exemplified πορνεία. However, there is no evidence that Paul, Philo, or any other first-century Greek-speaking Jew used the term πορνεία to refer to a man's exploitation of a woman who was his property.

In 1 Cor 7, Paul restricts sexual activity to marriage "because of cases of πορνεία" (v. 2). Harper writes, "It is revealing that, whereas authors of the Roman period saw sex with prostitutes or slaves as the solution to adultery, Paul saw marriage as the solution to temptations of easy sex with dishonored women."[48] As I have shown, there is no precedent to support Harper's contention that the term πορνεία would be understood to include a male slaveholder's sexual use of enslaved women in his household.

Although 1 Cor 7 does not advance the project of defining πορνεία, can we nonetheless infer Paul's attitude toward sexual use of slaves from his arguments there? Harper's insistence on situating Paul squarely in the trajectory of Hellenistic Jewish attitudes toward (free) men's sexual use of women without claim to sexual honor is at odds with his conclusions about the lessons of 1 Corinthians. To a twenty-first-century reader, it may seem obvious that Paul's endorsement of conjugal sexuality rules out sexual exploitation of slaves.[49] However, in Jewish sources,

---

[46] Ibid.

[47] Similarly, in *Slavery in the Late Roman World*, Harper holds that, for Paul, "*Porneia* was a metonym for the casual sex permitted in Roman culture, drawing on the ideological association between prostitution and sexual dishonor. *Porneia* must be understood in terms of a system in which male sexuality was given free rein to exploit dishonored women: prostitutes, concubines, and slaves. Paul's use of *porneia* operated by reference to an entire culture of sexuality that permitted casual sex with dishonorable women" (p. 322).

[48] Harper, "*Porneia*," 379.

[49] As an instance of such assimilation to twenty-first-century sexual logic, I cite my earlier verdict that "by limiting the legitimate range of sexual expression to marriage, Paul implicitly

encouragement of conjugal sexuality is coupled with tolerance for the sexual use of domestic slaves and enslaved concubines. Is this an attitude Paul shares?[50] Perhaps it is best to remain in some measure agnostic on a question Paul never addresses, but if we extend his argument according to the logic of first-century Jewish sexual norms rather than the logic of sexual norms in our own day, it is a probability.[51]

I do not mean to suggest that Paul or Philo would rate a man's sexual liaison with an enslaved woman as praiseworthy, a model to emulate.[52] However, praiseworthy/encouraged and blameworthy/forbidden are not the only possible moral verdicts on behavior. Behavior may also be categorized as licit—tolerated, not penalized—and indeed, this is how reliance on enslaved women as sexual outlets figures in the Jewish writings Harper positions as crucial context for understanding Pauline sexual ethics.

---

suggests that slaves who oblige their masters are engaged in *porneia*" (Glancy, *Slavery in Early Christianity*, 69, 67).

[50] Compare, for example, assumptions about the dynamics of sexual relationships between slaveholders and enslaved women that Paul and Philo share in their references to the story of Abraham and Hagar. (On Paul's assumptions in Gal 4, see Glancy, *Corporal Knowledge*, 65–66.)

[51] Cf. Osiek, "Female Slaves, *Porneia*," 274.

[52] In the course of arguing that Paul's characterization of Onesimus as "useful" is sexual, Marchal anticipates objections based on 1 Cor 7 ("Usefulness of an Onesimus," 768–69). His argument that endorsement of conjugal sexuality did not necessarily entail repudiation of the sexual use of household slaves parallels my own. I am nonetheless unable to reconcile Paul's advice on sexual abstention in 1 Cor 7, his self-description in 1 Cor 7:8, and his expressed antipathy toward same-sex eroticism in Rom 1:26–27 with the hypothesis that he found Onesimus sexually useful. Marchal does not consider Jewish writers other than Paul (see 760 n. 43). Because Harper argues that Paul, Philo, and other Hellenistic Jewish writers importantly distinguished themselves from the surrounding culture in their attitudes toward the sexual use of women without claims to honor, I have focused on the degree to which Jewish sources share those attitudes with coeval writings. There are, however, differences in tone between Jewish moralists and the preponderance of Greek and Latin sources cited by Marchal, sources often delighting in the sexual availability of slaves. I have argued that Philo seems close to Plutarch in reserved tolerance for a free man's sexual use of his own slaves, an attitude consistent with cryptic references to sex with slaves in other Jewish sources. Marchal, moreover, does not attempt to reconcile his thesis with Paul's words on same-sex passion in Rom 1:26–27. (My reading of male-male passion in Rom 1:26–27 adheres closely to that of Dale Martin, "Heterosexism and the Interpretation of Romans 1:18–32," in *Sex and the Single Savior: Gender and Sexuality in Biblical Interpretation* [Louisville: Westminster John Knox, 2006], 51–64, esp. 51–60.) For further discussion, see Jennifer A. Glancy, "The Utility of an Apostle: On Philemon 11," *Journal of Early Christian History* (forthcoming). Although I am unconvinced by Marchal's thesis, his reminders about the ubiquity of sexual reliance on slaves are certainly relevant to my argument.

Conclusion

Carolyn Osiek considers possible reasons why Paul and other Christian writers from the first centuries did not address the sexual exploitation of slaves:

> [B]ecause a prohibition was self-evident (unlikely), because it was not done by Christians (also unlikely given the prevailing acceptance in the culture), because it was too much of a problem to tackle (ignore it and maybe it will go away), or because they did not consider it a problem? I would argue that this was a part of the culture that they had not yet sorted out as something to reject explicitly.[53]

According to Harper, the situation is otherwise. On his view, Paul followed other Jewish moralists in refusing to countenance extramarital sexual relations between free men and women without claim to sexual honor. However, his account of the logic of Jewish sexual ethics is misleading. The attention to Jewish sources he commends leads to a conclusion different from the one he reaches.

Completing his survey of Hellenistic Jewish references to πορνεία, Harper concludes that, by the first century CE, "in a culture where sex with dishonored women, especially prostitutes and slaves, was legal and expected, the term condensed the cultural differences between the observers of the Torah and Gentile depravity."[54] Harper is correct, of course, that a woman's social status factored into whether a *blameworthy* extramarital sexual liaison qualified as πορνεία or as μοιχεία, but Jewish moralists did not subsume all extramarital sexual acts in those two categories. In particular, a male slaveholder's sexual use of enslaved women in his household was licit. In Jewish writers from Ben Sira's grandson to Philo and Josephus, advocacy of conjugal fidelity was coupled with ho-hum tolerance for the sexual use of household slaves. We have no evidence that Paul challenged that sexual norm.

[53] Osiek, "Female Slaves, *Porneia*," 274.
[54] Harper, "*Porneia*," 374–75.

Language Resources in Paperback from SBL Press

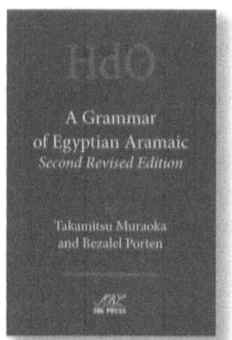

A GRAMMAR OF EGYPTIAN ARAMAIC, SECOND REVISED EDITION
Takamitsu Muraoka and Bezalel Porten
Paper $59.95, 978-1-62837-037-9   470 pages, 2014   Code: 069557
HdO 32, Brill Reprints 57

A DICTIONARY OF THE UGARITIC LANGUAGE IN THE ALPHABETIC TRADITION, SECOND REVISED EDITION (2 Volumes)
Gregorio del Olmo Lete and Joaquín Sanmartín
Wilfred G. E. Watson, translator
Paper $99.95, 978-1-62837-035-5   1124 pages, 2014   Code: 069559
HdO 67, Brill Reprints 59

A GRAMMAR OF THE UGARITIC LANGUAGE, SECOND IMPRESSION WITH CORRECTIONS
Daniel Sivan
Paper $39.95, 978-1-58983-285-5   356 pages, 2007   Code: 069515
HdO 28, Brill Reprints 15

A PHOENICIAN-PUNIC GRAMMAR
Charles R. Krahmalkov
Paper $42.95, 978-1-62837-031-7   330 pages, 2014   Code: 069556
HdO 54, Brill Reprints 56

SUMERIAN GRAMMAR
Dietz Otto Edzard
Paper $25.95, 978-1-58983-252-7   212 pages, 2006   Code: 069511
HdO 71, Brill Reprints 11

A GRAMMAR OF EPIGRAPHIC HEBREW
Sandra Landis Gogel
Paper $56.95, 978-1-55540-288-4   544 pages, 2009   Code: 060323
Resources for Biblical Study 23

SBL Press • P.O. Box 2243 • Williston, VT 05495-2243
Phone: 877-725-3334 (toll-free) or 802-864-6185 • Fax: 802-864-7626
Order online at www.sbl-site.org/publications

SBL 2015 International Meeting

Don't Miss It

The SBL International Meeting is held annually outside North America. It provides a unique forum for international scholars who are unable to attend the North American meeting. Each meeting showcases the latest in biblical research, fosters collegial contacts, advances research, and focuses on issues of the profession.

Buenos Aires, Argentina • July 20–24

Register Now at sbl-site.org and Save!

NOW AVAILABLE FROM SBL PRESS
THE SBL HANDBOOK OF STYLE, SECOND EDITION

"Every graduate program should make *The SBL Handbook of Style* a required text."
— Carol A. Newsom, Candler School of Theology, Emory University

The SBL Handbook of Style has been thoroughly updated to reflect the latest practices among scholars, editors, and publishers as well as to take into account current trends in scholarly publishing. This edition has been meticulously supplemented with important new subject matter that fills gaps in the first edition. Chapters and sections have been reorganized and restructured to be more intuitive and logical.

Hardcover $39.95, 978-1-58983-964-9
E-book $39.95, 978-1-58983-965-6

Instructors may request a complimentary copy of the *Handbook* when it is adopted for a course and ten or more copies are ordered.

New Material in the Second Edition includes
- Clearer and more comprehensive guidelines for authors in preparing manuscripts for publication, including a discussion of Unicode fonts
- A list of ancient Near Eastern archaeological site names
- An expansive discussion of the treatment of qur'anic sources
- An expanded and improved list of capitalization and spelling examples
- Addition of a section on Islamic dates
- An introduction on the principles of transliteration and transcription
- A substantially revised and updated discussion of Akkadian transliteration
- Addition of Sumerian, Hittite, Old Persian, Moabite, Edomite, Ammonite, Syriac, Mandaic, Ethiopic, Arabic, and Turkish to the list of ancient languages treated
- A more complete discussion of the rules of citation
- New rules for the treatment of Latin titles
- A comprehensive list of publishers and their places of publication
- Detailed guidelines for citing a variety of electronic sources
- Expanded coverage of rabbinic works and ancient codices
- A thoroughly updated and expanded list of secondary sources

SBL PRESS

SBL Press • P.O. Box 2243 • Williston, VT 05495-2243
Phone: 877-725-3334 (toll-free) or 802-864-6185 • Fax: 802-864-7626
Order online at www.sbl-site.org/publications

Biblia Hebraica Stuttgartensia: A Reader's Edition

An essential language reference tool for students, pastors, and scholars. The BHS Reader's Edition *is for those who have a basic understanding of Biblical Hebrew and desire to read and study the Hebrew Bible.*

Main Features Include:

- **Complete text** of the Biblia Hebraica Stuttgartensia, checked against the Leningrad Codex
- **All words that occur** fewer than 70 times are parsed and contextually defined in the apparatus
- **Glossary** listing of all other words
- **Improved layout** of poetic text
- **All weak verb** forms are parsed
- **High-quality paper** does not bleed through

Brown Hardcover • 978-1-59856-342-9 • Retail $59.95
Black Imitation Leather • 978-1-59856-749-6 • Retail $79.95

Available at local bookstores, online retailers and STORE.HENDRICKSON.COM

www.ingramcontent.com/pod-product-compliance
Lightning Source LLC
Chambersburg PA
CBHW021825300426
44114CB00009BA/331